U.S. SUBMARINE ATTACKS DURING WORLD WAR II

(Including Allied Submarine Attacks in the Pacific Theater)

John D. Alden

NAVAL INSTITUTE PRESS
Annapolis, Maryland

First printing

Library of Congress Cataloging-in-
Publication Data

Alden, John D. (John Doughty), 1921-
    U.S. submarine attacks during World
War II: including Allied submarine attacks in the Pacific theater/John D.
Alden.
        p.   cm.
    Bibliography: p.
    Includes index.
    ISBN 0-87021-767-4
    1. World War. 1939-1945--Naval
operations--Submarine. 2. World War,
1939-1945--Naval operations. American. I.
Title. II. Title: US submarine attacks
during World War II.
D783.A54 1989
940.54'51--dc19
89-30878

CIP

Printed in the United States of America

DEDICATION

This book is dedicated to the commanding
officers and crews of the U.S. and Allied
submarines that served in World War II,
especially those still on eternal patrol.

Contents

Acknowledgments   v

Preface   vi

Explanation   viii

Chronological Listing of Submarine Attacks   1

Bibliography   227

Appendix A   230

  Submarine Minelaying Activities   230

  Chronological Listing of Submarine Mineplants   233

Appendix B   236

  Commanding Officers of U.S. Submarines
  with Attacks Listed in the Data Tables   236

  Commanding Officers of British Submarines
  with Attacks Listed in the Data Tables   243

  Commanding Officers of Dutch Submarines
  with Attacks Listed in the Data Tables   244

Index   246

Acknowledgments

Many people have helped me in this project. I particularly want to acknowledge the assistance of Rear Admiral John D. H. Kane, Jr., Dean C. Allard, Bernard F. Cavalcante, and Stanley Kalkus of the Naval Historical Center in Washington, D.C.; Theresa M. Cass, Archivist, and Robert M. Banas, MMC(SS), of the Submarine Force Library and Museum in Groton, Conn.; Commander P. Richard Compton-Hall and Gus Britton of the Royal Navy Submarine Museum in Gosport, England; Roger W. Allan, my industrious colleague in Japan; and Dr. Thomas O. Paine of the Submarine Warfare Library, Santa Monica, California. Prof. Dr. Jürgen Rohwer of Stuttgart, Germany, provided a model in his book <u>Axis Submarine Successes, 1939-1945</u> in addition to clarifying several attacks by U.S. submarines in European waters. Christopher Wright of the International Naval Records Organization and Stefan Terzibaschitsch of Leonberg, Germany, steered me to sources I would not have found on my own, which are listed in the bibliography. John Taylor of the Military Reference Branch, National Archives, guided me to documents filed in that institution. Paul Wilderson, Marilyn Wilderson, and John Cronin of the Naval Institute Press have done much to improve the presentation of my material. I regret that I cannot mention all of the other staff members at the institutions cited above who helped make my visits fruitful and pleasant.

Finally, I thank my wife, Ann, whose patience in putting up with my hours on the computer and my frequent absences from home during the preparation of this volume made its completion possible.

John D. Alden
Pleasantville, New York

Preface

The idea for this book originated when I became aware of complaints by World War II submarine commanding officers that the statistics on Japanese ship sinkings compiled by the Joint Army-Navy Assessment Committee (JANAC) shortly after the war failed to reflect the full results of their attacks. More complete records of Japanese losses were said to have been prepared later, but never used to update JANAC. I expressed an interest in this problem to Rear Admiral John D. H. Kane, Jr., then the Director of Naval History, and he immediately provided copies of two key compilations of data for me to work with: a monograph prepared by the Military History Section, Special Staff, General Headquarters, U.S. Army Far East Command during the 1950s, The Imperial Japanese Navy in World War II; and the basic list of U.S. attacks compiled by the Submarine Operations Research Group during the war.

It soon became apparent to me that many of the JANAC assessments of Japanese submarine losses were inaccurate. This finding led me to undertake a broader study of the sinkings and damage wrought by U.S. submarines as reflected in the major postwar sources.

When I broached the idea to the United States Naval Institute of publishing an updated and expanded list of U.S. submarine successes, it was suggested that I consider including the ships attacked by U.S. submarines in the Atlantic theater and those attacked by our British and Dutch allies in the Pacific and Indian oceans. This apparently simple request, to which I readily agreed, ultimately took me far afield in my efforts to find reliable data. Even before then, however, two new compilations of Japanese ship losses came to my attention, so it seemed only fitting that I include them in my comparison with JANAC. Had I known what kind of "can of worms" I was opening, I might never have dared to undertake the project. Once begun, however, the task became one I was determined to finish. The results are published in this volume.

Knowing what I do now, I must warn the reader that the data compiled herein by no means constitute the final word on the achievements of U.S. and Allied submarines during World War II. Careful research in the Japanese archives should help to fill in many heretofore inexplicable gaps in the record and identify some of the "Unknown Marus" that were seen to blow up or sink but have not yet been recognized. It is my hope that this volume will facilitate the work of future researchers by providing a handy compilation of the data recorded by others, including those entries that have turned out to be false leads in the search for the truth.

Preparation of the data tables in this volume would have been impracticable without the aid of a personal computer, and the availability of the "hard disk" proved to be a tremendous help. Since the data tables are being published exactly as I have prepared them, the editors and the publisher cannot be blamed for any errors that may have crept into them.

Explanation

The primary objective of this compilation is to provide a side-by-side listing of data on U.S. submarine attacks and Japanese ship losses during World War II; what the submarine commanders reported when they made attacks against ships, most of which they could not identify precisely, is compared with information from Japanese sources on ships that were sunk or damaged by known or suspected enemy submarines. In the interest of completeness, the record has been expanded to include the few attacks made by U.S. submarines in the Atlantic, the attacks made by British and Dutch submarines operating in the Pacific and Indian oceans, and casualties caused by mines laid in those areas by U.S. and Allied submarines.

Although reported sinkings and other casualties are matched with the attacks that appear most likely to have caused them, it is not my intent to provide a definitive attribution of credit to the individual submarines listed. Especially in controversial cases where two or more submarines may have attacked the same ships, the source documents used are not detailed enough or, in many cases, reliable enough to resolve conflicting claims. Published attributions of credit, both official and unofficial, that have been made since the end of the war are included as part of the record. Wherever it appeared to me that sources were not in reasonable agreement, I have labeled the attribution questionable. There may be reason to challenge any of these or other attributions, but it is my contention that such questions can be resolved, if at all, only through careful study of original records that may still exist in Japan.

A major problem exists in evaluating submarine attacks because of the very nature of submarine warfare. Submarine commanding officers are not usually able to make positive identification of their targets or to verify the extent of damage caused by an attack. War records are replete with examples of submarine commanders who believed they had eyewitnessed sinkings only to find out later that they had been deceived by premature explosions of their torpedoes. It was even more common for commanders to overestimate the size of their targets, in part because of the magnification provided by periscope lenses and also because of the limited opportunity to examine a target ship. Both warships and merchant ships of common types tend to have family resemblances. Tankers, for example, look alike whether large or small; similarly, small warships like destroyers can look like cruisers when viewed under conditions of poor visibility. Submarine officers also tended to overestimate damage based on unseen explosions or "breaking-up" noises heard by sonar. On the enemy side, surface ships seldom saw an attacking sub-

marine; often they were unsure whether an explosion was caused by a torpedo or a mine. In some cases ships simply disappeared, and the cause, location, or time of loss may therefore have been unknown when the Japanese records were made.

Since submerged submarines during World War II often could not know their position precisely, and ships under attack may not have had time to establish their position accurately, the reported locations of ship sinkings or damagings are likely to be only approximate and therefore difficult to correlate. The problem is compounded when sinkings occurred hours or days after the initial damage, when several submarines engaged in a "wolf pack" attack on a convoy at night, or when ships vanished without trace. Matching particular submarine attacks to specific ship casualties is therefore imprecise if not impossible in many cases.

Another problem results from differences in the amount and quality of information provided by the various sources of data on submarine attacks. Such differences include ship classification systems, methods of measuring and reporting tonnage, identification of geographic locations, ways of reporting time, and others. In the case of English-language summaries of data from Japanese records, translation, transcription, and typographical errors can be expected to occur occasionally, and several are noted in the data tables. Certain Japanese characters can be translated in more than one way, and this has led to confusion in some ship names.

A puzzling feature of the compilations of Japanese data available in the U.S. is that the various sources frequently report different positions for a given ship casualty. Although the differences in latitude and longitude are usually small enough to be disregarded, they ap-pear to reflect different basic records of the event rather than errors in translation or transcription. It is likely that separate reports could have been made by the ship that was hit, naval escorts, other ships in company, rescue ships, or survivors of sinkings. The existence of multiple reports would obviously increase the possibility of errors and confusion in data compiled from different sets of records at different times.

Because this tabulation incorporates data from many sources in a necessarily condensed format, users are urged to study carefully the information that follows on the sources as well as the method, conventions, and abbreviations used in presenting the data. In all cases it is important to bear in mind the distinction between data, whether from U.S. or Japanese sources; the assessment by each side of the causes and results of the attack; and the attribution, or assignment of credit,

for a particular sinking or case of damage. The first is a matter of reporting
actual or perceived events, the second is
a matter of interpreting the data, and the
third is a matter of judgment in relating
one set of data to another.

SOURCES OF DATA ON SUBMARINE ATTACKS

1. Patrol reports constitute the
original source of data on most submarine
attacks. These detailed reports by the
submarine commanders were the principal
basis for the official assessments of
results during the war, and have also been
used by the authors of most published histories or accounts of wartime submarine
actions. I have not attempted to review
all U.S. patrol reports but have examined
many where it appeared desirable to verify
data in the various compilations and
source documents described below. Such
cases include those where Japanese
casualties apparently were caused by at-

tacks judged unsuccessful by the U.S.
evaluators, those where submarines were
given official credit for sinking "Unknown
Marus," and those where two or more submarines made "wolf pack" attacks in the same
area. Attacks by submarines that were
lost on patrol could have been credited to
those boats on the basis of radio messages
sent before the submarine was lost, events
seen or heard by nearby submarines or
other observers, information discovered by
intelligence methods, inference from the
last known position or assigned patrol
area of the submarine, or reports by survivors.

2. During the war the Submarine Operations Research Group (SORG), under Commander Submarines, Pacific (ComSubPac),
listed and assessed all reported submarine
attacks, taking into account the commanding officers' patrol reports, the comments
of higher commanders in their endorsements
to the reports, and the limited informa-

tion available from radio traffic with submarines that were lost. This information was tabulated by date and hour of attack and also by boat and patrol number. The compilation (hereafter abbreviated SORG; see bibliography for full title) was classified SECRET until well after the war. It is not clear whether communications intelligence (ComInt) derived from intercepted Japanese radio traffic was available to SORG. So-called Ultra information obtained from decrypted Japanese messages was probably not provided, in view of the highly classified and closely guarded nature of such information until long after the war. Data entries in SORG are: date (month/day/year), hour, light condition, operational command (headquarters), latitude, longitude, type of approach and attack, torpedo model, torpedoes fired, hits, target type, result, estimated target tonnage, submarine hull number, and patrol number. The "result"

column represents SORG's assessment of the success of the attack with, in most cases, no knowledge of the identity of the actual target. SORG's assessments of sinkings and damage, as well as those of target tonnage, largely agree with those of the operational commanders and are considerably overestimated in comparison with postwar analyses. The SORG assessments, however, have been cited in various publications, particularly in the individual submarine histories given in the U.S. government publication United States Submarine Losses, World War II (hereafter abbreviated USSL).

3. Both U.S. and Allied submarines laid minefields in Japanese waters and these are known to have sunk or damaged shipping. A number of sinkings that the Japanese attributed to submarines were probably caused by mines. Because such sinkings usually occurred some time after the mines were laid and seldom can be pin-

pointed to the location of the minefield, they are very difficult to attribute to specific submarines. The problem is compounded because mines were often laid in the same areas by Allied aircraft or even by the Japanese themselves. Casualties that have been officially attributed to, or appear likely to have been caused by, submarine-laid mines are included in this compilation. A complete tabulation of submarine-laid minefields and further discussion of the subject will be found in Appendix A.

BRITISH AND DUTCH DATA SOURCES

1. Little information on British and Dutch submarine attacks, much of it incomplete and inaccurate, has appeared in published secondary sources. However, European sources have provided reasonably complete official records of both British and Dutch submarine attacks. Most Dutch submarine patrols were conducted under British operational command. Except where specifically noted in the data tables, all British and Dutch entries are drawn from Naval Staff History Second World War, Submarines, Vol. 3, Operations in Far Eastern Waters, published in 1956 and referred to hereafter as the British Staff History or BSH. This volume contains brief summaries of each patrol report, data on mine fields, and an assessment of ships sunk. Although it gives much information (especially on small craft attacked) only in general terms, supplementary data were found in the so-called "Success Book" kept during the war, in which attacks made by most of the British submarines are recorded in handwritten entries. These entries correlate quite well with the information in BSH and give dates for many attacks that are not dated in that publication.

2. A detailed listing of Dutch submarine attacks appears in the official

publication De Nederlandse Onderzeedienst 1906-1966, hereafter referred to as DNO. This includes a few attacks not made under British operational control, but otherwise is in excellent agreement with the British records.

SOURCES OF DATA ON JAPANESE SHIP CASUALTIES

1. Japanese war records are reputed to be incomplete because of poor reporting, wartime losses, deliberate destruction, and postwar confusion; in addition, the available original records were largely inaccessible for many years after 1945, especially to persons unable to read them in the original Japanese. The English-language compilations listed below do not include references to the specific Japanese records and must therefore be accepted more or less on faith. This is particularly unfortunate when separate compilations are in conflict, which is the case rather frequently. In some cases it is impossible to judge which source is more likely to be correct. In order to provide a complete cross-reference of the major data sources, this tabulation lists all major differences, even if these are known or believed to be erroneous.

2. Immediately after the war, the Joint Army-Navy Assessment Committee made an assessment of Japanese war losses (sinkings only) based on Japanese records seized after the surrender. This was published in the report hereafter referred to as JANAC (see bibliography). To date, this has been the only official U.S. effort to attribute Japanese losses to specific agents; including submarines, surface warships, aircraft, mines, and marine casualties. The main tables in JANAC contain entries for date, name of vessel, type of vessel, standard tonnage, location, flag of agent, type of agent, and assessment (sunk or probably sunk).

Unfortunately, the JANAC assessment was limited to Japanese warships and those merchant ships of 500 or more gross tons that were believed to have been sunk; it does not list any ships that were assessed as damaged short of sinking, or many small merchant-type craft that were taken over as naval auxiliaries. German and Italian ships sunk in the Pacific and Indian ocean theaters are not included, nor are U.S., Allied, or neutral ships sunk by mistake. JANAC does not identify the ships or units responsible for the sinkings, except for a special appendix listing the sinkings for each U.S. submarine by name. These listings do not include ships sunk by mines laid by the submarines, nor are British and Dutch submarines individually identified. Specific original source documents are not cited or described, and the records used were reportedly packed up and returned to Japan after the assessment was completed. In spite of known errors,

JANAC data are widely cited, even in recent publications, because no later or more complete official assessment exists.

3. The other principal semiofficial English-language tabulation of Japanese ship casualties available up to this time is The Imperial Japanese Navy in World War II, a monograph prepared by Japanese researchers for the U.S. Far East Command in 1952, hereafter referred to as IJN (see bibliography). This is still the only comprehensive source of data on Japanese ship damages short of sinking or total loss. Data in IJN are reported in monthly lists accompanied by charts showing the approximate location of most casualties. In a few cases the charts do not agree with the data in the tables. No effort was made in IJN to identify the specific submarines responsible for the listed attacks.

4. Roger W. Allan, a researcher living in Japan, has recently made an in-

dependent analysis of Japanese wartime shipping losses, using a variety of Japanese sources not available in the U.S. The information compiled by Mr. Allan in an unpublished manuscript (hereafter referred to as <u>Allan</u>) appears to be very reliable; it has been given high priority in the tabulations that follow.

5. The German naval researchers Jentschura, Jung, and Mickel in 1970 published <u>Die Japanischen Kriegsschiffe, 1869-1945</u>, a major work based on information gathered by the late historian Erich Groner and Shizuo Fukui, a Japanese naval constructor. This was translated into English in 1977 as <u>Warships of the Imperial Japanese Navy, 1869-1945</u>, hereafter referred to as <u>WIJN</u>. The book covers mainly ships that were part of the Japanese Navy, including a large number of requisitioned and converted merchant ships. It also has a separate listing of standardized merchant types built in war programs. The attributions of credit for sinkings (few cases of damage are mentioned) appear to have been derived from JANAC or secondary sources; several erroneous attributions seem to have resulted from misreadings of U.S. submarine names or hull numbers, or from errors in translation.

6. The major published histories of World War II submarine operations appear to have relied almost entirely on JANAC in describing submarine successes and identifying the ships sunk. (As noted above, JANAC does not list damage short of total loss or merchant ships smaller than 500 gross tons.) Samuel Eliot Morison's fifteen-volume <u>History of United States Naval Operations in World War II</u> and the books by Roscoe, Holmes, and Blair (see bibliography) contain much information on U.S. but very little on British and Dutch submarine operations. These books, however, were written primarily from a U.S.

submarine point of view and none of them include complete listings of the ships sunk or damaged.

ATTRIBUTION OF CREDIT

As noted above, JANAC is the only source of official attributions of Japanese losses to specific U.S. submarines. The British and Dutch official histories agree with JANAC in most, but not all, attributions. In the tables that follow, all of these official attributions are shown. In the relatively few cases where I have questioned the official assignments of credit, this is noted as a comment. Where I have matched specific attacks to casualties that are not listed in JANAC or the British and Dutch histories, however, the attribution is based solely on my own evaluation of the data.

Three attacks that resulted in known sinkings do not appear in the tables. On 26 March 1944 the TULLIBEE (SS-284) under Charles F. Brindupke was sunk by a circular run of her own torpedo; one man survived to be taken prisoner and tell the tale after the war. The same fate befell the TANG (SS-306) on 24 October 1944, except that commanding officer Richard H. O'Kane and seven others were ultimately returned from a Japanese prisoner-of-war camp. On 23 January 1945 the GUARDFISH (SS-217) fired four torpedoes at what her commanding officer, Douglas T. Hammond, identified as a Japanese submarine; two hit and sank the target, which turned out to be the USS EXTRACTOR (ARS-16). Six men were killed, but 73 survivors were picked up by the GUARDFISH.

DESCRIPTION OF THE DATA TABLES

Each data column will be described in some detail, because the information contained therein is a compilation derived from the several sources described above. Because of the various ways in which data are presented in the different sources, it would be impractical to repeat each source's entry in detail. For instance, the sources vary in their use of abbreviations for ship types and include many minor differences in dates, locations, and ship tonnages. Some important discrepancies exist in these areas as well as in the identification of ships, extent of damage, cause of damage, or other data. Where sources give significantly different information, the leading entry is the one I have judged most reliable; conflicting information is indicated in the appropriate data column beneath the main entry, or in the comments. Minor differences are generally ignored.

The listing is basically chronological, according to the order in which the attacks were made, insofar as this could be determined from the records. Casualties for which no submarine attack could be found, and those caused by mines, have been inserted into the sequence according to the date given in the Japanese records.

The first ten columns, whose headings are listed immediately below, present information from U.S. and Allied sources, mainly SORG for U.S. submarines and the British and Dutch official histories for their boats. In many cases, information taken directly from U.S. patrol reports has been used to provide greater detail or resolve questionable cases.

Dt/Hr: date and sometimes hour of attack. Where the sinking or damage is attributed to a mine laid by the submarine indicated, the date is that when the casualty occurred; the date when the minefield was laid is given in the comments. The absence of a date (indicated by --) means that no record of an attack associated with a reported case of sinking or damage could be found. A few entries derived from sources other than the three official ones mentioned above (SORG, BSH, and DNO)

are indicated by the following letters in
this column:

   J - attack listed only in JANAC

   N - note; see comment column

   S - British attack listed only in the
       Success Book

   U - U.S. attack described only in USSL

   W - attack listed only in WIJN Submarine: hull number and name for U.S. submarines. British and Dutch submarines did
not use hull numbers; their names are
preceded by the designations HMS (British)
or HNMS (Dutch).

Pt (Patrol): patrol number. U.S. patrols
were numbered consecutively for each boat
whether made in the Atlantic or Pacific
theater. For British and Dutch submarines, the numbers are for patrols in
the Far East theater only. The letter A
in this column indicates an attack by a
U.S. submarine in the Atlantic theater.
The letter L in this column indicates that
the submarine was lost on this patrol.

Position: latitude and longitude are
generally given for U.S. submarines. Many
positions for British and Dutch submarines
are given only as the general patrol area.

Tgt (Target): abbreviation of ship type as
reported by the U.S. or Allied source.
Note that two or more targets (usually
small craft) may be listed in a single
entry where no identification is available. (See separate list and explanation
of ship type abbreviations below.)

Size: estimated tonnage of target. Note
that the target's size was almost always
overestimated by the submarine personnel.
This was partly because of observational
difficulties but also because U.S. recognition manuals often gave figures different from those used by Japanese
sources. For instance, submarine officers
frequently cited deadweight rather than
gross tonnage when both figures were
listed in the recognition manuals. (See
separate discussion below of the various

ways of measuring tonnage.)

Attack: type of attack. Torpedo attacks
are indicated by T followed by the number
of hits out of the number fired and a
three-letter combination showing the nature of the attack.

    1st letter D = day, N = night,
                T = twilight or moon-
                light
    2nd letter U = underwater, S =
                surfaced
    3rd letter V = visual, P = peri-
                scope, R = radar, S =
                sonar

    Gun attacks are indicated by G fol-
lowed by D, N, or T for the time of day,
as above.

    Because of space limitations, if
several attacks were made on a target, the
total number of torpedoes used is given
but usually only the final attack is described. In some cases, salvos fired at
one ship resulted in hits on others in a
group; in these instances the total number
of torpedoes fired appears only for the
first target listed, but the hits claimed
are indicated for each ship separately.
Where entries are incomplete, the missing
information was not given in the sources
studied.

    Note that most submarine attacks
early in the war were made with the boat
submerged. Later, night surface attacks
were found to be very effective, especially after radar became available.

    Because of a shortage of torpedoes at
various times during the war, target
priorities were set by higher commands and
changed to suit circumstances. Many
targets were missed at times when salvos
were deliberately kept small. Torpedo
problems existed throughout the war but
were particularly serious during the first
two years; cases of dud hits, premature
explosions, and erratic running torpedoes
are well documented, and at least two U.S.

submarines are known to have been sunk by circular runs of their own torpedoes.

In the final year of the war, some submarines were issued experimental homing torpedoes (called CUTY or DOGY) for use against attacking escorts. A single homing torpedo was usually fired "blind" with the aid of sonar, as the submarine maneuvered to evade the enemy.

As the war progressed and large targets became scarcer, surface gun attacks on small craft became more and more common. Although some of these targets were naval picket boats or converted naval types, many were obviously fishing boats and not all were Japanese owned. Relatively few of these craft are listed in the Japanese records of losses; however, in most cases their sinking or damage was clearly observed by the submarine. Some were identified by boarding the craft, taking prisoners, or recovering material. The data tables include a few such names

found in the patrol reports and other material that I examined; others could probably be found by a more thorough search.

Cl (Claim): damage claimed. Abbreviations used are as follows:

S   sunk

P   sunk, with partial credit to the submarine listed

D   damaged

0   no damage claimed

U   unknown (used for submarines lost on patrol)

The next seven columns present data on casualties from postwar Japanese sources, with preference generally given to data confirmed by Allan. The final column provides space to note discrepancies between the various sources or to make explanatory comments.

So (Source): source(s) of information on

Japanese losses. Abbreviations used are as follows:

A   Allan

I   IJN

J   JANAC

N   Netherlands source (described in Comments column)

U   USSL

W   WIJN

Other sources in specific cases are identified by comments.

Date: date as given in the sources on Japanese losses. If the dates given by different sources vary by no more than one day from the date reported by the submarine, it is assumed that the variation is due to differences in reporting the time, and the range of dates is shown. Greater differences are indicated separately below the main entries. If the Japanese date is later than the submarine's reported attack date, it is presumed that the sinking resulted from the attack but occurred somewhat later. If the Japanese date is more than one day earlier than the submarine date, either the date was recorded incorrectly or attribution of the loss to the attack in question must be considered doubtful.

Type: ship type as given in Japanese source(s). Minor differences in the type symbols used by the various sources are ignored. The type reported by Allan is usually preferred. (See separate list and explanation of ship type abbreviations below.)

Name: ship name as given in Japanese source(s), with the preferred identification listed first. Variant spellings or identifications are shown by separate entries or comments. The abbreviation M. stands for Maru (merchant). I-Go, a designation meaning "the first," was often applied to captured ships. Note the many cases where the same name was used for two or more different ships, either with or

without the addition of numerical designations. Regular Japanese Navy ship names
do not include <u>Maru</u>, but most merchant
ships taken into naval service during the
war retained their names. The following
classes of ships had letter/number designations instead of names.

CD   Escort and Patrol Vessels
      (WIJN Types C & D)

Ch   Submarine Chasers

Cha   Auxiliary Submarine
      Chasers, including converted
      fishing vessel and captured
      types

Comm. Apparently a type of communica-
Ship tion ship (not listed in WIJN)

I   Large Submarines

Ma   Coastal Minelayers

P   Escort and Patrol Vessels
      (former old destroyers and
      captured ships)

RO   Medium Submarines

T   Landing Ships (WIJN type

T1 was a fast amphibious
transport resembling the
U.S. APD; the T 101 type
resembled the U.S. LST)

Tx1,   Symbols used by IJN to
etc.   designate unidentified losses

U   German Submarines

UIT   Ex-Italian Submarines taken
       over by Germany

W   Minesweepers

Wa   Auxiliary Minesweepers
       (trawler types and captured
       ships)

<u>Tons</u>: tonnage as given in Japanese
source(s). Differences between sources
are ignored if less than 10 tons; larger
differences are shown in this column or
noted in the comments. Ships of merchant
types are measured in gross registered
tons. Warships are measured in displacement tons; usually the "standard" figure
from WIJN or Watts is given. (IJN does
not give warship tonnages and JANAC fig-

ures for warships are almost always smaller than those from postwar sources. Also
see discussion of tonnage below.)

Dm (Damage): extent of damage and agent as
reported by Japanese source(s). Separate
entries or comments appear in all cases
where sources disagree as to either extent
of damage or agent. All listed attacks
were reported as made by submarines unless
a different agent is indicated. Abbreviations used are as follows:

Extent of Damage   Agent

S sunk   A aircraft

J sunk, joint credit   W surface

P probable (see note)   warship

H heavy damage   M mine

M medium damage   C casualty,
                         other

L light damage   U unknown
                         agent

D disabled

? unknown extent

   Note: P alone indicates JANAC's

evaluation that a ship was probably sunk;
PS indicates a probable attribution to the
designated submarine.

Location: position as given by Japanese
source(s). I have generally given preference to the source that indicated latitude
and longitude. Where sources used
references to landmarks, I checked to see
whether these were consistent with the ge-
ographical coordinates; if not, the attribution is indicated as questionable.
Note that JANAC locates sinkings at the
submarine's rather than the target's position, with only rare exceptions. Therefore, where JANAC locations are the only
ones given, they are usually listed as
"sub position" only.

Comments: Most are self-explanatory, but
have had to be heavily condensed because
of space limitations. Sources are indicated by the same letters as used in the
"Source" column; PR indicates information
from patrol reports. I have enclosed ex-

pressions of my own judgment or opinion in brackets to distinguish them from information repeated from the data sources. The expression "attribution?" means that the attribution to the particular submarine is questionable. Where I consider a JANAC attribution questionable, the phrase "J attribution?" is used.

COMMANDING OFFICERS

The names of the commanding officers of all submarines included in the data tables are given in Appendix B. The one responsible for a particular attack can be found readily by using the submarine name and patrol number to enter this list.

TONNAGE MEASURES

Because of the widely different methods of measuring ship tonnage, especially between warships and merchant types, tonnage totals for individual submarines are, at best, mere approximations resulting

from the addition of "apples and oranges." The "gross registered tonnage" of merchant ships is actually a measurement of volume, one ton being equal to 100 cubic feet of carrying capacity. Obviously, this figure could vary depending on when the ship was surveyed, because of structural alterations as well as the accuracy of the measurements. Bulk carriers such as tankers and ore carriers are frequently rated in "deadweight" tons, which represent the maximum weight of cargo that can be carried safely.

Warships are measured in displacement tons, referring to the weight of the ship. Since ships cannot be weighed directly, displacement is calculated according to the volume of water displaced, using a standard value of 35 cubic feet of sea water per long ton (2,240 pounds). (Note that long tons are traditionally used rather than the common short tons of 2,000 pounds. Some countries, however, use metric tons, or "tonnes," of 1,000 kilo-grams, or 2,204.6 pounds.) Since the volume of water displaced will vary according to how deeply a ship is loaded, "standard" displacement was defined in naval treaties as that of a ship fully manned and equipped for sea in wartime, but without fuel or reserve feed water. "Light" displacement refers to the ship and its machinery without crew, provisions, fuel, ammunition, and other expendable items. "Full load" displacement is the standard displacement plus fuel and feed water. The term "normal displacement" is also used in some references without being clearly defined. In wartime, ships were almost always loaded beyond their nominal full load displacement, with extra crew members, stores, ammunition, guns, and other supplies. The actual displacement would, of course, change as stores and fuel were used during a cruise. The displacement of submarines

is usually given either surfaced or submerged, with the surfaced figure measured in one of the ways described above. The difficulty of establishing a warship's displacement is reflected in the variety of figures to be found in different reference publications.

A rough idea of the relationships among different measures of ship tonnage can be obtained from the following ratios derived from average figures for World War II types compiled by Frederic C. Lane in Ships for Victory:

Type	Disp. (Light)	Dead-weight	Gross
Standard Cargo	1.00	2.14	1.54
Liberty Ship	1.00	3.10	2.07
Victory Ship	1.00	2.44	1.70
Tanker	1.00	3.07	1.90
Military	1.00	1.04	1.43

SHIP TYPE ABBREVIATIONS

In identifying targets ("Tgt"

column), SORG uses a mixture of standard Navy classification symbols plus non-standard abbreviations for types that do not fit exactly into the U.S. system. No distinction is made between naval auxiliaries and merchant ships of similar types.

Each source of Japanese data uses a different system for indicating ship types: JANAC does not use abbreviations but spells out all ship types; WIJN uses type designations peculiar to the Japanese Navy, some of which do not have exact U.S. equivalents; IJN uses a mixture of standard and nonstandard U.S. symbols for combatant and naval noncombatant ships but spells out the common merchant types and also uses prefixes to indicate whether a ship was under army, navy, or civilian control. Since it would be meaningless to try to show all of the different type classifications in the data tables, I have given preference to the one that appears

to be the most useful or meaningful whenever two or more sources are referenced for a single attack. For warships and noncombatant ships under naval control, I generally classified the ships according to the WIJN type designations. Wherever possible, I have used standard U.S. abbreviations for ship types; otherwise, the preferred abbreviation is the one that gives the most information.

Certain common prefixes are used with many of the ship classification symbols listed below, with the following meanings.

X at the beginning of a ship type designation signifies a merchant ship taken into naval service. An exception to this rule exists in the case of merchant ships fully converted into warship types (such as aircraft carriers) rather than merely adapted to a naval role. In such cases the Japanese assigned new warship names in place of the original Maru names. Note that the symbol XPG, for example, means a merchant ship that was armed and used as a gunboat, not a "former gunboat" as stated in some sources. Larger ships used as armed merchant cruisers are designated XCL; these are not "former light cruisers."

A indicates ships under army control, B signifies navy control, and C shows civilian control. (These are prefixes used in IJN that are helpful in establishing the identity of many ships.)

The following basic symbols appear in the "Tgt" and "Type" columns. Variant nomenclature used in some sources but not in the data columns is indicated in parentheses; other comments are in brackets.

AC   Collier (IJN--Coal)
ACV Auxiliary Aircraft Carrier
     [Same as CVE]
AD   Destroyer Tender
AE   Ammunition Ship (IJN--Weps)

AF   Supply Ship
AG   Miscellaneous Auxiliary
AGP Motor Torpedo Boat Tender
AGS Surveying Ship
AH   Hospital Ship
AK   Cargo Ship (IJN--Cargo or Ore)
AKV Cargo Ship & Aircraft Ferry
AM   Minesweeper
AMc Coastal Minesweeper (JANAC--
     Special Minesweeper)
AN   Netlayer (JANAC--Net Tender)
AO   Oiler (IJN--also Oil or
     Tanker; JANAC--Tanker)
AOG Gasoline Tanker
AOR Replenishment Oiler
AP   Transport (IJN--also Pass)
APc Transport, Coastal
APD High-Speed Transport (WIJN--
     Landing Ship, Fast Transport)
APH Hospital Transport
APK Passenger-Cargo Ship
APV Transport & Aircraft Ferry
AR   Repair Ship

ARC	Cable Ship		CVS	Seaplane Carrier
ARL	Landing Craft Repair Ship or Tender		DD	Destroyer
			DE	Destroyer Escort [See Note 2]
ARS	Salvage Vessel		DL	Destroyer Leader
AS	Submarine Tender (WIJN-- Submarine Depot Ship)		Esc	Escort [See Note 2]
			Fish	Fishing Vessel
AT	Tug		Hulk	Hulk
Aux	Auxiliary, type unspecified		Jk	Junk [See Note 1]
AV	Seaplane Tender		LBV	Landing Barge
AW	Water Tanker		LC	Landing Craft
BB	Battleship		LS	Landing Ship
Bge	Barge		LSM	Landing Ship, Medium
CA	Heavy Cruiser		LST	Landing Ship, Tank
CL	Light Cruiser [Also see XCL, Armed Merchant Cruiser]		Ltr	Lighter [See Note 1]
			Lug	Lugger [See Note 1]
CM	Minelayer		Mis	Miscellaneous [See Note 1]
CMc	Coastal Minelayer (JANAC-- Special Minelayer)		ML	Motor Launch
			Ms	Motor-sail [See Note 1]
Crab	Crab Fishing Vessel		MV	Merchant Vessel
Cstr	Coaster [sometimes abbrev. Cst] [See Note 1]		ODD	Old Destroyer [See Note 2]
			Ore	Ore Carrier
CV	Aircraft Carrier		Pat	Patrol Vessel, type unspecified
CVE	Escort Aircraft Carrier			

PC   Submarine Chaser [Japanese
      Ch type]

PCE   Submarine Chaser, Escort

PF   Frigate [See Note 2]

PG   Gunboat

PGE   Gunboat/Escort

PGM   Motor Gunboat

Pkt   Picket Boat (WIJN--Guardboat)

PR   River Gunboat

Prau Prau [See Note 1]

PY   Yacht

PYc   Coastal Yacht

      Q-ship [Decoy]

Sail Sailing Vessel [See Note 1]

Sam   Sampan [See Note 1]

SC   Submarine Chaser [Japanese
      Cha type] (IJN--SCs; JANAC--
      Special Submarine Chaser;
      WIJN--Auxiliary Submarine
      Chaser)

Sch   Schooner [See Note 1]

SCs   Special Submarine Chaser [See
      SC]

Smc   Small Craft [sometimes abbrev.
      Sm] [See Note 1]

SS   Submarine

TB   Torpedo Boat

Tra   Trawler

Trk   Sea Truck [a small motor
      freighter] [See Note 1]

Tug   Tug

UB   U-boat [German Submarine]

Unk   Unknown

Wh   Whaling Vessel

XCL   Armed Merchant Cruiser

XPG   Auxiliary or Converted Gunboat

YP   Small Patrol Craft

YTL   Small Harbor Tug

Note 1: Small craft are listed under
various names for which there are no standard definitions. None of these type
designations can be considered definitive
in distinguishing one kind of small craft
from another.

Note 2: The Japanese (WIJN) classifi-

cation of Escort and Patrol Vessel includes types similar to the U.S. destroyer
escort and frigate, as well as converted
old destroyers, trawlers, and captured
ships of various types. SORG, IJN, and
JANAC use the symbols DE, PF, and ODD for
different ships in this group, but the
usage is not consistent. I use PF for all
types listed in IJN as Escort and Patrol
Vessels, and DE only for Matsu-class escort destroyers. The former names of
patrol vessels converted from old
destroyers are given under comments.

Dt/Hr	Submarine	Pt	Position	Tgt	Size	Attack	Cl	So	Date	Type	Name	Tons	Dm	Location	Comments
DEC	1941														
9	193 SWORDFISH	1	14-30N 119-00E	AK	3900	T1/2NSV	S								
10 N	201 TRITON	1	S of Wake I.	DD	Unk	T1/4NUS	D								Attack not in SORG; in Holmes and Blair; TRITON on practice patrol.
12	143 S-38	1	12- N 120- E	AP	5000	T1/1NSV	S								
12	HNMS K-XII	1	Off Kota Bharu	AK	1932	T		S	AJ I	12-3	A-AK	Toro M.	1932	S M	06-00N 102-20E Kuantan	Holmes credits HNMS O-16.
12	HNMS O-16	1L	Patani/Singora	AP	Unk	Unk	D	AI	12	A-AK	Tozan M.	8666	H	Off Patani	I lists as 3 unk ships (Tx3); DNO gives name Tosan M; Stove gives date 9 Dec; ship later salvaged.
12	HNMS O-16	1L	Patani/Singora	AP	Unk	Unk	D	AI	12-3	A-AP	Kinka M.	9306	H	Off Patani	I lists as Tx3; DNO gives name Ayata M, 9788T; Hervieux - Kinkasan M, 4980T; Von Münching - Ayato M; later salvaged.
12	HNMS O-16	1L	Patani/Singora	AP	Unk	Unk	D	AI	12	A-AK	Asosan M.	8811	H	Off Patani	I lists as Tx3; later salvaged.
12	HNMS O-16	1L	Patani/Singora	AP	Unk	Unk	D	N			Sakura M.	7170			Identification from DNO. [Attribution ?]
13	144 S-39	1	13-14N 124-21E	AK	5000	T1/4DUP	S								
13	192 SAILFISH	1	08-39N 120-06E	DD	1500	T1/2N	S								
13	HNMS K-XII	1	Off Kota Bharu	AO	3500	T		S	AI	12-3	A-AK	Taizan M.	3525	?	Near C. Camau	BSH says sunk in Gulf of Siam; Mars credits HNMS K-XIII. [Attribution ?; Kota Bharu not near Cape Camau.]
14/18	193 SWORDFISH	1	18-05N 109-18E	AK	9200	T1/2NSV	S	AIJ	13	C-AK	Nikkoku M.	2728	SC	Off Hainan I.	PR says seen stopped, listing & sinking; A says ran aground. [Attribution ?]
14	193 SWORDFISH	1	18-08N 109-22E	AK	9200	T1/2DUP	D								
14	193 SWORDFISH	1	18-08N 109-22E	AK	9200	T1/1DUP	S	AI	15	A-AP	Kashii M.	8407	M	Off Samah	
14	197 SEAWOLF	1	Not given	AV		T0/8DUP	0	AI	14	AV	Sanyo M.	8360	L	Aparri	PR claims no hits; Dull says hit by dud torp.
16	193 SWORDFISH	1	18-06N 109-44E	AK	9400	T1/3DUP	S	AJ I	16	A-AP	Atsutasan M.	8663	S D	S of Samah	

1

Dt/Hr	Submarine	Pt	Position	Tgt	Size	Attack	Cl	So	Date	Type	Name	Tons	Dm	Location	Comments
DEC	1941														
22	143 S-38	1	16- N 120- E	AP	5000	T1/2DUP	S	AJ I	21-2	A-AP	Hayo M.	5445	S H	Lingayan Gulf	
23	182 SALMON	1	16- N 119- E	DD	1500	T2/2NSV	S								
23	183 SEAL	1	17-35N 120-12E	AK	5000	T1/2DUP	S	AI J	23	A-AK	Soryu M. Hayataka M.	856	S	Off Badoc	
23	HNMS K-XIV	2	Kuching	AP	9849	T	S	AIJ	23	A-AP	Katori M.	9849	S	Off Kuching	Later salvaged.
23	HNMS K-XIV	2	Kuching	AP	4943	T	S	AI J	23	A-AK	Hiyoshi M. Hie M.	4943	D S	Off Kuching	BSH & DNO claim sunk; later salvaged.
23	HNMS K-XIV	2	Kuching	AP	Unk	Unk	D	I	23	XAP	Hokkai M.	8416	L	Off Kuching	
23	HNMS K-XIV	2	Kuching	AO	Unk	Unk	D	I	23	A-AK	Nichinan M.	6503	M	Kuching	DNO gives name Nichiran M; Dull says 1 AP at Kuching sunk by K-XVI, 3 damaged by K-XIV.
24	HNMS K-XVI	2L	Kuching	DD	1950	T2/?	S	AI J	24	DD	Sagiri	2090 1950	S	01-34N 110-21E	K-XVI lost 25 Dec; DNO gives tons as 1700.
27/09	176 PERCH	1	22-14N 115-13E	AK	5000	T1/2DUP	S	W I	27	XAE AG	Nojima M. Nojima	7190	M	SW Hong Kong	
JAN	1942														
1	141 S-36	1L	13- N 120- E	APK	5000	T1/1DUP	S								S-36 ran aground; lost, all crew saved.
5	180 POLLACK	1	34-15N 140-08E	AK	4000	T3/6NSV	S	I	5	B-AK	Heijo M.	2700	L	SE Izu Oshima	W lists XPG, 2627T; see 218 ALBACORE 4 Sep 43. [Attribution ?]
7	180 POLLACK	1	34-27N 139-59E	AK	6000	T1/2DUP	S	A IJW 7	10	XAC	Unkai M. #1	2225	S	Mikomoto I.	I lists as B-XPG, 2250T; J as AK, 2225T; W as XAC, 2250T. See Unyo M #1 below.
--							-	I	10	B-XPG	Unyo M. #1	2225	S	Mikomoto I.	A says same ship as Unkai M #1 above; W lists Unyo M #1 as XPG, not sunk; J as AK, 2039T, sunk 14 Jul 45 by a/c.
9	180 POLLACK	1	35-00N 140-36E	AK	6000	T1/4NSV	S	AIJ	9	C-AK	Teian M.	5387	S	SE Inubo Saki	
10	177 PICKEREL	2	05-52N 125-52E	AK	5000	T2/3NUP	S								
10	177 PICKEREL	2	06-19N 125-54E	AK	5000	T2/2NUP	S	AIJW	10	XPG	Kanko M.	2929	S	06-15N 125-50E	W confuses ship with 909T XAN of same sunk 5 Jan 45.

Dt/Hr	Submarine	Pt	Position	Tgt	Size	Attack	Cl	So	Date	Type	Name	Tons	Dm	Location	Comments
JAN	1942														
10	186 STINGRAY	2	17-40N 109-20E	AP	10700	T1/3DUP	S	AJ I	10	A-AK	Harbin M.	5167	S L	S Hainan I.	
10	191 SCULPIN	1	10-05N 123-55E	AK	5000	T2/4NSV	S								
10	211 GUDGEON	1	31-56N 132-16E	AK	5000	T2/3NSV	S								
10	HNMS O-19	2	07-35N 103-13E	AK	4000	T?/3	S	AJ I	10	A-AK	Akita M.	3817	S L	07-40N 102-50E 07-52N 120-53E	Bach Kolling in temporary command. [I longitude appears to be misprint.]
10	HNMS O-19	2	07-35N 103-13E	AK	5000	T?/3	S	N			Tairyu M.	4944			Attack not in BSH or DNO; other N sources say CO fired at smaller ship, saw hits on both; ship later salvaged; Stove & Hervieux give name Tarya M, 5600T. [Attribution ?]
12	181 POMPANO	1	09- N 169- E	APK	16500	T3/4DUP	S								
18	179 PLUNGER	1	34- N 134- E	AK	7200	T2/2DUP	S	AIJ	18	C-AK	Eizan M.	4702	S	Shionomisaki	
22	187 STURGEON	2	01- N 119- E	Unk	10000	T1/1	S								
23	194 SEADRAGON	1	12- N 109- E	AK	5000	T1/1DUP	S	I	23	A-AK	Fukuyo M.	5463	H	N Indochina	
24/12	193 SWORDFISH	2	01-25N 126-10E	AK	5000	T2/2DUP	S	AIJW	24	XPG	Myoken M.	4124	S	01-26N 125-10E	SORG gives incorrect posit 08S 116E.
24/13	193 SWORDFISH	2	01-25N 126-10E	AK	5000	T2/2DUP	S								Same as above.
24	HNMS K-XVIII	1	Balikpapan	DD	Unk	T	S	AJW I	24	PF	P 37	935	SW H	Balikpapan	Ex-DD Hishi; J says sunk; W beached & broken up after damage by US surface ships; BSH credits K-XVIII; DNO says target was Ch 12, no damage. [Attribution ?]
24	HNMS K-XVIII	1	00-10N 118-00E	APK	Unk	T	S	A IJ	24	A-AP	Tsuruga M.	6987	S SW	01-20S 117-01E	W lists as XAP, no other history; DNO claims sunk; BSH gives name Buruga M, damaged. [Attribution ?]
26	187 STURGEON	2	01- S 117- E	AP	5000	T1/4	S								
26/12	192 SAILFISH	2	05-30N 125-44E	CL	7500	T1/4DUP	D								
27/09	211 GUDGEON	1	28-24N 178-35E	SS	1400	T2/3DUP	S	IW J	27	SS	I-73 I-173	1400 1785	S	SW of Oahu	I says missing 27 Jan; subs not renumbered until 20 May.
31	187 STURGEON	2	00- N 119- E	AO	5000	T1/3NUP	S								SORG entry incomplete, gives incorrect longitude 019E.

Dt/Hr	Submarine	Pt	Position	Tgt	Size	Attack	Cl	So	Date	Type	Name	Tons	Dm	Location	Comments
FEB	1942														
2	194 SEADRAGON	1	17-16N 119-48E	APK	6400	T2/2NUP	S	AIJ	2	A-AK	Tamagawa M.	6441	S	17-32N 120-22E	
2	194 SEADRAGON	1	17-16N 119-48E	AP		T0/1DUP	O	I	2	A-AK	Nisshu M.	7785	?	Vigan	PR says torp missed ship previously hit. [Attribution ?]
3	196 SEARAVEN	2	00-05N 126-11E	DD	1500	T1/2	S								
4	191 SCULPIN	2	04-00S 123-00E	DD	1500	T2/3DUP	S	I	4	DD	Suzukaze	1685	D	Off Kendari	
4	200 THRESHER	2	13- N 145- E	AK	4500	T1/3DUP	S								
6	191 SCULPIN	2	04-30S 123-30E	CL	7500	T2/2NSV	D								
8	142 S-37	3	05-10S 119-24E	DD	1900	T1/1NSV	S	AIW J	8-9	DD	Natsushio	2033 1900	S	05-36S 119-16E	
8	HMS TRUSTY	1	Gulf of Siam	MV	Unk	G	0	I	8	C	Se Go	200	H	Poulo Condore	TRUSTY in gun action with MV about this time, no damage claimed. [Attribution ?]
9	202 TROUT	2	25-30N 122-38E	AK	5000	T2/3DUP	S	AIJW	10	XPG	Chuwa M.	2719	S	25-23N 122-42E	
9	202 TROUT	2	25-30N 122-38E	Same	Same	Same	0	AI J	9	A-AP	Kurama M. Kurama	6788	S SU	28-25N 122-13E	A credits unk sub. No sub attacks at location given; 202 TROUT closest, but PR says only 1 ship attacked 9 Feb. [Attribution ?]
14	193 SWORDFISH	2	06-45N 126-54E	AK	5000	T1/2DUP	S	A I	14	XAP	Amagisan M.	7620 9620	M	Off Davao	
17	201 TRITON	2	32-12N 127-32E	AK	6000	T1/4DUP	D								
17	201 TRITON	2	32-14N 127-14E	AK	6000	T1/2DUP	S	AIJW	17-8	XPG	Shinyo M. #5	1498	S	32-25N 126-23E	
18	146 S-41	2	00- N 119- E	AP	5000	T1/4DUP	S								
19	193 SWORDFISH	2	14-32N 120-08E	AO	5000	T1/2DUP	S								
19	197 SEAWOLF	4	08-39S 115-18E	AP	5000	T1/2DUP	D								
19	197 SEAWOLF	4	08-39S 115-18E	AP	5000	T1/2DUP	D								
20	202 TROUT	2	28-43N 142-41E	PC	200	T1/3NSV	S								
21	201 TRITON	2	32-10N 126-28E	AK	6000	T2/2DUP	S	AJ I	21	A-AK	Shokyu M.	4486	S ?	32-25N 126-23E	

Dt/Hr	Submarine	Pt	Position	Tgt	Size	Attack	Cl	So	Date	Type	Name	Tons	Dm	Location	Comments
FEB	1942														
24	183 SEAL	2	06-45S 117-24E	AP	5000	T2/2NSV	S								
24	183 SEAL	2	06-32S 117-10E	AK	5000	T2/2NSV	S								
25	197 SEAWOLF	4	08- S 115- E	AP	5000	T2/3DUP	S								
25	197 SEAWOLF	4	08- S 115- E	DD	1500	T2/2DUP	S								
25	197 SEAWOLF	4	08- S 115- E	AK	5000	T1/1	D								
27	167 NARWHAL	1	28-55N 138-15E	AO	7000	T2/2NUP	S	I	28	XAO	Manju M.	6515	M	29-04N 137-56E	SORG gives incorrect latitude 38N.
27	201 TRITON	2	31-50N 129-03E	APK	9000	T1/3DUP	D								
--							-	A I	27	XPkt	Palau M.	35	SA ?	Kwajalein SW of Pagan I.	No likely sub attack; W says sunk 6 Feb 45 at Kwajalein.
28/22	203 TUNA	1	32-31N 132-28E	AK	2000	T1/3NUP	D	I	28	?	Tx1	?	?	?	PR says 1 explosion heard but target did not slow. No other sub attacks 28 Feb. [Attribution ?; location not given.]
MAR	1942														
1/20	207 GRAMPUS	1	04-50N 157-20E	AO	10000	T2/3NSV	S	I	1	?	Tx2 #1	?	S	?	[Attribution ?; location not given.] Also see GRAMPUS 4 Mar.
--							-	I	1	?	Tx2 #2	?	S	?	Insufficient info to identify attack.
1	HNMS K-XV	2	Bay of Bantam	AO	Unk	T?/2	D	I	1	AO	Tsurumi	15050	?	E Nicholas Pt.	DNO gives tons as 8000; some sources identify ship as Erimo; see 144 S-39, 4 Mar.
2	143 S-38	4	06-27S 112-12E	CL	7500	T1/4NUP	D								
2	192 SAILFISH	3	08-06S 115-57E	CV	10000	T2/4NUP	D	AIJ	1-2	XAPV	Kamogawa M.	6440	S	N of Lombok I.	J lists as AV; ship not in W.
4	144 S-39	3	04-19S 108-25E	AO	5000	T3/4DUP	S	A J	4	AO	Erimo	14050 6500	S	S Billiton I.	I says heavy damage; W gives tons as 15450, says beached on Bali but credits HNMS O-15, which was never in Far East. [May be confused with K-XV.]
4	167 NARWHAL	1	28-37N 129-10E	AK	5000	T2/4NUP	S	AIJ	4	A-AK	Taki M.	1235	S	Amami Oshima	
4	203 TUNA	1	32-33N 132-26E	AK	6000	T1/1DUP	S	J	4	AK	Unknown M.	4000	S	Sub position	PR says target afire but not seen to sink. [J attribution ?]

Dt/Hr	Submarine	Pt	Position	Tgt	Size	Attack	Cl	So	Date	Type	Name	Tons	Dm	Location	Comments
MAR	1942														
4	207 GRAMPUS	1	00-56N 149-31E	AO	10000	T2/3NSV	S	AIW J	5 1	XAO	Kaijo M. #2	8632	S	S of Truk	J credits GRAMPUS attack of 1 Mar.
5	182 SALMON	2	05-35S 112-35E	CL	7500	T2/2NUP	D	I	4	XAP	Taito M.	4466	L	N of Lombok	[Attribution ?]
5	208 GRAYBACK	1	13- N 144- E	AK	4500	T1/2DUP	S								
5	208 GRAYBACK	1	13- N 144- E	PG	300	T1/1DUP	S								
7	210 GRENADIER	1	36-27N 141-06E	AK	5000	T1/6DUP	D	I	7	XAP	Asahisan M.	4551	M	S Shioyasaki	
11	180 POLLACK	2	30-53N 126-20E	AK	5400	T1/4NSV	S	AJ I	11	A-AK	Fukushu M.	1454 1434	S	30-45N 126-25E	
11	180 POLLACK	2	31-00N 126-32E	AK		T0/6NSV	0	A I	11 12	A-APK	Baikal M.	5266	S	31-00N 126-45E ?C N of Masinloc	A says torp by unk sub. [Attribution ?]
13	172 PORPOISE	2	07-45S 116-15E	AK	5000	T1/4DUP	D	I	13	?	Tx1	?	H	N Lombok Str.	Insufficient info for positive identification of attack. [Attribution ?]
13	206 GAR	1	33-53N 135-30E	AO	10000	T3/4DUP	S	AIW J	13	XAF	Chichibu M.	1462 1520	S	SW Mikura I.	I gives tons as 1320.
17	208 GRAYBACK	1	28- N 130- E	AK	7000	T1/2DUP	S	AIJW	17	XAC	Ishikari M.	3291	S	Chichi Jima	
26	211 GUDGEON	2	32-32N 127-11E	AK	5000	T2/3NSV	S	J	26	AK	Unknown M.	4000	S	Sub position	PR says turned over, sank by stern, lifeboats in water. [J attribution ?]
27	211 GUDGEON	2	33-50N 127-33E	APK	10000	T2/3NSV	S	AI J	27	C-AK	Nissho M. Unknown M.	6526 4000	S	SE Kumun I.	
28	191 SCULPIN	3	04- S 122- E	AK	5000	T2/3DUP	D								SORG listing incorrect; PR says sub posit 02-21 124-04E, no hits or damage claimed.
--							-	I	28	?	Tx1	?	?	Shionomisaki	No likely sub attack.
30	187 STURGEON	3	05-39S 119-00E	AK	5000	T1/2DUP	S	AIW J	28 30	XAP	Choko M.	842	S	Makassar City	PR says sank, lifeboats in water. [28 Mar date ?]
30	198 TAMBOR	2	13-00N 157-30E	AK	6300	T0/3NSV	0	I	30	XAP	Tatsuho M.	6334	L	Brown Atoll	PR says may have been dud hit.
31	185 SNAPPER	2	06-44N 125-44E	XCL	3000	T3/3DUP	S								
31	197 SEAWOLF	4	10- S 105- E	CL	7500	T1/4DUP	S								

6

Dt/Hr	Submarine	Pt	Position	Tgt	Size	Attack	Cl	So	Date	Type	Name	Tons	Dm	Location	Comments
APR	1942														
1	197 SEAWOLF	4	10- S 105- E	CL	7500	T1/3DUP	D	AI	1	CL	Naka	5195	H	Christmas I.	
1	197 SEAWOLF	4	10- S 105- E	CL	7500	T1/2DUP	D								
1	HMS TRUANT	2	05-42N 098-57E	AK	6000	T1/?	S	AIJ	1	A-AK	Yae M.	6780	S	06-07N 099-12E	
1	HMS TRUANT	2	05-42N 098-57E	AK	5000	T1/?	S	AIJ	1	A-AK	Shunsei M.	4939	S	06-07N 099-12E	
3	187 STURGEON	3	00-36N 119-19E	DD	1500	T1/3NUP	S	J	3	PF	Unknown	750	P	Sub position	PR says hit under bridge, not seen to sink. [J attribution ?]
3	187 STURGEON	3	00-36N 119-19E	AK	5000	T1/4NUP	D								
--							-	A I	9	CL	Kuma	5100	LA ?	S Cebu I.	No likely sub attack.
10	200 THRESHER	3	34-59N 139-29E	AK	5000	T1/1	S	AI J	10	C-AK	Sado Go Sado M.	3039	S	ENE of Oshima	
10	202 TROUT	3	33-26N 135-38E	AK	15000	T1/3DUP	D	AIW	11	XAO	Nisshin M.	16801	D	Shionomisaki	
11	209 GRAYLING	2	31- N 130- E	Sam		G	D								
13	209 GRAYLING	2	31-51N 132-50E	AK	6000	T1/4DUP	S	AIJ	13	C-AK	Ryujin M.	6243	S	Okinoshima	
16	078 R-1	2A	36-50N 060-52W	SS	700	T1/3DUP	D								
16	198 TAMBOR	2	03- S 152- E	AO	7000	T1/2NSV	S	AIW	17	XAF	Kitami M.	394	S	SE Kavieng	
17	190 SPEARFISH	3	10-53N 121-35E	AP	5000	T2/4DUP	S	J	17	AK	Unknown M.	4000	S	Sub position	PR says seen stopped, listing, stern awash, boats in water. [J attribution ?]
23	201 TRITON	3	28-22N 153-18E	Tra	1100	G	S	J	23	Tra	Unknown M.	1000	P	Sub position	PR says seen settling, bow down. [J attribution ?]
24	202 TROUT	3	33-30N 135-28E	AO	10000	T2/2DUP	S								
24	202 TROUT	3	33-31N 135-29E	AK	8000	T1/2DUP	S	I	24	C-AO	Tachibana M.	6521	LU	Off Susami Kii	PR says explosion seen; thought target may have beached.
25	190 SPEARFISH	3	17-01N 120-15E	AK	5000	T1/2DUP	S	AJ I	25	A-AP	Toba M.	6995	P DU	Lingayan Gulf W of Luzon	A says definitely sunk.
--							-	I	25	A	Tottori M.	6995	L	San Fernando	A says same ship as Toba M.; Tottori M was 5973T.

Dt/Hr	Submarine	Pt	Position	Tgt	Size	Attack	Cl	So	Date	Type	Name	Tons	Dm	Location	Comments
APR	1942														
26	177 PICKEREL	4	03- S 127- E	AK	7100	T1/7N	D	I	26	XAH	Takasago M.	9347	L	Manipa Str.	SORG shows no hits or damage; PR says 1 hit, then CO saw lighted red crosses on boat deck.
26/10	199 TAUTOG	2	18-11N 166-54W	SS	1500	T1/1DUP	S	J	26	SS	RO-30	965	S	Sub position	No sub lost here; RO-30 survived war. [J attribution incorrect.]
28	202 TROUT	3	32-59N 135-17E	PC	1000	T1/1NUP	S								
30	213 GREENLING	1	09-32N 156-03E	AK	7100	T0/6+G	D	I	30	XAE	Seia M.	6659	D	09-24N 156-18E	PR says hit by 3" fire.
MAY	1942														
1	201 TRITON	3	28-06N 123-47E	AK	5300	T1/2DUP	S	AIJ	1	A-AK	Calcutta M.	5338	S	28-05N 124-00E	
1	210 GRENADIER	2	32-00N 128-25E	AK	9500	T1/4NUP	S								
2	202 TROUT	3	33-26N 135-52E	AK	7000	T1/2DUP	S	AIJ	2	C-AK	Uzan M.	5019	S	Kashinosaki	
2/00	228 DRUM	1	34-26N 138-14E	AV	9000	T1/2NSV	S	AIW J	1-2	CVS	Mizuho	10930 9000	S	34-06N 137-46E	
4	202 TROUT	3	33-32N 136-05E	AK	5000	T1/2DUP	S	AIJW	4	XPG	Kongosan M.	2119	S	SW Daiosaki	
4	206 GAR	2	08- N 167- E	AK	4000	T1/2DUP	S								
4	213 GREENLING	1	08-44N 150-56E	AK	5800	T1/1DUP	S	AIJ	4	XPG	Kinjosan M.	3262	S	09-25N 151-51E	W lists ship but no info on loss.
6	184 SKIPJACK	3	12-33N 109-30E	AK	6000	T1/3DUP	S	AIJ	6-7	C-APK	Kanan M.	2567	S	Camranh Bay	
6	201 TRITON	3	28-42N 123-50E	AK	7000	T1/2NSV	S	AIJ	6	A-AK	Taiei M.	2208	S	28-00N 123-37E	
6	201 TRITON	3	28-19N 123-28E	APK	9000	T1/4NUP	S	AIJ	6	A	Taigen M.	5665	S	28-40N 124-00E	
8	184 SKIPJACK	3	12-18N 111-13E	AK	10000	T2/2DUP	S	AIJ	8	A-AK	Bujun M.	4804	S	12-18N 111-17E	
8	184 SKIPJACK	3	12-18N 111-13E	AK	7000	T1/4DUP	S								
8	210 GRENADIER	2	30-40N 127-54E	AP	14900	T2/4DUP	S	AIJ	8	A-AP	Taiyo M.	14457	S	30-45N 127-40E	
8/16	172 PORPOISE	3	03-50S 127-57E	AK	5000	T0/4DUP	0	I	16	XAH	Takasago M.	9347	L	03-19S 127-27E	PR says all torps missed. [Dud hit?]
9/14	228 DRUM	1	34- N 137- E	AK	6000	T1/4DUP	S	J	9	AK	Unknown M.	4000	P	33-49N 136-08E	PR says listing, down by stern. [J attribution ?]
10	236 SILVERSIDES	1	33-14N 150-58E	Tra	300	G		S							

Dt/Hr	Submarine	Pt	Position	Tgt	Size	Attack	Cl	So	Date	Type	Name	Tons	Dm	Location	Comments
MAY	1942														
11	153 S-42	1	05-06S 153-48E	CM	9800	T3/4NUP	S	AIW J	11	CM	Okinoshima	4470 4400	S	W of Buka I.	
12	155 S-44	1	05-06S 152-30E	AK	1900	T3/4DUP	S	AIJW	12	XAR	Shoei M.	5644	S	C. St. George	
12/12	180 POLLACK	3	30-55N 155-38E	Tra	600	GD	S								
13/10	228 DRUM	1	34 N 139 E	AK	6000	T1/1DUP	S	AI J	13	C-AK	Shonan M.	5356 5264	S	NE Mikomoto	
13/16	236 SILVERSIDES	1	33-52N 137-09E	SS	1400	T1/4DSV	S									
15	201 TRITON	3	28-22N 133-02E	Sam	100	G	S								
15	201 TRITON	3	28-22N 133-02E	Sam	100	G	S								
15	203 TUNA	2	33-34N 125-09E	AK	8000	T1/3	S	AIJW	15	XAP	Toyohara M.	805	S	Shokokuzan	
16	199 TAUTOG	2	07- N 152- E	AK	5000	T1/2DUP	S	I	16	XAO	Goyo M.	8469	H	S Truk I.	W says beached Truk, later salvaged.
17	184 SKIPJACK	3	06-22N 108-36E	AP	5300	T1/2DUP	S	AJ I	17	A-AP	Tazan M. Taizan M.	5477	S	06-55N 109-05E	
17	206 GAR	2	07- N 151- E	Q	2000	T1/2DUP	D									
17/17	236 SILVERSIDES	1	33-28N 135-33E	AK	5500	T2/3DUP	S	I J	17	A-AK	Thames M. Unknown M.	5871 4000	L PS	33-28N 135-35E	PR says blew up after heading for beach. J attribution ?; see 267 POMPON 25 Jul 43.]
17/17	236 SILVERSIDES	1	33-28N 135-33E	AK	8800	T2/2DUP	S	I	19	XAP	Tottori M.	5978	H	-> Manila	PR says 4 explosions after torps hit. [Attribution ?; location too indefinite.]
17/07	199 TAUTOG	2	07- N 152- E	SS	1500	T1/2DUP	S	IW J	16-7	SS	I-28	2198 2212	S	N of Rabaul	
17/11	199 TAUTOG	2	07- N 152- E	SS	1500	T2/3DUP	S								
17/18	201 TRITON	3	29-25N 134-06E	SS	1600	T1/1DUP	S	W IJ	?	SS	I-64 I-164	1635 1625	S	South Sea Area	I says missing after 25 May; subs not renumbered until 20 May.
17/21	180 POLLACK	3	31-00N 133-22E	Sam	100	GN	D								
--							-	A I	17	A-AK	Ryoga M.	5307	? S	Poulo Condore	No likely sub attack; A says sunk by mine 15 Feb 44; I & J list that sinking as Ryoka M, which A says is same ship.

Dt/Hr	Submarine	Pt	Position	Tgt	Size	Attack	Cl	So	Date	Type	Name	Tons	Dm	Location	Comments
MAY	1942														
20/00	180 POLLACK	3	31-00N 131-25E	Sam		GN	S								
20/00	180 POLLACK	3	31-00N 131-25E	Sam	100	GN	S								
22	199 TAUTOG	2	07- N 151- E	AK	5000	T1/1N	S	I	22	XAP	Sanko M.	5461	D	SW of Truk	
22	236 SILVERSIDES	1	33-30N 135-27E	AK	9600	T2/2DUP	S	I	22	XAP	Asahisan M.	4551	H	S of Ichiesaki	
23	193 SWORDFISH	4	02-21S 118-34E	AK	5000	T1/2	D								
24	181 POMPANO	2	25-16N 122-41E	Sam		GN	S	I	21	Fish	Kotoku M.	?	D	Uotsuri I.	[Attribution ?; dates do not agree.]
25	178 PERMIT	5	00-20N 118-20E	AK	6000	T0/4DUP	0	I	26	XAP	Senko M.	4472	D	00-13N 118-45N	PR says 1 torp could have hit.
25	181 POMPANO	2	25-56N 125-21E	AO	5000	T1/4	S	AIJ	25	C-AO	Tokyo M.	902	S	WNW of Naha	
25	182 SALMON	3	10-00N 110-00E	CL	2800	T4/4NUP	S	AIJW	25	AR	Asahi	11441	S	SE Camranh Bay	
25	199 TAUTOG	2	07- N 151- E	AK	5000	T1/2DUP	S	AIJW	25	XAP	Shoka M.	4467	S	04-05N 114-11E	
25/17	228 DRUM	1	34- N 139- E	AK	3000	T1/1DUP	S	AIJ	25	C-AK	Kitakata M.	2380	S	E Nojimasaki	
28	182 SALMON	3	09-00N 111-00E	AK	7000	T2/3NUP	S	AIJ	28	C-AK	Ganges M.	4382	S	09-07N 110-56E	
28/23	183 SEAL	3	07-27N 116-17E	AO	5000	T1/4NUP	S	J	28	A-AK	Tatsufuku M.	1946	S	Sub position	PR says hit seen & heard but ship continued on course. [J attribution ?; see 193 SWORDFISH 29 May.]
29/03	193 SWORDFISH	4	07-33N 116-18E	AO	3500	T2/3NUP	S	AI J	28-9	A-AK	Tatsufuku M. Unknown M.	1946 1900	S	Balabac Strait	PR says 2 explosions, sank in 2 minutes. J credits Tatsufuku M to 183 SEAL.
30	181 POMPANO	2	26-07N 129-06E	AP	10900	T2/2DUP	S	AJ I	30	A-AP	Atsuta M.	7983 7882	S	26-22N 129-20E	SORG gives incorrect posit 31N 134E.
31/03	180 POLLACK	3	31-38N 133-45E	Tra	200	GN	S	I W	31	XSC	Shunsei M. #5	92	S	Off Murotosan S Kii Channel	PR says hit & left burning; W credits 236 SILVERSIDES, which reported no likely attack in PR. [Attribution ?]
JUN	1942														
--							-	AJ I	1	A-AK	Kofuku M.	5822	SA S	16-16N 096-18E	No likely sub attack.
3	181 POMPANO	2	25-35N 141-12E	AK	400	T0/1+G	S								
3	236 SILVERSIDES	1	33-26N 135-33E	AO	10100	T1/2DUP	D								

10

Dt/Hr	Submarine	Pt	Position	Tgt	Size	Attack	Cl	So	Date	Type	Name	Tons	Dm	Location	Comments
JUN	1942														
4	168 NAUTILUS	1	30-13N 179-17W	CV	10000	T3/3DUP	S	AI J	5 4	CV	Soryu	15900 17500	SA JS	30-20N 179-17E	J credits a/c & NAUTILUS; Japanese sources say Kaga hit but undamaged. [J attribution ?]
4	HMS TRUSTY	3	Malacca Strait	AP	8000	T2/?	S	AIJ	4	A-AK	Toyohashi M.	7031	S	07-14N 098-06E	
5	181 POMPANO	2	25-04N 143-02E	Tra	100	G	S								
6	193 SWORDFISH	4	05-00N 104-00E	AK	6500	T1/2DUP	D								
12	193 SWORDFISH	4	10-08N 102-34E	AK	6900	T2/2NSV	S	AIJ	12	C-AK	Burma M.	4585	S	10-12N 102-29E	
13	191 SCULPIN	4	08- N 115- E	AK	4000	T1/3DUP	D								
14	191 SCULPIN	4	06- N 114- E	AO	8000	T1/4NSV	D								
14	191 SCULPIN	4	06- N 114- E	AO	8000	T1/3DUP	D								
15	197 SEAWOLF	5	14- N 120- E	AK	4500	T1/3DUP	D	A IJW	15	XPG	Nanpo M. Nampo M.	1206	S	Corregidor	
17	229 FLYING FISH	1	26-08N 157-24E	AO	5000	T2/7DUP	D								
18	191 SCULPIN	4	14- N 109- E	AK	7000	T1/1NSV	S								
21	155 S-44	2	09-00S 160-00E	XPG	1100	Unk	S	AIJW	21	XPG	Keijo M.	2626	S	W of Gavutu	
22	170 CACHALOT	2	32-15N 140-05E	AO	9200	T1/2DUP	D								
--							-	A	24	C-AK	Nissho M. #2	344	S	Etorofu I.	A says this is same ship as Nissho Maru; see 167 NARWHAL 24 Jul; no likely sub attack 24 Jun.
25	168 NAUTILUS	1	34-34N 140-26E	DD	1700	T2/2DUP	S	AW J	25	DD	Yamakaze	1685 1580	S	Off Katsuura	I says sunk by unk agent, E coast Japan, 24 Jun.
25	187 STURGEON	4	15-47N 119-33E	AK	7000	T1/3DUP	D								
25/10	214 GROUPER	1	28-46N 136-36E	AO	19600	T1/4DUP	D	A I	25	XAO	Tonan M. #3	19209 19262	?	28-54N 136-54E	SORG gives incorrect latitude 24N.
26	169 DOLPHIN	2	31-00N 133-53E	AO	8000	T2/3NUP	D								

11

Dt/Hr	Submarine	Pt	Position	Tgt	Size	Attack	Cl	So	Date	Type	Name	Tons	Dm	Location	Comments
JUN	1942														
27	168 NAUTILUS	1	34-38N 140-08E	PG	1500	T1/1NUP	S	IW	16 Jul	XAM	Musashi M.	227	S	NE Nojimasaki	PR says seen to sink by stern; W says possibly sunk by 167 NARWHAL or 170 CACHALOT, but NAUTILUS attack is only likely one. [Attribution ?; dates do not agree.]
28	186 STINGRAY	4	12-41N 136-22E	AK	9000	T2/4DUP	D	AIJW	28	XPG	Saikyo M.	1296	S	12-34N 136-20E	
30	179 PLUNGER	2	30-04N 122-54E	AK	9500	T1/1DUP	S	AIJ	29-30	C-AK	Unkai M. #5	3282	S	30-00N 123-00E	
JUL	1942														
1	187 STURGEON	4	18-37N 119-29E	APK	10000	T1/4NUP	S	AIJW	1	XAP	Montevideo M.	7266	S	18-35N 120-25E	
2	179 PLUNGER	2	30- N 123- E	AK	9500	T2/3NSV	S	AJ I	2	A-AK	Unyo M. #3	2997 2977	S	30-25N 123-25E	
2	179 PLUNGER	2	30- N 123- E	AK	6000	T1/1NSV	D								
2	179 PLUNGER	2	30- N 123- E	AK	4000	T1/2NSV	D								
3	HMS TRUANT	4	Malacca Strait	MV	Unk	T0/2	0	A I	4	A-AK	Tamon M. #1	3019	S M	03-14N 099-48E	BSH claims no damage. [Attribution ?]
4	201 TRITON	4	52-15N 173-51E	DD	1400	T1/2DUP	S	AIW J	4-5	DD	Nenohi	1715 1600	S	Agattu	Chart in I shows location Kiska.
4	229 FLYING FISH	1	26-18N 121-00E	DD	1200	T1/2NSV	D								
5	215 GROWLER	1	52-00N 177-40E	DD	1700	T1/1DUP	S	AIW J	5	DD	Arare	1960 1850	S	Kiska Bay	
5	215 GROWLER	1	52-00N 177-40E	DD	1700	T1/1DUP	S	AI	5	DD	Kasumi	1961	H	Kiska Bay	
5	215 GROWLER	1	52-00N 177-40E	DD	1700	T1/2DUP	D	AI	5	DD	Shiranui	2033	H	Kiska Bay	
5	230 FINBACK	1	51- N 177- E	DD	1500	T1/3DUP	D								
5/10	187 STURGEON	4	16-07N 119-13E	AO	4000	T0/3DUP	0	I	7	XAO	San Pedro M.	7268	M	S of Palavig	PR says torps heard running, only 2 end-of-run explosions; no likely sub attack 7 Jul. [Attribution ?]
6	200 THRESHER	4	08-36N 170-57E	AO	5000	T1/2DUP	D								

12

Dt/Hr	Submarine	Pt	Position	Tgt	Size	Attack	Cl	So	Date	Type	Name	Tons	Dm	Location	Comments
JUL	1942														
6	214 GROUPER	1	29-37N 127-36E	AP	9000	T3/6DUP	D								
7	191 SCULPIN	4	04- N 119- E	AO	10000	T1/3DUP	D								
8	142 S-37	5	04- S 151- E	AK	10000	T2/3DUP	D	A IJW	8	XAP	Tensan M. Tenzan M.	2775	S	N of Rabaul	
9	192 SAILFISH	5	11-31N 109-21E	AK	7000	T1/2DUP	S	I	9	A-AK	Aobasan M.	8811	M	11-40N 109-40E	
9	200 THRESHER	4	08-43N 167-33E	APK	6000	T2/2DUP	S	AIJ W	9	XAGP XAG	Shinsho M. Shinshu M.	4836	S	Kwajalein	W lists as torp recovery ship.
11	145 S-40	5	08-20S 158-47E	AK	5000	T1/4	D								
12	194 SEADRAGON	3	13-47N 109-33E	AK	4100	T2/2NSV	S	A IJ	12	C-AK	Nichizan M. Hiyama M.	6171	S	Qui Nhon, FIC	
13	194 SEADRAGON	3	13-05N 109-29E	AK	7000	T1/2DUP	S	AIJ	13	B-AG	Shinyo M.	4163	S	Cape Varella	Ship not in W.
15	216 GRUNION	1L	52-02N 177-42E	PC	300	Unk	S	AIW J	15	PC	Ch 25	460 300	S	Kiska Bay	
15	216 GRUNION	1L	52-02N 177-42E	PC	300	Unk	S	AIW J	15	PC	Ch 27	460 300	S	Kiska Bay	
16	194 SEADRAGON	3	12-55N 109-29E	AK	7000	T1/4DUP	S	AIJ	16	C-AK	Hakodate M.	5303	S	N Camranh Bay	
--							-	IW	16	XAM	Musashi M.	227	S	E Nojimasaki	See 168 NAUTILUS 27 Jun.
24	167 NARWHAL	3	45-09N 147-31E	AK	1000	G	S	I J	24	? AK	Nissho M. Unknown M.	344 1500	S	Etorofu I. Sub position	A says ship is Nissho M #2 but gives date 24 Jun; see listing that date. [Attribution ?]
24	167 NARWHAL	3	45-14N 147-31E	AK	1500	G	S	AI	24	C-AK	Kofuji M.	134	S	Off Oito	
24/16	236 SILVERSIDES	2	32-35N 158-54E	Tra	500	GD	S	I	24	?	Name Unknown	?	?	?	PR says left afire from 50 hits. [Attribution ?; no location given.]
24/20	167 NARWHAL	3	44-53N 147-09E	Sam	200	G	S	IW	24	XPkt	Shinsei M. #83	63	S	Utasutsu Bay	
24/21	167 NARWHAL	3	44-55N 147-03E	Sam	200	G	S								
26	167 NARWHAL	3	44-50N 147-55E	Sam	100	G	S								
27	190 SPEARFISH	4	11-28N 110-52E	APK	12000	T2/4NUP	S	I	27	XAS	Rio de Jan. M.	9627	M	E Camranh Bay	

13

Dt/Hr	Submarine	Pt	Position	Tgt	Size	Attack	Cl	So	Date	Type	Name	Tons	Dm	Location	Comments
JUL	1942														
27	HNMS O-23	1	05-07N 098-50E	Cstr	Unk	G	D	I	27	B-AG	Shofuku M. #2	729	?	S of Penang	Ship not in W.
28	236 SILVERSIDES	2	33-21N 139-24E	APK	7500	T3/3DUP	S	J	28	AP	Unknown M.	4000	S	Sub position	PR says not seen after attack, believed sank immediately. [J attribution ?]
30	210 GRENADIER	3	07-11N 151-22E	AO	15000	T2/3DUP	S								
31	211 GUDGEON	4	07-37N 150-10E	AK	8500	T2/3NSV	S								
31 W	216 GRUNION	1L	Unk	Unk	Unk	Unk	U	AI	31	XAP	Kashima M.	8572	M	NE of Kiska	Attack not in SORG or U; W says beached on Kiska 21 Jul after attack by GRUNION, destroyed 7-8 Aug by surface ships & a/c; J identifies that ship as Kano M., 8572T. [Attribution ?]
AUG	1942														
1	167 NARWHAL	3	41-12N 141-36E	AK	6500	T3/3DUP	S	AIJ	1	C-AK	Meiwa M.	2921	S	41-17N 141-34E	
1	167 NARWHAL	3	41-03N 141-28E	AO	4000	T1/2DUP	D	AI	1	C-AK	Koan M.	884	M	41-14N 141-30E	
1	177 PICKEREL	5	14- N 145- E	AK	4800	T1/2NUP	D								
2	197 SEAWOLF	6	02-44S 118-36E	AO	7000	T1/4DUP	D								
2	HNMS O-23	1	Off Penang	MV	Unk	T		S	AIJ	2	A-AK	Zenyo M.	6440	S	05-36N 099-53E	
2	HNMS O-23	1	Off Penang	MV	Unk	T1/2		S	Note 2		A-AP	Ohio M.	5873	S	Malacca Strait	BSH & DNO claim sinking; see 199 TAUTOG 6 Aug. [Attribution ?]
3	211 GUDGEON	4	07-37N 150-11E	AK	9500	T2/3DUP	S	AIJW	3	XAP	Naniwa M.	4853	S	07-17N 150-46E	
4	167 NARWHAL	3	40-26N 141-50E	AK	Unk	T0/2DUP	0	A I	4	C-AK	Fukuyama M.	6040 6020	M	40-18N 141-51E	PR says dud hit heard.
5	213 GREENLING	2	09-50N 150-38E	AP	13000	T2/7NSV	S	AIW J	5	XAP	Brazil M. Brasil M.	12752	S	09-51N 150-46E	I gives tons as 12733; W says ship was to be converted to CV.
6	213 GREENLING	2	09-04N 150-54E	AP	11000	T3/3NSV	S	AI J	5 6	C-APK	Palau M. Palao M.	4495	S	08-00N 150-42E	
6	228 DRUM	2	06-53N 152-04E	AK	4000	T1/3DUP	D								
6/00	199 TAUTOG	3	13-51N 113-15E	AK	7000	T2/3		S	AI J	5 6	A-AP	Ohio M.	5873	S PS	S China Sea	SORG gives incorrect date 16 Aug. See HNMS O-23 2 Aug. [J attribution ?]

14

Dt/Hr	Submarine	Pt	Position	Tgt	Size	Attack	Cl	So	Date	Type	Name	Tons	Dm	Location	Comments
AUG	1942														
7	143 S-38	7	04-52S 152-42E	AP	8000	T2/2	S	AIJW	8	XAP	Meiyo M.	5627	S	04-50S 152-40E	
7	198 TAMBOR	3	09- N 170- E	AK	7000	T1/1DUP S	A IJW		7	XAN	Shofuku M. #1 Shofuku M.	891	S	09-25N 170-11E	
8	167 NARWHAL	3	41-14N 141-32E	AK	5000	T1/2DUP S	AIJW	8	Crab	Bifuku M.	2559	S	41-30N 141-10E	
8	236 SILVERSIDES	2	33-33N 135-23E	APK	7000	T1/2DUP S	AI J		8	C-AK	Nikkei M.	5783 5811	S	33-33N 135-24E	
10	155 S-44	3	02-15S 152-15E	CA	7100	T4/4DUP S	AIW J		9-10	CA	Kako	8700 8800	S	02-30N 152-10E	
--							-	AI	10	C-AK	Eifuku M. #15	867	S	Off Timor I.	No likely sub attack.
12	181 POMPANO	3	33-31N 136-00E	AK	6900	T1/1DUP S	J		12	AK	Unknown M.	4000	S	Sub position	PR says target down by stern. [J attribution ?]
12	181 POMPANO	3	33-31N 136-00E	DD	1200	T1/1DUP S									
12	231 HADDOCK	1	29-45N 132-45E	AK	8500	T3/5NSV S									
13	209 GRAYLING	3	07- N 151- E	AK	10000	T2/4DUP S									
14	197 SEAWOLF	6	05-07N 119-37E	APK	3100	T1/3DUP S	AIJ		14-5	C-APK	Hachigen M.	3113	S	05-03N 114-37E	
14	236 SILVERSIDES	2	33-25N 135-31E	AO	5400	T1/3DUP D									
15	201 TRITON	4	52-45N 175-49E	DL	1700	T1/4NSV S									
15	212 GATO	2	51-05N 162-07E	AK	9300	T4/5	S								
17	211 GUDGEON	4	07-43N 151-13E	AK	8500	T3/3DUP S	I	17	XAO	Shinkoku M.	10020	L	07-40N 151-05E	
17	211 GUDGEON	4	07-43N 151-13E	APK	8500	T2/3DUP S	I	17	XAO	Nichiei M.	10020	L	NW of Truk	
17/07	168 NAUTILUS	2	03- N 172- E	PY	1500	GD	S								
17/07	168 NAUTILUS	2	03- N 172- E	AP	3500	GD	S								
20	146 S-41	4	06-01N 152-35E	AK	4000	T2/2NSV D									
20	146 S-41	4	06-01N 152-35E	AK	4000	T2/2NSV D									
21	171 CUTTLEFISH	3	31- N 130- E	AK	10000	T2/3DUP S	I	21	XAP	Nichiro M.	6534	L	30-00N 132-25E	

Dt/Hr	Submarine	Pt	Position	Tgt	Size	Attack	Cl	So	Date	Type	Name	Tons	Dm	Location	Comments
AUG	1942														
21	171 CUTTLEFISH	3	31- N 130- E	DD	1500	T1/1DUP	D								
21	198 TAMBOR	3	06-45N 158-10E	AK	5000	T3/3DUP	S	AIJW	21	XAC	Shinsei M. #6	4928	S	07-02N 158-03E	
22	217 GUARDFISH	1	39-40N 142-10E	Tra	400	G	S								
22	231 HADDOCK	1	26-07N 121-29E	AK	6300	T2/4DUP	S	AIW J	22	XAP	Tatsuho M. Unknown M.	6334 4000	S	25-52N 121-29E	
23	184 SKIPJACK	4	03-52S 127-54E	AO	5000	T1/4DUP	D	I	23	AO	Hayatomo	14050	L	SW of Ambon	W gives name Hayamoto.
23	217 GUARDFISH	1	39-15N 142-08E	Sam	100	G	S								
23/06	146 S-41	4	08-22S 158-45E	SS	1500	T2/3DUP	S								
24	189 SAURY	4	14-15N 120-19E	AO	9000	T1/2DUP	D	I	24	C-AO	Otowasan M.	9024	H	14-20N 120-08E	
24	217 GUARDFISH	1	38-12N 141-30E	APK	7200	T2/3DUP	S	AIJ	24	C-APK	Seikai M.	3109	S	Off Kinkazan	
25/07	197 SEAWOLF	6	03-55N 118-59E	AO	5000	T1/2DUP	S	J I	25 22	AK	Showa M.	1349	P S	Sub position Off Manila	PR says debris and survivors seen. No likely sub attack 22 Aug; A says records show ship salvaged off Manila, date not given. [J attribution ?]
25	215 GROWLER	2	22-33N 120-10E	AP	6000	T2/4DUP	S	AIJ W	25	XPG	Senyo M. Sen-Yo	2904	S	SSW of Takao	
25/06	217 GUARDFISH	1	40-04N 142-05E	AK	7000	T0/3DUP	D								PR says dud hit; torp seen floating without warhead.
26	213 GREENLING	2	05-13N 160-17E	Sam		G	S								
26	231 HADDOCK	1	26-27N 121-23E	AK	9500	T1/6DUP	S	AIJ	26	C-AK	Teishun M.	2251	S	26-53N 121-23E	
28	229 FLYING FISH	2	07- N 151- E	BB	29300	T2/4	D								
31	215 GROWLER	2	25-29N 122-37E	AK	5500	T2/2NUP	S	AJ I	31	C-AK	Eifuku M.	5866 5816	S	Off Sankaku I.	
31	236 SILVERSIDES	2	33-51N 149-39E	Tra	300	G	S								
SEP	1942														
1	198 TAMBOR	3	07- N 151- E	AO	10000	T1/4DUP	D								
1/01	236 SILVERSIDES	2	34-10N 150-05E	Tra	300	GN	D								

Dt/Hr	Submarine	Pt	Position	Tgt	Size	Attack	Cl	So	Date	Type	Name	Tons	Dm	Location	Comments
SEP	1942														
2	142 S-37	6	09-02S 159-51E	DD	1500	T2/2NSV	D								
2	217 GUARDFISH	1	41-49N 143-04E	AK	7500	T2/4DUP	S	AIJ	2	C-AK	Teikyu M.	2332	S	SSW Erimozaki	
3	183 SEAL	4	11- N 109- E	APK	4000	T1/1DUP	D	I	3	C-APK	Kanju M.	7267	H	SE C. Padaran	See SEAL 5 Sep.
3	229 FLYING FISH	2	07- N 151- E	PC	400	T1/2NSV	S								
4	181 POMPANO	3	35-22N 151-40E	PC	900	G		S	IW	15	XPkt	Nanshin M. #27	83	S	37N 152E	PR says ship had id. #163, took prisoner. A lists this ship as 834T A-AO, sunk 12 Sep 44. [Attribution ?]
4	215 GROWLER	2	25-41N 122-34E	Sam		G		S								
4	215 GROWLER	2	25-43N 122-38E	AO	10000	T3/4DUP	S	AIW J	4	AE AF	Kashino	10360 4000	S	25-45N 122-41E	W says ship specially designed to transport guns for BB Yamato.
4	217 GUARDFISH	1	40-14N 141-51E	AK	11000	T1/1DUP	S	AIJ	4	C-AK	Kaimei M.	5253	S	Kuji Bay	
4	217 GUARDFISH	1	40-14N 141-51E	AK	9000	T1/2DUP	S	AJ I	4	C-APK	Tenyu M.	3738 1118	S	Kuji Bay	
4	217 GUARDFISH	1	40-12N 141-49E	AK	5800	T1/1DUP	S	AIJ	4	C-AK	Chita M.	2276	S	Kuji Bay	
4	217 GUARDFISH	1	40-10N 141-53E	AK	9000	T2/3DUP	S								
5	171 CUTTLEFISH	3	34- N 133- E	AO	19600	T3/5NUP	S								
5/02	183 SEAL	4	11-00N 109-32E	AK		T0/3DUP	O	I	4	C-APK	Kanju M.	7267	D	SE Camranh Bay	PR says explosion thought premature; this ship damaged by SEAL attack 4 Sep.
7	215 GROWLER	2	25-31N 121-38E	AK	4500	T1/2DUP	S	AIJ	7	C-AK	Taika M.	2204	S	S of Fukikaku	
11	189 SAURY	4	03-15S 118-27E	AV	10000	T1/3NSV	S	AIJW	11	XAPV	Kanto M.	8606	S	NW C. Kendari	
12/21	158 S-47	3	05-29S 152-17E	CA	7100	T3/4NSV	S								
13	218 ALBACORE	1	08-34N 151-40E	AK	8000	T1/3DUP	D								
16	187 STURGEON	5	05-28S 152-58E	AO	10000	T2/4NUP	S								
18	219 AMBERJACK	1	04-50S 154-37E	AP	7000	T1/4NSV	D								
19	200 THRESHER	5	07-36S 116-15E	AK	6000	T1/1DUP	D								
19	200 THRESHER	5	07-36S 116-15E	AK	5000	T1/1DUP	D								

Dt/Hr	Submarine	Pt	Position	Tgt	Size	Attack	Cl	So	Date	Type	Name	Tons	Dm	Location	Comments
SEP	1942														
19	219 AMBERJACK	1	06-33S 156-05E	AP	5000	T2/2DUP	S	AIJW	19	XAP	Shirogane M.	3130	S	06-25S 156-20E	
20	238 WAHOO	1	07-43N 150-36E	AK	6500	T1/4NUP	S								
20/16	214 GROUPER	2	31-18N 123-27E	AK	5000	T1/1NSV	S	AJ	21	A-AK	Tone M.	4070	S	Formosa Strait	A says records show both dates.
								AI	17						
21	202 TROUT	5	06-54N 151-51E	AP	8200	T3/3DUP	S	AIJW	21	XAN	Koei M.	863	S	06-45N 152-34E	
24	168 NAUTILUS	3	40-41N 146-36E	PC	1000	G	D								
24	190 SPEARFISH	5	11-32N 121-07E	CM	3000	T1/3DUP	S								
25	168 NAUTILUS	3	39-47N 142-40E	Sam	200	G	S								
25	188 SARGO	5	10-31N 109-31E	AK	7000	T2/6DUP	S	AIJ	25	C-AK	Teibo M.	4472	S	10-35N 109-30E	
25	234 KINGFISH	1	33-27N 135-40E	AK	5300	T1/3DUP	D								
26	168 NAUTILUS	3	38-43N 142-20E	Sam	400	G	S								
27	168 NAUTILUS	3	40-35N 141-50E	APK	8700	T1/5+G	D	AJ	28	C-AK	Tamon M. #6	4994	S	40-33N 141-52E	PR says hit by 6" guns after torp attack.
								I	26						
28	191 SCULPIN	5	03-47S 151-36E	AO	9200	T2/4DUP	S	AI	28	CVS	Nisshin	11317	LC	E of Kokoda I.	PR says 2 hits seen. [Attribution ?]
28	202 TROUT	5	06-59N 151-45E	CV	17200	T2/5DUP	D	AI	28	CVE	Taiyo	17830	M	E of Truk	
30	194 SEADRAGON	4	12-27N 109-28E	AK	5500	T1/2NSV	S								
OCT	1942														
1	168 NAUTILUS	3	41-20N 141-35E	AK	5900	T2/3DUP	S	AIJ	1	C-AK	Tosei M.	2432	S	E Shiriyazaki	
1	187 STURGEON	5	05-51S 153-18E	AK	7000	T3/4DUP	S	AIJW	1	XAPV	Katsuragi M.	8033	S	05-38S 153-08E	
1	214 GROUPER	2	29-57N 122-56E	AK	7000	T2/6DUP	S	AIJ	1	A-AP	Lisbon M.	7053	S	30-17N 123-13E	
1	218 ALBACORE	1	09-02N 150-42E	AO	6000	T2/2DUP	D								
1	234 KINGFISH	1	33-31N 135-26E	AK	7000	T1/3DUP	S	AIJ	1	C-AK	Yomei M.	2860	S	33-32N 135-27E	
3	213 GREENLING	3	38-46N 142-02E	AK	4000	T1/3DUP	S	AJ	3	C-AK	Kinkai M.	5852	S	39-00N 142-00E	
								I				5552			
4	155 S-44	4	07-52S 157-40E	DD	1500	T3/4DUP	S								

Dt/Hr	Submarine	Pt	Position	Tgt	Size	Attack	Cl	So	Date	Type	Name	Tons	Dm	Location	Comments
OCT	1942														
4	213 GREENLING	3	39-48N 142-08E	AK	8000	T2/3DUP S		AIJ	4	C-AK	Setsuyo M.	4146	S	Off Sanriku	
5	196 SEARAVEN	5	10-25S 105-42E	AK	6900	T1/1DUP D									
5	214 GROUPER	2	32-06N - E	AK	4000	T1/4DUP D	I		4	?	Tx1	?	S	E of Izu I.	[Attribution ?; insufficient info to identify ship.]
5	234 KINGFISH	1	32-55N 133-45E	AK	5000	T1/4NSV D									
5	237 TRIGGER	2	31-40N 142-06E	AK	4000	T2/5NSV D	I		5	XAP	Shinkoku M.	3991	L	31-40N 142-00E	
7	191 SCULPIN	5	03-14S 150-01E	AP	4700	T3/4DUP S		AIJ	7	A-AP	Naminoue M.	4731	S	Off Rabaul	
7	219 AMBERJACK	1	01-55N 153-01E	AK	4000	T2/4NSV S		AIJW	7	XAF	Senkai M.	2101	S	01-10N 153-31E	
8	228 DRUM	3	34-06N 136-22E	AK	5300	T1/2DUP S		AIJ	8	C-AK	Hague M.	5641	S	34-01N 135-06E	SORG gives incorrect posit 33N 136E.
9	190 SPEARFISH	6	15-26N 117-05E	AK	7000	T2/3DUP D									SORG incorrectly shows no hits.
9	228 DRUM	3	33-27N 136-01E	AK	7000	T1/3DUP S		AJ I	8-9	C-AK	Hachimanzan M. Yawatasan M.	2461	S	33-30N 136-06E	
10	194 SEADRAGON	4	01-01S 117-22E	AK	7000	T2/2DUP S		AIW J	10	XAP	Shigure M.	1579 2445	S	01-07S 117-19E	
10	218 ALBACORE	1	08-20N 151-29E	AK	4000	T1/2DUP D									
10	219 AMBERJACK	1	02-36S 150-48E	AO	19600	T2/2DUP S		A I	10	C-AO B-AG	Tonan M. #2 Tonan M.	19262	S M	Kavieng Anch.	A says Tonan Maru #2 salvaged, towed to Japan & repaired.
10	219 AMBERJACK	1	02-36S 150-48E	AK	7000	T1/2DUP D	I		10	XAP	Tenryu M.	4861	M	Kavieng Anch.	
12	196 SEARAVEN	5	06-10S 105-37E	AK	7900	T1/4DUP S									
14	184 SKIPJACK	5	05-35N 144-25E	AK	7000	T2/2DUP S		AIJ	14	A-AK	Shunko M.	6780	S	05-45N 144-25E	
14	191 SCULPIN	5	03-51S 151-21E	AO	10200	T2/4NSV S		AI J	14	A-AK	Sumiyoshi M.	1921	S	03-15S 149-50E 03-20S 150-03E	
14	213 GREENLING	3	39-33N 142-15E	AK	9000	T3/3DUP S		AIJ	14	C-AK	Takusei M.	3509	S	40-10N 142-20E	
14/15	230 FINBACK	2	25-20N 121-25E	Aux	8000	T1/2	D								PR says down by bow, being abandoned 3 hrs after after attack.

Dt/Hr	Submarine	Pt	Position	Tgt	Size	Attack	Cl	So	Date	Type	Name	Tons	Dm	Location	Comments
OCT	1942														
14/15	230 FINBACK	2	25-20N 121-25E	AP	5400	T1/2	D	AIJ	14	C-AP	Teison M.	7007	S	25-20N 121-01E	PR says missing when FINBACK surfaced; SORG shows no hits.
17	213 GREENLING	3	38-46N 142-03E	AK	11000	T2/6NSV	S	AIJW	18	XAP	Hakonesan M.	6673	S	37-35N 141-30E	
17	237 TRIGGER	2	32-21N 132-04E	AK	5000	T2/4NSV	S	AIJ	17	C-AK	Holland M.	5870	S	E of Hososhima	
18	191 SCULPIN	5	05-31S 156-05E	AK	4000	T2/4DUP	D								
18	207 GRAMPUS	4	07-47S 157-19E	CL	5100	T1/4DUP	D	I	18	CL	Yura	5170	L	?	SORG incorrectly shows no hits or damage.
18	230 FINBACK	2	25-11N 122-01E	APK	5800	T2/4DUP	D								
18/10	137 S-32	5	50-01N 156-00E	AK	6000	T2/4DUP	D								
19	217 GUARDFISH	2	26- N 126- E	AK	7200	T1/6DUP	D								
20	199 TAUTOG	4	06-59N 119-20E	Sam	100	G	S	I	19	C	Nanshin M.	33	S	07-00N 119-40E	
20	228 DRUM	3	34- N 136- E	AK	7200	T1/2DUP	S	AIJ	20	C-AK	Ryunan M.	5106	S	34-09N 136-46E	
20	230 FINBACK	2	24-26N 120-25E	AK	7000	T2/2NUP	S	AIJ	20-1	A-APK	Africa M.	9476	S	24-26N 120-26E	
20	230 FINBACK	2	24-26N 120-25E	AK	7000	T1/2NUP	S	AJ I	20 19	A-AK	Yamafuji M.	5359	S HC	25-20N 121-01E Off Pescadores	
20	236 SILVERSIDES	3	06-45N 151-30E	APK	9500	T2/3NUP	S								
20	237 TRIGGER	2	31-13N 132-50E	AO	10000	T2/4NUP	D								
21	211 GUDGEON	5	03-30S 150-30E	AK	7000	T2/3DUP	S	AJW I	21	XAP	Choko M.	6783	S H	S of Kavieng	
21/00	213 GREENLING	3	39-37N 142-45E	Sam	50	GN	S								
21/14	217 GUARDFISH	2	27-03N 122-42E	AK	6700	T1/4DUP	S	AIJ	21	C-AK	Nichiho M.	6362	S	27-25N 123-05E	PR says seen to sink.
21/14	217 GUARDFISH	2	27-03N 122-42E	AO	8700	T1/3DUP	S	J	21	AK	Unknown M.	4000	S	Sub position	PR says hit, sank in 2 min, lifeboat launched. [J attribution ?]
22	208 GRAYBACK	4	04-45S 152-53E	AP	8000	T2/4DUP	S								
22	213 GREENLING	3	37-30N 145-00E	CVE	22000	T2/5DUP	D	I	20	CVE	Hiyo	26949	LU	?	[Attribution ?]
23	234 KINGFISH	1	33-20N 135-27E	AK	5000	T2/2DUP	S	AIJW	23	XPG	Seikyo M.	2608	S	33-12N 135-14E	

Dt/Hr	Submarine	Pt	Position	Tgt	Size	Attack	Cl	So	Date	Type	Name	Tons	Dm	Location	Comments
OCT	1942														
24	168 NAUTILUS	3	41-24N 141-50E	AK	3200	T2/3DUP	S	AIJ	24-5	C-AK	Kenun M.	4643	S	41-10N 141-38E	
24	237 TRIGGER	2	32-06N 132-34E	AO	10100	T1/4DUP	D	I	24	XAO	Nissho M.	10526	H	Bungo Channel	
25/11	168 NAUTILUS	3	41-45N 145-32E	Sam	400	GD	S								
25	239 WHALE	1	33- N 135- E	AK	9400	T2/3NUP	S	I	26	XAO	Kirishima M.	5959	?U	Hinomisaki	I gives tons as 8267 (A says this is DWT); W says ship was former AK converted to AO 1942.
25	239 WHALE	1	33- N 135- E	AK	7500	T1/1DUP	D								
25	239 WHALE	1	33- N 135- E	AK	5100	T1/1DUP	D								
25	HNMS O-23	3	Off Penang	MV	Unk	T1/?	D	I	25	A-AK	Shinyu M.	4621	M	05-28N 099-56E	
26/09	136 S-31	5	50-10N 155-36E	CM	3000	T2/2DUP	S	AIJW	26	XAP	Keizan M.	2864	S	50-10N 155-44E	
27/22	199 TAUTOG	4	10-20N 108-43E	APK	5000	T2/2NUP	S	J	27	APK	Unknown M.	4000	S	Sub position	PR says bow rose up & ship sank 7 min after hit. [J attribution ?]
27	228 DRUM	3	33- N 135- E	AK	6700	T1/4DUP	D								
28	199 TAUTOG	4	10-32N 109-15E	AK	3000	T1/2DUP	D								
29	239 WHALE	1	33- N 135- E	AK	5500	T1/2DUP	D								
--						-		IW	30	XPkt	Roshu M.	99	S	Sagami-Nada	W says sunk by 228 DRUM gunfire S of Honshu; DRUM PR shows no gun attacks. No likely sub attack.
31/18	200 THRESHER	5	04-40S 118-54E	AO	3000	GN	S	J	31	AK	Unknown M.	3000	P	Sub position	PR says ship aground on reef, under salvage; left afire & adrift after gun hits. [J attribution ?]
31	208 GRAYBACK	4	04-37S 152-30E	AP	7200	T1/3DUP	S	I	31	A-AK	Noto M.	7191	H	Rabaul area	
NOV	1942														
2	153 S-42	4	07-10S 156-00E	DD	1500	T1/4DUP	D								
2	158 S-47	4	06-50S 154-40E	CA	7100	T1/4NSV	D								
2	197 SEAWOLF	7	06-14N 126-07E	APK	3500	T1/3DUP	D	AIJ	2-3	A-AK	Gifu M.	2933	S	San Augustin	
3	179 PLUNGER	3	07-59S 159-52E	CL	5200	T2/4NSV	D								

Dt/Hr	Submarine	Pt	Position	Tgt	Size	Attack	Cl	So	Date	Type	Name	Tons	Dm	Location	Comments
NOV	1942														
3	197 SEAWOLF	7	07-02N 125-33E	APK	9300	T3/6DUP	S	AIJW	3	XAP	Sagami M.	7189	S	Davao harbor	
3	197 SEAWOLF	7	07- N 125- E	AK	5000	T1/3DUP	D								
3	198 TAMBOR	4	21-18N 108-39E	APK	10000	T1/2DUP	S	A IJ	3	C-AK	Chikugo M.	2444 2461	S	NW Hainan I.	
3	230 FINBACK	2	25-25N 126-31E	Sam	100	G	S								
3/02	231 HADDOCK	2	32-02N 126-13E	AO	10000	T1/3NSV	S	AJ I	5 3	C-AK	Tekkai M. Tekka M.	1925	S	32-18N 126-52E	PR says broke in two & sank in 4 mins; Japanese records show sinking 2 days later.
4	208 GRAYBACK	4	05-00S 152-36E	AK	8500	T1/4NSV	D								
6	207 GRAMPUS	4	07-48S 157-29E	DD	1500	T1/3DUP	D								
6	209 GRAYLING	4	06-44N 151-25E	AV	9000	T2/3DUP	D								
6/13	231 HADDOCK	2	33-46N 127-28E	AK	5000	T0/3DUP	0	A I	6	A-AK	France M.	5828 ?	H	33-49N 127-28E	PR says torps went under target without exploding.
8	182 SALMON	5	16-20N 119-11E	AK	7000	T2/2DUP	D								
8	197 SEAWOLF	7	07- N 125- E	APK	4000	T2/2DUP	S	AIJW	8	XPG	Keiko M.	2929	S	06-24N 125-59E	
8	233 HERRING	1A	33-34N 007-52W	AK	7000	T2/4DUP	S	Note	8	AK	Ville du Havre	5083	S	33-34N 007-52W	Hervieux says Vichy French AK.
9	207 GRAMPUS	4	07-32S 157-07E	DD	1400	T2/6DUP	S								
9	221 BLACKFISH	1A	Unk	AK	7000	T1/2	D	Note							Roscoe says believed to be French ship.
9	236 SILVERSIDES	3	02-26S 149-36E	DD	1300	T2/5NSV	S								
10	182 SALMON	5	15-10N 119-42E	Sam	100	G	S								
10	198 TAMBOR	4	09-03N 120-30E	Sam		G	S								
10	209 GRAYLING	4	07-12N 150-47E	AO	5300	T1/2NSV	S	A J	10	? AK	Sendai M. Unknown M.	472 4000	SU	07-12N 150-47E	PR says small AO broke in half & sank; W lists as XAF, sunk 20 Jan 42 in Davao Gulf by collision. [Attribution ?]
11	211 GUDGEON	5	03-31S 148-12E	AK	7500	T1/3NSV	D								

Dt/Hr	Submarine	Pt	Position	Tgt	Size	Attack	Cl	So	Date	Type	Name	Tons	Dm	Location	Comments
NOV	1942														
11	211 GUDGEON	5	03-31S 148-12E	AK	7500	T2/3NSV	S								
11	231 HADDOCK	2	35-36N 123-44E	AK	7000	T1/4NSV	S	AIJ	11	C-AK	Venice M.	6571	S	35-40N 123-45E	
12	210 GRENADIER	4	11-18N 109-02E	AK	Unk	T0/3NSV	0	AI	?	A	Hokkai M.	400	S	S coast FIC	PR says torps ran under target without exploding. [Attribution ?]
13	193 SWORDFISH	6	05-27S 152-29E	AK	6300	T1/4DUP	D								
13	231 HADDOCK	2	36-10N 125-56E	AK	7000	T1/3NSV	S								
13	231 HADDOCK	2	36-01N 125-57E	AO	17500	T1/3NSV	D								
16	183 SEAL	5	06-18N 135-20E	AP	5500	T2/2DUP	S	AJ I	16-7	A-AK	Boston M.	5477 5487	S	06-10N 135-19E	
16	231 HADDOCK	2	31-52N 126-14E	AO	10000	T1/2DUP	D	I	16	C-AK	Nichinan M.	2732	H	31-58N 126-12E	
17	182 SALMON	5	14-16N 119-44E	AO	6000	T2/2NUP	S	AJW	17-8	XAR	Oregon M.	5873	S	W of Manila	
17	182 SALMON	5	14-16N 119-44E	AO	5000	T1/2NUP	D								
17	182 SALMON	5	14-16N 119-44E	AK	6000	T1/2NUP	D								
17	193 SWORDFISH	6	05-00S 152-26E	AK	4400	T1/4DUP	S								
17	196 SEARAVEN	5	10-24S 105-41E	AO	14000	T2/2DUP	S	A IW	17	XAP	Nissei M.	833 333	S	10-30S 105-35E	
18	HMS TRUSTY	7	Off Penang	MV	7000	T1/3	D	AI	18	A-AK	Columbia M.	5617	M	06-21N 099-05E	BSH identifies as Kara M; A says no record of that ship.
21	186 STINGRAY	5	06-32S 156-05E	AK	7500	T2/4DUP	D	AI	21	XAV	Sanyo M.	8360	H	Shortland	
DEC	1942														
4	209 GRAYLING	4	03- S 128- E	Sch		G	S								
4	229 FLYING FISH	3	08-13S 158-19E	DD	1500	T1/6NUP	S								
6/17	187 STURGEON	6	08-14N 149-15E	AK	5500	T1/4DUP	D								
7/21	234 KINGFISH	2	23-59N 138-43E	AK	7100	T2/6NSR	S	AIJW	7	XAK	Hino M. #3	4389	S	23-00N 138-20E	
8	214 GROUPER	3	04-45S 154-13E	AK	4000	T1/4DUP	D								

Dt/Hr	Submarine	Pt	Position	Tgt	Size	Attack	Cl	So	Date	Type	Name	Tons	Dm	Location	Comments
DEC	1942														
8	229 FLYING FISH	3	07-43S 157-27E	DD	1500	T1/4DUP	S								
8/12	206 GAR	5	00-52N 118-54E	AK	2000	GD	D	AJW I	8	XAK	Heinan M.	661	S D	00-49N 138-51E	
10	238 WAHOO	2	04-06S 154-58E	AK	5600	T3/4DUP	S	AIJW	10	XAC	Kamoi M.	5355	S	Off Buin	
10/00	232 HALIBUT	3	40-40N 141-58E	AP	10000	T1/3NSR	S	I	9	XAP	Uyo M.	6376	M	Off Hachinohe	W lists ship as both XAP & Std AK 1A.
10/00	232 HALIBUT	3	40-40N 141-58E	AP	8000	T2/2NSR	D	I	16	C	Kosei M.	233	?	SW of Kushiro	PR says fired at 2 APs & 2 escorts. [Attribution ?; sinking not near attack, but no other sub attack likely.]
11/07	194 SEADRAGON	5	04-55S 152-44E	AK	4800	T1/2DUP	D	I	11	A-AK	Johore M.	6187	H	C. St. George	
12/11	228 DRUM	4	32-04N 142-30E	CVE	7600	T2/4DUP	D	I	12	CV	Ryuho	13360	L	Hachijo Jima	
12/24	232 HALIBUT	3	40-37N 142-40E	AK	7000	T3/3NSR	S	AJ I	12 16	C-AK	Gyokusan M. Gyokuzan M.	1970	PS S	40-19N 142-27E	
14/13	238 WAHOO	2	06-30S 156-09E	SS	2000	T1/3DUP	S								
16	232 HALIBUT	3	41-18N 141-32E	AK	6800	T2/3DUP	S	AJ I	16	C-AK	Shingo M.	4740	S ?	Cape Shiriya	
16	232 HALIBUT	3	41-18N 141-32E	Same	Same	Same	0	AJ I	16	AK	Genzan M.	5708	PS ?	Cape Shiriya	PR says fired at last of 3 AKs, thought others out of range.
17	214 GROUPER	3	04-54S 154-17E	APK	8400	T2/4DUP	S	AIJ	17	A-APK	Bandoeng M.	4003	S	04-55S 154-25E	
17/00	179 PLUNGER	4	08- S 157- E	DD	1300	T2/4NUP	S								
17/24	179 PLUNGER	4	08- S 157- E	DD	1300	T2/4NUP	D								
--							-	I	17	XAP	Tenryu M.	4861	M	Kavieng	No likely sub attack.
18/21	218 ALBACORE	2	05-10S 145-57E	AP	6000	T1/4DUP	S	I	18	XCL	Gokoku M.	10438	?A	Madang	PR says hit seen, much floating debris. W says XCL reclassified XAP 1943, tons are displacement as XCL. [Attribution ?]
18/22	218 ALBACORE	2	05-12S 145-56E	CL	3200	T2/2NUP	S	AIW J	18	CL	Tenryu	3230 3300	S	N of Madang	

24

Dt/Hr	Submarine	Pt	Position	Tgt	Size	Attack	Cl	So	Date	Type	Name	Tons	Dm	Location	Comments
DEC	1942														
18/07	281 SUNFISH	1.	34-10N 136-52E	AK	4500	TO/3DUP	O	I	18	XAP	Kyowa M.	1917	L	36-06N 136-55E	PR says all torpedoes missed. [Attribution ?; sinking not near attack, but may be misprint.]
19/01	191 SCULPIN	6	06-06N 150-30E	AO	7500	T2/4NUP	D								
19/19	207 GRAMPUS	5	05-49S 153-08E	AK	6000	T1/3DUP	S								
19/19	207 GRAMPUS	5	05-49S 153-08E	DD	1500	T2/3DUP	D								
--							-	I	19	XAO	Hoyo M.	8691	M	18-55N 150-16E	No likely sub attack.
20/23	237 TRIGGER	3	35-45N 140-55E	AK	8400	Mine	S	I	20	C-AK	Mitsuki M.	3893	SC	S of Daiozaki	PR says ship hit mine during mineplant.
								J			Unknown M.	4000	SM		[Attribution ?]
21/07	194 SEADRAGON	5	05-02S 152-33E	SS	1400	T2/4DUP	S	I	?	SS	I-4	1970	S	New Guinea	W says probably sunk 25 Dec by PT-122,
								J				1995			08-32S 148-17E; most authorities credit SEADRAGON.
22/02	213 GREENLING	4	05-05S 156-04E	DD	1500	T4/5NUP	S	J	22	PF	P 35	750	S	Sub position	A & W say P 35 (ex-DD Tsuta, 935T) sunk 2 Sep 43 by US a/c. [J attribution ?]
22/09	232 HALIBUT	3	40-59N 141-33E	AK	6500	T1/3DUP	S	I	22	?	Tx1	?	?	Cape Shiriya	PR says new coal-burner sank until only masts & stack visible. [Attribution ?; ship not identified.]
22/14	237 TRIGGER	3	34-52N 139-49E	AK	5400	T2/4DUP	S	I	22	C-AK	Yoshu M.	5711	L	Off Tokyo Bay	PR says deck awash forward, screw out of
								J			Teifuku M.	5198	S	Sub position	water. [J attribution ?; see TRIGGER 29 Dec.]
24/09	201 TRITON	5	19-16N 166-36E	AO	7000	T3/3DUP	S	AJ	24	XAW	Amakasu M. #1	1913	S	19-20N 166-20E	W gives name Amakusa M #1.
								I			Amakusu M. #1				
25/00	192 SAILFISH	7	06-30S 150-00E	SS	1400	T1/2	D								
25/02	208 GRAYBACK	5	07-50S 156-04E	4LC		GM	S								
25/03	199 TAUTOG	5	09- S 124- E	APK	5000	T2/3NUP	S	A	25	A-AK	Banshu M. #2	998	S	08-40S 124-30E	I says heavy damage.
								J				1000			
25/14	190 SPEARFISH	6	02-56S 149-55E	AK	7000	T1/2DUP	D								
25/14	190 SPEARFISH	6	02-56S 149-55E	AK	7000	T1/2DUP	D								
25/15	200 THRESHER	6	06-38S 112-44E	AK	6000	T1/2DUP	D								

Dt/Hr	Submarine	Pt	Position	Tgt	Size	Attack	Cl	So	Date	Type	Name	Tons	Dm	Location	Comments
DEC	1942														
25/15	200 THRESHER	6	06-38S 112-44E	AK	7000	T1/2DUP	S	A I	28	A-AP	Tokiwa M. #1 Tokiwa M.	892	SM	06-50S 112-47E	
25/22	194 SEADRAGON	5	05-05S 152-28E	AK	6000	T1/4NUP	S	AI	25	XAP	Nankai M.	8416	M	C. St. George	W gives name Nankei M.
26 N	220 BARB	2A	C. Finisterre	AO	Unk	T1/2	S	Note	26-7	AO	Campomanes	6276	H	42-07N 008-54W	PR reported no attacks but CO said policy was to sink all tankers; BARB returned with only 20 torpedoes. Attack not in SORG; USN records identify ship as Spanish tanker en route Bilbao-Aruba. No U-boat reported attack (Rohwer). [Attribution ?]
26	237 TRIGGER	3	35-45N 140-55E	AK	5000	Mine	U	A I	29	C-AK	Teifuku M.	5198	S M	NE Inubosaki	PR says AK ran into minefield laid 20 Dec; J credits TRIGGER attack 22 Dec. [Attribution ?]
28/01	201 TRITON	5	06-24N 160-18E	AK	3300	T3/3NUP	S	AIJ	27-8	C-APK	Omi M.	3394	S	06-10N 160-10E	
28/22	234 KINGFISH	2	24-46N 120-40E	AK	6600	T1/6NSR	S	AJ I	28	C-AK	Choyo M.	5388	S SM	25-05N 120-59E	
29	198 TAMBOR	4	20-04N 109-19E	-	-	Mine	U	J AI	29	C-AK	Fukken M.	2558	PM S	20-04N 109-18E NW of Hainan I.	No likely torpedo attack; minefield laid 2 Nov.
--							-	AI	29	C	Kinkai M.	3393	S	06-10S 156-00E	A says gutted by gunfire, agent unk; no likely sub attack.
30/03	200 THRESHER	6	04-45S 113-54E	AP	10000	T0/6+G	S	AJ I	29-30	C-AK	Hachian M. Kanayama M.	2733	S	05-30N 114-50E	
30/23	213 GREENLING	4	00-41N 148-52E	AK	9000	T2/4NSR	S	AJ I	30	A-AK	Hiteru M. Nissho M.	5857	S	00-34N 148-58E	
30/23	213 GREENLING	4	00-41N 148-52E	AK	5000	T2/2NSR	S	I J	30	? AK	Ryufuku M. Unknown M.	? 4000	L S	00-34N 148-58E	
31/07	188 SARGO	6	02-39S 149-59E	AO	7500	T1/4DUP	D								
31/16	196 SEARAVEN	6	03-54S 127-50E	CM	2000	T2/3DUP	D	I	1 Jan	C-AK	Osaka M.	3740	M	W of Ambon	
31/18	237 TRIGGER	3	34-29N 140-38E	AK	8500	T2/3DUP	S	I	1 Jan	XAP	Shozan M.	5859	?	35-55N 140-55E	

Dt/Hr	Submarine	Pt	Position	Tgt	Size	Attack	Cl	So	Date	Type	Name	Tons	Dm	Location	Comments
JAN	1943														
1/07	206 GAR	5	14-30N 118-35E	AK	5000	T1/3DUP	D								
1/09	172 PORPOISE	4	39-11N 141-04E	AK	4000	T1/1DUP	D								
1/09	172 PORPOISE	4	39-11N 141-04E	AK	5300	T2/2DUP	S	AJ I	1	C-AK	Renzan M.	4999 4571	S	39-11N 142-02E	
2/05	190 SPEARFISH	6	03-24S 151-22E	AK	7000	T1/4NUP	D	AI	2	A-AK	Akagisan M.	4634	M	03-22S 151-24E	PR says attacked convoy of 2 APKs & 2 TBs, 1 AK left dead in water, TB alongside.
--							-	W I	2	XPkt	Ebon M.	198	S H	04-30S 151-30E	190 SPEARFISH attack is closest but does not appear likely; 166 ARGONAUT (sunk 10 Jan) possibly in area. W gives 212 GATO as possible agent, but GATO not in area.
3/00	208 GRAYBACK	5	08-49S 157-09E	SS	2000	T1/2NSV	S	J	2	SS	I-18	2180	S	Sub position	No sub lost here. [J attribution incorrect.]
4/05	235 SHAD	2A	43-55N 002-42W	Tra	600	GN	S	Note 4		AM	M 4242	212	S	Sub position	German XAM, ex-French trawler Odet II per Rohwer & Hervieux.
4/05	235 SHAD	2A	43-55N 002-42W	Bge		GN	S								PR says ore barge towed by M 4242.
5/23	228 DRUM	4	32-09N 132-10E	AO	8000	T1/3NSR	D								
6/16	236 SILVERSIDES	4	07-06N 151-17E	SS	2000	T1/3DUP	D								
7/07	234 KINGFISH	2	25-46N 138-09E	Sch	200	GD	S								
7/18	234 KINGFISH	2	25-21N 136-28E	Sch	200	GT	S								
9	166 ARGONAUT	3L	05- S 149- E	DD	1200	Unk	D								U says attack seen by a/c before ARGONAUT was sunk.
9/03	168 NAUTILUS	4	06-13S 156-00E	AP	9300	T2/3NUP	D	AIJW	9	XAP	Yoshinogawa M.	1422	S	06-10S 156-00E	
9/10	199 TAUTOG	5	04-07S 128-32E	CL	5600	T2/3DUP	D	AI	9	CL	Natori	5170	L	SE of Ambon	
9/16	206 GAR	5	01-46N 119-01E	Aux	14100	T2/3DUP	D	AI	9	AO	Notoro	14050	L	Makassar Strait	
9/18	196 SEARAVEN	6	07-38N 134-12E	AK	5200	T0/1TUP	O	I	9	A-AK	Yubae M.	3217	H	07-30N 134-12E	PR says explosion heard but target steamed away. [Attribution ?]
10/06	213 GREENLING	4	01-09S 150-16E	AO	9000	T1/4TSR	D								

Dt/Hr	Submarine	Pt	Position	Tgt	Size	Attack	Cl	So	Date	Type	Name	Tons	Dm	Location	Comments
JAN 1943															
10/07	210 GRENADIER	5	06-18S 112-44E	Sam	100	GD	S								
10/13	237 TRIGGER	3	35-02N 140-12E	DD	1400	T2/3DUP	S	AIW J	10	DD	Okikaze	1215 1300	S	Katsura Lt.	
10/16	207 GRAMPUS	5	05-01S 152-22E	AP	8000	T3/3DUP	S								
10/16	207 GRAMPUS	5	05-01S 152-22E	AP	10000	T3/3DUP	S								
--							-	I	10	A-AK	Sumatra M.	5861	M	12-44N 124-08E	No likely sub attack; other sources say sunk 12 May 43 at above location; see 211 GUDGEON that date.
11/21	202 TROUT	7	04-40N 114-00E	AO	17500	T2/4NSV	D	AI	11	XAO	Kyokuyo M.	17549	M	Miri	
--							-	I	11	XAP	Kaiko M.	3548	M	03-24N 154-13E	No likely sub attack.
12/21	210 GRENADIER	5	06-33S 112-31E	AK	500	GN	S								
12/21	210 GRENADIER	5	06-33S 112-31E	AK	700	GN	S								
12/24	217 GUARDFISH	3	02-51S 149-43E	DD	1400	T1/3NUR	S	AIW J	12-3	PF	P 1	1215 750	S	S Tingwon I.	Ex-DD Shimakaze.
13/09	201 TRITON	5	00-45S 148-56E	AO	10200	T1/8TSV	D	I	13	XAO	Akebono M.	10182	L	00-45S 148-44E	
13/14	239 WHALE	2	09-54N 167-07E	AP	9500	T3/4DUP	S	AIW J	15 13	XAC	Iwashiro M.	3559	S	Off Kwajalein	
14/06	168 NAUTILUS	4	05-13S 155-09E	AO	10400	T3/5TUP	D								
14/12	196 SEARAVEN	6	09-12N 130-38E	PC	200	T2/2DUP	S	AIW	14	XSC	Ganjitsu M. #1	216	S	09-00N 130-50E	
14/12	196 SEARAVEN	6	09-12N 130-38E	AK	5700	T2/2DUP	S	A J	14	A-AK	Shiraha M.	5682 5693	S	09-00N 130-05E	I lists as Shirahane M, 5693T.
16/07	201 TRITON	5	01-39S 148-20E	AK	7000	T2/3DUP	S								
16/07	201 TRITON	5	01-39S 148-20E	AK	4000	T1/2DUP	D								
16/10	215 GROWLER	4	04-00S 151-55E	AK	5400	T2/2DUP	S	AJ I	16	A-APK	Chifuku M.	5857	S H	04-03S 151-55E	
16/18	213 GREENLING	4	02-47S 149-10E	AK	5000	T2/3TSP	S	AJ IW	16	XAP	Kinposan M. Kimposan M.	3261	S	W of Kavieng	

28

Dt/Hr	Submarine	Pt	Position	Tgt	Size	Attack	Cl	So	Date	Type	Name	Tons	Dm	Location	Comments
JAN	1943														
16/20	213 GREENLING	4	02-45S 149-20E	Pat	200	GN	S								
17/10	231 HADDOCK	3	34-32N 137-48E	AO	6500	T1/3DUP	S	J	17	AK	Unknown M.	4000	S	Sub position	PR says AO blew up & sank in 2 min. [J attribution ?]
17/18	239 WHALE	2	10-13N 151-25E	AP	9800	T7/9TUP	S	AJ AIW	17 21	XAP	Heiyo M.	,9816	S	10-10N 151-25E	A says sources give both dates; I gives tons as 9615.
17/22	230 FINBACK	3	30-33N 132-25E	PC	200	GN	S	I	17	C	Yachiyo M.	?	M	Tanega Shima	
18/02	236 SILVERSIDES	4	06-21N 150-23E	AO	10000	T3/4NUP	S	AIJW	18	XAO	Toei M.	10022	S	SW of Truk	
18/05	213 GREENLING	4	02-04S 150-37E	PC	500	T0/1NSR	0	I	18	AE	Soya	3800	L	Q. Carola Chan	PR says torp ran under target, did not explode. [Attribution ?]
18/11	202 TROUT	7	12-37N 109-30E	Sam		GD	S								
18/11	202 TROUT	7	12-37N 109-30E	Sam	100	GD	S								
19/05	213 GREENLING	4	01-35S 150-57E	AK	1000	T0/1NSR	0	I	20	A-AK	Shinai M.	3793	H	N of Rabaul	[Attribution ?; location not specific.]
19/11	180 POLLACK	5	41-10N 141-24E	AK	7000	T1/2DUP	D	Note	Note	C-APK	Seikai M.	3109	S	Note	PR says target beached, believed same hit by 217 GUARDFISH 25 Aug 42.
19/11	231 HADDOCK	3	34-13N 136-59E	AK	6800	T2/2DUP	S	I	19	XAO	Genyo M.	10018	?	Off Shiranuka	
19/16	193 SWORDFISH	7	05-25S 156-00E	AK	4200	T2/2DUP	S	AIJ	19	A-AK	Myoho M.	4122	S	05-38S 156-20E	
19/24	168 NAUTILUS	4	05-57S 156-00E	DD	1900	T1/5NUP	D	I	19	DD	Akizuki	2700	M	W of Tulagi	
20/20	236 SILVERSIDES	4	03- N 155- E	AK	5200	T2/2TUP	D	AJ I	20	A-AP	Surabaya M. Soerabaja M.	4391 4351	S	03-24N 154-13E	
20/20	236 SILVERSIDES	4	03- N 155- E	AK	7200	T2/2TUP	D	J I	20 Note	APK	Somedono M.	5154	S LA	03-52N 153-56E	A says sources show ship sunk by a/c either 20 Jan, 19 Feb, or 23 Feb 43; ship salvaged at Buin, date not given. [J attribution ?]
20/20	236 SILVERSIDES	4	03- N 155- E	AK	4000	T0/2TUP	0	AJ I	20-1	A-AP	Meiu M.	8230	S	03-24N 154-13E 33-48N 140-13E	PR says 5 hits heard on convoy of 4 AKs, 2 escorts. [IJN location appears incorrect.]
21/08	202 TROUT	7	11-25N 109-22E	AK	3000	T1/2DUP	S	I J	21	XPG	Eifuku M. Unknown M.	3520 2984	M S	11-49N 109-21E	PR says seen drifting with stern under. All sources show Eifuku M sunk 7 Feb 45; see 383 PAMPANITO that date. [J attribution ?]

Dt/Hr	Submarine	Pt	Position	Tgt	Size	Attack	Cl	So	Date	Type	Name	Tons	Dm	Location	Comments
JAN	1943														
21/18	212 GATO	4	06-12S 155-51E	AP	4600	T1/2TUP	S	AJ I	21	A-AP	Kenkon M.	4575	S HA	ENE of Buin	
21/23	180 POLLACK	5	42-41N 145-37E	AK	9300	T0/3NSP	O	I	26	C-AK	Asama M.	4891	S	Off Kushiro	PR says 3 explosions but target did not appear damaged. [Attribution ?]
22/06	217 GUARDFISH	3	03-55S 152-07E	AP	8600	T1/3DUP	S	J	22	AK	Unknown M.	4000	S	Sub position	PR says left with only masts visible on reef W of Cape Tawui. [J attribution ?]
22/12	210 GRENADIER	5	01-22S 116-52E	AK	7000	T2/2DUP	D								
22/23	199 TAUTOG	5	05-40S 120-30E	AK	1900	T2/2NUP	S	AI J	23 22	A-AK	Yashima M. Hasshu M.	1873	S	Kabaena I.	
23/18	217 GUARDFISH	3	02-47S 150-38E	DD	1500	T1/3TUP	S	AIW J	23	DD	Hakaze	1215 1300	S	W of Kavieng	
24/15	203 TUNA	5	07-40S 156-50E	AO	6500	T2/4DUP	D								
24/15	238 WAHOO	3	03-23S 143-34E	DD	1500	T1/3DUP	S	AI	24	DD	Harusame	1685	H	W of Wewak	
24/18	203 TUNA	5	07-36S 156-52E	AK	8000	T1/4DUP	D								
25/03	212 GATO	4	06-00S 156-04E	CL	7000	T2/6NUS	D								
25/11	235 SHAD	2A	43-28N 002-59W	AK	1200	T1/2DUP	D	Note	25	AK	Nordfels	1214	D	43-28N 002-59W	German blockade runner per Rohwer & Hervieux.
25/16	203 TUNA	5	07-41S 156-51E	AK	6000	T1/3DUP	D								
26/00	239 WHALE	2	08-30N 156-40E	AO	7500	T1/3NUP	D								
26/11	238 WAHOO	3	01-55N 139-14E	AK	7200	T2/2DUP	S	AJ I	26	A-AK	Buyo M.	5447 6446	S	01-54N 134-57E	
26/12	238 WAHOO	3	01-55N 139-14E	AP	7200	T3/5DUP	S	AJ I	26	A-AK	Fukuei M. #2	1901 1701	S	02-04N 140-10E	
26/13	209 GRAYLING	5	13-26N 121-16E	AK	3800	T1/2DUP	S	J A	26 25	C-AK	Ushio M.	749	S SM	N of Mindoro	I says sunk by unk agent. PR says bow broke off, stern sank, #477 on bridge, photos.
26/17	229 FLYING FISH	4	13- N 144- E	AK	7200	T1/2DUP	D	I J	26	XAP	Tokai M.	8359	M JS	Guam	PR says ship anchored in Apra harbor. J credits FLYING FISH and 185 SNAPPER (see 27 Aug); also see 178 PERMIT 5 May.

Dt/Hr	Submarine	Pt	Position	Tgt	Size	Attack	Cl	So	Date	Type	Name	Tons	Dm	Location	Comments
JAN	1943														
26/20 238	WAHOO	3	02-37N 139-42E	AO	6500	T2/5NSV	S	W J	26	XCL AK	Ukishima M. Unknown M.	4730 4000	H S	SE of Palau	PR says target back broken; W says hit by 3 torps; A says Ukishima M was at Tsingtao 26 Jan. [Attribution ?]
26/21 238	WAHOO	3	02-30N 139-44E	AK	9500	T4/6NSR	S	I	26	A-AK	Pacific M.	5872	L	20-09N 139-45E	PR says AK sank after 4 hits. [Attribution ?; latitude does not agree but may be misprint.]
27/14 239	WHALE	2	14-15N 153-43E	AK	5600	T1/8DUP	D	AI J	27	XAP	Shoan M.	5624	M S	14-24N 153-30E	Japanese records agree ship sunk by a/c at Saipan 23 Feb 44. [J attribution ?]
27/17 209	GRAYLING	5	12-43N 122-01E	APK	4500	T2/3DUP	S								
28/09 168	NAUTILUS	4	05-12S 154-29E	AK	4500	T2/3DUP	D								
29/03 168	NAUTILUS	4	06-27S 154-05E	DD	1000	T1/1NUP	S								
29/16 212	GATO	4	06-22S 156-04E	AK	7200	T1/2DUP	S	AIJ	29	A-AK	Nichiun M.	2723	S	N of Buin	
30	POMPANO 181	4	08-24N 149-20E	AO	10000	T2/4DUP	D								
30/19 215	GROWLER	4	01-14S 148-55E	AK	6400	T1/4TUP	D								
FEB	1943														
1/23 175	TARPON	6	34-16N 138-17E	AO	9000	T3/6NSV	S	AJ I	1	C-APK	Fushimi M.	10935	S L	34-08N 138-11E	
2/11 275	RUNNER	1	20- N 142- E	AK	6800	T2/3DUP	S								
2/11 275	RUNNER	1	20- N 142- E	AK	6800	T2/3DUP	D								
3/06 282	TUNNY	1	22- N 114-30E	AO		T0/10TUP	0	I	3	A-AK	Shinto M. #1	1933	M	22-03N 114-23E	PR says dud hit. I gives tons as 1983.
3 U	219 AMBERJACK	3L	Off Buka	Sch		G	S								Attack not in SORG; info from U.
4	219 AMBERJACK	3L	08- S 157- E	AK	4000	Unk	S								
4/04 282	TUNNY	1	21-30N 113-42E	AK	10000	T2/3NSR	S	I	5	XAP	Tatsuwa M.	6345	L	21-30N 113-42E	I gives tons as 6335.
4/10 181	POMPANO	4	08-07N 149-34E	AO	7300	T1/2DUP	D								
6/15 229	FLYING FISH	4	14-57N 145- E	AK	7000	T1/3DUP	S	I	6	XAP	Nagisan M.	4391	M	Tinian	

31

Dt/Hr	Submarine	Pt	Position	Tgt	Size	Attack	Cl	So	Date	Type	Name	Tons	Dm	Location	Comments
FEB	1942														
7/02	215 GROWLER	4	03-34S 151-09E	PG	2500	Ram	S	I	7	AF	Hayasaki	950	L	NW of Rabaul	GROWLER CO Gilmore killed during this attack.
7/15	202 TROUT	7	04-31N 114-52E	AO	17600	T1/2DUP	D	AI	7	XAO	Nisshin M.	16801	M	Off Miri	
8	282 TUNNY	1	22-40N 119-12E	AK	6600	T2/5NSV	S	AJ I	8		C-AK Kusuyama M.	5306	S L	22-30N 119-03E	
8/22	175 TARPON	6	33-45N 140-25E	AP	12000	T4/4NUP	S	AJW I	8	XAP	Tatsuta M.	16975	S M	Mikura Shima	I lists ship again 8 Feb 44 [misprint?]
9	282 TUNNY	1	22-40N 120-02E	AP	12800	T2/2DUP	D								
9/21	275 RUNNER	1	10-10N 133-50E	AK	5900	T1/2NUP	S								
10/10	177 PICKEREL	6	40-10N 142-04E	AK	6000	T0/3DUP	0	I	12		C-AK Amari M.	2184	S	Off Sanriku	PR says no torps hit. SORG gives incorrect posit 34N 134E; A says no record of this ship. [Attribution ?]
11/14	209 GRAYLING	5	14-16N 120-28E	AK	6100	T1/2DUP	S	A I	11	A-AK	Hoeisan M. Hoeizan M.	6032	M	Corregidor	
11	HMS TRUSTY	8	Java Sea	MV	3000	T1/4	S									BSH says CO saw target sink.
12/05	177 PICKEREL	6	38- N 141- E	8Sam	300	GN	D								
14/08	202 TROUT	7	04-11N 117-45E	AO	7700	T1/1DSV	S	AIJW	14	XPG	Hirotama M.	1911	S	03-59S 117-30E	
14/14	275 RUNNER	1	07-31N 134-21E	AK	7100	T2/3DUP	S								
14/11	200 THRESHER	7	06-05S 105-47E	SS	1600	T0/3DUP	0	I	14	SS	I-62 (I-162)	1635	L	Lesser Sundas	PR says dud hit on I-65 class SS; posit in Sunda Strait.
15	282 TUNNY	1	25- N 147- E	Sam	100	GD	S								
15/09	177 PICKEREL	6	39- N 142- E	AK	6000	T2/3DUP	S	AIJ	15	B-AG	Tateyama M.	1990	S	39-12N 142-03E	Ship not in W.
15/21	212 GATO	4	06-28S 156-02E	AK	7900	T1/2NUP	S	AIJW	15	XAF	Suruga M.	991	S	06-25S 156-05E	
16	229 FLYING FISH	4	18-30N 145-57E	AK	6000	T2/4DUP	S	AIJW	16	XAF	Hyuga M.	994	S	18-35N 145-55E	
17/07	276 SAWFISH	1	30-50N 135-42E	Q	3800	T1/3TUP	S	Note	17	AK	Ilmen	2369	S	30-36N 136-30E	Soviet ship; PR says not on reported route to USA, no USSR ident seen. Survivors taken to Portland, Ore by another Soviet ship.

Dt/Hr	Submarine	Pt	Position	Tgt	Size	Attack	Cl	So	Date	Type	Name	Tons	Dm	Location	Comments
FEB	1943														
17/22	276 SAWFISH	1	30-50N 135-35E	AK	4300	T2/3NUP	S	Note	?	AK	Kola	?	?	?	Soviet ship; loss reported by USSR, apparently no survivors. US intel gave date of loss 7 Mar; no likely sub attack that date.
19	207 GRAMPUS	6L	05-04S 152-18E	AK	6400	Unk	D	AI	18	XAPV	Keiyo M.	6442	L	04-55S 152-26E	
19/13	177 PICKEREL	6	38-15N 141-30E	AK	4000	T1/3DUP	D								
19/15	275 RUNNER	1	07-35N 134-25E	AK	7400	T2/3DUP	D								
19/18	221 BLACKFISH	3A	43-30N 002-54W	PC	1000	T1/4NUP	D	Note	19	PC	VP 408	445	S	Sub position	German aux patrol boat (Vorpstenboot), ex-trawler Haltenbank per Rohwer & Hervieux.
19/21	212 GATO	4	06-27S 156-01E	AK	7900	T1/3NUP	S	I J	19	XAE	Hibari M.	6550	L JS	06-25S 156-05E	PR says target sinking by stern; J credits GATO & a/c; A & I say sunk by a/c 17 Apr at Shortland.
20/08	218 ALBACORE	3	00-50S 146-06E	Esc	1300	T2/2DUP	S	J	20	PF	Unknown	750	S	Sub position	PR says fired at CM & DD, no sign of CM after attack. [J attribution ?]
20/08	218 ALBACORE	3	00-50S 146-06E	DD	1500	T1/4DUP	D	AIW J	20	DD	Oshio	1960 1850	S	NW of Manus	
20/19	177 PICKEREL	6	38- N 141- E	Sam	100	GN	S								
20/20	177 PICKEREL	6	38- N 141- E	Sam		GN	S								
20/21	232 HALIBUT	4	15-09N 159-30E	AK	5600	T3/3NUP	S	J IWA	20 18	XAP	Shinkoku M.	3991	S	S of Saipan	PR says target sank, no survivors. No likely attack 18 Feb. [Attribution ?; dates do not agree.]
20	281 SUNFISH	1	34-28N 137-20E	--	--	Mine	U	I	20	XPF	Yoshida M.	2920	M	34-30N 137-20E	No likely torp attack. Minefield laid 14-17 Dec 42; W says ship was XPG rerated XPF, converted to AO 1943. [Attribution ?]
21/14	200 THRESHER	7	07-54S 119-13E	AP	12000	T2/3DUP	D								PR says 2 ships hit & left dead in water.
21/19	200 THRESHER	7	07-55S 119-14E	AP	12000	T2/3TUP	D								See above.
21/23	276 SAWFISH	1	29-29N 132-48E	AO	4400	T1/6NUP	D	I	21	AO	Ose	7986	L	Oagari Jima	
21	HNMS O-24	4	Salang I.	MV	4000	G	D	AI	21	C	Bandai M.	165	S	07-50N 098-09E	DNO gives tons as 4147.

Dt/Hr	Submarine	Pt	Position	Tgt	Size	Attack	Cl	So	Date	Type	Name	Tons	Dm	Location	Comments
FEB	1943														
22/07	200 THRESHER	7	08-15S 119-15E	AP	7000	T0/4DUP	S	AI J	21-2	A-AK	Kuwayama M.	5724	S	06-30S 110-30E Sub position	PR says ship hit 21 Feb & abandoned, decks awash; hit by 2 more dud torpedoes, broke in two & sank, photos. [J attribution ?; sinking not near attack, but may be misprint.]
--							-	AIW	24	XPkt	Otori M. #2	302	S	06-50N 121-25E	No likely sub attack.
27	N 207 GRAMPUS	6L	Unk	Unk	Unk	Unk	U	I	27	AM	W 22	755	L	Kolombangara	GRAMPUS lost in this area between 18 Feb & 6 Mar. Attack not listed in SORG. [Attribution ?]
28/09	179 PLUNGER	5	06-09N 167-18E	AO	14000	T1/5DUP	D	I	27	AO	Iro	14050	M	W of Jaluit	I gives tons as 15450.
MAR	1943														
2/10	178 PERMIT	7	39-00N 141-54E	AK	6000	T3/4DUP	S	I	2	A-AK	Tsurushima M.	4645	L	38-53N 141-45E	
2/15	200 THRESHER	7	03-29S 117-17E	AO	7000	T2/4DUP	S	AIJW	2	XAO	Toen M.	5232	S	03-28S 117-23E	
3/24	232 HALIBUT	4	10-22N 145-21E	APK	9500	T2/4NSP	S	AI J	3	XAG	Nichiyu M.	6818	M S	10-25N 145-25E	W lists as XCM; A & W say sunk 16 Jun 44 (I says 26 Jun) at Guam. [J attribution ?]
--							-	I	3	C-APK	Teisho M.	9849	S	38-34N 122-23E	See 238 WAHOO 24 Mar.
4	234 KINGFISH	3	24-23N 143-18E	Sam	200	GD	S								
4/07	178 PERMIT	7	39-30N 142-08E	AK	5600	T1/3DUP	D	AI J	4-5	C-AK	Hokuto M. Hokutu M.	2267	S PM	S of Muroran 42-00N 141-00E	PR says heard "magnetic" explosion. A says hit by dud torp, started leaking next day & sank. [J attribution ?]
6	201 TRITON	6L	02- S 152- E	AK	4000	T3/6D	S	A IJ	4 6	A-AK	Kiriha M.	3057	S	00-37N 145-30E	TRITON lost this patrol; some info from U. [Date & posit may be inaccurate.]
6	201 TRITON	6L	02- S 152- E	AK	4000	T?/6D	S	I	6	A-AP	Mito M.	7061	L	00-37N 145-30E	See above.
6	U 201 TRITON	6L	02- S 152- E	AK	Unk	T?/6D	D								Attack not in SORG; infor from U.
6/16	276 SAWFISH	1	31-04N 131-48E	APK	5200	T1/3DUP	S	I	6	A-AK	Clyde M.	5497	L	SE of Toizaki	
7/05	178 PERMIT	7	41-55N 143-50E	Sam	100	GN	S	I	7	C	Shoshin M.	30	L	45-45N 143-30E	[Attribution ?; sinking not near attack but may be misprint.]
7/22	281 SUNFISH	2	27-02N 122-28E	AK	5500	T3/7NSP	S									

34

Dt/Hr	Submarine	Pt	Position	Tgt	Size	Attack	Cl	So	Date	Type	Name	Tons	Dm	Location	Comments
7 U	201 TRITON	6L	Unk	AK	Unk	T5/8N	S								Attack not in SORG; info from U.
7 U	201 TRITON	6L	Unk	AK	Unk	T /8N	S								See above.
8/18	178 PERMIT	7	41-16N 142-27E	AK	4200	T2/3DUP	S	AIJ	8		C-AK Hisashima M.	2747	S	41-21N 141-22E	
9/17	281 SUNFISH	2	27-04N 121-14E	AP	17000	T3/4DUP	D								
9/21	137 S-32	6	53-03N 173-15E	DE	1200	T1/4NSR	S								
10/07	199 TAUTOG	6	00-52S 117-47E	Sam		GD	S								
11/19	199 TAUTOG	6	01-39S 117-42E	Sch		GT	S								
12/02	179 PLUNGER	5	07-15N 159-10E	AK	9000	T2/2NSR	S	AIJW	12	XAW	Taihosan M.	1804	S	07-15N 158-45E	
12/04	232 HALIBUT	4	09-19N 132-50E	AK	5000	T1/3NSR	D								
12/04	232 HALIBUT	4	09-19N 132-50E	AK	5000	T2/3NSR	D								
12/04	232 HALIBUT	4	09-19N 132-50E	AK	5000	T2/3NSR	D								
13/18	208 GRAYBACK	6	00-01S 151-00E	AK	6400	T2/4DUP	S	AI	13	XAP	Noshiro M.	7184	L	00-07S 150-58E	
13/21	137 S-32	6	53-14N 173-15E	SS	1100	T1/2NSV	S								
13/22	281 SUNFISH	2	29-04N 129-17E	AK	6700	T2/3NUP	S	AJ I	13		C-AK Kosei M.	3262	S L	29-08N 129-10E	
13	HNMS O-21	1	11-40N 092-50E	MV	4000	T2/4	S	A IJW	13	XAP	Kasuga M. #3 Kasuga M. #2	3967	S	Port Blair	BSH gives name Kasuga M #2, date 13 Feb 42 [misprint].
15/12	237 TRIGGER	4	00-00N 145-00E	AK	7100	T2/3DUP	D	AJ I	15	A-AK	Momoha M. Toka M.	3103	S	00-02S 145-05E	
15/17	137 S-32	6	52-54N 173-13E	SS	2000	T1/3DUP	S	I	15	SS	RO-103	525	LC	Silipuaka I.	Unable to identify location; sub posit in Aleutians. [Attribution ?]
15/22	237 TRIGGER	4	00-00N 145-00E	AK	7200	T2/9DUP	D	I	15	XAP	Florida M.	5854	M	00-09N 144-55E	
16/12	277 SCAMP	1	38-19N 141-38E	AK	4100	T1/3DUP	D								
17/08	199 TAUTOG	6	05-35S 122-53E	AO	4000	T1/1DUP	D								
17/23	234 KINGFISH	3	24-32N 120-15E	AK	4600	T2/4NUP	S	I	17	XAP	Tenryugawa M.	3883	M	24-30N 129-09E	

MAR 1943

Dt/Hr	Submarine	Pt	Position	Tgt	Size	Attack	Cl	So	Date	Type	Name	Tons	Dm	Location	Comments
18/15	199 TAUTOG	6	05- S 120- E	Sch	100	GD		S							
19/05	238 WAHOO	4	38-29N 122-19E	AK	4100	T1/1TUP	S	AIJ	19	C-AK	Zogen Go Zogen M.	1428	S	38-39N 122-19E	
19/09	234 KINGFISH	3	26-00N 122-18E	AP	8200	T2/4DUP	S	AIJ	19	A-AH	Takachiho M.	8154	S	25-50N 122-30E	PR say troops with packs left ship; no hospital markings.
19/09	238 WAHOO	4	38-27N 122-18E	AK	6000	T1/4DUP	D	AIJ	19-20	C-AK	Kowa M.	3217	S	38-34N 122-28E	
20/08	239 WHALE	3	16-03N 143-08E	AK	7500	T2/3DUP	S								
20/08	239 WHALE	3	16-03N 143-08E	AK	9600	T2/3DUP	S								
20/12	276 SAWFISH	1	32-55N 152-11E	PC	300	GD	D	AWI	20	XPkt	Shinsei M.	148	S M	32-50N 152-00E	
20/14	237 TRIGGER	4	03-44N 144-12E	AK	7500	T1/3DUP	D	AI	20	XPG	Choan M. #2	2613 2629	H	03-48N 144-12E	
20/17	277 SCAMP	1	41-06N 141-26E	AK	2600	T3/3DUP	D	I	20	C	Seinan M.	1450	L	Off Tomari	
21/01	233 HERRING	3A	44-13N 008-23W	SS	500	T2/2NSR	S	U	21	SS	U-163	1120	S	Sub position	Rohwer & Hervieux disagree with attribution; U-163 left Lorient 10 Mar, missing after 15 Mar, should have been far from this posit; Rohwer believes sunk 13 Mar by HMCS PRESCOTT.
21/05	277 SCAMP	1	41-45N 142-14E	AO	6500	T3/9NUP	D	I	21	B-AP	Manju M.	6541	M	41-37N 142-30E	W lists 3 ships this name: XAO, 6516T; XAP, 5874T; XAG, 7266T; no indication which damaged here.
21/07	180 POLLACK	6	05-26N 171-32E	AK	6700	T2/4DUP	D								
21/07	238 WAHOO	4	38-11N 124-33E	AK	7200	T1/3DUP	S	AIJ	20-1	C-AK	Hozan M.	2260	S	38-05N 124-33E	
21/10	238 WAHOO	4	38-05N 124-33E	AK	6500	T2/3DUP	S	AIJ	21	C-AK	Nittsu M.	2183	S	38-07N 124-32E	
21/11	230 FINBACK	4	07-40N 139-48E	AP	9300	T2/3DUP	D	I	21	XAP	Sanuki M.	7158	L	07-43N 139-54E	W says ship was XAV rerated XAP 1942, 7189T; I gives tons as 9246.
22/06	198 TAMBOR	6	08-58N 123-08E	AO	2500	T1/3TUP	D	I	22	XAP	Bugen M.	691	L	09-00N 123-08E	
22/19	211 GUDGEON	7	06-31S 112-47E	AK	5300	T2/2TUP	S								

Dt/Hr	Submarine	Pt	Position	Tgt	Size	Attack	Cl	So	Date	Type	Name	Tons	Dm	Location	Comments
MAR	1943														
22/19	211 GUDGEON	7	06-31S 112-47E	AK	7000	T1/2TUP	S	AIJ	22	A-AK	Meigen M.	5434	S	06-23S 112-43E	
22/19	211 GUDGEON	7	06-31S 112-47E	AK	5700	T2/2TUP	D								
23/04	239 WHALE	3	17-16N 144-56E	AK	9300	T3/4NUP	S	AIJW	23	XAP	Kenyo M.	6486	S	17-20N 145-00E	
23/04	239 WHALE	3	17-16N 144-56E	AK	7100	T2/3NUP	S								
23/05	238 WAHOO	4	38-37N 121-01E	AK	2400	T1/1TUP	S	J	23	AK	Unknown M.	2427	S	Sub position	PR says target sank by stern. [J attribution ?]
24/04	211 GUDGEON	7	06-25S 113-48E	PC	300	GN	D								
24/21	238 WAHOO	4	39-00N 122-16E	AO	7500	T1/7NUP	S	AI J	3 25	C-APK	Teisho M. Unknown M.	9849 2556	S	38-34N 122-23E 38-13N 123-24E	PR says AO seen to sink. [Dates do not agree but this is only attack to account for Teisho M in location given; attribution ?]
25/05	238 WAHOO	4	38-13N 123-24E	AK	2600	T0/2+G	S	AJ I	24-5	C-AK	Takaosan M.	2076 2056	S	39-05N 122-25E	PR says hit by torp but not stopped; set afire & sunk by gunfire.
25/06	238 WAHOO	4	38-10N 123-26E	AK	1000	GT	S	AIJ	25	C-AK	Satsuki M.	830	S	38-16N 123-14E	
25/22	209 GRAYLING	6	03- S 118- E	Sch		GN	S								
26/22	230 FINBACK	4	05-02N 139-10E	AK	6000	T1/3NSR	D								
26/22	230 FINBACK	4	05-02N 139-10E	AK	6600	T2/3NSR	D								
27/10	238 WAHOO	4	33-39N 125-23E	PC	100	GD	S								PR says hit & set afire but believed to escape.
28/07	282 TUNNY	2	19-20N 166-35E	APK	10600	T1/2DUP	P	AI J	28	XAP	Suwa M.	10672	S JS	Wake I.	J credits TUNNY, 230 FINBACK (5 Apr) & 194 194 SEADRAGON (27 Jul); W credits FINBACK & SEADRAGON only; SORG credits TUNNY & FINBACK. PR says stern blown off but did not sink.
28/10	209 GRAYLING	6	03-04N 118-05E	AO	10000	T1/4DUP	D								
28/18	238 WAHOO	4	31-39N 127-41E	Sam	100	GD	S								PR says hit by 20mm, not seen to sink.
28/18	238 WAHOO	4	31-39N 127-41E	Sam		GD	S								Same as above.

Dt/Hr	Submarine	Pt	Position	Tgt	Size	Attack	Cl	So	Date	Type	Name	Tons	Dm	Location	Comments
MAR	1943														
29/04	211 GUDGEON	7	00-00N 118-19E	AO	10000	T4/6NSV	S	AIW J	29	XAO	Toho M.	9987 9997	S	00-30S 118-26E	
29/04	238 WAHOO	4	30-26N 129-41E	AK	5200	T1/2NUP	S	AIJW	29		XARC Yamabato M.	2556	S	W of Yakujima	
29/08	198 TAMBOR	6	11-50N 121-48E	AK	5000	T1/3DUP	D								
29/12	211 GUDGEON	7	00-54N 119-01E	AO	7300	T2/2DUP	S	I	29	XAO	Kyoei M. #2	1192	L	00-53N 119-02E	
30/09	203 TUNA	6	00-22S 147-46E	AK	8500	T2/3DUP	S	AIJ	30		A-AK Kurohime M.	4697	S	00-35S 147-55E	
31/11	203 TUNA	6	01-53N 146-42E	AK	6600	T1/4DUP	D								
APR	1943														
1	235 SHAD	3A	44-37N 002-18W	AK	10000	T3/8		D	Note 1	AK	Pietro Orseolo	6344	D	Sub position	Italian blockade runner per Rohwer & Hervieux; Rohwer says hit by only 1 torp.
2/22	282 TUNNY	2	07-23N 149-13E	AK	3800	T1/3NSV	S	AJW I	2	XAP	Toyo M. #2	4162	S SA	07-22N 149-18E	
--							-	I	2		A-AK Gisho M.	543	L	Vella Lavella	No likely sub attack.
3/13	231 HADDOCK	4	10-26N 135-00E	AP	11900	T3/3DUP	S	AIJW	3	XAO	Arima M.	7389	S	10-12N 134-35E	
3/13	231 HADDOCK	4	10-26N 135-00E	Same	Same	Same	0	A J	8		C-AK Toyo M.	1916	S	05-04N 139-43E Sub position	PR says only 1 target attacked here, none 8 Apr; I says Toyo M sunk by a/c at Rabaul 8 Apr. [J attribution ?]
3	J 177 PICKEREL	7L	Unk		Unk	Unk	U	AIW J	3	PC	Ch 13	460 440	S	40-03N 141-58E	Attack not in SORG or U; PICKEREL lost off Honshu possibly this attack or later; no other sub attacks in area; I gives location 43-03N 141-58E [possible misprint].
4/12	172 PORPOISE	5	13-12N 161-57E	AK	3000	T1/3DUP	S	AIJ	4		C-Wh Koa M.	2023	S	13-30N 161-56E	
4/12	180 POLLACK	6	05-59N 169-48E	AK	5200	T2/2DUP	D								
4/17	202 TROUT	8	04-45N 113-58E	Aux	3500	T1/4DUP	D								
4	N 177 PICKEREL	7L	Unk		Unk	Unk	U	I	4	XAP	Shoei M.	3083	M	39-42N 142-05E	Attack not in SORG or USSL; no other sub attacks in area. [Attribution ?]

Dt/Hr	Submarine	Pt	Position	Tgt	Size	Attack	Cl	So	Date	Type	Name	Tons	Dm	Location	Comments
APR	1943														
5	230 FINBACK	4	19-20N 166-35E	APK	10600	T1/2DUP	P	AJ W	Note 5	XAP	Suwa M.	10672	JS	Wake I. S	J credits FINBACK, 282 TUNNY (28 Mar) & 194 194 SEADRAGON (27 Jul); W credits FINBACK & SEADRAGON only; SORG credits TUNNY & FINBACK; attack not in I. PR says made hit on ship already beached & down by stern.
--							-	I	6	A-AK	Tateyama M. #2	394	L	07-20N 098-52E	I gives tons as 349; no likely sub attack.
7/03	209 GRAYLING	6	13-30N 121-24E	AK	7200	T2/6NSR	D								
7/23	209 GRAYLING	6	13-08N 122-10E	AK	1500	GN		D							
7/24	282 TUNNY	2	08-50N 147-06E	AP	9600	T2/2NSR	S	AIJW	7-8	XAF	Kosei M.	8237	S	08-45N 147-10E	
7	J 177 PICKEREL	7L	Unk	Unk	Unk	Unk	U	AJ I	7	C-AK	Fukuei M.	1113	PS SC	41-00N 135-00E S Shiriyasaki	Attack not in SORG or USSL; PICKEREL only sub in area.
9/06	209 GRAYLING	6	13-12N 121-45E	AK	5900	T2/3DUP	S	AIJ	9	A-AK	Shanghai M.	4103	S	13-05N 121-43E	
9/06	209 GRAYLING	6	13-12N 121-45E	AK	6600	T1/2DUP	S								
9/08	199 TAUTOG	6	05- S 123- E	AK	5000	T2/5DUP	S	AIJ	9	A-AK	Penang M.	5214	S	05-31S 123-09E	
9/13	199 TAUTOG	6	05-26S 123-04E	DD	1700	T1/3DUP	S	AIW J	9	DD	Isonami	2090 1950	S	Boetoeng Str.	
9/14	228 DRUM	5	00-32N 150-05E	AK	3800	T1/3DUP	S	AIJ	9	A-AK	Oyama M.	3809	S	00-38N 150-17E	
9/23	282 TUNNY	2	06-07N 150-28E	CVE	14000	T4/4NUP	D								
9/23	282 TUNNY	2	06-07N 150-28E	CV	22500	T3/6NUP	D								
10/02	137 S-32	7	53-12N 173-05E	AK	9000	T2/4NSR	S								
10/03	181 POMPANO	5	35-03N 142-40E	CV	28900	T2/6NSR	D								
10/03	228 DRUM	5	01-37N 149-20E	AK	5000	T2/3NSR	S								
12	229 FLYING FISH	5	41-23N 141-30E	AK	6000	T1/4DUP	S	AIJ	12	C-AK	Sapporo M. #12	2865	S	41-22N 141-29E	
13	229 FLYING FISH	5	41-58N 141-10E	AK	7600	T2/4DUP	D								
13/20	209 GRAYLING	6	10-38N 121-27E	APK	2000	GN		S							

Dt/Hr	Submarine	Pt	Position	Tgt	Size	Attack	Cl	So	Date	Type	Name	Tons	Dm	Location	Comments
APR	1943														
14/05	173 PIKE	7	01-42N 148-45E	AK	7000	T2/4NUP	D	I	14	A-AK	Madras M.	3802	M	01-25N 148-22E	
14/05	173 PIKE	7	01-42N 148-45E	AK	5000	T2/2NUP	D								
15	229 FLYING FISH	5	41-55N 141-06E	AK	5000	T1/4DUP	D	I	15	A-AK	Seiryu M.	1904	S	N of Esansaki	No other record of this attack; I lists same ship sunk 11 May 44. [Attribution ?]
15/16	197 SEAWOLF	8	21-15N 152-00E	AK	10000	T4/9NUP	S	AIJW	15	XAP	Kaihei M.	4575	S	21-13N 152-24E	
17/10	229 FLYING FISH	5	42-04N 143-22E	AK	7000	T2/4DUP	S	AIJ	16-7	A-AK	Amaho M.	2774	S	42-00N 143-20E	
--							-	AJW I	16-7	XAO	Nisshin M. #2	17579	SU H	Ishigaki Jima 23-30N 124-19E	A says sunk by unk sub; W credits 197 SEAWOLF but PR shows no such attack; J says sunk by unk agent off Formosa. No likely sub attack.
18/14	228 DRUM	5	01-55N 148-24E	AK	7100	T4/8DUP	S	AIJW	18	XAP	Nisshun M.	6380	S	02-02N 148-27E	W lists ship as both XAE & Std AK 1A.
18/18	209 GRAYLING	6	06-10S 116-53E	Sch	100	GD	S								
19/11	197 SEAWOLF	8	26-15N 139-35E	AO	2000	T1/2DUP	S	AW I	15	XAG	Banshu M. #5	389	S ?U	Truk-Rabaul Truk-Yokohama	PR says #360 on bridge, life rings with name Banshu M #5; ship sank by head, 30 survivors in water. W says missing 15 Apr.
20/07	197 SEAWOLF	8	25-37N 135-52E	Sam	100	GD	S								PR says left damaged, crew still on.
20/12	278 SCORPION	1	37-10N 141-25E	AK	2900	T1/3DUP	S	AIJW	20	XPG	Meiji M. #1	1934	S	Off Kinkazan	
21/00	278 SCORPION	1	37-40N 141-30E	Sam		GM	S								
22/24	278 SCORPION	1	37-12N 141-29E	Sam	100	GN	S								
22	HNMS O-21	2	03-28N 099-47E	MV	7000	T2/4	S	AIJ	21-2	A-AK	Yamazato M.	6925	S	03-28N 099-47E	
23/01	278 SCORPION	1	37-06N 141-27E	Sam	100	GN	S								
23/01	278 SCORPION	1	37-08N 141-28E	Sam		GN	S								
23/04	278 SCORPION	1	37-03N 142-11E	AK	7500	T1/1NUP	D								
23/07	197 SEAWOLF	8	23-45N 122-45E	DE	900	T1/6DUP	D	AIW J	23	PF	P 39	935 820	S	23-48N 122-42E	Ex-DD Tade. PR says found DD & tugs with derelict AK, stern blown up, stack off, 30 deg list; sank DD. Derelict AK not identified.

Dt/Hr	Submarine	Pt	Position	Tgt	Size	Attack	Cl	So	Date	Type	Name	Tons	Dm	Location	Comments
APR	1943														
23/12	202 TROUT	8	03-22N 119-39E	Sam	200	GD	S								
23/12	202 TROUT	8	03-22N 119-39E	Sam	200	GD	S								
24	229 FLYING FISH	5	41-44N 141-21E	AK	9000	T3/4DUP	S	AJ I	24	C-APK	Kasuga M.	1374 1397	S	41-42N 141-20E	
24/13	275 RUNNER	2	21-41N 116-24E	AK	4800	T1/3DUP	D	I	25	A-AH	Buenos Aires M	9625	L	22-12N 114-47E	PR says ship zig-zagging with armed escort. Not listed as AH in W. [Attribution ?; location not close to attack.]
25/16	279 SNOOK	1	28-46N 129-47E	Sam		GD	S								
26/00	211 GUDGEON	8	01-48N 119-12E	AK	9000	T3/6NUR	D								
26/14	197 SEAWOLF	8	28-11N 137-33E	Sam	100	GD	S								
27/05	278 SCORPION	1	38-08N 143-03E	AK	9300	T4/4TUP	S	AIJ	27	C-AK	Yuzan M.	6380	S	37-54N 143-17E	
28/01	211 GUDGEON	8	10-18N 121-44E	AP	17500	T3/4NSP	S	AIJW	28	APH	Kamakura M.	17526	S	10-25N 121-50E	W says ship to have been converted to CVE.
29/06	278 SCORPION	1	38- N 147-30E	PC	100	GD	S								
30/10	278 SCORPION	1	37-37N 155-00E	PC	600	T1/1DSR	S	IW	30	XPkt	Ebisu M. #5	131	S	37-34N 155-00E	
MAY	1943														
1	229 FLYING FISH	5	41-19N 141-28E	AK	6000	T2/4DUP	S								
1/09	266 POGY	1	37-04N 141-06E	AK	7000	T1/3D	S	AIJW	1	XPG	Keishin M.	1434	S	37-00N 141-05E	
1/24	266 POGY	1	37-32N 142-08E	DE	800	T1/3NSR	D								
2/02	186 STINGRAY	7	27-18N 121-38E	AK	7500	T1/3NSR	S	I J	2	A-AP	Ussuri M. Tamon M.	6385 8156	L S	N of Formosa Sub position	[J attribution ?; A & I give Tamon M location 14-38N 149-23E.]
--							-	A I	1	C-AK	Tamon M.	8156 3156	S	14-38N 149-23E	No likely sub attack.
2/10	206 GAR	7	00-41S 117-50E	AK	500	GD	S	AI	2	XPkt	Jimbo M. #12	192	S	00-35S 117-50E	
2/19	266 POGY	1	37-11N 143-40E	Sam	100	GD	S								

Dt/Hr	Submarine	Pt	Position	Tgt	Size	Attack	Cl	So	Date	Type	Name	Tons	Dm	Location	Comments
MAY	1943														
2/08	183 SEAL	6	07-45N 134-02E	AK	4500	T0/3DUP	0	I	5	?	Genei M. #1	?	S	S of Palau	PR says torpedoes missed, heard bomb explosion. [Attribution ?]
--							-	A I	3	C-AK	Unyo M. #5	2054	SC S	36-07N 125-38E	A says ran aground. No likely sub attack.
4/06	238 WAHOO	5	45-20N 149-08E	AV	15600	T1/3DUP	D								
4/07	211 GUDGEON	8	10-11N 121-43E	Tra	500	GD	S	Note			Naku M.				PR says ship identified by survivors; A says not listed in Japan Registry.
4/17	183 SEAL	6	06-54N 134-55E	AO	10200	T3/3DUP	S	AJW I	4	XAO	San Clemente M	7354 10215	S	06-50N 134-28E	
5/08	178 PERMIT	8	13-27N 144-35E	AK	8400	T1/4DUP	D	I	5	XAP	Tokai M.	8359	L	13-30N 144-29E	J credits 229 FLYING FISH (26 Jan) & 185 SNAPPER (27 Aug). PR says ship in Apra harbor, already damaged.
5/09	211 GUDGEON	8	10-38N 122-20E	APK	1600	GD	S								
5/19	276 SAWFISH	2	34-11N 137-41E	XAV	8600	T2/4DUP	D	AIJW	5	XPG	Hakkai M.	2921	S	34-05N 137-35E	
5/22	279 SNOOK	1	38-39N 122-35E	AK	4000	T1/3NSR	S	AIJ	5	C-AK	Kinko M.	1268	S	38-39N 122-48E	
5/23	279 SNOOK	1	38-38N 122-39E	AK	5700	T1/5NSR	S	AJ I	5	C-AK	Daifuku M. Taifuku M.	3194	S	N of Formosa	
6/16	206 GAR	7	03-14N 117-58E	Sch	300	GD	S	AI	6	C-AK	Kotoku M.	164	S	Tarakan Harbor	
7/03	279 SNOOK	1	36-05N 123-21E	AK	7000	T1/4NSR	D	AIJ	7	C-AK	Tosei M.	4363	S	35-58N 123-31E	
7/03	279 SNOOK	1	36-05N 123-21E	Same	Same	Same	0	AI	7	C-AK	Shinsei M. #3	1258	S	36-05N 123-21E	PR says fired at 2 overlapping ships in convoy, heard 3 possible explosions.
7/06	206 GAR	7	04-19N 118-53E	Sam	100	GD	S								
7/11	238 WAHOO	5	40-05N 141-53E	AK	5700	T1/2DUP	S	AIJ	7	C-APK	Tamon M. #5	5260	S	40-04N 141-57E	
8/17	206 GAR	7	07-45N 122-02E	AK	500	GD	S								
9/03	179 PLUNGER	6	10-18N 150-46E	AK	7400	T2/3NUP	D								
9/05	238 WAHOO	5	38-57N 141-49E	AO	9500	T1/3TUP	S	AIJ	9	C-AK	Takao M.	3204	S	38-52N 141-43E	
9/05	238 WAHOO	5	38-57N 141-49E	AO	9500	T1/3TUP	S	AJ I	9	C-AK	Jinmu M. Jimmu M.	1912	S H	38-52N 141-43E	

Dt/Hr	Submarine	Pt	Position	Tgt	Size	Attack	Cl	So	Date	Type	Name	Tons	Dm	Location	Comments
MAY	1943														
9/08	266 POGY	1	37-05N 141-06E	AK	4100	T1/3DUP	D	I	9	XAP	Uyo M.	6376	L	36-59N 141-04E	W lists ship as both XAP & Std AK 1A.
9/12	206 GAR	7	09-09N 122-50E	AK	3000	T2/4DUP	S	IJW A	9	XPG	Aso M.	703	S	SE Cagayan I. 14-48N 120-14E	A says location doubtful. PR says target seen to sink, survivors in water.
9/17	179 PLUNGER	6	12-24N 149-55E	AK	8700	T3/3DUP	S								
9/17	179 PLUNGER	6	12-24N 149-55E	AK	7400	T1/1DUP	D								
10/09	179 PLUNGER	6	14-29N 149-00E	APK	7100	T2/2DUP	S	AIJ	10	C-APK	Tatsutake M.	7068	S	14-33N 149-23E	
11/01	178 PERMIT	8	16-15N 146-53E	AK	10000	T2/3NSR	S								
11/01	178 PERMIT	8	16-15N 146-53E	AK	5000	T2/2NSR	S								
11/01	178 PERMIT	8	16-15N 146-53E	AK	5000	T1/1NSR	D								
11/06	179 PLUNGER	6	14-29N 149-00E	AK	8300	GD	S	AIJW	10	XAP	Kinai M.	8360	S	14-33N 149-23E	
11/07	266 POGY	1	37-52N 143-12E	Sam	100	GD	S								
11/08	208 GRAYBACK	7	00-47S 149-02E	AK	6500	T2/3DUP	D	AIJW	11	XAC	Yodogawa M.	6441	S	00-40S 148-55E	
11/08	208 GRAYBACK	7	00-47S 149-02E	AK	5000	T1/1DUP	D								
11/08	208 GRAYBACK	7	00-47S 149-02E	AK	4000	T1/2DUP	D								
12/08	211 GUDGEON	8	12-43N 124-08E	AK	4500	T0/2DUP	O	A J	12	A-AK	Sumatra M.	5861	S PS	12-44N 124-08E	PR says ship moored, thought torp exploded on beach.
13/01	238 WAHOO	5	38-52N 143-00E	AK	9300	T2/4	D								
13/10	266 POGY	1	38-16N 141-36E	AK	6400	T1/3DUP	D								
13/21	279 SNOOK	1	32-08N 127-17E	AK	2200	T1/2NUP	S								
15/10	206 GAR	7	13-07N 121-49E	AK	6000	T1/3DUP	S	AIJ	15	A-AK	Meikai M.	3197	S	13-10N 121-50E	
15/17	206 GAR	7	13-07N 121-49E	AK	6000	T3/9	S	AIJ	15	A-AK	Indus M.	4361	S	Baltasar I.	
16/13	208 GRAYBACK	7	01-00S 148-44E	DD	1800	T2/6DUP	D	AI	16	DD	Yugure	1715	H	NW of Kavieng	
16/14	279 SNOOK	1	30-29N 141-55E	Tra	100	GD	S								
17/18	208 GRAYBACK	7	01-00S 148-40E	AK	5300	T2/4DUP	D	AIJ	17	A-AK	England M.	5829	S	00-45N 148-30E	

43

Dt/Hr	Submarine	Pt	Position	Tgt	Size	Attack	Cl	So	Date	Type	Name	Tons	Dm	Location	Comments
MAY	1943														
17/19 208 GRAYBACK		7	01-00S 148-40E	AK	6000	T2/4DUP	D								
18/18 180 POLLACK		7	08- N 171- E	AK	1900	T2/2DUP	S	AI JW	20 18	XPF	Terushima M.	3110	S P	08-33N 171-00E	
19/12 206 GAR		7	01-02N 119-03E	Sam	100	GD	S	IW	25	XPkt	Asuka M.	37	S	Makassar Str.	PR says burned & sunk after boarding.
20/14 206 GAR		7	03-18S 118-18E	Sam		GD	S	Note			Note				PR identifies as sailing vessel Noesutana Salemo, Makassar; not seen to sink.
20/15 180 POLLACK		7	06-47N 169-42E	AK	7400	T3/4DUP	S	AIJW	20	XCL	Bangkok M.	5351	S	E of Jaluit	
20/20 199 TAUTOG		7	06-37S 120-28E	Sam	100	GM	S								
21/20 199 TAUTOG		7	05-44S 122-29E	AK	1000	GN	D								
26/00 239 WHALE		4	14-17N 144-53E	AK	4400	T1/3NUS	S	AIJW	25-6	XPG	Shoei M.	3580	S	14-17N 144-50E	
26/10 189 SAURY		6	28-49N 129-40E	AK	4500	T2/3DUP	S	AIJ	26	C-AP	Kagi M.	2346	S	28-50N 129-32E	
26/14 266 POGY		1	37-03N 141-09E	AK	1900	T2/3DUP	S	AIJ	26	C-AK	Tainan M.	1989	S	36-59N 141-16E	
26 202 TROUT		8	02-00N 109-15E	--	--	Mine	U	I	26	C-AO	Palembang M.	5236	M	02-03N 109-11E	Minefield laid 7 Apr. [Attribution ?]
27/02 230 FINBACK		5	08-41N 134-02E	AK	6000	T2/3NUP	S	AIJ	27	A-AK	Kochi M.	2910	S	08-28N 134-06E	
27/16 197 SEAWOLF		9	24-40N 134-40E	Sam	100	GD	S								
28/09 146 S-41		6	50-38N 155-15E	AK	1200	T1/2DUP	S	AJ I	28	Sail C-AK	Seiki M.	1036	S SU	50-35N 155-13E	PR says 4-masted barkentine.
28/15 237 TRIGGER		5	34-33N 138-50E	AO	7500	T1/3DUP	D	I	29	C-AO	Koshin M.	975	L	Off Irosaki	[Attribution ?; size discrepancy.]
28/19 189 SAURY		6	27-32N 126-08E	AO	10400	T5/10DUP	S	AIJW	28	XAO	Akatsuki M.	10216	S	27-40N 125-55E	
29/01 277 SCAMP		2	01-40S 150-24E	AK	15600	T2/2NSR	S	AIJW	28	XAV	Kamikawa M.	6853	S	01-00S 150-18E	
29/10 198 TAMBOR		7	17-35N 110-45E	AK	4400	T3/3DUP	S	AIJ	29-30	C-AK	Eisho M.	2486	S	17-30N 110-55E	
29/23 283 TINOSA		1	32-03N 131-56E	AK	6700	T2/14NSV	D								
30/01 189 SAURY		6	30-07N 124-32E	AO	10000	T2/6NSV	S	AJ I	29-30	C-AK	Shoko M. Matsue M.	5385	S	29-37N 125-00E	PR says fired at AO in convoy, 1 possible dud hit, sank ship with 2nd salvo.

Dt/Hr	Submarine	Pt	Position	Tgt	Size	Attack	Cl	So	Date	Type	Name	Tons	Dm	Location	Comments
MAY	1943														
30/01	189 SAURY	6	30-07N 124-32E	Same	Same	Same	0	A J	30	A-AK	Takamisan M.	1992	S	31-20N 122-34E Sub position	I says sunk by mine, 31-20N 122-39E; see 279 SNOOK 30 May. [J attribution ?; sinking not near attack.]
30/01	189 SAURY	6	30-07N 124-32E	Same	Same	Same	0	I	30	C-AK	Hakozaki M.	3948	SM	31-20N 122-39E	See above note & 233 HERRING 14 Dec. [Attribution ?]
30	279 SNOOK	1	30-21N 122-30E	--	--	Mine	U	I	30	A-AK	Takamisan M.	1992	SM	31-20N 122-39E	Minefield laid 30 Apr; see 189 SAURY 30 May. [Attribution ?]
30	279 SNOOK	1	30-21N 122-30E	--	--	Mine	U	I	30	C-AK	Hakozaki M.	3948	SM	31-20N 122-39E	Same as above. [Attribution ?]
31/19	139 S-34	6	50-29N 156-28E	AK	3000	T2/3DUP	S								
JUN	1943														
1/01	146 S-41	6	50-04N 156-32E	AK	5000	T1/3TSR	S								
1/11	237 TRIGGER	5	35-02N 140-14E	AK	8200	T1/3DUP	S	AIJ	1	C-AC	Noborikawa M.	2182	S	35-03N 140-28E	
2/03	198 TAMBOR	7	20-30N 107-57E	AK	6600	T1/3NSV	S	AJ	2	APK	Eika M.	1248	S	Sub position	J gives date 2 Jun 45 [apparently misprint].
2/05	230 FINBACK	5	07-11N 134-45E	APK	7100	T1/3TUP	D								
3/17	182 SALMON	6	30-04N 137-36E	AK	7500	T2/3DUP	D								
3/17	182 SALMON	6	30-04N 137-36E	AK	6400	T2/3DUP	D								
5/09	283 TINOSA	1	30-55N 125-46E	APK	10900	T2/2DUP	D								
5/22	239 WHALE	4	14-34N 151-33E	AV	15600	T3/4NUS	D								
6/01	197 SEAWOLF	9	30-45N 126-47E	DE	1000	T1/1NSV	D								
6/19	135 S-30	7	50-45N 156-56E	Sam	100	GD	S	I	6	C-AK	Nagashige M #2	30	S	S Kamchatka	
6/23	199 TAUTOG	7	07-00N 123-37E	AK	5000	T1/3NSR	S	AIJ	6	A-AK	Shinei M.	970	S	07-13N 123-23E	
7/02	198 TAMBOR	7	20-23N 107-47E	AK	6000	T1/3NSV	S								
7/19	209 GRAYLING	7	03-12S 108-47E	AK	5500	T1/3TUS	S								
8/02	230 FINBACK	5	09-07N 134-31E	AK	5700	T2/3NSV	S	AIW J	8	XCM	Kahoku M.	3277 3350	S	08-58N 134-14E	

Dt/Hr	Submarine	Pt	Position	Tgt	Size	Attack	Cl	So	Date	Type	Name	Tons	Dm	Location	Comments
JUN	1943														
8/02	230 FINBACK	5	09-07N 134-31E	AK	7000	T1/3NSV	D								
8/03	230 FINBACK	5	09-07N 134-31E	AK	5400	T1/2NSV	S								
8/19	230 FINBACK	5	11-36N 134-10E	AP	6400	T1/3TUP	D								
9/02	213 GREENLING	6	02-20N 145-45E	AO	10200	T3/4N	D	I	9	XAO	Akebono M.	10182	H	20-17N 145-39E	[Latitude in I may be misprint.]
9/07	202 TROUT	9	02-10N 118-28E	AK	4200	T2/4DUP	D								
9/22	239 WHALE	4	11-58N 149-03E	AK	7600	T1/4NUP	D								
9/22	239 WHALE	4	11-58N 149-03E	AK	8600	T2/2NUP	S								
10/05	283 TINOSA	1	31-14N 132-44E	AO	14000	T2/4TUP	D	I	10	AO	Iro	14050	L	SE of Fuka I.	I gives tons as 15400.
10/08	213 GREENLING	6	01-01N 145-37E	AK	5400	T1/3DUP	S								
10/12	229 FLYING FISH	6	24-55N 145-36E	AK	8600	T1/3DUP	D								
10/20	237 TRIGGER	5	34-13N 139-50E	CV	27500	T4/6TUP	D	A I	10	CV	Hiyo	26949	H M	NE Miyake I.	
11/01	236 SILVERSIDES	5	02-47N 152-00E	APK	10000	T3/4NSV	S	AJ IW	10-1	XAK	Hide M. Hinode M.	5256	S	02-43N 152-00E	
11/10	230 FINBACK	5	07-36N 134-17E	AP	6100	T2/3DUP	S	AJ I	11	A-AK	Genoa M.	6784	S	07-39N 134-17E 09-40N 134-20E	[Latitude in I may be misprint.]
11/14	135 S-30	7	50-23N 155-36E	AK	10000	T2/3DUP	D	A IJ	11	C-AK	Jinbu M.	5131 5228	S	50-23N 155-38E	I gives name Jimbu M.
11 J	275 RUNNER	3L	Unk	Unk	Unk	Unk	U	J	11	AK	Seinan M.	1338	PS	41-00N 141-30E	Attack not in SORG or U; I lists ship of same name about same location, 20 Mar; see 277 SCAMP that date. [J attribution ?]
13/04	217 GUARDFISH	5	03-14S 151-31E	AK	7000	T1/4NSR	D								
13/15	194 SEADRAGON	6	09-30N 167-30E	AK	6900	T2/4DUP	D								
13/15	217 GUARDFISH	5	03-08S 151-24E	AK	4000	T1/2DUP	S	AJ I	13	A-AK	Suzuya M.	897 201	S	03-00S 151-18E	
13/22	188 SARGO	7	06-08N 138-28E	AK	6600	T2/2NUP	S	AIJ	13	A-AP	Konan M.	5226	S	06-05N 138-25E	

Dt/Hr	Submarine	Pt	Position	Tgt	Size	Attack	Cl	So	Date	Type	Name	Tons	Dm	Location	Comments
JUN	1943														
14/12	188 SARGO	7	06-40N 136-59E	AK	8300	T1/3DUP	D								
14/19	191 SCULPIN	7	38-26N 141-45E	AK	4500	T1/4DUP	D								
14/23	282 TUNNY	3	08-35N 152-37E	AP	9300	T3/4NUP	D								
15/02	258 HOE	1	06-32N 134-51E	AK	5900	T1/3NUR	D								
15/03	253 GUNNEL	2	33-55N 127-38E	AK	7500	T2/7NSR	S	AIJ	15	C-APK	Koyo M.	6426	S	33-53N 128-30E	
15/13	202 TROUT	9	05-09N 119-38E	AO	6500	T3/3DUP	S	AIJW	15	XAO	Sanraku M.	3000	S	04-58N 119-37E	
15/14	192 SAILFISH	8	39- N 142- E	AK	5000	T1/3DUP	D	AIJ	15	C-AK	Shinju M.	3617	S	39-15N 142-03E	
17/07	228 DRUM	6	02-03S 153-44E	AK	8700	T3/4DUP	S	AIW J	17	XAP	Myoko M.	5086	S PS	04-04N 154-03E	[J attribution ?; sinking not near attack.]
17/23	209 GRAYLING	7	03- N 105- E	Sam		GN	S									
18/03	138 S-33	7	50-25N 155-02E	Sam	100	GT	S	I	19	Fish	Tx2 # 1	?	H	Paramushiro I.	PR says left afire. [Attribution ?; insufficient identification.]
18/03	138 S-33	7	50-25N 155-02E	Sam		GT	S	I	19	Fish	Tx2 # 2	?	H	Paramushiro I.	Same as above.
18/04	138 S-33	7	50-25N 155-02E	Sam	100	GT	S								PR says hit & appeared to be sinking.
19/04	191 SCULPIN	7	37-11N 142-30E	Pat		GT	S	IW	19	XPkt	Miyasho M. #1	79	S	E Inubo Saki	
19/08	253 GUNNEL	2	32-40N 126-37E	AK	7200	T1/3DUP	S	AIJ	19	C-AK	Tokiwa M.	6971	S	32-31N 126-17E	PR says old AK broke in two & sank.
19 N	253 GUNNEL	2	32-40N 126-37E	AK	Unk	T1/3DUP	U	AIW J	21	XPG	Hong Kong M.	2797	S SU	Shirase Lt.	Attack not in SORG; PR says possible hit on 2nd AK; W credits GUNNEL. [Attribution ?]
19/16	215 GROWLER	5	01-38N 148-14E	AK	7400	T2/4DUP	D								
19/16	215 GROWLER	5	01-38N 148-14E	AK	4500	T2/2DUP	S	IJ A	19 17	A-AK	Miyadono M.	5196	S	01-42N 147-23E	No likely sub attack 17 Jun.
19/17	191 SCULPIN	7	37-04N 142-54E	PC	100	GD	S	AI	19	A-AK	Sagami M.	135	S	36-40N 142-55E	
19/22	253 GUNNEL	2	32-40N 126-31E	DE	900	T1/2NSR	S	I	19	CMc	Tsubame	450	M	32-30N 126-15E	
20/05	199 TAUTOG	7	15-57N 140-30E	AO	9200	T3/4TUP	S	AIJW	20	XAP	Meiten M.	4474	S	15-57N 140-57E	

Dt/Hr	Submarine	Pt	Position	Tgt	Size	Attack	Cl	So	Date	Type	Name	Tons	Dm	Location	Comments
20/10	197 SEAWOLF	9	24-39N 118-58E	APK	4200	T1/4DUP	S	AJ I	20	C-AK	Shojin M.	4739	S H	24-32N 118-53E	
21/23	258 HOE	1	08-58N 131-13E	AP	9500	T3/4NUR	S								
22	209 GRAYLING	7	04-03N 103-57E	AO	8700	T1/3NUP	D	AI	22	C-AO	Eiyo M.	8673	M	04-08N 103-52E	
22/01	257 HARDER	1	34-30N 137-32E	AK	7000	T3/4NUR	S	I	21	XAO	Kyoei M. #3	1189	D	E of Daio Saki	W lists ship as both XAO & Std AO 1TS.
23/05	257 HARDER	1	33-45N 138-10E	APK	9100	T1/4NUP	D	AIJW	23	XAV	Sagara M.	7189	S	33-52N 138-20E	A & W say beached, total loss.
24/07	257 HARDER	1	34-10N 136-30E	AK	7100	T1/7DUP	D								
24/11	279 SNOOK	2	28-50N 126-56E	AO	9500	T2/4DUP	D	I	24	AO	Ose	7986	H	W Amami Oshima	
25/02	209 GRAYLING	7	05- N 107- E	Sam	100	GN	S								
25/10	192 SAILFISH	8	39- N 142- E	AK	6500	T1/3DUP	D	IA J	28 25	A-AC	Iburi M.	3291	S	39-53N 142-06E	
25/16	257 HARDER	1	33-30N 135-55E	AK	4400	T1/4DUP	S								
25/16	257 HARDER	1	33-30N 135-55E	AK	4400	T1/3DUP	D								
25/20	191 SCULPIN	7	37-02N 141-02E	AK	4500	T1/4TUP	D								
26/05	259 JACK	1	33-22N 138-56E	AK	8200	T2/3DUP	S	AIJW	26	XAP	Toyo M.	4163	S	33-10N 139-00E	
26/05	259 JACK	1	33-22N 138-56E	AK	6000	T3/7DUP	D								
26/06	259 JACK	1	33-22N 138-56E	AK	9300	T1/2DUP	S	AIJW	26	XAP	Shozan M.	5859	S	33-10N 139-00E	
26/17	202 TROUT	9	10-14N 121-46E	AK	600	GD	S								
26/18	202 TROUT	9	10-14N 121-46E	Sch	400	GD	S								
26/19	202 TROUT	9	10-14N 121-46E	Sch	200	GD	S								
26 J	275 RUNNER	3L	Unk	Unk	Unk	Unk	U	AJ I	26	A-AK	Shinryu M.	4935	PS SC	48-06N 153-15E	Attack not in SORG or U.
28/13	282 TUNNY	3	14-10N 145-03E	AK	3100	T2/3DUP	S	AJW I	28	XPG	Shotoku M.	1964	S	14-07N 145-07E 14-07N 148-07E	[Longitude in I may be misprint.]
28/11	265 PETO	2	01-47N 151-46E	Q		2000	T1/2DUP	S	AI W	29 Note XAGOR	B-AG	Tenkai M. #2	359 1200	SA SU	01-30N 151-24E	W says presumably lost Truk to Rabaul, Jun 43. [Attribution ?]

48

Dt/Hr	Submarine	Pt	Position	Tgt	Size	Attack	Cl	So	Date	Type	Name	Tons	Dm	Location	Comments
JUN	1943														
29/12	254 GURNARD	2	07-34N 134-26E	AK	8200	T3/3DUP S									
29/12	254 GURNARD	2	07-34N 134-26E	AK	7400	T2/3DUP D									
29/14	257 HARDER	1	34-33N 137-42E	AK	4000	T1/1DUP S									
29/14	257 HARDER	1	34-33N 137-42E	AO	6500	T1/1DUP D									
30/12	172 PORPOISE	6	08-36N 171-02E	AK	4000	T1/2DUP D									
30/18	200 THRESHER	9	01-11S 117-26E	AK	7000	T1/3DUP D									
JUL	1943														
1/01	188 SARGO	7	10-36N 146-04E	AK	4000	T1/2NSV D									
1/09	254 GURNARD	2	07-38N 134-23E	DD	1000	T3/3DUP S									
1/09	254 GURNARD	2	07-38N 134-23E	AK	7300	T1/2DUP D									
1/09	254 GURNARD	2	07-38N 134-23E	AK	6100	T1/1DUP D									
1/12	254 GURNARD	2	07-40N 134-20E	CV	17000	T3/4DUP D									
1/15	187 STURGEON	7	33-33N 135-23E	AK	5500	T2/4DUP D									
1/19	200 THRESHER	9	00-43N 119-34E	DD	1800	T2/3TUP D	AI	1		DD	Hokaze	1215	M	00-43N 119-33E	
1/24	200 THRESHER	9	00-20N 119-32E	AO	10000	T1/1NSV S	AIJ	1-2		A-AK	Yoneyama M.	5274	S	01-30N 119-33E	
1/24	200 THRESHER	9	00-20N 119-32E	AO	10000	T1/1NSV S									
2/04	202 TROUT	9	13-36N 121-49E	AO	9500	T2/4NSV S	AIJ	2		A-AK	Isuzu M.	2866	S	Lombok Channel	
2/05	229 FLYING FISH	6	25-07N 119-18E	APK	8500	T3/4TUP S	AIJ	2		C-AP	Canton M.	2822	S	24-42N 119-00E	
2/14	140 S-35	6	52- N 156- E	AK	8200	T2/3DUP S	AI J	2		Crab	Banshu M. #7	5490 5430	S	Kamchatka	
--						-	AJW I	2		A-AK	Kashi M.	654	SA S	08-06S 157-20E	W lists as XAN. No likely sub attack.
3/02	172 PORPOISE	6	08-22N 169-20E	AK	6900	T2/3NUP S									
3/10	278 SCORPION	2	38- N 124- E	AK	4000	T2/3DUP D	AIJ	3		C-AK	Anzan M.	3890	S	38-21N 124-24E	

Dt/Hr	Submarine	Pt	Position	Tgt	Size	Attack	Cl	So	Date	Type	Name	Tons	Dm	Location	Comments
JUL	1943														
3/10	278 SCORPION	2	38- N 124- E	AK	4000	T3/3DUP	D	AIJ	3	C-AK	Kokuryu M.	6112	S	38-08N 124-30E	
4/01	279 SNOOK	2	28-40N 124-10E	AK	10000	T2/3NSR	D	I	4	XAP	Atlantic M.	5872	H	28-29N 124-06E	
4/03	279 SNOOK	2	28-40N 124-10E	AO	17600	T3/6NSV	S	AIJ	4	C-AK	Liverpool M.	5865	S	28-29N 124-15E	
4/04	279 SNOOK	2	28-40N 124-10E	AK	5000	T3/5NSV	S	AIJ	4	C-AK	Koki M.	5290	S	28-45N 124-06E	
4/16	259 JACK	1	34-31N 138-35E	AK	6800	T3/3DUP	S	AIJ	4	C-AK	Nikkyu M.	6529	S	34-33N 138-37E	
4/22	181 POMPANO	6	34-38N 137-53E	AK	9100	T2/3NSR	D	Note 4		XAV	Sagara M.	7189	S	Sub position	PR says target was grounded ship previously hit by 257 HARDER; see 23 Jun.
5/19	266 POGY	2	07-25N 149-33E	AK	3000	T1/3TUP	D								
5/21	200 THRESHER	9	01-33N 121-25E	AO	10000	T1/4NSV	D								
6/22	178 PERMIT	9	43-35N 140-21E	AK	3100	T1/2NSR	S	AIJ	6	C	Banshu M. #33	787	S	43-30N 140-20E	
7/02	178 PERMIT	9	43-14N 139-53E	AK	5000	T1/2NSR	S	AIJ	6-7	C-AK	Showa M.	2212	S	Off Otaru	
7/02	178 PERMIT	9	43-14N 139-53E	AK	5000	T2/2NSR	D								
7/14	179 PLUNGER	7	37-14N 132-57E	AK	3000	T0/4+GD	0	I	7	C-AK	Anzan M.	5493	M	37-02N 133-30E	PR says possible dud hit; no gun hits but target appeared damaged.
7/17	265 PETO	2	00-37N 148-06E	AO	10000	T2/3DUP	D								
8/00	178 PERMIT	9	42-45N 139-52E	AK	8000	T2/3NSV	S								
8/02	178 PERMIT	9	42-41N 139-49E	AK	3000	T1/7NSV	D								
9 N	178 PERMIT	9	See note	Tra	55	GD		S	Note 9		Tra	Seiner No. 20	55	S	See note	Soviet trawler; attack not in SORG but in Holmes & Blair. PR gives posit 27 mi 251 deg off Kaiba To, 12 survivors taken to Akutan, Alaska.
10/21	232 HALIBUT	5	10-37N 150-45E	CL	10500	T3/6NUP	D								
10/23	280 STEELHEAD	2	10-02N 150-46E	CVE	18000	T4/5NSR	D								
10/22	181 POMPANO	6	33-34N 136-07E	AO	Large	T0/2NSR	0	AI	11	XAO	Kyokuyo M.	17549	L	33-31N 135-24E	PR says torps appeared to miss ahead.
11/05	254 GURNARD	2	12-53N 131-49E	AK	6400	T2/3TUP	S	AIJ	11	A-AK	Taiko M.	1925	S	12-45N 131-50E	
11/05	254 GURNARD	2	12-53N 131-49E	AK	5700	T1/1TUP	D								

Dt/Hr	Submarine	Pt	Position	Tgt	Size	Attack	Cl	So	Date	Type	Name	Tons	Dm	Location	Comments
JUL	1943														
11/15	260 LAPON	1	41- N 129- E	Sam	100	GD	S								
11/17	229 FLYING FISH	6	24-05N 135-33E	Sch	200	GD	S	IW	11	XPkt	Takatori M. #8	51	S	24-00N 135-25E	
--							-	W I	11	XPkt	Seiun M.	39	S ?	51-20N 164-30E	W credits 140 S-35; PR posit not near location; no likely sub attack.
12/04	179 PLUNGER	7	43-02N 140-00E	AK	5100	T1/4TUP	S	AIJ	12	C-AK	Niitaka M.	2482	S	43-02N 139-56E	
12/17	190 SPEARFISH	7	11-12N 161-50E	DD		T0/3DUP	0	I	12	DD	Kawakaze	1580	L	?	PR says premature explosions. [Attribution ?; location not given.]
12/18	261 MINGO	1	01-00N 142-59E	AK	5900	T2/3DUP	D								
12/18	261 MINGO	1	01-00N 142-59E	AK	6000	T2/3DUP	D								
14/12	206 GAR	8	05-38S 120-30E	AK	500	GD	D								
15/08	283 TINOSA	2	10-16N 151-27E	CVE		T0/4DUP	0	I	16	XCL	Aikoku M.	10437	L	10-27N 150-50E	PR says torps apparently missed. [Attribution ?]
15	236 SILVERSIDES	5	02-36S 150-34E	--	--	Mine	U	I	15	CA	Nagara	5170	LM	Kavieng	Minefield laid 4 Jun. A says damage negligible. [Attribution ?]
17/20	181 POMPANO	6	33-03N 137-35E	Sam	100	GN	S								PR says left 2/3 submerged.
19/02	172 PORPOISE	6	18-45N 166-40E	APK	10400	T3/4NUP	S	IJW A	18-9 Note	XAP XAC	Mikage M. #20	2718	S	18-50N 166-21E	A gives date 31 Aug; no likely sub attack then.
19/10	218 ALBACORE	5	00-37N 149-25E	AP	6400	T1/3DUP	D								
20/03	181 POMPANO	6	33-55N 136-26E	AK	8000	T0/2NUP	0	I	20	XAP	Uyo M.	6376	L	E of Miki Zaki	PR says explosions heard but torps appeared to miss. W lists ship as both XAP & Std AK 1A. [Attribution ?]
21/04	276 SAWFISH	3	30-44N 128-21E	AK	9900	T2/2NUP	D								
21/04	276 SAWFISH	3	30-44N 128-21E	APK	6900	T2/3NUP	S								
21/04	276 SAWFISH	3	30-44N 128-21E	AK	6900	T1/1NUP	D								
21/13	231 HADDOCK	5	16-18N 134-09E	AP	10900	T3/4DUP	S	AJ I	21	A-AP	Saipan M.	5532	S	16-29N 133-57E 16-29N 123-57E	[Longitude in I may be misprint.]
21/13	231 HADDOCK	5	16-18N 134-09E	AP	9900	T1/1DUP	D								

Dt/Hr	Submarine	Pt	Position	Tgt	Size	Attack	Cl	So	Date	Type	Name	Tons	Dm	Location	Comments
JUL	1943														
21/13	231 HADDOCK	5	16-18N 134-09E	AP	6200	T1/1DUP	D								
21/13	231 HADDOCK	5	16-18N 134-09E	AP	9000	T1/2DUP	D								
22/22	184 SKIPJACK	7	34-21N 138-40E	AK	7100	T1/4NSR	D								
22/24	276 SAWFISH	3	31-04N 125-33E	AP	17000	T3/6NSR	S	I	23	XAE	Seia M.	6659	M	30-54N 125-15E	
24/12	283 TINOSA	2	06-56N 147-53E	AO	19400	T2/15DUP	D	AI	24	XAO	Tonan M. #3	19209	H	06-56N 148-35E	PR says 8 dud hits.
--							-	AJ I	24		A-AK Mie M.	2913	SM S	02-31S 133-26E Babo Harbor	No likely sub attack.
25/19	267 POMPON	1	02-40N 148-26E	AK	5700	T2/4TUP	D	I	25	XAP	Kinsen M.	3081	H	02-46N 148-35E	
25/19	267 POMPON	1	02-40N 148-26E	AK	6600	T3/4TUP	S	AIJ	25		A-AK Thames M.	5871	S	02-46N 148-35E	
27/02	231 HADDOCK	5	04-59N 139-04E	AO	10500	T2/7NUP	D								
27/03	277 SCAMP	3	02-38S 149-20E	AO	10000	T2/6NUP	D	I	27	AO	Kazahaya	18300	M	02-44N 149-29E	
27/11	194 SEADRAGON	7	19-20N 166-32E	AK	5000	T1/2DUP	D	AIJW	Note	XAP	Suwa M.	10672	JS	Wake I.	J credits SEADRAGON, 282 TUNNY (28 Mar) & 230 FINBACK (5 Apr); W credits FINBACK & SEADRAGON only; I does not list this attack. [J attribution ?]
27/12	276 SAWFISH	3	32-32N 127-41E	DD	1700	T1/4DUP	S	AIJW	27	CMc	Hirashima	720	S	Goto I.	
27/18	277 SCAMP	3	02-50S 149-01E	SS	2300	T1/4DUP	S	IW J	? 27	SS	I-168 I-24	1400 2180	S	E of Australia Sub position	I says given up 4 Aug; most authorities agree I-168 sunk by this attack.
27	198 TAMBOR	4	20-04N 109-18E	--	--	Mine	U	A J	27		C-AK Teikin M.	1972	SA PM	Hainan I. 19-57N 109-05E	Minefield laid 2 Nov 42; I says sunk by sub. No likely sub attack. [Attribution ?]
28/14	135 S-30	8	51-02N 154-55E	AK	7500	T2/3DUP	D								
30/23	230 FINBACK	6	06-31S 111-26E	APK	10800	T1/3NSR	S	AJ I	30-1		A-AK Ryuzan M.	4719	S	06-30S 111-30E 06-30N 111-30E	[Latitude in I misprint.]
31/03	189 SAURY	7	27-03N 135-27E	DD	1500	Ram	D								PR says DD hit periscope shears.
31/13	194 SEADRAGON	7	17-40N 163-58E	AK	3000	T1/3DUP	D								

Dt/Hr	Submarine	Pt	Position	Tgt	Size	Attack	Cl	So	Date	Type	Name	Tons	Dm	Location	Comments
AUG	1943														
1/00	266 POGY	2	11-16N 153-34E	AV	15600	T2/4NUP	S	AIW J	31-1	XAKV	Mogamigawa M.	7469 7497	S	11-04N 153-18E	
1/06	280 STEELHEAD	2	10-20N 153-30E	AK	4800	T2/4DUP	S	I	1	XAP	Seiko M.	5385	?	10-00N 153-30E	PR says 2 hits, breaking-up noises heard. I & J say sunk by a/c 17 Feb 44. [Attribution ?]
1/07	230 FINBACK	6	04-19S 112-09E	AK	5700	T1/4DUP	D	I	31 Jul	XAP	Atlas M.	7349	M	04-10S 112-10E	I gives tons as 7400.
1/16	135 S-30	8	51-03N 155-53E	AK	7500	T2/3DUP	D								
3/16	198 TAMBOR	8	09-56N 117-31E	AK	4400	T2/3DUP	S								
3/23	230 FINBACK	6	05-18S 111-52E	AK	5500	T2/5NSR	S	A IJ	7 3-4	A-AK	Kaisho M.	6070	S	05-18S 111-50E	
4/19	194 SEADRAGON	7	07-40N 160-45E	AK	5000	T1/2TUP	D	I	4	XAP	Kembu M.	4519	?C	07-30N 161-12E	PR says hit & smoking.
5/03	173 PIKE	8	24-37N 152-45E	AO	5000	T3/3NSR	S	AIW J	5	XAP	Shoju M.	1992 2022	S	24-30N 158-50E	I & W give tons as 1911.
5/10	236 SILVERSIDES	6	01-53N 153-52E	AS	10000	T0/4DUP	0	I	5	CM	Tsugaru	4000	M	NNE of Rabaul	PR says 1 possible hit.
6/10	261 MINGO	1	13-49N 133-15E	AK	3100	T1/1DUP	D								
6/14	173 PIKE	8	21-03N 153-31E	CVE	22500	T3/6DUP	D								
6/23	180 POLLACK	8	27-54N 140-51E	AK	7600	T1/6NSV	D								
7/02	194 SEADRAGON	7	08-49N 167-23E	AK	5000	T2/2NSV	D								
7/02	194 SEADRAGON	7	08-49N 167-23E	AK	5000	T1/1NSV	D								
8/07	239 WHALE	5	24-12N 142-52E	APK	10000	T2/4TUP	S	AIJW	8	XAPV	Naruto M.	7148	S	24-03N 142-45E	
8/24	182 SALMON	7	46-48N 145-20E	AK	7000	T3/4NUP	S								
9/06	191 SCULPIN	8	24-51N 122-12E	APK	4500	T1/3DUP	S	AIJ	9	C-APK	Sekko M.	3183	S	24-10N 122-10E	
9	278 SCORPION	1	36-05N 140-45E	--	--	Mine	U	I	9	C	Esutoru M.	3295	LM	36-07N 140-45E	Minefield laid 19 Apr. [Attribution ?]
10/13	182 SALMON	7	46-58N 143-30E	AK	4100	T3/8DUP	S	AJ I	10	Fish	Wakanoura M.	2408 2460	S	46-55N 143-30E	PR says target rolled over and sank. A says owner's records show sinking off Hachinohe, Sanriku (40-44N 143-50E). [Latitude error?]

Dt/Hr	Submarine	Pt	Position	Tgt	Size	Attack	Cl	So	Date	Type	Name	Tons	Dm	Location	Comments
AUG	1943														
13/06	263 PADDLE	1	34-42N 136-13E	AK	7100	T2/4DUP	D	I	13	XAP	Hidaka M.	5486	L	33-45N 136-17E	W gives name Hikade M.
13/23	281 SUNFISH	4	23-24N 142-26E	AO	9200	T3/6NUP	S	AIJW	13	XPG	Edo M.	1299	S	24-04N 142-21E	
13/23	281 SUNFISH	4	23-24N 142-26E	AK	9900	T3/4NUP	S									
15/01	238 WAHOO	6	43-12N 140-00E	AK	3000	TO/1NUP	O	I	14	Fish	Ryokai M.	4643	L	43-24N 140-26E	PR says hit by dud torps; I gives tons as 4655; A says ship was fishery mother ship; see 179 PLUNGER 22 Aug.
15/04	238 WAHOO	6	43-15N 140-03E	AK	6000	TO/1TUP	O	I	15	XAO	Terukawa M.	6433	L	43-46N 140-30E	PR says dud hit, air flask explosion. (PR).
18/09	238 WAHOO	6	45-35N 146-50E	Sam		GD	S									
18/13	179 PLUNGER	8	43-30N 140-30E	AK	4500	TO/2DUP	O	I	18	C-AK	Okuni M.	5633	L	43-24N 140-28E	PR says no explosion seen, ship speeded up & left. [Dud hit?]
19/14	230 FINBACK	6	03-01S 125-50E	AK	1500	GD	D									
19/14	230 FINBACK	6	03-01S 125-50E	PC	800	GD	D	A J	14 19	SC	Cha 109	75 200	S	Balikpapan	PR says small steamer & 2 escorts, 1 burned & sank; I says heavily damaged by a/c 19 Aug; W says sunk by a/c 14 Aug; no likely sub attack then; Cha 109 was ex-Dutch Kawi. [J attribution ?]
19/14	230 FINBACK	6	03-01S 125-50E	Pat	800	GD	S									
--							-	AI	19	C-AK	Amoy M.	1350	S	38-52N 121-02E	No likely sub attack.
19	U 209 GRAYLING	8L	Balikpapan	AK	6000	T	D								Attack not in SORG; info from U.
20/17	206 GAR	9	00-58N 119-01E	AK	4000	T1/3DUP	S	AIJW	20	XAP	Seizan M.	955	S	01-00N 119-00E	
20/17	238 WAHOO	6	45-50N 148-22E	Sam	100	GD	S	I	20	C	Inari M. #1	33	S	45-30N 146-30E	
20/19	179 PLUNGER	8	42-15N 139-58E	AK	4500	T2/6DUP	S	AIJ	20	C-AK	Seitai M.	3404	S	41-43N 139-55E	
20/19	238 WAHOO	6	45-47N 148-42E	Sam		GD	S									
20	HNMS O-24	8	S of Penang	MV	3000	T1/4	S	AIJW	20	XPG	Chosa M.	2538	S	05-09N 100-10E	
20	U 209 GRAYLING	8L	Sibutu Passage	AO	250	G	S								Attack not in SORG; U says sub reported taking prisoner.
21/20	175 TARPON	8	33-45N 139-45E	AK	6300	T1/3NUP	D									

Dt/Hr	Submarine	Pt	Position	Tgt	Size	Attack	Cl	So	Date	Type	Name	Tons	Dm	Location	Comments
AUG	1943														
21/20	175 TARPON	8	33-45N 139-45E	AK	6500	T2/3NUP	D								
22/13	193 SWORDFISH	8	02-40N 137-10E	AP	8600	T1/2DUP	D	AIJ	22	A-AK	Nishiyama M.	3016	S	02-53N 136-21E	
22/13	193 SWORDFISH	8	02-40N 137-10E	AP	8400	T2/2DUP	D								
22/14	179 PLUNGER	8	42-40N 139-48E	AK	4500	T1/1DUP	S	A IJ	22	Fish	Ryokai M.	4643 4655	S	42-39N 139-47E	Fishery mother ship.
22/18	284 TULLIBEE	1	10-09N 147-25E	AK	5000	T1/3DUP	D								
22/18	284 TULLIBEE	1	10-09N 147-25E	AK	7000	T2/3DUP	S	AIJW	22	XAP	Kaisho M.	4164	S	10-13N 147-20E	
22/23	173 PIKE	8	21-52N 137-50E	AK	2000	T1/2NSR	D	I	22	A-AK	Toun M.	1915	L	21-50N 137-52E	
23/12	263 PADDLE	1	34-37N 137-53E	AK	5500	T2/6DUP	S	AIJ	23	C-APK	Ataka M.	5248	S	34-36N 138-50E	
23/18	173 PIKE	8	24-28N 137-36E	AK	4000	T1/2DUP	D								
23/22	281 SUNFISH	4	19-55N 117-20E	AP	7400	T2/3NSR	D								
24/02	239 WHALE	5	31-15N 129-00E	AO	10000	T1/2NUP	D								
24/02	239 WHALE	5	31-15N 129-00E	AK	7000	T1/2NUP	D								
25/06	282 TUNNY	4	10-01N 133-32E	AK	5400	T1/7DUP	D								
25/06	282 TUNNY	4	10-01N 133-32E	AK	5400	T1/1DUP	D								
25/09	202 TROUT	10	00-32N 125-18E	Sam		GD	S								
26/11	282 TUNNY	4	07-30N 134-20E	AK	8900	T2/3DUP	D								
27	209 GRAYLING	8L	13-35N 120-45E	APK	5500	Unk	S	AIJ	27	A-AK	Meizan M.	5480	PS	13-36N 129-23E	GRAYLING lost between 9-12 Sep, Lingayan Gulf area.
27/03	180 POLLACK	8	32-27N 132-24E	AK	6000	T1/4NSV	D	AIJ	27	A-AK	Taifuku M.	3520	S	32-28N 132-23E	
27/15	185 SNAPPER	7	13-31N 144-37E	APK	8600	T2/3DUP	S	AIW	27	XAP	Tokai M.	8359	S	Guam	J credits SNAPPER & 229 FLYING FISH (26 Jan); also see 178 PERMIT 5 May.
28/01	228 DRUM	7	01-30S 148-35E	AK	5000	T2/4NSR	S	I	27	XAP	Yamagiri M.	6438	M	01-31S 148-41E	
28/01	228 DRUM	7	01-30S 148-35E	AK	5000	T1/2NSR	S								
28/04	175 TARPON	8	33-42N 139-44E	AK	5500	T1/4TUP	D	I	28	XAF	Shinsei M.	4746	M	33-39N 139-28E	I gives tons as 4758.

55

Dt/Hr	Submarine	Pt	Position	Tgt	Size	Attack	Cl	So	Date	Type	Name	Tons	Dm	Location	Comments
AUG	1943														
29	HMS TRIDENT	1	Pulo Weh	CL	5800	T1/8	U								
30/15	232 HALIBUT	6	41-53N 141-10E	AK	3800	T1/3DUP	S	AIJ	30	C-AK	Taibun M.	6581	S	41-50N 141-13E	
31/09	197 SEAWOLF	10	28-27N 123-03E	AK	8500	T2/4DUP	S	AIJ	31	A-AK	Shoto M.	5253	S	28-30N 123-06E	
31/09	197 SEAWOLF	10	28-27N 123-03E	AK	7500	T1/4DUP	D	AIJ	31	C-AK	Kokko M.	5486	S	28-30N 123-06E	
31	197 SEAWOLF	10	28-27N 123-03E	Same	Same	Same	0	AI	31	TB	Sagi	840	M	28-30N 123-06E	PR says TB last seen heading toward port.
SEP	1943														
1	N 181 POMPANO	7L	Unk	Unk	Unk	Unk	U	I	1	C	Nankai M.	451	S	Off Miyako	Attack not in SORG or U. [Attribution ?]
2/01	197 SEAWOLF	10	31-28N 127-24E	AK	6700	T1/8+GN	S	AIJ	1	A-AK	Fusei M.	2256	S	31-16N 127-14E	
2/15	185 SNAPPER	7	08-40N 151-31E	DD	1800	T3/3DUP	S	AIW J	2	PF	Mutsure	870 860	S	N of Truk I.	
3/20	180 POLLACK	8	34-10N 140-12E	AK	5000	T2/4NUP	D	AIJW	3	XAP	Tagonoura M.	3521	S	33-43N 140-00E	
3	J 181 POMPANO	7L	Unk	Unk	Unk	Unk	U	AI J	3	C-AK	Akama M.	5600	S PS	41-00N 144-34E	Attack not in SORG or U.
4/00	281 SUNFISH	4	22-22N 120-04E	AP	10000	T2/4NSR	S	AJ I	4	A-AK	Kozan M.	4180	S H	22-06N 119-50E	
4/03	264 PARGO	1	30-06N 128-02E	AO	10000	T2/4NSR	S	I	4	XAO	Ryuei M.	5144	M	30-13N 128-16E	W lists ship as both XAO & Std AO 1TM.
4/04	218 ALBACORE	6	05-32N 156-23E	AK	4200	T3/4NSR	S	AIJW	4	XPG	Heijo M.	2627	S	05-26N 156-37E	W lists ship as both XPG & Std AK 1C.
4/23	175 TARPON	8	35-56N 157-59E	PC	1000	T1/2NUP	S	W IW	4	XPkt	Yurin M. Yulin M.	97	S	35-40N 159-02E	W says Yulin was Chinese name.
5/08	197 SEAWOLF	10	29-48N 140-20E	Sam	100	GD	S								
5/08	197 SEAWOLF	10	29-48N 140-20E	Sam		GD	S								
5/09	218 ALBACORE	6	03-50N 160-20E	AK	5000	T1/3DUP	D	I	5	XAP	Hokusho M.	4211	L	03-48N 160-38E	PR says 1 dud hit seen.
5/03	193 SWORDFISH	8	01-10N 142-10E	AK	7000	T4/4DUP	S	IJ A	5	A-AP	Tenkai M.	3203	S	01-35N 141-45E 01-35S 141-45E	[South latitude misprint?]
6/06	232 HALIBUT	6	42-13N 142-16E	AK	5900	T2/4DUP	S	AIJ	6	C-AK	Shogen M.	3362	S	42-13N 142-00E	
6/10	304 SEAHORSE	1	07-31N 134-21E	AP	7500	T3/4DUP	D								

Dt/Hr	Submarine	Pt	Position	Tgt	Size	Attack	Cl	So	Date	Type	Name	Tons	Dm	Location	Comments
SEP	1943														
6/21	232 HALIBUT	6	41-40N 142-24E	DD	1000	T1/4NUP	D	AI	6	CA	Nachi	13380	L	40-07N 142-20E	PR says 1 dud hit.
7/01	264 PARGO	1	31-25N 129-07E	APK	9800	T2/2NSR	D								
7/01	264 PARGO	1	31-25N 129-07E	AK	5900	T2/2NSR	S								
7/01	264 PARGO	1	31-25N 129-07E	AK	5900	T1/1NSR	S								
7/01	264 PARGO	1	31-25N 129-07E	AK	5800	T1/1NSR	S								
7/21	197 SEAWOLF	10	30-28N 155-30E	Sam	100	GM		D							
7/24	232 HALIBUT	6	40-51N 145-38E	Sam	200	GN		D							
8/14	228 DRUM	7	02-44S 141-36E	AK	2900	T1/3DUP	S	AIJ	8	A-AK	Hakutetsu M 13	1334	S	02-30S 141-44E	
8/17	286 BILLFISH	1	11-04N 110-27E	AK	5900	T1/4DUP	D								
9/05	257 HARDER	2	35-30N 140-40E	AK	4000	T0/3NSR	O	IJA	9	C-AK	Koyo M.	3010	PS	35-23N 140-38E	PR says torps apparently missed ahead.
9/14	202 TROUT	10	10-33N 125-32E	SS	1600	T2/3DUP	S	J	9	SS	I-182	1630	S	Sub position	I-182 believed sunk earlier; no sub lost here. [J attribution ?]
9/23	178 PERMIT	10	08-55N 168-12E	AK	6800	T1/3NUP	D								
9	N 181 POMPANO	7L	Unk	Unk	Unk	Unk	U	I	9	A-AK	Nanking M.	3005	M	40-12N 141-55E	Attack not in SORG or U. [Attribution ?]
10/17	214 GROUPER	7	05-05N 149-55E	APK	6400	T1/4DUP	D								
11/01	257 HARDER	2	33-50N 139-53E	AK	4000	T1/3NUR	S	AIJW	11-2	XAP	Yoko M.	1050	S	Mikura I.	
11/02	190 SPEARFISH	8	30-56N 132-47E	AK	5500	T1/2NUP	D	I	11	A-AP	Tsuyama M.	6962	H	30-56N 132-47E	
11/02	190 SPEARFISH	8	30-56N 132-47E	AK	5500	T2/2NUP	S								
11/08	167 NARWHAL	6	00-28S 166-52E	AK	4500	T1/2DUP	S	AIJW	11-2	XAP	Hokusho M.	4211	S	NW of Nauru I.	
12/04	178 PERMIT	10	08-33N 164-40E	AK	8600	T3/3NSP	S	I	12	XAPV	Fujikawa M.	6938	M	08-23N 165-12E	I gives tons as 9524.
12/07	178 PERMIT	10	08-33N 164-40E	AK	8600	T2/2DUP	S								
--							-	I	12	PC	Ch 13	460	L	?	Ch 13 sunk 3 Apr (see 177 PICKEREL). [This listing in I appears incorrect.]
13/01	279 SNOOK	3	30-06N 123-03E	AP	9000	T1/6NUR	S	AIJ	13	A-AP	Yamato M.	9655	S	30-18N 123-35E	

Dt/Hr	Submarine	Pt	Position	Tgt	Size	Attack	Cl	So	Date	Type	Name	Tons	Dm	Location	Comments
SEP	1943														
13/03 178 PERMIT		10	08-33N 164-40E	CL	5600	T2/2NUP	D								
13/07 178 PERMIT		10	08-33N 164-40E	AO	10500	T6/6DUP	S	AI	12	AO	Shiretoko	14050	M	08-23N 165-12E	
16/00 231 HADDOCK		6	09-32N 150-38E	AK	4000	T1/6NUP	D	I	15	XAC	Sansei M.	641	L	09-42N 150-36E	
16 236 SILVERSIDES		5	02-36S 150-34E	--	--	Mine	U	IW J	16	XPG	Seikai M.	2693 2663	SM	02-30S 150-48E	Minefield laid 4 Jun. J credits Australian mine; I gives location Kavieng harbor. [Attribution ?]
17/03 268 PUFFER		1	04-14S 127-09E	AK	5300	T2/2NUP	S								
17/03 268 PUFFER		1	04-14S 127-09E	AP	7500	T1/1NUP	D								
17/06 211 GUDGEON		9	13-51N 145-02E	PC	600	GD	D								
18/00 237 TRIGGER		6	27-31N 126-57E	AK	8500	T1/8NUS	S	J A	18 14	C-AK	Yowa M.	6435	PS S	Sub position Off Formosa?	PR says 2 dud hits 17 Sep, target sunk by 2nd attack; no likely sub attack 14 Sep. [J attribution ?]
18/05 190 SPEARFISH		8	29-07N 134-30E	AK	7100	T2/4NUP	S								
18/05 190 SPEARFISH		8	29-07N 134-30E	AK	5500	T2/3NUP	D								
18/05 190 SPEARFISH		8	29-07N 134-30E	AK	5500	T1/1NUP	D								
18/07 222 BLUEFISH		1	05-38S 120-48E	AK	500	GD	S								
18/17 153 S-42		5	50-22N 155-43E	AK	6000	T0/3DUP	0	I	18	XPG	Chowa M.	2719	L	50-25N 155-35E	
18/17 281 SUNFISH		4	25-02N 145-12E	AK	5700	T1/3DUP	D								
18/19 277 SCAMP		4	00-36N 146-27E	DE	500	T1/1TUP	D								
19/01 277 SCAMP		4	00-25N 146-21E	APK	8600	T1/1NUP	S	AIJ	18	A-AK	Kansai M.	8614	S	01-05N 146-27E	
19/17 257 HARDER		2	33-30N 135-40E	AO	7300	T1/3DUP	S	AJ I	19	C-AK	Kachisan M. Kachiyama M.	814	S	33-25N 135-38E	
20/16 133 S-28		7	49-05N 151-45E	AK	4000	T2/4DUP	S	AJ IW	19-0 12	XPG	Katsura M. #2	1368	S	48-07N 149-20E	No likely sub attack 12 Sep. [Date misprint?]
20/17 214 GROUPER		7	00-02N 150-29E	APK	6000	T1/4DUP	D								
20/23 231 HADDOCK		6	07-34N 150-12E	AO	19400	T3/6NSR	S	AI	20	AO	Notoro	14050	M	07-23N 150-11E	

Dt/Hr	Submarine	Pt	Position	Tgt	Size	Attack	Cl	So	Date	Type	Name	Tons	Dm	Location	Comments
SEP	1943														
21/19	231 HADDOCK	6	08-53N 148-30E	AP	10400	T3/8NSR	S								
21/20	231 HADDOCK	6	08-53N 148-30E	AP	9400	T4/4NSR	S	I	21	XAC	Shinyubari M.	5354	M	08-46N 148-43E	
21/20	277 SCAMP	4	01-05N 142-38E	AK	6000	T2/3TSP	S								
21/21	237 TRIGGER	6	26-27N 122-40E	AO	10000	T2/3NSS	S	AIW J	21	AO	Shiriya	14050 6500	S	NE of Keelung	
21/21	237 TRIGGER	6	26-27N 122-40E	AO	7500	T1/2NSV	S	AIJW	21	XAO	Shoyo M.	7498	S	26-33N 123-10E	
21/21	237 TRIGGER	6	26-27N 122-40E	AO	7300	T1/1NSS	S								
21/21	237 TRIGGER	6	26-27N 122-40E	AK	6700	T1/1NSV	S	AIJ	21	C-AK	Argun M.	6661	S	26-33N 123-10E	
--							-	I	21	DD	Oite	1270	L	18-46N 148-43E	No sub attack near location given.
21 N	238 WAHOO	7L	Unk	Unk	Unk	Unk	U	AJ I	21-2	Fish	Hokusei M.	1394	SU M	45-45N 145-46E	Attack not in SORG or U. [Attribution ?]
22/00	237 TRIGGER	6	26-27N 122-40E	AK	7000	T2/6NSS	D	I	21	A-AK	Gyoku M.	6854	M	26-33N 123-10E	
22/06	257 HARDER	2	34-15N 137-00E	AK	7000	T1/3TUP	S	AI J	23	C-AO	Daishin M.	5957 5878	S	34-20N 137-05E	
22/06	257 HARDER	2	34-15N 137-00E	AK	7000	T1/3TUP	S	AIJ	23	C-AK	Kowa M.	4520	S	34-20N 137-05E	
22/09	279 SNOOK	3	39-11N 123-20E	AK	3400	T1/4DUP	S	AIJ I	22 23	C-AK	Katsurahama M. Yokahama M.	715	S	39-05N 123-25E	I lists 2 ships, same tons; A says they are same ship. PR says ship sank, survivors in water.
22/15	258 HOE	2	10-07N 146-57E	AO	10000	T2/6DUP	D								
22/18	279 SNOOK	3	39-15N 123-30E	AK	4000	T0/4DUP	0	I	22	C-AK	Hakutetsu M 30	762	L	39-18N 123-00E	PR says 1 dud hit.
23/09	202 TROUT	10	21-17N 142-00E	AK	5400	T2/3DUP	S	AIJ	23	C-AK	Yamashiro M.	3427	S	20-45N 142-10E	
23/09	202 TROUT	10	21-17N 142-00E	AP	8000	T2/3DUP	S	AIJ W	23 22	XAP	Ryotoku M. Ryotaku M.	3483	S	20-45N 142-10E	
23/20	203 TUNA	8	04-39N 105-02E	APK	4000	T1/4NSV	D								
24/08	288 CABRILLA	1	27-55N 146-05E	CVE	17200	T2/6DUP	D	AI	24	CVE	Taiyo	17830	H	NE Chichi Jima	
25/06	222 BLUEFISH	1	06-18S 119-01E	AP	8200	T3/10DUP	S								

Dt/Hr	Submarine	Pt	Position	Tgt	Size	Attack	Cl	So	Date	Type	Name	Tons	Dm	Location	Comments
SEP	1943														
25/13	287 BOWFIN	1	09-44N 111-56E	AK	8600	T3/4DUP	S								
25/13	287 BOWFIN	1	09-44N 111-56E	AP	6000	T2/2DUP	S	AW IJ	25	XAO B-AP	Kirishima M.	5959 8120	S	09-53N 112-10E	W says ship converted from AK to AO.
25/13	287 BOWFIN	1	09-44N 111-56E	AO	9200	T2/4DUP	S								
25/19	223 BONEFISH	1	11-05N 112-24E	AO	9200	T3/4NUP	S								
25/20	286 BILLFISH	1	10-49N 113-18E	AK	6000	T1/5NSR	D								
25 J	181 POMPANO	7L	Unk	Unk	Unk	Unk	U	AI J	25	B-AG	Taiko M.	2958	S PS	41-30N 139-00E	Attack not in SORG or U. W lists as XPG, 2984T; see 381 SAND LANCE 14 Jul 44.
25 N	238 WAHOO	7L	Unk	Unk	Unk	Unk	U	AI	25	B-AG	Taiko M.	2958	S	41-30N 139-00E	O'Kane claims WAHOO sinking; attack not in SORG or U; J credits 181 POMPANO.
26/23	222 BLUEFISH	1	05-50S 121-57E	DE	600	T2/3NSR	S	AIW J	26-7	TB	Kasasagi	840 595	S	05-00S 121-57E	PR says target disintegrated. A says some records give location 05-45S 150-50E, probably incorrect. W misspells sub name Bluefin.
26/23	222 BLUEFISH	1	05-50S 121-57E	AK	6900	T1/5NSR	D								
27/02	262 MUSKALLUNGE	1	08-22N 133-55E	APK	8600	T2/5NSR	D								
27/06	223 BONEFISH	1	10-13N 109-45E	AP	9900	T2/2DUP	S	AIJ	27	A-AP	Kashima M.	9908	S	10-10N 109-40E	
27/06	223 BONEFISH	1	10-13N 109-45E	AK	5900	T2/2DUP	D								
--							-	A I	27	C-AK	Taisei M.	1957	SA S	Off Wewak Off Wake I.	Chart in I shows location off Wewak; [Wake I probably misprint]. No likely sub attack.
28/15	211 GUDGEON	9	15-22N 145-38E	AK	7000	T2/4DUP	S	AJ I	28	C-AK	Taian M.	3158	S	15-17N 145-39E 15-10N 143-39E	[Location in I may be misprint.]
28/23	222 BLUEFISH	1	06-11S 126-00E	AK	6900	T2/2NSR	S	A IJ	27 28-9	C-AK	Akashi M.	3228	S	06-05S 125-55E	
29/10	211 GUDGEON	9	15-38N 145-52E	AK	8600	T1/2DUP	D	AI W	29	XPG	Santo M.	3266	M S	15-28N 145-58E	A says ship was repaired & rerated AP, believed renamed Sansei M; see 276 SAWFISH 8 Dec.
29/10	211 GUDGEON	9	15-38N 145-52E	AK	8000	T1/2DUP	S								

Dt/Hr	Submarine	Pt	Position	Tgt	Size	Attack	Cl	So	Date	Type	Name	Tons	Dm	Location	Comments
SEP	1943														
29/11	279 SNOOK	3	30-25N 145-50E	Smc	300	GD	D								
29 J	238 WAHOO	7L	Unk	Unk	Unk	Unk	U	AI J	Note 29	C-AK	Masaki M. #2	1238	S PS	Sea of Japan 40-00N 130-00E	Attack not in SORG or U; A & I give date 1 Oct; I lists as Misaki M, 1229T, location unk.
30/07	266 POGY	3	06-01N 139-08E	AK	6600	T2/4TUP	S	AIJ	30	A-AP	Maebashi M.	7005	S	01-00N 139-28E	
30/08	287 BOWFIN	1	08-17N 121-57E	LC	100	GD	S								
30/18	257 HARDER	2	34-10N 14 - E	Pat	200	GD	D								
OCT	1943														
1/14	234 KINGFISH	5	07-00S 117-10E	Sam	100	GD	S								
1/19	265 PETO	3	04-01N 143-47E	AK	5000	T1/2TUP	S	AIJ	1	A-AK	Kinkasan M.	4980	S	04-00N 143-50E	
1/19	265 PETO	3	04-01N 143-47E	AK	5500	T2/4TUP	S	AIJW	1	XAP	Tonei M.	4930	S	04-00N 143-50E	
2/15	287 BOWFIN	1	00-55S 118-13E	Sam		GD	S								
2/21	262 MUSKALLUNGE	1	11-26N 134-10E	AK	4900	T2/3NSV	D								
2	236 SILVERSIDES	5	02-36S 150-34E	--	--	Mine	U	I	2	AM	W 28	648	LM	Kavieng Bay	Minefield laid 4 Jun. [Attribution ?]
4/05	283 TINOSA	3	08-02N 150-19E	AO	9500	T2/4TUP	D								
5	238 WAHOO	7L	34- N 129- E	AK	7100	Unk	S	AIJ	5	A-AP	Konron M.	7903	S	34-20N 130-18E	
6/03	280 STEELHEAD	3	10-26N 146-30E	AO	10500	T2/4NSR	D	AI J	6	AO	Kazahaya	18300 8000	JS	10-50N 148-30E	J credits STEELHEAD & 283 TINOSA. PR says hit & slowed but not sunk.
6/07	223 BONEFISH	1	12-21N 109-24E	AK	3900	T1/3DUP	S								
6/07	223 BONEFISH	1	12-21N 109-24E	AK	4000	T1/3DUP	S								
6/19	283 TINOSA	3	10-01N 148-31E	AO	10500	T8/16NUP	S	AI J	6	AO	Kazahaya	18300 8000	JS	10-50N 148-30E	J credits TINOSA & 280 STEELHEAD. PR says ship steaming at 6 knots when sunk by this attack.
6 J	238 WAHOO	7L	Unk	Unk	Unk	Unk	U	AIJ	6	A-AK	Kanko M.	1283	PS	37-18N 129-33E	Attack not in SORG or U.
8/01	254 GURNARD	3	18-24N 119-09E	AP	10800	T2/4NSR	S	AIJ	8	A-AK	Taian M.	5655	S	18-48N 119-21E	
8/01	254 GURNARD	3	18-24N 119-09E	AK	7200	T3/4NSR	S	AIJ	8	A-AP	Dainichi M.	5813	S	18-48N 119-21E	

Dt/Hr	Submarine	Pt	Position	Tgt	Size	Attack	Cl	So	Date	Type	Name	Tons	Dm	Location	Comments
OCT	1943														
8/03	217 GUARDFISH	6	00-35S 146-07E	AK	8200	T2/6NSR	S	AIJ	8	A-AK	Kashu M.	5460	S	00-26S 146-17E	
9/05	269 RASHER	1	03-36S 127-44E	AK	3100	T2/3TUP	S	AIJ	9	A-AK	Kogane M.	3131	S	03-30S 127-45E	
9/06	234 KINGFISH	5	05-10N 119-11E	AO	14000	T2/4DUP	S	AI W	9	AO	Hayatomo Hayamoto	14050	M H	05-09N 119-18E	W says towed to Singapore as hulk.
9/11	268 PUFFER	1	01-08N 119-31E	AK	7500	T2/6DUP	D	I	9	XAO	Kumagawa M.	7508	M	01-07N 119-30E	W says AK converted to AO 1943.
9 J	238 WAHOO	7L	37-18N 129-33E	Unk	Unk	Unk	U	A IJ	9	C-AK	Hankow M. Kanko M.	2995	S PS	Off Oga Pen.	Attack not in SORG or U.
10/01	217 GUARDFISH	6	01-06N 145-55E	AK	4800	T1/7NUP	S								
10/04	254 GURNARD	3	18-34N 118-48E	AO	9000	T3/10NUP	D								
10/14	223 BONEFISH	1	14-44N 110-19E	AP	9200	T2/2DUP	S	AIJ	10	A-AP	Teibi M.	10086	S	14-49N 110-16E	
10/14	223 BONEFISH	1	14-44N 110-19E	AK	4000	T2/2DUP	S	AIJ	10	C-AK	Isuzugawa M.	4214	S	14-49N 110-16E	
10/17	208 GRAYBACK	8	28-36N 138-35E	AK	6200	T1/4DUP	D								
--							-	AI J	10	A-AK	Hino M. #5	2935 2725	SA	Buka 05-35S 154-25E	W lists ship as XPG & credits 234 KINGFISH at 23-59N 138-42E; not near KINGFISH's area. No likely sub attack.
12/05	225 CERO	1	29-00N 137-23E	AK	6000	T2/3TUP	S								
12/12	225 CERO	1	28-50N 137-20E	AK	8000	T4/6DUP	D	I	12	AF	Mamiya	15820	HU	Chichi Jima	PR says identified as Mamiya after attack.
13/06	194 SEADRAGON	8	08-45N 167-08E	APK	8200	T2/4DUP	S								
13/15	269 RASHER	1	03-47S 127-41E	AK	3100	T2/3DUP	S	AI J	13	A-AK	Kenkoku M.	3377 3127	S	03-49S 127-40E	
13/15	269 RASHER	1	03-47S 127-41E	AK	4000	T2/3DUP	D								
14/06	157 S-46	4	50-30N 154-46E	AO	7000	T1/4NUP	D								
14/17	208 GRAYBACK	8	27-35N 127-27E	AK	7100	T1/4DUP	S	AIJW	14	XAO	Kozui M.	7072	S	27-35N 127-30E	
14/18	223 BONEFISH	1	00-10N 119-15E	Sch		GD	S								
15/01	284 TULLIBEE	2	24-35N 120-31E	AP	8000	T1/3NUP	D								

Dt/Hr	Submarine	Pt	Position	Tgt	Size	Attack	Cl	So	Date	Type	Name	Tons	Dm	Location	Comments
OCT	1943														
15/01	284 TULLIBEE	2	24-35N 120-31E	AP	6000	T2/3NUP	S	AIJ	15	A-AP	Chicago M.	5866	S	24-30N 120-26E	
15/14	182 SALMON	8	46-45N 145-45E	AK	6000	T1/7DUP	D								
16/18	261 MINGO	2	11-03N 151-23E	CV	17200	T2/6DUP	D								
17/02	175 TARPON	9	33-42N 140-08E	Unk	10000	T4/8NUP	S	Note I	17 ?	XCL	Michel Michael M.	4740 ?	S	Sea S of Izu	German commerce raider, identified in Holmes; tons per Rohwer.
18	236 SILVERSIDES	7	01-00N 143-16E	AK	7000	T2/6NUP	S	AIJ	18	A-AK	Tairin M.	1915	S	00-22N 143-23E	
18/04	229 FLYING FISH	7	19-31N 145-20E	CVE	17200	T1/6NUP	D								
18/10	260 LAPON	2	34-00N 136-24E	AK	2900	T1/3DUP	S	AIJ	18	C-AK	Taichu M.	1906	S	33-59N 136-21E	
18/10	260 LAPON	2	34-00N 136-24E	Same	Same	Same	0	AI	18	XAM	Keijin M. #2	433	?	Kumano Nada	PR says convoy of 2 AKs & 3 escorts, not aware of hitting this ship; made 2 dud hits on ship near this posit 13 Oct.
19/03	212 GATO	6	02-45N 151-30E	AK	7000	T1/3NUP	D								
19/03	212 GATO	6	02-45N 151-30E	AK	8500	T1/3NUP	D								
20/15	234 KINGFISH	5	12-36N 109-30E	AK	5000	T2/4DUP	S	AJ I	20	C-AK	Sana M.	3365	S L	12-30N 109-30E	
21/02	280 STEELHEAD	3	08-26N 141-50E	AK	8500	T2/3NUP	D	I	20	XAPV	Goshu M.	8592	H	SE of Ulithi	
--							-	I	21	Fish	Hokusei M.	1394	SU	45-45N 145-46E	I lists ship twice; see 238 WAHOO 21 Sep. [This I listing appears to be duplicate.]
22/02	235 SHAD	6	28-40N 124-07E	CA	7000	T2/3NUP	D								
22/02	235 SHAD	6	28-40N 124-07E	CA	7000	T1/2NUP	D								
22/04	208 GRAYBACK	8	26-48N 124-56E	XCL	7400	T4/6NUR	S	AIJW	22	XAP	Awata M.	7398	S	26-30N 125-05E	
23/00	285 BALAO	2	00-34N 147-40E	AK	5000	T2/6NSR	S								
23/01	285 BALAO	2	00-34N 147-40E	AK	4000	T4/4NSR	D								
23/12	260 LAPON	2	34-34N 137-46E	AK	4600	T1/1DUP	D								
24/01	236 SILVERSIDES	7	02-05N 144-39E	AK	7000	T3/3NSR	S	AIJW	23-4	XAO	Tennan M.	5407	S	02-00N 144-46E	W lists ship as both XAO & Std AO 1TM.
24/01	236 SILVERSIDES	7	02-05N 144-39E	AK	6200	T1/1NSR	S	AIJ	23-4	A-AK	Johore M.	6187	S	02-00N 144-46E	

Dt/Hr	Submarine	Pt	Position	Tgt	Size	Attack	Cl	So	Date	Type	Name	Tons	Dm	Location	Comments
OCT	1943														
24/19	236 SILVERSIDES	7	02-05N 144-39E	AK	1900	T2/3DSV	S	AIJ	23-4	A-AK	Kazan M.	1893	S	02-00N 144-46E	PR says sinking completed by gunfire.
25/23	284 TULLIBEE	2	26-01N 121-03E	AO	9000	T1/10NUS	S								
26/01	236 SILVERSIDES	7	02-45N 140-41E	AK	5000	T1/2NSR	D								
27/00	235 SHAD	6	28-25N 128-04E	AP	9100	T1/1NSR	S								
27/00	235 SHAD	6	28-25N 128-04E	AP	8500	T2/4NUS	P	AJ I	26-7	C-APK	Fuji M.	9130	JS M	28-20N 128-05E	J credits SHAD & 208 GRAYBACK. PR says fired at convoy of 3 APs & 1 AK, heard 2 explosions. GRAYBACK PR says SHAD hit 3 APs, AK collided with 1 in melee.
27/00	235 SHAD	6	28-25N 128-04E	AP	7400	T1/2NSR	D								
27/00	235 SHAD	6	28-25N 128-04E	AK	3500	0	D								Damaged by collision as above.
27/06	208 GRAYBACK	8	28-26N 128-04E	AP	8500	T1/2DUP	P	AJ I	26-7	C-AK	Fuji M.	9130	JS M	28-20N 128-05E	J credits GRAYBACK & 235 SHAD. PR says saw 2 APs, 1 smoking, AK down by bow, torpedoed smoking AP.
27/10	229 FLYING FISH	7	10-59N 134-35E	AK	7000	T2/6DUP	S								
27/22	229 FLYING FISH	7	12-34N 134-48E	AK	8000	T1/8NUR	D	AIJ W	27	XAP	Nanman M. Namman M.	6550	S	12-02N 134-28E	
28/02	182 SALMON	8	45-50N 145-40E	AK	5000	T1/4NUP	D	I	29	XPG	Nagata M.	2969	L	45-30N 146-00E	
28/02	229 FLYING FISH	7	12-54N 134-06E	AK	7000	T1/4NUR	D	AI	31	B-AO	Koryo M.	589	S	12-02N 137-28E	J credits 269 RASHER, 31 Oct. Ship not in W. [Attribution ?]
29/02	197 SEAWOLF	11	22-30N 115-25E	CM	4000	T2/4NSR	S	AJ I	29	C-AK	Wuhu M. Wufu M.	3222	S	22-45N 116-10E	
29/14	304 SEAHORSE	2	31-24N 138-24E	Sam	200	GD	S								
30/17	304 SEAHORSE	2	30-48N 135-36E	Sam	200	GD	S								
31/17	304 SEAHORSE	2	31-19N 134-13E	Sam	200	GT	S								
31/22	269 RASHER	1	01-25N 120-46E	AO	7500	T2/3NSR	S	J	31	B-AO	Koryo M.	589	S	Sub position	A & I give different location; see 229 FLYING FISH 28 Oct. [J attribution ?]
NOV	1943														
1/22	237 TRIGGER	7	29-12N 134-37E	AK	7000	T1/2NSR	S								

Dt/Hr	Submarine	Pt	Position	Tgt	Size	Attack	Cl	So	Date	Type	Name	Tons	Dm	Location	Comments
NOV	1943														
1/22	237 TRIGGER	7	29-12N 134-37E	AK	7000	T1/1NSR	S								
1/24	231 HADDOCK	7	09-02N 150-43E	AP	7000	T3/5NSR	S								
1/24	231 HADDOCK	7	09-02N 150-43E	AK	4100	T1/1NSR	S								
2/01	304 SEAHORSE	2	28-37N 134-47E	AP	10400	T3/3NSR	S	AI	2	A-AK	Yawata M.	1852	S	28-20N 135-22E	A says timing of hits matches this attack; I gives longitude 147-22 [misprint]; J credits 237 TRIGGER. [Attribution ?]
2/02	237 TRIGGER	7	28-49N 134-50E	AK	7000	T3/6NSV	S	AJ I	2	A-AP	Delagoa M.	7148	PS	28-20N 135-20E 28-20N 147-22E	A says timing of hits matches this attack. [I longitude is misprint.]
2/03	237 TRIGGER	7	28-49N 134-50E	AO	8000	T3/3NSV	S	J	2	A-AK	Yawata M.	1852	PS	Sub position	A says timing of hits matches 304 SEAHORSE attack, above. [J attribution ?]
2/04	304 SEAHORSE	2	28-37N 134-45E	AO	10400	T2/3NSR	S	AI J	2	A-AK	Ume M.	5859	S PS	28-40N 135-25E	A says timing of hits matches this attack.
2/04	304 SEAHORSE	2	28-37N 134-45E	AK	3000	T2/3NSR	S	AIW J	2	XAP	Chihaya M.	7089	S PS	28-31N 134-50E	A says timing of hits matches this attack. I gives longitude 147-22 [misprint].
2/09	232 HALIBUT	7	28-18N 134-48E	AK	3500	T2/3DUP	S	AIJ	2	A-AK	Ehime M.	4653	S	28-20N 134-48E	PR says seen to sink. A says timing of hits matches this attack; I gives longitude 147-22E [misprint].
2/21	231 HADDOCK	7	09-18N 150-09E	DD	1500	T1/4NSR	S								
--							-	A J	3 13	C-AK	Tango M.	6893	H SU	Amami Oshima E China Sea	I says sunk by mine at Naze 19 Sep; A says ran aground off Naze that date, later torp by unk sub & abandoned. No likely sub attack either date.
4/11	199 TAUTOG	8	07-34N 134-09E	AK	3800	T1/3DUP	S	IW J	4	SC	Cha 30	270 100	SA S	06-10S 155-35E Sub position	I & W say Cha 30 attacked by a/c near Kieta. [J attribution ?]
4/11	199 TAUTOG	8	07-34N 134-09E	AK	3800	T1/3DUP	D								
4/20	277 SCAMP	5	00-28N 152-03E	AP	8000	T1/6NUP	D								
4/22	197 SEAWOLF	11	21-22N 113-20E	APK	10000	T3/4DUP	S	AIJ	4	C-AK	Kaifuku M.	3177	S	21-00N 113-05E	

Dt/Hr	Submarine	Pt	Position	Tgt	Size	Attack	Cl	So	Date	Type	Name	Tons	Dm	Location	Comments
NOV	1943														
4	236 SILVERSIDES	5	02-36S 150-34E	--	--	Mine	U	JW I	4	XAP	Ryuosan M.	2455	SM	02-40S 150-40E Edmago I.	Minefield laid 4 Jun; J credits Australian mine. [Attribution ?]
4	236 SILVERSIDES	5	02-36S 150-34E	--	--	Mine	U	I	4	CL	Isuzu	5170	LM	Edmago I.	Minefield laid 4 Jun. [Attribution ?]
4	236 SILVERSIDES	5	02-36S 150-34E	--	--	Mine	U	I	4	DD	Isokaze	2033	LM	Edmago I.	Minefield laid 4 Jun. [Attribution ?]
4	236 SILVERSIDES	5	02-36S 150-34E	--	--	Mine	U	I JW	4	AGS	Tsukushi	1400 2000	SM	Edmago I. 02-40S 150-40E	Minefield laid 4 Jun; J credits Australian mine. [Attribution ?]
5/01	225 CERO	1	32-28N 125-18E	AP	10000	T1/3NSV	D								
5/01	225 CERO	1	32-28N 125-18E	AK	15800	T2/3NSV	D								
5/06	232 HALIBUT	7	32-19N 132-58E	CV	15000	T3/8TUP	D	AI	5	CV	Junyo	24140	H	Bungo Channel	
5/13	199 TAUTOG	8	07-39N 134-22E	AK	4000	T1/3DUP	D								
5/13	199 TAUTOG	8	07-39N 134-22E	AK	4000	T1/3DUP	D								
6/02	231 HADDOCK	7	07-54N 150-06E	AO	10000	T1/1NSR	S								
6/02	231 HADDOCK	7	07-54N 150-06E	AO	10000	T3/3NSR	S	AI	6	XAO	Hoyo M.	8691	H	08-08N 149-45E	W says towed to Truk, sunk there later.
6/24	199 TAUTOG	8	13-05N 134-05E	AO	8000	T1/2NUP	D								
7/05	247 DACE	1	34-14N 137-15E	AK	6800	T1/2NSR	D								
8/04	222 BLUEFISH	2	16-44N 116-22E	AO	10000	T2/2NSP	S								
8/04	222 BLUEFISH	2	16-44N 116-22E	APK	6800	T1/1NSP	D								
8/04	222 BLUEFISH	2	16-44N 116-22E	AK	7600	T1/2NSP	D								
8/04	222 BLUEFISH	2	16-44N 116-22E	APK	6900	T2/2NSP	D								
8/04	222 BLUEFISH	2	16-44N 116-22E	APK	8400	T2/2NSP	D								
8/06	222 BLUEFISH	2	16-44N 116-22E	AO	12000	T5/9DSP	S	AIJ	8	A-AO	Kyokuei M.	10570	S	17-00N 116-17E	
8/16	269 RASHER	1	00-22N 119-44E	AO	7600	T2/3DUP	S	AIJ	8	C-AO	Tango M.	2046	S	00-25N 119-45E	
9/01	269 RASHER	1	00-39N 119-04E	AO	10000	T1/4NUP	D								

Dt/Hr	Submarine	Pt	Position	Tgt	Size	Attack	Cl	So	Date	Type	Name	Tons	Dm	Location	Comments
NOV	1943														
9/04	197 SEAWOLF	11	20-37N 118-10E	AK	5000	T1/2NSR	D								
9/11	287 BOWFIN	2	03-37S 118-20E	Sch	100	GD	S								
9/11	287 BOWFIN	2	03-37S 118-20E	Sch		GD	S								
9/11	287 BOWFIN	2	03-37S 118-20E	Sch		GD	S								
9/17	188 SARGO	9	21-38N 131-19E	AO	10000	T2/5DUP	S	AIJ	9	A-AK	Taga M.	2868	S	21-40N 131-12E	
9/22	287 BOWFIN	2	02-22S 118-16E	Sch	100	GN	S								
10/05	220 BARB	6	24-41N 122-11E	AK	8000	T2/2NSR	S								
10/05	220 BARB	6	24-41N 122-11E	AK	5600	T1/2NSR	D								
10/13	291 CREVALLE	1	12-52N 121-46E	AK	5600	T1/10DUP	D								
10/15	277 SCAMP	5	03-39N 150-37E	APK	6500	T1/7DUP	S	AIJW	10	XAP	Tokyo M.	6481	S	04-06N 150-17E	PR says ship was towed away. W says damaged by a/c & sank in tow.
10	HMS TALLY HO	1	06-12N 099-25E	MV	5000	T1/5	S	AIJW	10	XAW	Kisogawa M.	1914	S	06-12N 099-27E	
11/02	291 CREVALLE	1	12-00N 121-00E	AK	700	GN	S								
11/07	228 DRUM	8	00-20N 148-35E	AP	11900	T2/6DUP	D	AIW J	12 22	XAP	Kanayamasan M.	2869	SA	01-00N 149-20E	All sources say sunk by a/c, but location is close to sub posit. [Attribution ?]
11/12	188 SARGO	9	27-36N 130-32E	APK	5900	T2/4DUP	S	AIJW	11	XAP	Kosei M.	3551	S	27-40N 130-24E	
11/12	222 BLUEFISH	2	08-00N 118-36E	Sam		GD	S								
11/13	225 CERO	1	30-50N 150-07E	Sam	200	GD	D								
11/18	289 CAPELIN	1	03-27S 127-52E	AK	4000	T2/5NUP	S								
11/22	287 BOWFIN	2	04-58N 119-42E	AO	800	GM	S								
11/22	287 BOWFIN	2	04-58N 119-42E	AO	1200	GM	S								
11/23	289 CAPELIN	1	03-08S 127-38E	AK	3400	T3/6NUP	S	AIJ	11	A-AK	Kunitama M.	3127	S	NW of Ambon	
12/09	277 SCAMP	5	01-10N 149-02E	CA	8500	T1/6DUP	D								
12/16	257 HARDER	3	21-10N 144-50E	AK	4000	T2/3DUP	S								

Dt/Hr	Submarine	Pt	Position	Tgt	Size	Attack	Cl	So	Date	Type	Name	Tons	Dm	Location	Comments
12/19	257 HARDER	3	21-10N 144-50E	PC	800	GN	S	I	14	PC	Ch 20	460	M	?	PR says stern blown off, afire & sinking, photos. [Attribution ?; location not given.] See HMS TAURUS 14 Nov. (PR).
13/00	200 THRESHER	10	08-57N 152-36E	AK	5600	T3/3NUP	S	AIJW	12-3	XAP	Muko M.	4862	S	09-02N 152-46E	
13/06	237 TRIGGER	7	32-57N 125-06E	AP	10500	T2/4DUP	S	AIJ W	13	XAP	Nachisan M. Nachizan M.	4433	S	32-55N 125-09E	
13	HMS TAURUS	1	05-17N 100-05E	SS		T1/6	S	IW J	12-3	SS	I-34	2198 2212	S	05-26N 108-06E	
13/08	278 SCORPION	3	18-18N 142-48E	AO	8500	T1/4DUP	D	AI	13	AO	Shiretoko	14050	M	18-22N 142-50E	W says taken to Singapore as hulk.
14/11	308 APOGON	1	08-14N 154-05E	AK	5200	T1/3DUP	D									
14	HMS TAURUS	1	Sembilan Is.	PC	Unk	G	D	I	14	PC	Ch 20	460	M	?	[Attribution ?; location not given.] See 257 HARDER 12 Nov.
15/09	291 CREVALLE	1	14-54N 119-54E	AK	7100	T1/4DUP	S	AJ I	15 13		A-AK	Kyokko M.	6783	S	14-53N 119-56E	
16	281 SUNFISH	1	34-28N 137-20E	--	--	Mine	U	AI JW	16	CMc	Ukishima	720	S SU	SE Hatsushima Off Japan	Minefield laid 14-17 Dec 42; I says missing; W says lost, cause unk, at 34-55N 139-22E; A says torp by unk sub. No likely sub attack. [Attribution ?; mines 11 months old.]
17	226 CORVINA	1L	07-08N 151-53E	SS	1600	Unk	S									CORVINA believed sunk by Japanese sub 16 Nov, 05-50N 151-10E. [Basis for SORG listing is not clear.]
17/15	228 DRUM	8	01-48N 148-24E	AS	11900	T1/4DUP	S	AIJW	17	XAS	Hie M.	11621	S	01-45N 148-45E	
--								AI	17	A-AK	Yoshitomo M#22	392	S	07-40S 130-23E	No likely sub attack.
18/20	291 CREVALLE	1	15-08N 119-38E	CVE	18000	T4/6NSR	S									
18/23	222 BLUEFISH	2	04-52N 122-07E	DE	800	T3/3NSR	S	AIW J	18	DD	Sanae Sanaye	820	S	05-00N 122-00E	
18/23	222 BLUEFISH	2	04-52N 122-07E	AO	14100	T1/3NSR	D	AIW	18	AO	Ondo	14050	H	05-00N 122-00E	A says beached off Cavite until sunk by a/c 13 Nov 44; W says beached, no further disposition.

Dt/Hr	Submarine	Pt	Position	Tgt	Size	Attack	Cl	So	Date	Type	Name	Tons	Dm	Location	Comments
NOV	1943														
19/06	257 HARDER	3	22-27N 147-15E	APK	6600	T2/3DUP	S	A IJW	Note 19	XAP	Hokuko M. Hokko M.	5385	S	22-28N 147-22E	PR says 1 target sank, 1 taken under tow. A gives date 8 Dec; no likely sub attack then.
19/06	257 HARDER	3	22-27N 147-15E	APK	6900	T5/6DUP	S	AIJW	19	XAP	Udo M.	3936	S	22-28N 147-22E	See above note.
20/01	257 HARDER	3	22-47N 147-20E	APK	6500	T2/12NUP	S	AIJW	20	XAP	Nikko M.	5949	S	23-10N 147-22E	
21/03	203 TUNA	9	06-15S 113-14E	AK	4000	T1/4NSR	D								
21/23	237 TRIGGER	7	36-40N 125-31E	AK	5200	T2/4NSR	S	A J	23 21	C-AK	Eizan M.	1681	S PS	Yellow Sea	
22/03	304 SEAHORSE	2	33-36N 128-35E	AK	3800	T2/4NUP	S	AJ I	22	C-AK	Daishu M. Taishu M.	3322	S	33-41N 128-35E	
22/09	283 TINOSA	4	07-10N 134-34E	AK	4000	T3/3DUP	S	AIJ	22	A-AK	Kiso M.	4070	S	Off Palau	
22/09	283 TINOSA	4	07-10N 134-34E	AK	4100	T2/3DUP	S	AJ I	22	A-AK	Yamato M.	4379 4398	S	07-08N 134-33E	
--							-	AI	22-3	A-AK	Yoshitomo M#21	389	S	New Guinea	No likely sub attack.
23/00	221 BLACKFISH	6	02-28N 140-06E	AK	4500	T3/6NSV	D	AIW	22-3	XAP	Yamato M. #2	439	S	Wewak->Palau	[Attribution ?; location indefinite.]
23/04	211 GUDGEON	10	28-49N 122-12E	AK	1000	T1/2NSR	S								
23/04	211 GUDGEON	10	28-49N 122-12E	AO	10100	T2/2NSR	D								
23/04	211 GUDGEON	10	28-49N 122-12E	CL	1800	T1/1NSR	S	AIW J	23	PF	Wakamiya	870 860	S	S Shushan I.	
23/05	211 GUDGEON	10	28-49N 122-12E	AP	10900	T5/11NUR	S	AIJ	23	A-AP	Nekka M.	6783	S	28-43N 122-07E	
23	N 289 CAPELIN	2L	Unk	Unk	Unk	Unk	U	AI J	23	A-AK	Kizan M.	2841	S SA	01-50N 127-55E Near Kaoe Bay	Attack not in SORG; U says anti-sub attack made at 01-34N 123-07E may have sunk CAPELIN. [Attribution ?]
24/03	185 SNAPPER	8	33-26N 139-37E	AO	6500	T2/2NSR	S								
24/03	185 SNAPPER	8	33-26N 139-37E	AK	5000	T2/6NSR	D								
24/23	221 BLACKFISH	6	00-56N 144-52E	AK	4500	T2/6NSR	S								
25/05	308 APOGON	1	07-38N 152-39E	AK	3000	T1/3TSV	D								

NOV   1943

Dt/Hr	Submarine	Pt	Position	Tgt	Size	Attack	Cl	So	Date	Type	Name	Tons	Dm	Location	Comments
25/12	218 ALBACORE	7	00-51N 145-56E	AK	9000	T2/5DUP S		AIJ	25	A-AK	Kenzan M.	4704	S	00-46N 144-52E	
25/15	196 SEARAVEN	9	08-20N 158-01E	AO	10100	T2/4DUP S		AJW I	25	XAO	Toa M.	10050 10032	S	08-22N 158-00E	
26/01	291 CREVALLE	1	15-24N 119-44E	AK	4000	T2/4NSR S									
26/03	287 BOWFIN	2	12-48N 109-34E	APK	12000	T1/2NSV S									
26/03	287 BOWFIN	2	12-48N 109-34E	AO	17500	T3/6NSV S		AJ I	26	A-AO	Ogurasan M.	5069 5200	S	13-25N 109-30E	
26/05	271 RAY	1	02-27N 147-50E	AK	4500	T3/4NUR S									
26/10	283 TINOSA	4	06-56N 134-38E	AK	3800	T2/3DUP S		A I	26	A-AK	Taiyu M.	1873	H	06-22N 134-48E 06-22N 143-48E	[Location in I may be misprint.]
26/10	283 TINOSA	4	06-56N 134-38E	AK	7200	T2/3DUP D		A J	26	A-AK	Shini M.	3811	S	06-22N 134-48E	
26/10	287 BOWFIN	2	13-02N 109-38E	APK	5500	T4/4DUP S		AIJ	26	C-AK	Tainan M.	5407	S	13-25N 109-30E	
26/19	271 RAY	1	04-00N 147-50E	APK	9800	T4/6DUP S		AIJW	26	XAP	Nikkai M.	2562	S	04-12N 148-20E	
26/23	270 RATON	1	00-40N 148-14E	AK	6700	T3/5NSR S		AIJW	26	XAE	Onoe M.	6667	S	00-40N 148-20E	
26/23	270 RATON	1	00-40N 148-14E	Same	Same	Same	0	IW	26	XAP	Kamoi M.	2811	S	00-46N 148-20E	PR says smaller target "milled around" but did not sink.
26/23	304 SEAHORSE	2	33-36N 128-57E	AO	10000	T2/3NSR S		J	26	AK	Unknown M.	4000	S	Sub position	PR says broke in two, both parts sank. [J attribution ?]
27/00	304 SEAHORSE	2	33-38N 129-05E	AO	10500	T2/4NSR S		AIJW	27	XAO	San Ramon M.	7309	S	33-34N 128-35E	
27/16	287 BOWFIN	2	13-01N 109-30E	AK	1500	T2/3DUP S		J	27	AK	VanVollenhoven	691	S	Sub position	PR identifies as French coastal steamer.
28/03	287 BOWFIN	2	12-45N 109-42E	APK	12000	T4/4NUP S		AIJ	28	A-AK	Sydney M.	5425	S	12-50N 109-35E	
28/03	287 BOWFIN	2	12-45N 109-42E	APK	10000	T2/2NUP S		AI J	28	C-AO	Tonan M.	9839 9866	S	12-50N 109-35E	
28/03	287 BOWFIN	2	12-45N 109-42E	AK	9900	T2/2NUP S									
28/05	286 BILLFISH	2	12-33N 109-36E	AK	6000	T1/4NSV D									
28/12	270 RATON	1	01-40N 141-45E	AK	6000	T3/3DUP S		AIJ	28	A-AK	Yuri M.	6787	S	01-40N 141-51E	

Dt/Hr	Submarine	Pt	Position	Tgt	Size	Attack	Cl	So	Date	Type	Name	Tons	Dm	Location	Comments
NOV	1943														
28/12 270 RATON		1	01-40N 141-45E	AK	6000	T2/3DUP	S	AIJ	28	A-AK	Hokko M.	5346	S	01-40N 141-51E	
28/22 264 PARGO		2	18-34N 140-09E	DD	1700	T1/3NSR	D								
28/22 264 PARGO		2	18-34N 140-09E	Same	Same	Same	O								SORG gives half credit with 279 SNOOK for 8000T AK. PR says fired only at DD.
28/23 279 SNOOK		4	18-48N 139-50E	AK	8000	T1/6NSR	D								SORG gives half credit with 264 PARGO. PR says fired at 4 AKs, hit 1 previously damaged by PARGO & 1 other.
28/23 279 SNOOK		4	18-48N 139-50E	AK	6000	T1/ NSR	D	I	28	C-AK	Kotobuki M.	5874	S	NW of Saipan	Ship not in other sources. [Attribution ?]
28/23 279 SNOOK		4	18-48N 139-50E	AK	3500	T1/4NSR	D								
28 S HMS TRESPASSER		1	Car Nicobar	MV	4000	T3/6	S								BSH says attack unsuccessful.
29/01 279 SNOOK		4	18-37N 139-45E	AK	7000	T4/6NSR	S	AIJW	28-9	XAP	Yamafuku M.	4928	S	18-21N 140-08E	[Location closer to 264 PARGO posit.]
29/03 264 PARGO		2	18-23N 140-18E	AK	5700	T2/4NSR	S	AIJW	29	XAP	Manju M.	5874	S	18-34N 139-58E	PR says target seen to sink. [Location closer to 279 SNOOK posit.]
29/03 279 SNOOK		4	18-38N 139-35E	AK	7500	T2/6NUP	S	AJ IW	28-9 Note	XAP	Shiganoura M.	3512	S	18-24N 139-41E	I & W give date 1 Dec.
29/06 224 COD		1	11-42N 118-30E	AK	7100	T2/4DUP	S								
29/06 224 COD		1	11-42N 118-30E	AP	4700	T1/2DUP	D								
29/08 223 BONEFISH		2	06-22S 116-35E	AK	8200	T2/4DUP	S	AIJ	29	A-AK	Suez M.	4645	S	06-20S 116-30E	
29/10 185 SNAPPER		8	33-19N 139-34E	AK	8500	T2/3DUP	S								
29/10 185 SNAPPER		8	33-19N 139-34E	AK	5300	T2/3DUP	S	AIJW	29	XAP	Kenryu M.	4575	S	Hachijo Jima	
29/12 263 PADDLE		2	11-20N 162-29E	AO	10000	T2/5DUP	D								
30/11 305 SKATE		2	09-03N 151-29E	CV	20000	T1/3DUP	D								
30/17 212 GATO		7	01-57N 147-24E	AK	5600	T2/4DUP	S	AJ I	30	A-AP	Columbia M.	5617	S H	01-54N 147-20E	
DEC	1943														
1/01 264 PARGO		2	14-24N 140-40E	AO	12000	T7/11NSR	S	AIJW	30-1	XAP	Shoko M.	1933	S	18-02N 138-55E	

Dt/Hr	Submarine	Pt	Position	Tgt	Size	Attack	Cl	So	Date	Type	Name	Tons	Dm	Location	Comments
DEC	1943														
1/01	304 SEAHORSE	2	26-34N 140-47E	AK	4800	T2/4NSR	D								
1/09	265 PETO	4	01-02N 146-42E	APK	8200	T3/6DUP	S	AIJW	1	XAP	Konei M.	2338	S	01-16N 146-45E	
1/21	223 BONEFISH	2	01-31N 120-51E	AK	7200	T1/4NSV	S	AIJW	1	XAP	Nichiryo M.	2721	S	01-30N 120-44E	
1/21	223 BONEFISH	2	01-31N 120-51E	DD	1200	1/ NSV	D								
2/10	287 BOWFIN	2	03-25S 118-20E	Sch	100	GD	S								
3/21	283 TINOSA	4	06-29N 131-32E	AK	6600	T3/7NUP	S	AIJW	3	XAO	Azuma M.	6646	S	06-34N 131-40E	
4/01	253 GUNNEL	3	29-45N 145-54E	AK	9500	T4/4NSR	S	AIJW	4	XAP	Hiyoshi M.	4046	S	29-36N 145-54E	
4/06	192 SAILFISH	10	32-27N 143-49E	CV	22500	T4/7NSR	D	I	?	CV	Ryuho	13360	?	Off Yokosuka	PR says CV dead in water, crew on deck, believed this was same ship sunk in later attack. SORG evaluates as unsuccessful attack on Chuyo. [Attribution ?]
4/10	192 SAILFISH	10	32-27N 143-49E	CVE	22500	T2/3DUP	S	AIW J	3-4	CVE	Chuyo	17830 20000	S	Hachijo Jima	See above. PR says attacks made in typhoon.
4/18	308 APOGON	1	08-15N 159-06E	AK	3000	T2/3TUP	S	AIJW	4	XPG	Daido M.	2962	S	09-06N 159-02E	
4/21	309 ASPRO	1	27-46N 156-16E	Sam	100	GN	D								
5/07	167 NARWHAL	8	09-09N 124-29E	APK	4000	GD	S	J	5	AK	Himeno M.	834	S	Sub position	PR says set afire, seen to sink. [J attribution ?]
7/16	266 POGY	4	14-04N 152-09E	AK	5400	T1/2DUP	S	AIJW	7	XAC	Soyo M.	6081	S	14-03N 152-20E	
8/02	276 SAWFISH	5	25-19N 141-44E	AK	6000	T2/4NSR	S	AJW I	8	XAP	Sansei M.	3266	S M	26-32N 141-36E	
8/03	266 POGY	4	14-11N 151-41E	AK	8800	T4/6NSV	S								
8/18	212 GATO	7	01-06N 145-14E	AK	4500	T2/4TUP	D								
11/11	267 POMPON	3	07-13N 115-01E	Sam	100	GD	S								
11/12	223 BONEFISH	2	04-03N 118-22E	CM	700	GD	D								
11/13	267 POMPON	3	07-03N 114-50E	Sam		GD	S								

Dt/Hr	Submarine	Pt	Position	Tgt	Size	Attack	Cl	So	Date	Type	Name	Tons	Dm	Location	Comments
DEC	1943														
12/08	203 TUNA	9	02-44N 126-14E	AK	8200	T1/5DUP	D	AJW I	12	XAP	Tosei M.	5484 5434	S M	02-43N 126-56E	
13/05	268 PUFFER	2	14-36N 119-58E	AP	9200	T1/4TUP	D								
13/08	266 POGY	4	07-07N 134-31E	AP	5300	T2/3DUP	S	AIJ	13		A-AK Fukkai M.	3829	S	07-06N 134-40E	PR says fired at 2 AKs & PC, saw 1 hit & heard another.
13/08	266 POGY	4	07-07N 134-31E	Same	Same	Same	0	A I	23		C-AK Fukurei M.	5969 5800	L	07-06N 134-30E	Location agrees with this attack but date does not. [Attribution ?]
13/23	192 SAILFISH	10	30-55N 132-33E	AK	5800	T1/4NUP	S	AIJ	13		A-AK Totai M.	3195	S	30-25N 130-30E	
13/23	192 SAILFISH	10	30-55N 132-33E	AK	7100	T1/ NUP	D								
14/04	233 HERRING	6	33-10N 124-55E	AP	14000	T2/2NUP	S	AIJ	14		C-AK Hakozaki M.	3948	S	33-10N 125-00E	
14/04	233 HERRING	6	33-10N 124-55E	AO	7000	T1/1NUP	D								
15/08	309 ASPRO	1	26-07N 122-33E	AO	7300	T1/4DUP	D								
17/04	229 FLYING FISH	8	22-27N 120-08E	AK	5300	T3/3NUP	S	AIJ	15-6		C-AK Ginyo M.	8613	S	22-14N 120-06E	
17/22	309 ASPRO	1	23-59N 124-42E	AP	11600	T2/5NSR	S								
17/22	309 ASPRO	1	23-59N 124-42E	AK	7000	T2/ NSR	S								
17/22	309 ASPRO	1	23-59N 124-42E	AK	7000	T2/4NSR	S								
17/22	309 ASPRO	1	23-59N 124-42E	AO	10000	T1/ NSR	D								
18/02	309 ASPRO	1	23-31N 124-15E	AK	7000	T2/3NUP	D								
18/02	309 ASPRO	1	23-31N 124-15E	AK	7000	T2/3NUP	D								
18/22	208 GRAYBACK	9	26-22N 128-20E	AK	4000	T1/2NSR	D								
18/22	208 GRAYBACK	9	26-22N 128-20E	AK	4000	T2/2NSR	S	AIJ	18-20		C-AK Gyokurei M.	5588	S	26-30N 128-15E	
18/22	208 GRAYBACK	9	26-22N 128-20E	AK	7000	T1/2NSR	D								
19/03	208 GRAYBACK	9	26-30N 128-26E	PG	1200	T3/4NUS	S	AIW J	18-9	DD	Numakaze	1215 1300	S	26-30N 128-13E	I says missing, cause unk.
20/08	268 PUFFER	2	14-44N 119-55E	DD	1400	T2/4DUP	S	AIJW	20	DD	Fuyo	820	S	Subic Bay	

73

Dt/Hr	Submarine	Pt	Position	Tgt	Size	Attack	Cl	So	Date	Type	Name	Tons	Dm	Location	Comments
DEC 1943															
20/09 268 PUFFER		2	14-44N 119-55E	AK	5900	T2/5DUP	D								
20/17 212 GATO		7	01-30N 148-36E	AK	6500	T1/6DUP	S	AIJ W	20 Note	XAP	Tsuneshima M. Tsunushima M.	2926	S	01-26N 148-36E	W gives date 20 Oct. [Misprint?]
20/17 212 GATO		7	01-30N 148-36E	AK	9000	T2/ DUP	S								
21/03 208 GRAYBACK		9	30-24N 129-54E	AK	4100	T2/2NSR	S	AIJ	21	C-APK	Konan M.	2627	S	30-26N 129-58E	
21/03 208 GRAYBACK		9	30-24N 129-54E	AK	5500	T1/3NSR	S								
21/03 208 GRAYBACK		9	30-24N 129-54E	AK	6300	T2/4NSR	S								
21/06 208 GRAYBACK		9	30-24N 129-54E	XAM	2700	T1/2TSV	S	AIJW	21	XAN	Kashiwa M.	515	S	30-26N 129-58E	
21/06 305 SKATE		2	09-50N 151-55E	AK	6400	T3/4TUP	S	AIJW	21	XAO	Terukawa M.	6433	S	09-45N 151-56E	
21/12 192 SAILFISH		10	32-38N 132-04E	AK	7400	T2/3DUP	S	AIJW	21	XAP	Uyo M.	6376	S	32-29N 132-08E	W lists ship as both XAP & Std AK 1A.
22/21 254 GURNARD		4	33-30N 135-57E	AK	7000	T1/4NSR	D	I	22	C-AK	Haferland-go	6334	M	E Kashinosaki	
23/00 262 MUSKALLUNGE		2	10-04N 143-48E	APK	5600	T1/6NSR	D								
24/03 270 RATON		2	02-46N 127-41E	APK	8000	T3/6NSR	S	AIJW	24	XAP	Heiwa M.	5578	S	Kaoe Bay	
24/03 270 RATON		2	02-46N 127-41E	XAV	6000	T1/4NSV	D								
24/07 254 GURNARD		4	34-02N 136-20E	AK	5000	T2/2DSR	S	AIJW	24	XAP	Seizan M. #2	1898	S	E of Mikisaki	
24/07 254 GURNARD		4	34-02N 136-19E	AK	6000	T2/2DUP	S	AJ I	24	A-AK	Tofuku M.	5857	S	E of Mikisaki 07-06N 134-30E	[Location in I appears incorrect.]
24/07 254 GURNARD		4	34-02N 136-19E	Same	Same	Same	O	IW	25	XAM	Naruo M.	215	S	NE of Daiosaki	W credits GURNARD, but PR does not mention 2nd ship. [Attribution ?]
25/05 305 SKATE		2	10-13N 150-27E	BB	20000	T2/4TUP	D	I	25	BB	Yamato	64170	L	NE of Truk	
27/01 271 RAY		2	05-00S 121-22E	AO	10000	T5/6NUP	S	AIJW	27	XAO	Kyoko M.	5800	S	W Tioro Str.	
27/11 229 FLYING FISH	8		21-42N 117-48E	AO	10500	T6/10DUP	S	AIJW	27	XAO	Kyuei M.	10171	S	21-25N 118-05E	
27/12 199 TAUTOG		9	33-25N 135-40E	AK	8000	T2/3DUP	D	I	27	XAV	Kimikawa M.	6863	D	Shionomisaki	
27/12 208 GRAYBACK		9	30-29N 159-25E	Sam	200	GD	S								

Dt/Hr	Submarine	Pt	Position	Tgt	Size	Attack	Cl	So	Date	Type	Name	Tons	Dm	Location	Comments
DEC	1943														
27/24	254 GURNARD	4	34-22N 138-32E	AP	11000	T2/4NSR D	A I		27	XAP	Gokoku M. Gokuku M.	10438	M	34-23N 138-24E	
28/23	262 MUSKALLUNGE	2	09-13N 147-00E	AK	8200	T2/4NSR S									
29/02	236 SILVERSIDES	8	08-07N 133-59E	AK	4000	T1/2NSR D									
29/02	236 SILVERSIDES	8	08-07N 133-59E	AK	4000	T1/2NSR D									
29/03	236 SILVERSIDES	8	08-03N 134-04E	AO	7000	T3/3NSR S	AIJ		29	C-AK	Ryuto M.	3311	S	08-00N 134-00E	
29/04	236 SILVERSIDES	8	08-00N 133-51E	AK	5500	T3/8NSR S	AIJ		29	A-AK	Shichisei M.	1911	S	08-00N 134-00E	
29/05	236 SILVERSIDES	8	08-09N 133-51E	APK	6000	T1/1NSR S	AIW J		29	XAP	Temposan M. Tenposan M.	1970	S	08-00N 134-00E	W lists ship as both XAP & Std AK 1D.
30/22	222 BLUEFISH	3	02-45S 109-10E	AO	14100	T5/5NSR S	AJ		29-30	AO	Ichiyu M.	5061	S	Java Sea	
31/12	213 GREENLING	8	05-18N 160-16E	AK	1900	T1/4DUP S	AIJW		31	XAP	Shoho M.	1936	S	05-40N 160-20E	
31/22	233 HERRING	6	31-33N 138-32E	DE	500	T2/4NSV S									
JAN	1944														
1/03	233 HERRING	6	32-10N 138-37E	AP	9500	T2/3NSV S	AIJW		1	XAPV	Nagoya M.	6071	S	32-15N 138-02E	
1/03	233 HERRING	6	32-10N 138-37E	AK	6000	T1/3NSV S									
1/03	268 PUFFER	2	08-50N 122-56E	AP	7000	T1/3NSR D	AIJ		1	A-AK	Ryuyo M.	6707	S	08-36N 122-52E	
1/03	268 PUFFER	2	08-25N 122-56E	AV	9000	T1/3NSV D									
1/09	271 RAY	2	03-51S 128-04E	AK	7900	T3/6DUP S	AIJW		31-1 Ja	XPG	Okuyo M.	2904	S	03-52S 128-02E	
1/23	285 BALAO	3	04-32N 147-23E	AK	8500	T3/6NSR D	AI W		1	XAP	Kiyosumi M. Kiyozumi M.	8613	H	04-35N 147-15E	
2/04	230 FINBACK	7	29-30N 128-50E	AO	10000	T5/6NSR S	AI J		2	C-AO	Isshin M.	10044 10000	S	28-36N 129-03E	
--							-	I	2	?	Choun M.	?	S	Off Medan	No likely sub attack.
3/01	234 KINGFISH	6	08-06N 112-30E	AO	8700	T1/3NSR D	AIJW		2	XAO	Ryuei M.	5144	S	06-03N 110-02E	W lists ship as both XAO & Std AO 1TM.

Dt/Hr	Submarine	Pt	Position	Tgt	Size	Attack	Cl	So	Date	Type	Name	Tons	Dm	Location	Comments
JAN	1944														
3/01	234 KINGFISH	6	08-06N 112-30E	AK	6600	T2/7NSR	D								
3/03	270 RATON	2	08-18N 129-59E	AO	10000	T3/6NSR	S	I	3	XAO	Akebono M.	10182	M	08-22N 129-52E	
3/10	199 TAUTOG	9	33-44N 136-02E	AK	3000	T1/3DUP	S	AIJ W	3	XAP	Saishu M. Saisho M.	2073	S	33-44N 136-23E	I gives tons as 2083.
3/18	234 KINGFISH	6	06-58N 112-02E	AO	7500	T3/4DUP	S	AIW J	4 3	XAO	Bokuei M.	5135	SC S	Amami Oshima	A & W say sunk in collision; I gives tons as 5200. [J attribution ?]
4/05	199 TAUTOG	9	34-09N 136-50E	AK	6700	T4/6NSR	S	AIJ	4		C-AK Usa M.	3943	S	34-10N 136-48E	
4/10	271 RAY	2	10-01S 123-25E	APK	10800	T2/4DUP	D								
4/16	288 CABRILLA	2	11-05N 109-10E	AK	4100	T3/4DUP	S	AIJ	4		C-AK Tamon M. #8	2704	S	11-03N 109-29E	
4/21	222 BLUEFISH	3	07-10N 108-28E	AO	6000	T3/6NUP	S	AIJ	4		C-AO Hakko M.	6046	S	06-55N 109-29E	
4/22	288 CABRILLA	2	10-33N 109-47E	AK	3800	T1/5NUP	D								
5/04	269 RASHER	2	05-46N 108-36E	AO	7200	T5/14NSV	S	AJW I	4	XAO	Kiyo M. Kiyo M. I-Go	7251	S	06-55N 108-23E	
7/05	262 MUSKALLUNGE	2	10-38N 142-21E	AO	8000	T2/4NSR	D								
7/15	268 PUFFER	2	10-31S 115-20E	Tra	100	GD	S								
7/22	234 KINGFISH	6	09-27N 117-36E	AO	7500	T2/4NSR	S	AIJ	7		C-AO Fushimi M. #3	4289	S	09-35N 117-26E	
7/22	234 KINGFISH	6	09-27N 117-36E	AO	7300	T1/2NSR	S								
8/10	221 BLACKFISH	7	01-30S 148-06E	AO	4500	T2/3DUP	D								
9/02	194 SEADRAGON	9	10-20N 149-28E	AK	7400	T3/4NUP	S								
9/13	291 CREVALLE	2	00-30N 119-10E	Sam		GD	S								
10/06	280 STEELHEAD	4	31-28N 137-44E	APK	9000	T1/4NSR	S	AIJW	10	XAR	Yamabiko M.	6799	S	31-42N 137-50E	
10/10	200 THRESHER	11	23-34N 133-35E	Sam	200	GD	S	I	10	?	Horai M.	91	S	?	[Attribution ?; location not given.]
10/12	197 SEAWOLF	12	27-35N 127-30E	AK	5000	T1/3DUP	S	AIJ	10	A-AK	Asuka M.	7523	S	27-32N 127-30E	
10/12	197 SEAWOLF	12	27-35N 127-30E	AK	4000	T1/4DUP	D								
10/23	197 SEAWOLF	12	27-10N 127-28E	AK	4500	T2/5NUP	S	AIJ	10-1	A-AK	Yahiko M.	5747	S	27-18N 127-40E	

76

Dt/Hr	Submarine	Pt	Position	Tgt	Size	Attack	Cl	So	Date	Type	Name	Tons	Dm	Location	Comments
JAN	1944														
11/04	197 SEAWOLF	12	27-10N 127-28E	APK	10000	T7/9NSR	S	AIJ	10-1	C-AK	Getsuyo M.	6440	S	27-18N 127-40E	
11/13	187 STURGEON	9	32-56N 132-02E	AO	7300	T1/4DUP	D	AJ I	11	A-AK	Erie M. Erii M.	5493	S	32-31N 132-34E	
11/22	269 RASHER	2	11-39N 109-12E	AK	4500	T1/3NUP	D								
11/23	199 TAUTOG	9	34-10N 136-56E	AK	8000	T1/3NUP	D	I	11	XAE	Kogyo M.	6353	M	34-10N 136-55E	
11/23	199 TAUTOG	9	34-10N 136-56E	AK	4000	T1/1NUP	D								
11	HMS TALLY HO	3	Off Penang	CL	5100	T2/7	S	AIW J	11	CL	Kuma	5100 5700	S	W of Penang	
12/19	218 ALBACORE	8	03-30N 147-27E	AP	5000	T4/8TUP	S	AIW J	12	XPG	Choko M. #2 Choko M.	2629	S	03-37N 147-27E	
12/19	218 ALBACORE	8	03-30N 147-27E	Same	Same	Same	0	W	12	PGM	H 4	25	S	03-37N 147-27E	W says craft towed by Choko M #2, scuttled.
12/19	256 HAKE	3	23-15N 132-49E	AP	6400	T2/4NSV	S	AIJW	12	XAPV	Nigitsu M.	9547	S	23-15N 132-51E	
--							-	AJ I	12	A-AK	Kanjo M.	2197	SM M	22-37N 120-11E	No likely sub attack.
14/01	193 SWORDFISH	10	33-16N 139-30E	AK	7500	T2/4NUP	D	AIJW	14	XAP	Yamakuni M.	6925	S	33-15N 139-38E	
14/13	218 ALBACORE	8	05-15N 141-15E	DD	1800	T2/4DUP	S	AIW J	14	DD	Sazanami	2090 1950	S	05-30N 141-34E	
14/13	277 SCAMP	6	05-02N 140-43E	AO	10000	T2/6DUP	S	AIJW	14	XAO	Nippon M.	9974	S	05-02N 140-50E	
14/19	217 GUARDFISH	7	05-22N 141-27E	AO	10000	T5/6TUP	S	AIJW	14	XAO	Kenyo M.	10024	S	05-23N 141-32E	
14/20	197 SEAWOLF	12	28-30N 133-40E	AK	4500	T2/3NSR	S	AIW J	14	XAO	Yamazuru M. Yamatsuru M.	3651	S	28-25N 133-30E	I gives tons as 2651.
15/02	197 SEAWOLF	12	28-04N 134-25E	AK	4000	GM	D								
15/22	200 THRESHER	11	19-45N 120-40E	AK	4000	T2/4NSR	S	AIJ	14-5	A-AK	Toho M.	4092	S	20-05N 120-31E	
15/22	200 THRESHER	11	19-45N 120-40E	AK	8200	T3/3NSR	S	AJ I	15	C-AO	Tatsuno M.	6960 6353	S	20-05N 120-31E	
15	HMS TALLY HO	3	Car Nicobar	MV	6000	T1/6	S	AIJ	15	A-AK	Ryuko M.	2962	S	10-50N 093-00E	

Dt/Hr	Submarine	Pt	Position	Tgt	Size	Attack	Cl	So	Date	Type	Name	Tons	Dm	Location	Comments
JAN 1944															
16/00 193 SWORDFISH		10	34-04N 139-56E	AK	5900	T3/3NUP	S	AIW J	16	XPG	Delhi M.	2205 2182	S	34-12N 139-54E	
16/11 187 STURGEON		9	32-11N 132-22E	AK	7200	T3/3DUP	S								
16/11 187 STURGEON		9	32-11N 132-22E	DD	2000	T1/1DUP	D	IW	16	DD	Suzutsuki	2700	H	Bungo Channel	
16/16 221 BLACKFISH		7	04-03N 148-41E	AK	6000	T3/6DUP	S	AIJW	16	XAP	Kaika M.	2087	S	03-50N 148-44E	
16/16 221 BLACKFISH		7	04-03N 148-41E	AO	4500	T1/4DUP	D								
16/18 239 WHALE		6	23-09N 135-14E	AK	7000	T2/3TUP	S	AIJ	16	A-AK	Denmark M.	5869	S	23-15N 135-14E	
16/18 239 WHALE		6	23-09N 135-14E	AO	7000	T1/ TUP	D								
16/19 272 REDFIN		1	15-08N 114-58E	DD	1700	T4/4TSV	S	AI	17	DD	Amatsukaze	2033	H	N Spratley Is.	
16/19 287 BOWFIN		3	02-54S 118-24E	Sam		GT	S								
16/20 304 SEAHORSE		3	12-49N 150-19E	APK	6500	T3/4NSR	S	AIJ	16	C-AK	Nikko M.	784	S	12-48N 150-18E	
16/23 197 SEAWOLF		12	22-45N 135-00E	AK	6000	GM	D	AIW J	17-8	XAP	Tarushima M.	4865	S JS	22-34N 135-46E	J credits SEAWOLF & 239 WHALE. PR says chased target to WHALE, which sank it.
17/07 239 WHALE		6	23-08N 135-09E	AK	7000	T3/9TUP	S	AIW J	17-8	XAP	Tarushima M.	4865	S JS	22-34N 135-46E	J credits WHALE & 197 SEAWOLF; PR says sunk by WHALE.
--							-	I	18	C-AK	Shinano M.	6254	S	36-10N 140-40E	No likely sub attack; A says no record of ship.
18/03 287 BOWFIN		3	00-18N 118-37E	AK	7500	T6/12NUP	S	AIJ	17-8	C-AO	Shoyo M.	4408	S	00-17N 118-25E	
18/03 287 BOWFIN		3	00-18N 118-37E	DD	1200	T1/2NUP	D								
18/03 287 BOWFIN		3	00-18N 118-37E	DE	600	T2/ NUP	S								
18/20 249 FLASHER		1	23-50N 151-28E	AK	6000	T2/4NSP	S	AIW J	18	XAO	Yoshida M.	2920 2900	S	23-46N 151-30E	W says ship was XPF rebuilt as AO.
19/12 231 HADDOCK		8	12-50N 146-23E	CV	22500	T4/6DUP	D	AI	19	CVE	Unyo	17830	H	ESE of Guam	
20/01 310 BATFISH		1	31-30N 134-51E	APK	7100	T3/3NSR	S								
20/05 310 BATFISH		1	31-28N 134-52E	APK	8600	T2/5NSV	S	AIJ W	20 24	XAP	Hidaka M. Hikade M.	5486	S	31-32N 135-58E	

Dt/Hr	Submarine	Pt	Position	Tgt	Size	Attack	Cl	So	Date	Type	Name	Tons	Dm	Location	Comments
JAN	1944														
20/08	206 GAR	10	06-40N 134-17E	AK	7200	T2/3DUP	S	AIJ	20	A-AK	Koyu M.	5324	S	06-48N 134-13E	
20/11	194 SEADRAGON	9	08-04N 152-40E	AK	8400	T2/4DUP	D	I	20	AF	Irako	9570	M	NW of Truk	
20/11	194 SEADRAGON	9	08-04N 152-40E	AK	7200	T1/ DUP	D								
21/22	304 SEAHORSE	3	03-19N 137-02E	AK	4000	T1/3NSR	S	AIJ	21	A-AP	Ikoma M.	3156	S	03-25N 137-06E	
21/23	304 SEAHORSE	3	03-19N 137-02E	AK	5900	T4/9NSR	S	AIJ	21	A-AK	Yasukuni M.	3021	S	03-25N 137-06E	
22/07	223 BONEFISH	3	02-36S 118-06E	Sch	100	GD	S								
22/17	283 TINOSA	5	07-22N 115-05E	AK	4600	T2/3DUP	S	AIJ	22	C-AO	Seinan M.	5401	S	07-19N 116-52E	
22/17	283 TINOSA	5	07-22N 115-05E	AK	6000	T1/3DUP	S	AIJ	22	C-AO	Koshin M.	5485	S	07-27N 115-07E	
22/18	182 SALMON	9	29-33N 141-02E	AO	4000	T3/4TUP	D								
22/22	283 TINOSA	5	07-01N 114-58E	AK	3700	T1/6NSV	D								
22/23	206 GAR	10	06-08N 134-39E	APK	5200	T2/3NSR	D								
22/23	206 GAR	10	06-08N 134-39E	APK	5000	T1/3NSR	D								
22/23	206 GAR	10	06-08N 134-39E	APK	9300	T3/6NSR	S								
22/24	311 ARCHERFISH	1	25-45N 121-24E	APK	9000	T1/4NSR	S								
23/02	206 GAR	10	05-45N 134-45E	AK	5000	T1/2NSR	S	AIJW	23	XAP	Taian M.	3670	S	05-50N 134-14E	
23/03	279 SNOOK	5	29-49N 140-08E	AK	7000	T2/6NSR	S	AIJW	23-4	XPG	Magane M.	3120	S	30-06N 141-19E	
24/02	187 STURGEON	9	32-28N 132-23E	AK	5000	T1/4NSR	S	AIJ	24	A-AK	Chosen M.	3110	S	32-40N 132-18E	
24/03	187 STURGEON	9	32-28N 132-23E	AK	7000	T2/3NSR	S								
24/23	256 HAKE	3	07-10N 126-57E	AO	10000	T1/3NSR	D								
26/00	184 SKIPJACK	9	08-51N 157-10E	DD	1500	T4/4NUP	S	AIW J	25-6	DD	Suzukaze	1685 1580	S	NW of Ponape	
26/00	184 SKIPJACK	9	08-52N 157-10E	AK	5900	T1/4NUP	D								
26/04	184 SKIPJACK	9	09-22N 157-26E	AK	6900	T2/4NUP	S	AIJW	26	XAP	Okitsu M.	6666	S	09-24N 157-45E	

Dt/Hr	Submarine	Pt	Position	Tgt	Size	Attack	Cl	So	Date	Type	Name	Tons	Dm	Location	Comments
JAN 1944															
26/22 256 HAKE		3	05-50N 126-00E	Sam	300	GN	S	A	27	XAN	Shuko M.	889	S	Ambon	PR says 120-ft craft, Japanese flag painted on bow, left afire. Other sources credit 240 ANGLER (see 29 Jan). [Attribution ?]
26/22 291 CREVALLE		2	08-27N 109-12E	APK	6600	T1/4NSR	S	AIW J	26	XPG	Busho M.	2569 2552	S	08-30N 109-10E	
26 HMS TEMPLAR		4	W Malacca Str.	CL	5100	T1/8	S	AW I	27	CL	Kitakami Kitagami	5100	H	SW of Penang	
27/00 200 THRESHER		11	22-11N 119-12E	AO	7300	T2/3NSR	S	AIJW	27	XAP	Kosei M.	2205	S	22-10N 119-30E	
27/00 200 THRESHER		11	22-11N 119-12E	AK	6600	T1/3NSR	S	AIJ	27	C-AK	Kikuzuki M.	1266	S	22-10N 119-30E	
27/00 247 DACE		2	02-17N 149-02E	AO	10000	T2/6NSV	D	I	27	B-AG	Keikai M.	2827	S	03-45N 150-38E	Ship not listed in other sources. [Attribution ?; sinking not near attack.]
27/01 287 BOWFIN		3	07-07S 126-07E	AK	4400	T2/3NSR	S								
27/05 200 THRESHER		11	22-00N 118-42E	AO	9900	T1/7NSR	D								
27/13 240 ANGLER		1	23-58N 145-50E	Sam	200	GD	S								
27/24 193 SWORDFISH		10	33-31N 139-36E	APK	9300	T3/8NSV	S	AIJW	27-8	XPG	Kasagi M.	3140	S	33-30N 139-35E	
--								I	27	SC	Cha 61	135	?	06-02N 134-29E	No likely sub attack.
28/24 287 BOWFIN		3	03-25S 118-15E	AO	17000	T5/18NSR	D	I	28	AO	Kamoi	17000	D	Near Makassar	
--							-	I	28	AOR	Shioya	7950	?	05-44N 124-49E	No likely sub attack.
29/02 240 ANGLER		1	23-07N 142-27E	AO	8500	T1/3NSR	S								
29/02 198 TAMBOR		9	27-22N 128-29E	AK	7000	T2/2NSV	S	AIJ	29	C-AK	Shuntai M.	2254	S	27-50N 128-48E	
29/02 240 ANGLER		1	27-03N 142-27E	AO	5000	T2/3NSR	D								
29/02 240 ANGLER		1	27-03N 142-27E	AK	4000	T1/3NSR	D	JW	29	XAN	Shuko M.	889	S	SSE Iwo Jima	PR says believed hit in attack on AO above. A says sunk off Ambon 27 Jan; see 256 HAKE 26 Jan. [J attribution ?]
30/02 304 SEAHORSE		3	06-10N 138-14E	AK	7500	T3/3NSR	S	AIJ	30	A-AK	Toko M.	2747	S	06-20N 138-08E	

Dt/Hr	Submarine	Pt	Position	Tgt	Size	Attack	Cl	So	Date	Type	Name	Tons	Dm	Location	Comments
JAN	1944														
30/11	230 FINBACK	7	30-19N 134-00E	Sam	100	GD	S								
30/13	287 BOWFIN	3	05-50S 116-52E	Sch		GD	S								
30/13	287 BOWFIN	3	05-50S 116-52E	Sch	100	GD	S								
30/23	190 SPEARFISH	10	21-15N 149-18E	AK	5800	T1/4NSV	S	AIJW	30	XAP	Tamashima M.	3560	S	21-12N 149-28E	
30/23	190 SPEARFISH	10	21-15N 149-18E	AK	7000	T1/4NSV	S								
30/23	190 SPEARFISH	10	21-15N 149-18E	DE	500	T1/4NSR	S								
31/02	237 TRIGGER	8	09-50N 147-06E	DD	1800	T2/3NSR	S	AI J	31	DD CM	Michishio Nasami	1960 443	M S	09-48N 147-20E Sub position	A & W say Nasami sunk 1 by a/c at Rabaul. [J attribution ?]
31/05	237 TRIGGER	8	09-21N 147-02E	APK	10000	T2/5TSR	S	AIJW	31	XAS	Yasukuni M.	11933	S	09-15N 147-13E	
31/15	230 FINBACK	7	30-42N 139-49E	Sam	100	GD	S								
31/17	179 PLUNGER	10	34-37N 137-50E	AK	6500	T2/4DUP	S								
31/22	284 TULLIBEE	3	15-23N 145-35E	AK	2500	T2/3NUP	S	AIJW	31	XAN	Hiro M.	549	S	15-21N 145-31E	
31 S	HMS TEMPLAR	4	N Malacca Str.	SS		T2/3	S								BSH evaluates attack unsuccessful.
FEB	1944														
1/01	256 HAKE	3	01-35N 128-58E	AP	5800	T2/3NSR	S	AIJ	1	A-AP	Tacoma M.	5772	S	01-30N 128-50E	
1/01	256 HAKE	3	01-35N 128-58E	AK	4000	T1/3NSR	D								
1/01	256 HAKE	3	01-35N 128-58E	AK	4000	T1/ NSR	S	AIJ	1	A-AK	Nanka M.	4065	S	01-30N 128-50E	
1/02	308 APOGON	2	14-40N 146-42E	APK	17500	T2/3NSV	S								
1/02	308 APOGON	2	14-40N 146-42E	AK	6500	T2/4NSV	S								
1/04	304 SEAHORSE	3	04-21N 143-16E	AK	7000	T2/8NUR	S	AIJW	1	XAP	Toei M.	4004	S	04-24N 143-15E	
1/13	217 GUARDFISH	7	07-10N 151-44E	DD	1900	T1/4DUP	S	AIW J	1	DD	Umikaze	1685 1580	S	SW of Truk	
1/24	286 BILLFISH	3	04-58N 119-36E	AK	1000	GM	S								
1/24	286 BILLFISH	3	04-58N 119-36E	AK	900	GM	D								

81

Dt/Hr	Submarine	Pt	Position	Tgt	Size	Attack	Cl	So	Date	Type	Name	Tons	Dm	Location	Comments
FEB	1944														
--							-	I	1	A-AK	Minryo M.	2224	S	13-43N 120-39E	See 249 FLASHER 14 Feb.
2/10	179 PLUNGER	10	33-10N 136-10E	AK	5500	T2/2DUP	S	AIJ	2	C-AK	Toyo M. #5	2193	S	33-29N 135-59E	
2/10	179 PLUNGER	10	33-10N 136-10E	AK	3000	T2/2DUP	S	AIJ	2	C-AK	Toyo M. #8	2191	S	33-29N 135-59E	
3/03	198 TAMBOR	9	29-11N 124-45E	AK	8000	T2/3NSV	S	AIJW	3	XAO	Goyo M.	8469	S	28-32N 124-04E	
3/03	198 TAMBOR	9	29-11N 124-45E	AO	9500	T1/3NSV	S	AIJ	3	C-AO	Ariake M.	5149 5000	S	28-32N 124-04E	
3/09	221 BLACKFISH	7	01-36S 150-09E	DD	1800	T2/6DUP	D								
--							-	I	4	A-AK	Kibi M.	2759	?	Near Palau	No likely sub attack.
5/22	249 FLASHER	1	13-09N 120-24E	AK	4400	T2/4NUP	S	AIJ	5	A-AK	Taishin M.	1722	S	13-08N 120-26E	
5/22	249 FLASHER	1	13-12N 120-22E	Sam	100	GM	S								
5/22	249 FLASHER	1	13-12N 120-22E	Sam		GM	D								
5	HMS STONEHENGE	1	Off Penang	Cstr	800	G	S								
6/10	223 BONEFISH	3	11-59N 109-20E	XAO	19400	T2/4DUP	D								
6/10	223 BONEFISH	3	11-59N 109-20E	AK	3700	T1/2DUP	S								
6	HMS TAURUS	3	SW Sumatra	Tug	80	G	S								
6	HMS TAURUS	3	SW Sumatra	Ltr	50	G	S								
8/22	279 SNOOK	5	32-18N 129-20E	AK	6200	T1/2NUP	D	I	8	A-AK	Shiranesan M.	4739	H	31-05N 129-37E	I gives tons as 4939.
8/22	279 SNOOK	5	32-18N 129-20E	AK	6300	T2/2NUP	S	AIJ	8	A-AP	Lima M.	6989	S	31-05N 127-17E	
--							-	I	8	XAP	Tatsuta M.	16975	S	Mikurashima	Other sources give date 8 Feb 43; see 175 TARPON that date. [Listing in I appears incorrect.]
9/12	223 BONEFISH	3	11-30N 109-10E	XAO	17500	T4/5DUP	S	AI	9	C-AO	Tonan M. #2	19262	M	11-30N 109-08E	
10/03	266 POGY	5	23-12N 121-30E	DD	1400	T2/2NSV	S	AIWJ	10	DD	Minekaze	1215 1300	S	23-20N 121-30E	
10/03	266 POGY	5	23-12N 121-30E	AK	6100	T2/3NSV	S	AJI	10	C-AK	Malta M.	5499	S H	23-21N 121-35E	

Dt/Hr	Submarine	Pt	Position	Tgt	Size	Attack	Cl	So	Date	Type	Name	Tons	Dm	Location	Comments
FEB	1944														
10/03	266 POGY	5	23-12N 121-30E	AK	8400	T1/ NSV	D								
10/21	178 PERMIT	11	08-27N 149-24E	CA	8500	T1/4NSV	D								
10/22	190 SPEARFISH	10	21-53N 119-13E	APK	8500	T2/4NSV	S	I	10	XAP	Tatsuwa M.	6345	H	21-55N 119-30E	I gives tons as 6335.
10/22	190 SPEARFISH	10	21-53N 119-13E	AK	5500	T1/ NSV	D								
10/22	256 HAKE	3	01-58N 129-14E	AK	4000	T2/3NUP	D								
11/03	190 SPEARFISH	10	21-00N 119-07E	AK	6000	T1/4NSV	D								
11/16	291 CREVALLE	2	05-00N 119-06E	PC	200	GD	S								
11/23	211 GUDGEON	11	27-38N 121-15E	AP	10000	T2/3NUP	S	AIJ	11	C-AK	Satsuma M.	3091	SA	28-00N 121-30E	Sources credit Chinese aircraft. PR says ship appeared damaged earlier, saw bow down, stern high in air & heard breaking-up noises. [Attribution ?]
12/12	190 SPEARFISH	10	20-31N 117-47E	AK	6600	T2/4DUP	D								
12/21	198 TAMBOR	9	27-43N 128-35E	AK	5000	T1/3NSR	S	AIJ	12	C-AO	Ronsan M.	2735	S	27-44N 128-42E	
12	HMS STONEHENGE	1	W coast Malaya	AV	7000	T2/6	S	AJ I	12	XAN	Choko M.	889	S L	05-46N 099-52E	Escort hit by torp fired at main target.
13/14	227 DARTER	1	05-16N 149-22E	AK	7500	T1/10DUP	D								
13/16	256 HAKE	3	04-37S 125-26E	Sam		GD	S								
13/17	273 ROBALO	1	13-30N 121-13E	AK	6200	T1/4DUP	D								PR says hit aft but believed not sunk.
14/04	249 FLASHER	1	13-44N 120-40E	AK	7000	T1/4NUP	S	AIJ	14	C-AO	Hokuan M.	3712	S	13-44N 120-29E	PR says broke in two, breaking-up noises heard.
14/07	249 FLASHER	1	13-41N 120-27E	AK	9000	T2/4DUP	S	A J	14	A-AK	Minryo M.	2224 2193	S	13-43N 120-39E	I gives date 1 Feb [may be misprint].
14/20	279 SNOOK	5	33-48N 128-50E	APK	6000	T1/3NSV	S	AIJ	14	C-AK	Nittoku M.	3591	S	Off Tsushima	
15/07	212 GATO	8	04-00N 150-10E	Tra	100	GD	S	I W	16 Note	XPkt	Taiyo M. #3	36	S	Rabaul	PR says gutted by fire, crew in water. W gives date 16 Jan. [Attribution ?]
15/11	279 SNOOK	5	34-23N 128-23E	AK	1500	T1/2DUP	S	AI J	15	C-AK	Kamome M. Hoshi M. #2	875	SM S	34-27N 128-45E Sub position	PR says small AK sank. I lists as Hoshi M, sunk by mine at above location; A says Kamome M is correct name.

Dt/Hr	Submarine	Pt	Position	Tgt	Size	Attack	Cl	So	Date	Type	Name	Tons	Dm	Location	Comments
FEB	1944														
15/20	283 TINOSA	5	10-04N 126-54E	AK	5400	T1/6NSV	D	AIJ	15	A-AK	Odatsuki M.	1988	S	09-30N 127-00E	
15/21	291 CREVALLE	2	05-10N 128-43E	AK	6000	T2/6NSV	S								
15/21	291 CREVALLE	2	05-10N 128-43E	AK	6000	T1/ NSV	D								
14	HMS TALLY HO	4	Off Penang	SS	Unk	T1/3	S	U	14	SS	UIT-23	1031	S	04-25N 100-09E	ex-Reginaldo Giuliani.
15/21	291 CREVALLE	2	05-10N 128-43E	AK	6000	T1/ NSV	D								
15/21	291 CREVALLE	2	05-10N 128-43E	AK	4000	T1/3NSV	D								
15/21	291 CREVALLE	2	05-10N 128-43E	AK	4000	T1/ NSV	D								
15/22	309 ASPRO	2	10-23N 150-23E	SS	2200	T2/4NSR	S	IW J	?	SS	I-43	2230 2212	S	South Sea area	
15/25	291 CREVALLE	2	05-43N 128-30E	APK	7100	T1/6NUP	S								
15 S	HMS TRUCULENT	1	N Sumatra	MV	7000	T1/4	D								
15	HMS TRUCULENT	1	N Sumatra	Cstr	600	G	S								
16/00	283 TINOSA	5	09-15N 127-05E	AK	6300	T1/3NUP	S	AJ I	15-6	A-AP	Chojo M.	2610	S M	08-30N 126-58E	
16/18	224 COD	2	12-38N 117-33E	Sam		GT	S								
16/18	305 SKATE	3	10-11N 151-42E	CL	7000	T4/4DUP	S	AIW J	16-7	CL	Agano	6632 7000	S	N of Truk	
16/24	258 HOE	3	06-04N 126-22E	AK	6800	T2/6NSV	S								
16/24	258 HOE	3	06-04N 126-22E	AK	6800	T1/ NSV	S								
16/24	258 HOE	3	06-04N 126-22E	AK	5400	T1/2NSV	S								
17/00	225 CERO	3	00-53N 146-26E	AK	6200	T1/4NUP	D	AIW	17	XAP	Jozan M.	1086	S	Truk->New Ire.	SORG credits no hits or damage; PR says hit heard & screws stopped.
17/04	306 TANG	1	08-04N 149-28E	AK	7800	T3/4NUP	S	AIJ	17	A-AK	Gyoten M.	6854	S	08-00N 149-17E	
17/04	306 TANG	1	08-04N 149-28E	Same	Same	Same	0	I	17	C-AO	Kuniei M.	5184	S	08-00N 149-17E	Other sources have no record of ship. [Attribution ?]
17/17	211 GUDGEON	11	28-01N 123-23E	Sam	100	GD	S								

Dt/Hr	Submarine	Pt	Position	Tgt	Size	Attack	Cl	So	Date	Type	Name	Tons	Dm	Location	Comments
FEB	1944														
17/19	211 GUDGEON	11	28-01N 123-23E	Sam	100	GT	D								
17/22	188 SARGO	10	08-50N 135-57E	AO	14000	T1/8NSV	D	I	17	AO	Sata	14050	M	N of Palau	
17/22	188 SARGO	10	08-50N 135-57E	AK	7000	T2/ NSV	S	AIJW	17	XAP	Nichiro M.	6534	S	08-50N 135-40E	
18	HMS TRESPASSER	3	Burma coast	MV	3400	T1/6	S	I	18	XPG	Eifuku M.	3520	M	07-55N 093-03E	
19	208 GRAYBACK	10L	21-50N 119-50E	AK	4000	Unk	S	AI J	19	A-AK	Taikei M.	4739	S PS	21-48N 118-50E	
19	208 GRAYBACK	10L	21-25N 120-50E	AK	1900	Unk	S	AI J	19- 20	A-AK	Toshin M.	1917	S PS	21-45N 120-06E	
19/05	259 JACK	3	14-34N 114-11E	XAO	2500	T2/3NSP	S	AIJ	19	C-AO	Nanei M.	5019	S	14-28N 114-27E	
19/05	259 JACK	3	14-34N 114-11E	AO	8000	T3/3NUP	S	AJ	19	C-AO	Kokuei M.	5154	S	14-28N 114-27E	
19/19	259 JACK	3	15-40N 115-48E	AO	8000	T2/4TUP	S	AIJ	19	C-AO	Nichirin M.	5162	S	15-46N 115-57E	
19/19	259 JACK	3	15-40N 115-48E	AO	10000	T1/ TUP	S	I	19	XAO	Asanagi M.	5141	?	15-46N 115-57E	
19/20	225 CERO	3	03-22N 138-28E	AK	6100	T2/6TUP	S								
19/23	259 JACK	3	15-59N 115-35E	AO	10000	T3/7NSR	S	AIJ	19	C-AO	Ichiyo M.	5106	S	15-46N 115-57E	
19	236 SILVERSIDES	5	02-36S 150-34E	--	--	Mine	U	AJ I	19	A-AK	Shinto M. #1 Shinto M.	1933	SA S	02-50S 150-42E 02-50S 150-55E	Minefield laid 4 Jun 43. [Attribution ?; mines 8 months old.]
20/02	266 POGY	5	24-12N 123-20E	AK	6300	T2/2NSV	S	AIJ	20	ARC	Nanyo M.	3614	S	W Iriomote I.	A says cable layer owned by Dep't of Communications.
20/05	266 POGY	5	24-28N 123-31E	AK	5800	T1/3TSV	D	AJ I	20	C-AK	Taijin M.	5154	S H	24-15N 123-15E	
--							-	I	21	SC	Cha 52	135	M	Sunosaki	No likely sub attack.
21	HMS TALLY HO	4	Malacca Strait	MV	2500	T1/5	S	AJ I	21-2	A-AK	Daigen M. #6 Taigen M. #6	510	S	04-00N 101-00E 01-51N 139-00E	[Location in I appears incorrect.]
22/03	225 CERO	3	00-36S 139-31E	AK	8600	T2/13NSR	D	I	21	A-AK	Hasshu M.	2655	M	00-15S 139-40E	
22/17	268 PUFFER	3	03-03N 109-16E	AP	15100	T4/4DUP	S	AIJ	22	A-AP	Teiko M.	15105	S	03-12N 109-18E	
22/22	285 BALAO	4	00-07S 135-42E	AK	5900	T3/6NUP	S	AIJ	22-3	A-AK	Nikki M.	5857	S	00-11S 135-00E	

Dt/Hr	Submarine	Pt	Position	Tgt	Size	Attack	Cl	So	Date	Type	Name	Tons	Dm	Location	Comments
FEB	1944														
22/24	306 TANG	1	14-47N 144-50E	AK	6500	T4/4NSV	S	AIJW	22	XPG	Fukuyama M.	3581	S	W of Saipan	
--							-	A I	22	A-AK	Chiyoda M. #15 Chiyoda M. #5	408	SA S	South Pacific	Location too indefinite to identify sub attack. [Probably non-sub.]
--							-	A I	22	C-AO	Takatori M. #2 Takatori M.	521	SA S	Rabaul	No likely sub attack.
--							-	AJW I	22	XAN	Kyosei M.	556	SW S	02-44S 150-29E Kavieng	Sources say sunk by DesDiv 45. No likely sub attack.
22	236 SILVERSIDES	5	02-36S 150-34E	--	--	Mine	U	JW I	22	SC	Cha 29	130	SA SU	02-24S 151-45E Near Kavieng	Minefield laid 4 Jun 43. [Attribution ?; mines 8 months old.]
22/15	212 GATO	8	07-13N 151-38E	Unk	5000	TO/3DUP	O	AIW	22-3	XAR	Yamashimo M.	6777	S	Truk	PR says believed torps exploded on reef. [Attribution ?; see 306 TANG 23 Feb.]
23/01	306 TANG	1	14-45N 144-32E	AS	8700	T3/4NSV	S	AIJW	22-3	XAR	Yamashimo M.	6777	S	Truk	Sub position near Saipan, not Truk. [J attribution ?; see 212 GATO 22 Feb.]
23/02	281 SUNFISH	6	15-23N 145-03E	CV	25000	T3/6NSV	S	AW J	24 23	XAP	Kunishima M.	4083	DC S	34-11N 136-48E Sub position	W says stranded off Katata. PR says only 1 AK attacked later same day; see below. [J attribution ?]
23/04	266 POGY	5	26-22N 126-16E	AK	6000	T1/2NSV	D	I	23	C-AO	Teikon M.	5113	M	26-20N 126-11E	
23/05	266 POGY	5	26-22N 126-16E	AK	8600	T2/4NSV	S	AIJ	23	C-AK	Horei M.	5588	S	26-20N 126-11E	
23/09	281 SUNFISH	6	15-17N 145-03E	AK	5400	T4/7DSV	S	AIJW	23	XAC	Shinyubari M.	5354	S	W of Saipan	
23/12	179 PLUNGER	10	30-30N 140-20E	AK	7500	T1/1DUP	S	AIJ W	23 Note	XAP	Kimishima M.	5193	S	30-11N 140-49E	W gives date 23 Dec. [Probably misprint.]
23/23	224 COD	2	03-53N 129-17E	XAO	7400	T2/4NSV	S	AIJW	23	XAO	Ogura M. #3	7358	S	03-53N 129-05E	
23/23	279 SNOOK	5	28-58N 141-15E	AK	6000	T2/5NSV	S	AIJW	23	XAP	Koyo M.	5471	S	28-49N 141-13E	
24	208 GRAYBACK	10L	25- N 125- E	AO	10000	Unk	S	A IJW	24	XAO	Nanho M. Nampo M.	10033	S	24-20N 122-23E	W lists Nampo M as both XAO & Std AO 1TL.
24 U	208 GRAYBACK	10L	Unk	AK	Unk	Unk	D	AI	24	XAP	Asama M.	16975	L	24-15N 122-19E	Attack not in SORG; info from U. [Attribution ?]
24 U	208 GRAYBACK	10L	Unk	AO	Unk	Unk	D								Same as above.

Dt/Hr	Submarine	Pt	Position	Tgt	Size	Attack	Cl	So	Date	Type	Name	Tons	Dm	Location	Comments
FEB	1944														
24/22	306 TANG	1	15-16N 143-12E	AK	7000	T3/4NUP	S	AIJ	24	C-AK	Echizen M.	2424	S	15-15N 143-29E	
24	HMS TALLY HO	4	Malacca Strait	TB		Coll	D	I	24	TB	Kari	840		LC Malacca Strait	
25/01	258 HOE	3	05-46N 125-56E	AO	10100	T2/4NSR	D	AI	25	XAO	Kyokuto M.	10051	H	05-38N 126-00E	
25/03	258 HOE	3	05-46N 125-56E	AO	10500	T5/10NSR	S	AIJW	25	XAO	Nissho M.	10526	S	05-50N 126-00E	
25/07	306 TANG	1	15-50N 144-21E	AO	12000	T3/4DUP	S	AIJW	24-5	XAO	Choko M.	1790	S	15-46N 144-10E	
25/20	269 RASHER	3	07-46S 115-10E	APK	6500	T3/4NSR	S	AIJ	25	C-AK	Tango M.	6200	S	07-41S 115-10E	
25/21	269 RASHER	3	07-57S 115-14E	APK	4800	T3/4NSR	S	AIJ	25	A-AK	Ryusei M.	4805	S	07-55S 115-15E	
25 U	208 GRAYBACK	10L	Unk	AK	Unk	Unk	D								Attack not in SORG; info from U.
25 U	208 GRAYBACK	10L	Unk	AK	Unk	Unk	D								Same as above.
26/19	212 GATO	8	00-55S 139-02E	AK	8500	T2/4TUP	S	AJ I	26	A-APK	Daigen M. #3 Taigen M. #3	5255	S	01-51N 139-00E	
26/19	212 GATO	8	00-55S 139-02E	AK	6500	T1/2TUP	S								
27	202 TROUT	11L	22-40N 131-50E	APK	9200	Unk	S	AI	29	XAK	Aki M.	11409	?	Okino Oagari	[Attribution ?; date discrepancy.]
27	208 GRAYBACK	10L	Unk	APK	4900	Unk	S	AI J	28	XAP	Ceylon M.	4905	S PS	31-35N 127-47E	U says GRAYBACK probably sunk 26 Feb at 25-47N 128-45E; W credits 266 POGY, but PR shows no such attack.
27/03	224 COD	2	01-48N 127-33E	AK	2500	T2/4NSV	S	AJ I	27	A-AK	Taisoku M. Dairen M.	2473	S	02-00S 127-40E	
27/11	212 GATO	8	01-12S 134-22E	AK	4500	T1/4DUP	D								
28/16	381 SAND LANCE	1	50-02N 155-30E	AK	5200	T3/3DUP	S	AIJ W	28 23	XAP	Kaiko M.	3548	S	50-02N 155-26E	[W date may be misprint.]
28/23	285 BALAO	4	00-06N 132-53E	APK	7200	T2/6NSP	S	AIJ	28	A-AK	Akiura M.	6803	S	00-15N 133-02E	
28/23	285 BALAO	4	00-06N 132-53E	APK	4100	T2/3NSP	S	AIJ	28-9	A-AP	Shoho M.	2723	S	00-15N 133-02E	
28/23	285 BALAO	4	00-06N 132-53E	APK	3100	T1/1NSP	S								
28	HMS TACTICIAN	4	Off Penang	Cstr		T1/2+G	S								

Dt/Hr	Submarine	Pt	Position	Tgt	Size	Attack	Cl	So	Date	Type	Name	Tons	Dm	Location	Comments
FEB	1944														
29/20	202 TROUT	11L	22-40N 131-50E	AK	8000	Unk	D	AJ I	29	A-AP	Sakito M.	7126 9245	S	22-40N 131-50E	TROUT believed lost at this time.
29/24	188 SARGO	10	08-50N 132-56E	AK	7000	T2/8NSV	D	AI J	Note 29	A-AK	Uchide M.	5275	S	09-00N 132-45E	A gives date 1 Mar, I gives 2 Mar.
MAR	1944														
1/03	259 JACK	3	14-52N 117-48E	AK	7500	T2/3NUP	S								
1/03	259 JACK	3	14-52N 117-48E	AK	7500	T2/4NUP	S								
1/19	168 NAUTILUS	8	19-28N 134-41E	AK	6500	T2/4TUP	D								
2/23	382 PICUDA	1	06-25N 148-31E	APK	10800	T4/4NUP	S	AI J	2	A-AK	Shinkyo M.	5139 2672	S	06-22N 148-28E	2672T Shinkyo M sunk by 287 BOWFIN 24 Mar.
3/00	381 SAND LANCE	1	45-52N 149-16E	AK	8500	T4/6NUP	S	AIJW	2-3	XAP	Akashisan M.	4541	S	46-00N 149-08E	
3/02	271 RAY	3	09- N 113- E	AO	10000	T1/4NSR	D								
3/06	381 SAND LANCE	1	46-28N 149-18E	AK	5900	T3/4DUP	S	Note	3	AK	Belorussia		S	Sub position	Soviet AK. PR says mistaken for Japanese ship damaged earlier. Blair gives name Bella Russa.
3/18	167 NARWHAL	10	08-52N 123-23E	AP	3600	T1/4DUP	D	AIW J	3	PR	Karatsu	560	H S	Sulu Sea	Ex-USS LUZON. A says towed to Manila, scuttled there 3 Feb 45.
3/23	269 RASHER	3	03-17N 123-55E	AP	6900	T3/3NSR	S	AIJ	3	A-AP	Nittai M.	6484	S	03-18N 123-56E	
3	HMS SEA ROVER	1	Malacca Strait	Cstr	700	G	S								
4/00	265 PETO	5	01-28S 138-40E	AK	4400	T2/6NUP	S	AIJ	3-4	A-AK	Kayo M.	4368	S	01-40S 138-50E	
4/01	309 ASPRO	2	09-12N 153-38E	APK	11600	T1/6NSV	D								
4/07	222 BLUEFISH	4	05-32N 109-09E	AO	7500	T3/3DUP	S	AJ IW	4	XAO	Ominesan M. Taihosan M.	10536	S	05-29N 108-46E	W lists Taihosan M as both XAO & Std AO 1TL, sunk here; Ominesan M as XAO, same tons, fate unk.
5/03	269 RASHER	3	02-43N 126-44E	AK	7100	T1/4NSR	D								
5	HMS SURF	1	Aroa Is.	Ltr	800	G	D								
5	HMS SURF	1	Aroa Is.	Tug	250	G	S								

Dt/Hr	Submarine	Pt	Position	Tgt	Size	Attack	Cl	So	Date	Type	Name	Tons	Dm	Location	Comments
MAR	1944														
6/06	168 NAUTILUS	8	21-50N 143-54E	APK	6100	T2/2TUP	S	AIJW	6	XAP	America M.	6069	S	22-19N 143-54E	
6/06	168 NAUTILUS	8	21-50N 143-54E	APK	8400	T2/2TUP	D								
--							-	I	6	B-AG	Shofuku M. #2	729	M	15-52N 094-17E	No likely sub attack. Ship not in W.
6	HMS SEA ROVER	1	Malacca Strait	Cstr	750	G	D								
8	HMS SEA ROVER	1	03-38N 099-12E	MV	4000	T2/6	S	AIW J	8	XAP	Shobu M.	2005 1950	S	03-38N 099-22E	
9/01	260 LAPON	3	19-47N 115-56E	AO	10000	T2/4NUP	S	AIJ	8	C-AK	Toyokuni M.	5792	S	19-21N 116-09E	
9/01	260 LAPON	3	19-47N 115-56E	AK	6300	T2/3NUP	S	AIJ	9	C-AK	Nichirei M.	5396	S	19-44N 115-52E	
9/13	212 GATO	8	00-20S 135-23E	Tra	100	GD	S								
10/09	260 LAPON	3	19-27N 118-23E	Sam		GD	D								
11/15	287 BOWFIN	4	01-30S 128-18E	APK	6800	T6/7DUP	S	AI J	10-1	A-AK	Tsukikawa M.	4673 4470	S	01-18S 128-12E	
11/24	287 BOWFIN	4	02-18S 128-04E	APK	4700	T1/14NSP	D								
12/08	212 GATO	8	01- S 133- E	AK	2000	GD	S	AJ I	12	A-AK	Okinoyama M #3 Okinoyama M.	871	S	00-20S 132-08E	
12/08	212 GATO	8	01- S 133- E	Tra	100	GD	S								
12/09	229 FLYING FISH	9	25-53N 131-19E	AK	2000	T2/2DUP	S	A IJ	12	C-AK	Taijin M.	1924 1937	S	Kita-Oagari J.	
12	HMS STORM	1	Malacca Strait	Cstr	500	G	S								
13/03	381 SAND LANCE	1	32-58N 138-52E	CL	3500	T1/2NUP	S	AIW J	13	CL	Tatsuta	3230 3300	S	32-37N 139-17E	
13/03	381 SAND LANCE	1	32-58N 138-52E	AK	6000	T2/2NUP	D								
13/03	381 SAND LANCE	1	32-58N 138-52E	AK	5200	T2/2NUP	S	AIJW	12-3	XAK	Kokuyo M.	4667	S	32-52N 139-12E	
13/14	199 TAUTOG	10	47-40N 152-50E	AK	2900	T2/7DUP	S	AI J	13	A-AK	Ryua M.	1915 1925	S	47-39N 152-45E	
13/15	199 TAUTOG	10	47-41N 152-41E	AK	2800	T1/3DUP	S	AIJ	13	A-AK	Shojin M.	1942	S	47-39N 152-45E	

Dt/Hr	Submarine	Pt	Position	Tgt	Size	Attack	Cl	So	Date	Type	Name	Tons	Dm	Location	Comments
MAR	1944														
15/10	260 LAPON	3	19-57N 119-46E	Sam	100	GD	S								
16/02	229 FLYING FISH	9	27-41N 127-41E	AK	5000	T2/2NUP	S	AIJ	16	C-AK	Anzan M.	5493	S	27-38N 128-58E	
16/06	229 FLYING FISH	9	28-06N 128-57E	AO	7500	T2/12DUP	D								
16/16	236 SILVERSIDES	9	00-28N 136-56E	AK	4500	T2/3DUP	S	AIJ	16	A-AK	Kofuku M.	1919	S	00-07N 137-00E	SORG gives incorrect latitude 04-28N.
16/21	199 TAUTOG	10	42-35N 144-45E	AK	4000	T1/4NSV	S	AIJ	16	A-AK	Nichiren M.	5460	S	42-18N 145-11E	
16/21	199 TAUTOG	10	42-35N 144-45E	AK	4000	T2/ NSV	D	AIW J	16	DD	Shirakumo	2090 1950	S	42-20N 144-55E	
16/21	260 LAPON	3	18-22N 117-22E	APK	8400	T3/6NSR	S								
16/24	199 TAUTOG	10	42-25N 144-55E	AK	4000	T1/3NSV	S								
16/24	199 TAUTOG	10	42-25N 144-55E	AK	4000	T2/4NSV	S								
16/24	199 TAUTOG	10	42-25N 144-55E	AK	4000	T1/ NSV	D								
18/00	260 LAPON	3	19-22N 116-52E	AO	8000	T2/2NUP	S	AI J	18	XAP	Hokuriku M. Hokuroku M.	8359	S	19-24N 116-50E	W gives name Hokuriki M.
18/00	260 LAPON	3	19-22N 116-52E	CVS	6900	T2/2NUP	D								
18/14	382 PICUDA	1	12-36N 141-17E	AO	7500	T2/4DUP	D	I	20	XAE	Aratama M.	6783	?	Near Guam	Sunk 8 Apr by 304 SEAHORSE.
18/17	271 RAY	3	07-25S 115-20E	DE	500	T1/6DUP	D								
--							-	AIW	18	XPkt	Kunimiya M.	104	S	37-00N 151-00E	No likely sub attack.
--							-	AIW	18	XPkt	Bangame M. #3	99	S	38-00N 151-00E	No likely sub attack.
20/02	180 POLLACK	9	30-53N 140-42E	AK	5000	T1/2NSR	S	AJ IW	20	XAK	Hakuyo M. Shirataka M.	1327	S	30-40N 140-42E	
20/02	382 PICUDA	1	10-06N 138-10E	APK	6500	T2/4NUP	S	AIJ W	20	XAF	Hoko M. Hokko M.	1504	S	10-09N 138-10E	I gives tons as 1521.
21/23	241 BASHAW	1	06-55N 136-17E	AK	4200	T1/6NSR	D	A I	21	XARS	Uragami M. Urakami M.	4317	M	06-58N 136-29E	
22/07	282 TUNNY	5	07-12N 132-07E	AK	9000	T1/3DUP	D	I	20	AO	Iro	14050	H	07-22N 132-08E	
22/07	282 TUNNY	5	07-12N 132-07E	AK	9000	T3/3DUP	D								

MAR	1944														
22/07	282 TUNNY	5	07-12N 132-07E	DD	1200	T3/4DUP	D								
22/15	215 GROWLER	8	28-03N 129-21E	AK	3000	T1/4DUP	D								
23/21	255 HADDO	5	14-34N 109-25E	AK	2500	GN	D								
23/23	233 HERRING	7	31-42N 132-58E	DD	1400	T1/3DUP	D								
23/23	282 TUNNY	5	06-40N 134-03E	SS	2100	T2/4NSR	S	IW J	23	SS	I-42	2230 2212	S	Missing	I says given up 27 Apr.
24/23	287 BOWFIN	4	05-27N 125-39E	AK	7400	T3/5NSR	S	AIW J	25	XAP	Shinkyo M.	2672 5139	S	05-37N 125-58E	J confuses ship with 5139T Shinkyo M sunk by 382 PICUDA 3 Mar.
24/23	287 BOWFIN	4	05-27N 125-39E	AK	6800	T2/ NSR	S	AIJ	24-5	A-AK	Bengal M.	5399	S	05-38N 125-58E	
24/23	287 BOWFIN	4	05-27N 125-39E	AK	6800	T2/2NSR	D								
25/00	180 POLLACK	9	28-34N 142-14E	DD	1400	T1/4NSR	S	AIW J	25	PC	Ch 54	442 300	S	N Chichi Jima	A says sinking was joint with a/c.
25/00	180 POLLACK	9	28-34N 142-14E	AK	4000	T2/ NSR	D								
25/01	185 SNAPPER	9	28-55N 142-03E	AK	7000	T2/4NSR	D								
25/02	180 POLLACK	9	28-17N 142-14E	AK	7500	T2/4NSR	S								
25/02	180 POLLACK	9	28-17N 142-14E	AK	7500	T2/2NSP	S								
26 U	284 TULLIBEE	4L	N of Palau	AP	Unk	Unk	S								Attack not in SORG; U says survivor claimed this sinking.
27/09	269 RASHER	3	07-32S 115-57E	AK	5900	T1/4DUP	S	AI J	27	A-AK	Nichinan M.	2732 2750	S	07-27S 115-55E	
27/09	269 RASHER	3	07-32S 115-57E	APK	4500	T2/2DUP	S								
27/20	256 HAKE	4	03-52S 109-40E	AO	10000	T2/5NSV	S	AI J	27	C-AO	Yamamizu M.	5154 5174	S	03-53S 109-42E	
28/13	236 SILVERSIDES	9	00-55S 134-14E	AK	3000	T1/4DUP	S	W	27	LST	SS 3	948	S	01- S 134-10E	[Attribution ?]
28/24	220 BARB	7	24-25N 131-11E	Q	2200	T2/3NSR	S	AIJ	28-9	C-AK	Fukusei M.	2219	S	S of Daito Is.	

Dt/Hr	Submarine	Pt	Position	Tgt	Size	Attack	Cl	So	Date	Type	Name	Tons	Dm	Location	Comments
MAR	1944														
28	HMS TRUCULENT	2	Malacca Strait	AK	1000	T3/4	S	AJ I	28	A-AK	Yasushima M. Yasujima M.	1910	S	03-38N 100-50E	
29/05	255 HADDO	5	17-40N 109-54E	AK	6000	T2/4NSR	S	I	29	C-AK	Nichian M.	6197	L	17-42N 109-57E	
29/18	282 TUNNY	5	07-30N 134-30E	BB	42000	T2/6DUP	D	AI	29	BB	Musashi	64170	M	Off Palau	
30/03	227 DARTER	2	01-56N 133-00E	AK	6800	T4/6NSR	S	AIJ	30	A-AK	Fujikawa M.	2829	S	01-50N 133-25E	
30/05	186 STINGRAY	10	20-42N 143-00E	APK	8600	T3/8NSR	S	AIJ W	30 Note	XAP	Ikushima M.	3943	S	20-43N 143-04E	W gives date 30 Apr. [Probably misprint.]
30/18	382 PICUDA	1	12-15N 145-42E	AK	7100	T2/5DUP	S	AIJW	30	XAP	Atlantic M.	5872	S	12-20N 145-55E	
APR	1944														
1/02	255 HADDO	5	16-36N 109-07E	AK	2500	T1/2NSR	D								
1/08	229 FLYING FISH	9	25-56N 131-18E	AK	3500	T2/2DUP	S	AJ I	1	A-AK	Minami M.	2398	S	25-59N 131-19E 35-59N 131-19E	[Location in I probably misprint.]
1	HMS TRUCULENT	2	Malacca Strait	MV	200	S		S	Note			Mantai				Name from "Success Book."
2/04	256 HAKE	4	01-52N 106-25E	AK	6000	T2/3NSR	D	I	2	XAO	Tarakan M.	5135	H	01-52N 106-11E	W lists ship as both XAO & Std AO 1TM.
2/05	256 HAKE	4	01-52N 106-20E	AO	10400	T3/7NSR	S								
3/15	180 POLLACK	9	30-00N 139-44E	AK	7000	T2/4DUP	D	AIJ	3	A-AK	Tosei M.	2814	S	30-14N 139-45E	
4/18	277 SCAMP	7	02-43N 130-00E	Tra	200	GT	D								
5/05	193 SWORDFISH	11	20-23N 141-22E	AK	5000	T1/4NSR	D								
5/05	193 SWORDFISH	11	20-23N 141-22E	AK	5000	T2/4NSR	D								
8/02	304 SEAHORSE	4	13-16N 144-55E	AK	6800	T3/3NUR	S	AJW I	8	XAE	Aratama M.	6783	S H	13-16N 145-11E	
8/02	304 SEAHORSE	4	13-16N 144-55E	AK	3900	T1/3NUR	S	AIW J	8	XAW	Kizugawa M.	1915	H S	13-16N 145-11E	
8/04	237 TRIGGER	9	19-06N 142-31E	AO	10000	T2/4NUP	D								
8/04	237 TRIGGER	9	19-06N 142-31E	AK	4000	T1/ NUP	D								
8/04	237 TRIGGER	9	19-06N 142-31E	AK	4000	T1/ NUP	D								

Dt/Hr		Submarine	Pt	Position	Tgt	Size	Attack	Cl	So	Date	Type	Name	Tons	Dm	Location	Comments
APR	1944															
9/02	239	WHALE	7	33-45N 128-42E	AK	5000	T2/7NUP	S	IA J	20 9	C-AK	Honan M.	5401	S	33-50N 128-01E	PR says seen to sink. No likely attack 20 Apr. [Possibly delayed sinking or date incorrect; attribution ?]
9/17	304	SEAHORSE	4	15-22N 145-06E	AK	7500	T2/6DUP	S	AIW J	9	XAP	Mimasaka M. Bisaku M.	4667 4467	S	15-30N 145-00E	I & W give name Misaku M; W lists as both XAP & Std AK 1B; I gives tons as 4500.
10/14	215	GROWLER	8	24-28N 144-42E	Pat	300	GD	S								
10/22	383	PAMPANITO	1	09-40N 143-30E	AK	7000	T2/4NUP	D								
11/17	272	REDFIN	2	06-43N 122-23E	DD	1500	T3/4DUP	S	AIW J	11	DD	Akigumo	2077 1900	S	Zamboanga Lt.	
12/02	232	HALIBUT	9	28-07N 129-01E	AK	8000	T1/3NUP	D	AIJW	12	C-APK	Taichu M.	3213	S	28-08N 128-57E	
12/19	237	TRIGGER	9	10-26N 134-29E	Sam	100	GT	D								
12/21	230	FINBACK	8	09-39N 147-50E	AK	4000	T2/3NSR	D								
12/21	230	FINBACK	8	09-39N 147-50E	AK	4000	T2/3NSR	D								
12/21	230	FINBACK	8	09-39N 147-50E	AK	4000	T1/ NSR	D								
13/19	257	HARDER	4	10-13N 143-51E	DD	1700	T2/4DUP	S	AIW J	13-4	DD	Ikazuchi	2090 1950	S	10-00N 143-48E	I says missing, cause unk.
14	S	HMS STORM	2	Malacca Strait	AK	3500	T2/6	S								BSK evaluates attack unsuccessful.
15/23	272	REDFIN	2	06-41N 123-40E	AK	4000	T3/3NSR	S	AI J	16 15	A-AK	Shinyu M.	4621	H S	06-22N 123-42E	
15/23	272	REDFIN	2	06-41N 123-40E	AO	10000	T2/3NSR	S								
15	S	HMS STORM	2	Malacca Strait	AK	4000	T2/2	D								BSH evaluates attack unsuccessful.
15		HMS STORM	2	11-34N 093-08E	DD	Unk	T2/2	S	AIW J	15	AM	W 7	750 630	S	Andaman Is.	
15	280	STEELHEAD	1	42-07N 143-21E	--	--	Mine	U	AJ I	15	C-AK	Sumida M.	2022	PM S	42-04N 142-22E	Minefields laid 12 & 30 May 43. [Attribution ?; mines 10 months old.]
16/02	263	PADDLE	3	02-20S 127-20E	AK	9400	T3/6NUP	S	AIJ	15-6	A-AP	Mito M.	7061	S	02-25S 127-24E	
16/02	263	PADDLE	3	02-20S 127-20E	AO	7300	T1/2NUP	D	AIJ	15-6	C-AK	Hino M. #1	2671	S	02-25S 127-24E	

Dt/Hr	Submarine	Pt	Position	Tgt	Size	Attack	Cl	So	Date	Type	Name	Tons	Dm	Location	Comments
APR	1944														
16/02	263 PADDLE	3	02-20S 127-20E	DD	1400	T1/2NUP	S								
16/02	272 REDFIN	2	07-04N 123-27E	AK	7200	T2/3NSR	S	AIJ	16	A-AK	Yamagata M.	3807	S	06-51N 123-37E	
16/02	272 REDFIN	2	07-04N 123-27E	AK	7500	T2/3NSR	S								
17	257 HARDER	4	09-22N 142-18E	AK	3600	T1/4NUP	S	AJ I	17	A-AK	Matsue M.	7061	S	09-30N 142-35E 10-30N 142-44E	[Location in I may be misprint.]
17	257 HARDER	4	09-22N 142-18E	DD	1700	T1/ NUP	D								
17/18	196 SEARAVEN	11	25-52N 142-24E	AK	5500	T2/4DUP	S	AI W	17 1	XAM	Noshiro M. #2	216	S	S Haha Jima	W credits 231 HADDOCK 1 Apr; PR shows no such attack. [Attribution ?]
18/06	198 TAMBOR	10	22-07N 160-31E	Tra	300	GD	S								
19/12	230 FINBACK	8	08-22N 151-41E	Sam	100	GD	S								
19	HMS TANTALUS	1	Malacca Strait	Tug	300	G	S	Note			Kampung Besar				Name from "Success Book."
20/10	304 SEAHORSE	4	15-19N 145-31E	SS	700	T1/2DUP	D	Note J	20	SS	I-174 RO-45	1420 965	S	Sub position	RO-45 not sunk here; I-174 believed lost to either this attack or operational casualty; I says given up 13 Apr. [J attribution ?]
22/04	362 GUAVINA	1	27-37N 141-46E	Tra	500	GN	S								
22	HMS TAURUS	5	07-10N 099-20E	Cstr	500	G	S	AI JW	22	ARS	Hokuan I-Go Hokuan	558 534	S	07-14N 099-14E	I gives name Hokuan M I-Go; BSH Gio Hokuan; ship was ex-Dutch Rokan.
22	HMS TAURUS	5	Off Penang	Tug		G	S								
22	S HMS SEA ROVER	2	N Sumatra	Cstr	500	G	S								
23/07	194 SEADRAGON	10	33-35N 135-45E	AK	3500	T1/3DUP	D	AI J	23	C-AK	Taiju M. Daiju M.	6886 1279	S	Shionomisaki	J confuses ship with 1279T Daiju M sunk 18 Mar by a/c.
23	199 TAUTOG	4	02-10S 116-40E	--	--	Mine	U	IW J	23	DD	Amagiri	2090 1950	SM	02-12S 116-45E	Minefield laid 7 Mar 43. J credits US Army (a/c) mine. [Attribution ?; mines 13 months old.]
23	N HNMS K-XV	6	New Guinea	Prau	10	G	S								Patrol not in BSH; K-XV operated from Fremantle under US control for Neth Forces Intelligence Svc.
23	N HNMS K-XV	6	New Guinea	Cstr	50	G	S								See note above.

Dt/Hr	Submarine	Pt	Position	Tgt	Size	Attack	Cl	So	Date	Type	Name	Tons	Dm	Location	Comments
APR	1944														
24/02 231 HADDOCK		9	26-46N 130-56E	AK	1000	T1/2NSR	S								
25/07 362 GUAVINA		1	28-55N 140-28E	AK	9300	T3/7DUP	S	I	25	A-AK	Tetsuyo M.	2130	?	NW Chichi Jima	
25/12 291 CREVALLE		3	07-09N 116-48E	AK	7000	T2/6DUP	S	AIJW	25	A-AK	Kashiwa M.	976	S	07-10N 116-45E	W says ship former XAN.
25/13 276 SAWFISH		6	30-32N 140-10E	AK	5100	T2/4DUP	S								
26/02 259 JACK		4	18-14N 119-53E	AK	4000	T4/6NSR	D	I	27	A-AK	Wales M.	6586	L	19-20N 118-50E	[Attribution ?]
26/03 259 JACK		4	18-06N 119-47E	AK	4000	T2/4NSR	D	AIJ	26	A-AP	Yoshida M. #1	5425	S	18-06N 119-40E	
26/03 259 JACK		4	18-06N 119-47E	AK	4000	T2/3NSR	D								
26/03 259 JACK		4	18-06N 119-47E	AK	4000	T2/3NSR	D								
26/05 259 JACK		4	18-04N 119-48E	AK	4000	T2/2NSR	D								
26/08 188 SARGO		11	33-30N 135-27E	AK	5000	T3/4DUP	S	AIJ	26	A-AK	Wazan M.	4851	S	33-31N 135-24E	
26/10 362 GUAVINA		1	28-37N 141-00E	AK	5700	T3/3DUP	S	AI JW	26	XAP	Noshiro M I-Go Noshiro M.	2333	S	28-42N 141-26E	
26/10 362 GUAVINA		1	28-37N 141-00E	AK	4000	T2/3DUP	S								
26/23 223 BONEFISH		4	06-12N 125-47E	AK	4100	T2/4NSR	S	J	26	APK	Tokiwa M.	806	S	Sub position	A says no record of ship. [J attribution ?]
26/23 223 BONEFISH		4	06-12N 125-47E	Smc	500	T1/ NSR	D								
27/01 237 TRIGGER		9	08-20N 134-53E	APK	7500	T1/3NSR	S	AIJW	27	XAP	Miike M.	11738	S	08-34N 134-53E	
27/01 237 TRIGGER		9	08-20N 134-53E	APK	7500	T1/3NSR	S								
27/01 237 TRIGGER		9	08-20N 134-53E	APK	7500	T2/ NSR	S								
27/01 304 SEAHORSE		4	14-50N 142-23E	AK	7500	T3/4NUR	S	AIW J	27	XAP	Akikawa M. Akigawa M.	5244	S	14-46N 143-22E	
27/03 237 TRIGGER		9	08-29N 135-55E	APK	9800	T2/4NSR	S	I	27	A-AK	Asosan M.	8811	M	08-34N 134-48E	
27/03 237 TRIGGER		9	08-29N 135-55E	ODD	900	T1/9NSR	S	I	27	PF	Kasado	870	M	08-33N 134-48E	
27/03 232 HALIBUT		9	27-12N 128-13E	AK	5000	T1/3NSR	D								

Dt/Hr	Submarine	Pt	Position	Tgt	Size	Attack	Cl	So	Date	Type	Name	Tons	Dm	Location	Comments
APR	1944														
27/04	221 BLACKFISH	8	05-35N 133-17E	DD	3500	T1/4NSR	D								PR says possible hit on large DD or CL. [Probably Yubari.] See 242 BLUEGILL below.
27/05	232 HALIBUT	9	27-20N 128-15E	AK	4000	T2/3NSR	S	AJ I	27	C-AP	Genbu M. Gembu M.	1872	S	27-16N 128-21E	
27/06	223 BONEFISH	4	05-33N 125-21E	AK	4500	T3/4DUP	S								
27/09	232 HALIBUT	9	27-37N 128-11E	CM	600	T2/4DUP	S	AIJW	27	PF	Kamome	450	S	N of Naha	W lists as ex-CM.
27/11	242 BLUEGILL	1	05-20N 132-16E	CL	2900	T2/6DUP	S	AIW J	27-8	CL	Yubari	2890 3500	S	05-29N 131-45E	
27/11	259 JACK	4	19-32N 122-21E	Tra		GD	S								
27/12	194 SEADRAGON	10	33-32N 135-59E	AK	5000	T1/3DUP	D	I	27	C-AK	Hawaii M.	9467	H	33-16N 135-48E	
27/20	241 BASHAW	1	03-20N 131-35E	Tra	100	GT	S								
27/20	241 BASHAW	1	03-20N 131-35E	3Tra	200	GT	D								
27	HMS TAURUS	5	05-03N 100-12E	--	--	Mine	U	I	27	SS	I-37	2198	LM	S of Penang	Minefield laid 18 Apr; damage not claimed in BSH. [Attribution ?]
28	259 JACK	4	17-34N 124-06E	Tra	100	GT	S								
29/01	266 POGY	6	32-07N 133-03E	SS	1800	T1/4NSR	S	IJW	28-9	SS	I-183	1630	S	Sub position	I says given up 28 May.
29/21	385 BANG	1	19-26N 118-45E	AK	7000	T2/4NUP	D	AI J	29	A-AK	Takekawa M. Takegawa M.	1930	S	19-20N 118-50E	
29/21	385 BANG	1	19-26N 118-45E	AO	8000	T1/2NUP	D								
29/23	249 FLASHER	2	13-02N 109-28E	AK	6000	T1/3NUP	D	A J	29	AK	Song Giang Go Song Giang M.	1065	S	Hone Cohe FIC	
29	199 TAUTOG	4	02-10S 116-40E	--	--	Mine	U	I	29	XAP	Kunikawa M.	6863	MM	Balikpapan	Minefield laid 7 Mar 43. [Attribution ?; mines 10 months old.]
29	HMS TANTALUS	1	Malacca Strait	Cstr	400	G	S					Pulo Salanama				Name from "Success Book."
30/00	249 FLASHER	2	13-02N 109-28E	AK	4000	T1/4NUP	S	J	29	PR	Tahure	644	S	Sub position	No such Japanese ship. PR says believed sunk. [J attribution ?]
30/03	385 BANG	1	19-11N 119-10E	AP	10400	T2/14NSR	S	AIJ	30	C-AO	Nittatsu M.	2859	S	19-04N 119-14E	

Dt/Hr	Submarine	Pt	Position	Tgt	Size	Attack	Cl	So	Date	Type	Name	Tons	Dm	Location	Comments
APR	1944														
30/09	283 TINOSA	6	18-15N 120-18E	AO	7500	T1/6DUP	D								
30/09	283 TINOSA	6	18-15N 120-18E	AK	5500	T1/ DUP	S								
30/09	283 TINOSA	6	18-15N 120-18E	AK	5500	T2/ DUP	S								
30/10	384 PARCHE	1	18-22N 119-17E	AK	6500	T1/2DUP	D								
30/14	280 STEELHEAD	5	26-10N 125-34E	Tra	300	GD	S								
MAY	1944														
1/19	196 SEARAVEN	11	25-43N 142-41E	PY	1000	T1/3TUP	S								
2/02	264 PARGO	3	03-40N 128-40E	AO	10100	T2/4NSR	S								
2/07	242 BLUEGILL	1	07-07N 129-56E	AK	8800	T2/4+G	S	AIJ	1	A-AK	Asosan M.	8811	S	07-08N 130-00E	PR says left afire & abandoned after gun attack.
2/13	199 TAUTOG	11	48- N 152- E	AK	6000	T2/6DUP	S	AIJ	2	A-AP	Ryoyo M.	5973	S	N Pacific	
2	HMS TANTALUS	1	11-00N 092-00E	AK	4000	T2/7	S	AIJ	3	A-AK	Amagi M.	3165	S	10-52N 093-12E	
3/04	381 SAND LANCE	2	15-29N 145-42E	AK	5800	T1/6TUR	S	AIJW	3	XAP	Kenan M.	3129	S	15-20N 145-34E	
3/12	199 TAUTOG	11	45-28N 149-56E	AK	5600	T2/4DSR	S	AIJ	3	A-AK	Fushimi M.	4935	S	45-30N 149-10E	
3/12	249 FLASHER	2	12-54N 114-07E	AK	7500	T5/12DUP	S	AIJ	3	C-AK	Teisen M.	5050	S	12-50N 114-10E	
3/18	305 SKATE	4	29-46N 137-02E	AK	8600	T2/4DUP	D								
3/21	232 HALIBUT	9	27- N 128-22E	Sam	200	GN	S								
3/23	283 TINOSA	6	20-51N 118-02E	AO	10500	T2/3NUP	S	AIJ	4	C-AK	Toyohi M.	6436	S	20-50N 118-00E	PR says seen to sink.
3/23	283 TINOSA	6	20-51N 118-02E	AK	6000	T1/3NUP	D								PR says hit seen & heard.
3 N	283 TINOSA	6	20-51N 118-02E	AK	6000	T1/ NUP	D	Note							Attack not in SORG. PR says 2nd AK stopped & afire.
3/23	291 CREVALLE	3	05-05N 114-36E	XAO	7500	T2/4NUR	D								
4/01	384 PARCHE	1	20-48N 118-03E	AK	6700	T3/4NSR	S	AIJ	4	C-AK	Shoryu M.	6475	S	20-50N 117-55E	
4/01	384 PARCHE	1	20-48N 118-03E	AK	6800	T2/2NSR	S	AI J	4	C-AK	Taiyoku M.	5244	S PS	20-50N 117-55E	

Dt/Hr	Submarine	Pt	Position	Tgt	Size	Attack	Cl	So	Date	Type	Name	Tons	Dm	Location	Comments
MAY	1944														
4/01	384 PARCHE	1	20-48N 118-03E	AP	10400	T2/4NSR	S								PR says 3 ships hit, 2 sank, 3rd last seen with deck awash.
4/03	283 TINOSA	6	20-55N 118-12E	AK	9500	T3/4NSR	S	AI J	4	C-AK	Taibu M.	6440	S PS	20-50N 117-55E	PR says ship disintegrated.
4/04	385 BANG	1	20-58N 117-59E	AK	7500	T2/4NSR	S	AI J	4	C-AK	Kinrei M.	5945	S PS	20-50N 117-55E	PR says AK exploded.
4/04	385 BANG	1	20-58N 117-59E	DD	2300	T1/ NSR	S								
4/04	283 TINOSA	6	21-02N 118-03E	AK	6000	T1/4NSR	D								
4/10	203 TUNA	10	22-06N 166-47E	Tra	100	GD	S	AIW	4	XPkt	Tajima M.	89	S	22-10N 166-50E	
4/16	264 PARGO	3	07-04N 129-18E	AK	2100	T2/3DUP	S	AIJW	4	XAN	Eiryu M.	758	S	07-14N 129-12E	
4/17	264 PARGO	3	07-04N 129-18E	AK	3200	T1/5DUP	D								
5/10	266 POGY	6	33-31N 135-28E	AK	5200	T1/3DUP	S	AIJW	5	XAP	Shirane M.	2825	S	33-30N 135-31E	W lists ship as both XAP & Std AK 1C.
6/04	190 SPEARFISH	11	32-16N 127-08E	AK	6500	T2/4NSR	S	I	6	AF	Mamiya	15820	M	32-12N 127-02E	
6/07	291 CREVALLE	3	07-17N 116-15E	AO	19400	T3/4DUP	S	AIJW	6	XAO	Nisshin M.	16801	S	07-19N 116-52E	
6/12	190 SPEARFISH	11	32-16N 127-08E	AK	8400	T3/8DUP	S	AIJ	6	C-AK	Toyoura M.	2510	S	32-18N 127-11E	
6/13	254 GURNARD	5	02-42N 124-10E	AK	7500	T2/2DUP	S	AIJ	6	A-AK	Aden M.	5823	S	02-43N 124-07E	
6/13	254 GURNARD	5	02-42N 124-10E	AK	4000	T2/2DUP	S	AI J	6	A-AK	Tajima M. Taijima M.	6995	S	02-24N 124-07E	
6/13	254 GURNARD	5	02-42N 124-10E	AK	4000	T1/1DUP	D								
7/01	254 GURNARD	5	02-51N 124-07E	AK	5400	T1/1NSP	S	AI J	6-7	A-AK	Amatsusan M. Tenshinzan M.	6886	S	02-24N 124-07E	
7/05	249 FLASHER	2	08-37N 121-16E	AK	7500	T1/2TUP	D								
7/09	312 BURRFISH	2	33-13N 134-14E	AO	5000	T3/3DUP	S	J I	7	AO ?	Rossbach	5894 ?	S	S Murotosaki	
7/18	223 BONEFISH	4	07-07N 121-50E	AP	8800	T3/4DUP	S	I	7	A-AK	Aobasan M.	8811	L	07-10N 121-50E	
7	HMS TANTIVY	2	W coast Siam	Jk	150	G	S								

Dt/Hr	Submarine	Pt	Position	Tgt	Size	Attack	Cl	So	Date	Type	Name	Tons	Dm	Location	Comments
MAY	1944														
8/05	258 HOE	4	19-22N 120-13E	AK	7500	T1/4TUP	D	I	8	PF	Sado	870	?	19-19N 120-19E	PR says 2 hits heard on large convoy.
8/05	258 HOE	4	19-22N 120-13E	AO	4000	T1/2TUP	D	I	8	C-AO	Akane M.	10241	H	19-19N 120-19E	
8/10	199 TAUTOG	11	41-50N 141-12E	AK	4900	T2/5DUP	S	AIJ	8		C-AK Miyazaki M.	3943	S	41-52N 141-12E	
8/15	236 SILVERSIDES	10	13-33N 144-34E	AK	5000	T1/4DUP	D								
9/16	283 TINOSA	6	22-20N 146-40E	Tra	200	GD	S								
10/04	187 STURGEON	10	29-30N 141-40E	AK	5800	T3/4NUP	S								
10/06	224 COD	3	15-38N 119-25E	DD	1300	T2/3DUP	S	AJW	10	DD	Karukaya	820	S	Off Manila Bay	
10/06	224 COD	3	15-38N 119-25E	AP	6000	T1/2DUP	D								
10/06	224 COD	3	15-38N 119-25E	AK	8800	T3/3DUP	S	AIJW	10	XAP	Shohei M.	7255	S	15-38N 119-32E	
10/06	224 COD	3	15-38N 119-25E	AK	5400	T1/1DUP	D								
10/06	236 SILVERSIDES	10	11-26N 143-46E	AP	6300	T2/2TUP	S	AJW	10	XAP	Mikage M. #18	4319	S	Off Saipan	
10/06	236 SILVERSIDES	10	11-26N 143-46E	AP	4300	T1/1TUP	S	AIJW	10	XARC	Okinawa M.	2256	S	11-31N 143-41E	
10/06	236 SILVERSIDES	10	11-26N 143-46E	AK	5000	T1/2TUP	S	AJW I	10	XPG	Choan M. #2	2613 2631	S	11-31N 143-41E	
10/06	236 SILVERSIDES	10	11-26N 143-46E	AK	5000	T1/1TUP	D								
10/11	187 STURGEON	10	27-50N 141-45E	AK	4100	T2/4DUP	S								
10/18	198 TAMBOR	10	19-26N 140-19E	AK	6000	T2/4DUP	D	AI	10	XAPV	Keiyo M.	6442	L	19-27N 140-00E	
11/04	187 STURGEON	10	29-30N 141-40E	AK	5500	T2/4NUP	S	AIJ	11	A-AK	Seiryu M.	1904	S	29-42N 141-35E	
11/09	307 TILEFISH	1	33-27N 135-38E	AP	17100	T1/4DUP	D								
11/09	307 TILEFISH	1	33-27N 135-38E	ODD	900	T1/ DUP	D								
11/15	381 SAND LANCE	2	14-58N 145-26E	AK	6500	T2/4DUP	D	AIJW	11	XAP	Mitakesan M.	4441	S	14-57N 145-30E	
11/20	269 RASHER	4	03-08S 126-01E	CM	1700	T1/1NSR	D								
11/23	269 RASHER	4	03-30S 126-06E	AK	4000	T1/9NUR	S	AIJ	11-2	B-AG	Choi M.	1074	S	03-28S 126-03E	Ship not in W.
12/07	199 TAUTOG	11	40-01N 141-58E	AK	4000	T2/3DUP	S	AIJ	12	C-AC	Banei M. #2	1186	S	40-00N 141-58E	

Dt/Hr	Submarine	Pt	Position	Tgt	Size	Attack	Cl	So	Date	Type	Name	Tons	Dm	Location	Comments
MAY	1944														
12/10	269 RASHER	4	03-42S 127-16E	AP	4000	T1/14DUP	D								
12	HMS TAURUS	5	05-03N 100-12E	--	--	Mine	U	AIW J	12	XAP	Kasumi M.	971 1400	SM	03-24N 099-29E	Minefield laid 18 Apr. J & W confuse ship with 1400T ARS Kasumi M sunk 30 May 45.
13/21	266 POGY	6	34-31N 138-33E	AK	5800	T2/3NSR	S	AIW J	13	XAK	Awa M. Anbo M.	4532	S	34-25N 138-40E	
14/03	223 BONEFISH	4	05-08N 119-38E	AO	10000	T2/5NUP	S								
14/03	223 BONEFISH	4	05-08N 119-38E	DD	1800	T0/5NUP	O	AIW J	14	DD	Inazuma	2000 1950	S	05-03N 119-36E	PR says 2 hits seen on convoy of 3 AOs & 3 DDs.
14/06	287 BOWFIN	5	08-53N 133-35E	AK	6500	T2/6DUP	S	A J	14	XAK	Miyama M. Bisan M.	4667 4500	S JS	08-55N 133-42E	J credits BOWFIN & 309 ASPRO. PR says target down by stern after attack. I & W list as Bisan M, 4667T; I gives location 10-10N 131-42E.
14/06	309 ASPRO	3	09-04N 133-32E	AK	7500	T1/4DUP	S	A IJW	14	XAK	Miyama M. Bisan M.	4667 4500	JS	08-55N 133-42E	J credits ASPRO & 287 BOWFIN.
14/14	381 SAND LANCE	2	13-42N 144-43E	AK	4400	T2/4DUP	S	AIJ	14	A-AK	Koho M.	4291	S	13-43N 144-42E	
15/10	309 ASPRO	3	10-10N 131-25E	AK	4000	T1/2DUP	S	AIJW	15	XAP	Jokuja M.	6440	S	10-10N 131-48E	
16/17	266 POGY	6	33-56N 139-50E	Sam		GD	S								
17/00	273 ROBALO	2	11-13N 115-38E	AO	7500	T1/6NSR	S								
17/00	381 SAND LANCE	2	14-57N 144-47E	AK	8300	T2/4NUR	S	AIJW	17	XAP	Taikoku M.	2633	S	14-58N 144-49E	W lists ship as both XAP & Std AK 1C.
17/16	194 SEADRAGON	10	33-31N 155-25E	Tra	100	GD	S								
17/19	282 TUNNY	6	14-45N 142-40E	AK	5100	T1/3TUP	S	AIJ	17	A-AK	Nichiwa M.	4955	S	14-49N 142-27E	
17/21	381 SAND LANCE	2	14-55N 142-30E	AK	3800	T1/4NSR	S	AIJ	17	A-AK	Fukko M.	3834	S	14-49N 142-27E	
18/02	258 HOE	4	12-27N 116-35E	AK	4000	T1/5NSV	D								
18/05	268 PUFFER	4	07-36S 113-12E	AK	7500	T2/4TSR	S	AIJ	18	A-AK	Shinryu M.	3181	S	07-34S 113-18E	
18/08	254 GURNARD	5	06-06N 125-45E	BB	32700	T2/6DUP	D								
18	HMS TALLY HO	5	03-41N 099-04E	--	--	Mine	U	I	18	C-AO	Nichiyoku M.	1945	HM	03-40N 099-07E	Minefield laid 14 May.

Dt/Hr	Submarine	Pt	Position	Tgt	Size	Attack	Cl	So	Date	Type	Name	Tons	Dm	Location	Comments
MAY	1944														
19/11	305 SKATE	4	28-56N 141-38E	Sam	100	GD	S	I	19	XPkt	Meisho M.	31	S	Ogasawara	PR says 3 survivors picked up, target left afire & sinking. W credits 187 STURGEON but PR shows no such attack.
--							-	A I	19	A-AK	Ogi M.	200	SA S	Manokwari	No likely sub attack.
20/01	258 HOE	4	13-00N 119-10E	AK	4000	T2/3NSV	S								
20/02	258 HOE	4	13-00N 119-10E	AK	4000	T2/4NSV	D								
20/05	266 POGY	6	31-21N 140-03E	Sam	100	GD	S								
20/16	236 SILVERSIDES	10	13-32N 144-36E	AP	8000	T2/4DUP	D	AJW	20	XPG	Shosei M.	998	S	Off Saipan	
20/17	242 BLUEGILL	1	02-13N 128-01E	AK	1900	T3/4DUP	S	AIJ	20	A-AK	Miyaura M.	1856	S	02-14N 128-05E	
20/18	240 ANGLER	3	05-40S 105-28E	AP	5700	T1/4TUP	S	AJ IW	20	XAP	Otori M.	2105	S	05-57N 105-12E 05-57N 127-11E	W credits 271 RAY (see 22 May). A says owner gives location off Malaya, which agrees with ANGLER's position. [Location in I may be misprint.]
21	167 NARWHAL	11	07-52N 127-00E	AK	4000	T1/4NSR	D								
21	167 NARWHAL	11	07-52N 127-00E	AK	4000	T1/1NSR	D								
21/09	225 CERO	4	00-15N 128-55E	AK	4000	T1/4DUP	D								
21/09	286 BILLFISH	4	13-39N 140-45E	APK	8600	T1/3DUP	D	I	21	XAK	Bokuyo M.	2726	M	13-42N 140-41E	
21/09	286 BILLFISH	4	13-39N 140-45E	APK	8500	T3/3DUP	S								
22/01	271 RAY	4	05-42N 127-37E	AP	8600	T2/3NSR	S	AI J	22	A-AK	Tempei M. Tenpei M.	6097	S	05-16N 127-42E	
22/01	271 RAY	4	05-42N 127-37E	AO	10200	T1/1NSR	S								
22/01	271 RAY	4	05-42N 127-37E	AK	5800	T2/3NSR	S	IW	20	XAP	Otori M.	2105	S	05-57N 127-11E	J credits 240 ANGLER 20 May; A says owner gives location off Malaya. [Attribution ?; location in I may be misprint.]
22/01	271 RAY	4	05-42N 127-37E	CM	1400	T1/1NSR	S								
22/04	180 POLLACK	10	28-20N 138-57E	DD	1500	T3/4NSR	S	AIJW	22	DD	Asanagi	1270	S	NW Chichi Jima	

Dt/Hr	Submarine	Pt	Position	Tgt	Size	Attack	Cl	So	Date	Type	Name	Tons	Dm	Location	Comments
MAY	1944														
22/04	180 POLLACK	10	28-20N 138-57E	AK	4000	T1/ NSR	D								
22/10	268 PUFFER	4	04-37N 119-50E	CV	26900	T1/6DUP	D								
22/18	382 PICUDA	2	21-20N 117-10E	APK	7000	T1/4DUP	S	AIJ	22-3	C-APK	Tsukuba M.	3171	JS	21-18N 117-12E	J credits PICUDA & a/c. PR says ship damaged & stopped when found; Army plane reported down at this location.
22/18	382 PICUDA	2	21-20N 117-10E	Esc	1000	T1/ DUP	S	AIW J	22	PG	Hashidate	999 1200	S	21-08N 117-20E	
22	HMS SEA ROVER	3	04-55N 100-21E	AK	3000	T1/6	S	AIJW	22	XPG	Kosho M.	1365	S	04-52N 100-18E	
23/05	271 RAY	4	02-51N 128-00E	AP	8300	T4/6TSR	S	I	23	A-AO	Kenwa M.	6384	L	02-42N 128-08E	PR says target apparently sinking 1 hour after attack. See 225 CERO below. PRs indicate subs were not aware of each other. [Attribution ?]
23/05	271 RAY	4	02-51N 128-00E	AK	8200	T2/4TSR	S	AIJ	23	A-AK	Taijun M.	2825	S	02-42N 128-08E	PR says left with decks awash. J credits 225 CERO; see above note. [Attribution ?]
23/08	225 CERO	4	02-36N 128-08E	AK	4000	T2/3DUP	D	AIJ	23	A-AK	Taijun M.	2825	S	02-42N 128-08E	PR says not seen after attack. See 271 RAY above; PRs indicate subs were unaware of each other.
23/08	225 CERO	4	02-36N 128-08E	AK	7500	T2/3DUP	D	I	23	A-AO	Kenwa M.	6384	L	02-42N 128-08E	Same as above.
23/12	178 PERMIT	12	07-00N 150-20E	Sam	300	GD	D								
23/19	270 RATON	4	00-25N 107-34E	AK	1200	GD	S								
23/19	270 RATON	4	00-25N 107-34E	AK	600	GD	S	AI	23	C	Koshin M.	168	S	00-25S 107-45E	
23/23	260 LAPON	4	07-16N 109-04E	AK	7500	T1/10NSR	S	AIJ	24	A-AK	Wales M.	6586	S	07-20N 109-20E	
24/01	260 LAPON	4	07-26N 108-50E	AK	7500	T3/4NSR	S	AIJW	24	XAK	Bizen M.	4667	S	07-30N 109-08E	
24/01	270 RATON	4	01-17N 107-50E	DD	1700	T2/2NSR	S	AIW J	24	PF	Iki	870 860	S	01-17N 107-53E	
24/01	270 RATON	4	01-17N 107-50E	AP	10000	T1/2NSR	D	I	24	PF	Matsuwa	870	L	01-17N 107-53E	[Attribution ?]
24/03	260 LAPON	4	07-27N 108-42E	AK	7500	T2/6NSR	D								
24/03	313 PERCH	1	22-10N 118-30E	AO	5000	T4/6NSR	D								

102

Dt/Hr	Submarine	Pt	Position	Tgt	Size	Attack	Cl	So	Date	Type	Name	Tons	Dm	Location	Comments
MAY	1944														
24/06	269 RASHER	4	02-01S 127-28E	Mis		GD	S								
24/06	288 CABRILLA	4	02-04S 121-01E	AV	5500	T1/6DUP	D								
24/14	254 GURNARD	5	05-45N 125-45E	AO	10000	T3/4DUP	S	AIW J	24	XAO	Tatekawa M.	10009 10090	S	05-45N 125-43E	
25/10	229 FLYING FISH	10	11-30N 134-55E	AK	4000	T3/4DUP	S	AIJW	25	XAP	Taito M.	4466	S	11-12N 135-14E	
25/10	229 FLYING FISH	10	11-30N 134-55E	AK	4000	T1/4DUP	D	AIJ	25	C-AK	Osaka M.	3740	S	11-12N 135-14E	
26/15	178 PERMIT	12	07-05N 152- E	SS	2200	T1/6DUP	S	I	26	SS	I-44	2230	LU	?	[Attribution ?; location not given.]
26/15	288 CABRILLA	4	02-48N 124-19E	AK	8400	T4/5DUP	S	AIJW	26	XAP	Sanyo M.	8360	S	02-46N 124-22E	
26/23	198 TAMBOR	10	20-22N 141-45E	AK	6400	T2/4NSR	S	AIJW	26	XAF	Chiyo M.	657	S	20-08N 141-55E	
27	HMS TACTICIAN	6	W coast Siam	2Jk	40	G	S								
28	HMS TEMPLAR	7	Malacca Strait	MV	2700	T1/3	S	Note AW	28 Note	AK XPG	Tyokai M. Chokai M.	2658	S	Malacca Strait	BSH claims Tyokai M. A & W say Chokai M is correct name, sunk 1941 prior to hostilities. [Attribution ?]
29/02	236 SILVERSIDES	10	16-23N 144-59E	AK	5000	T2/3NSR	S	AIW J	29	XAP	Horaisan M. Horaizan M.	1998	S	16-19N 145-21E	
29/02	236 SILVERSIDES	10	16-23N 144-59E	AK	3000	T2/3NSR	S	AIJW	29	XAP	Shoken M.	1942	S	16-19N 145-21E	W lists ship as both XAP & Std AK 1D.
29/04	178 PERMIT	12	09- N 149- E	AK	2000	T1/2NSR	D								
30/01	269 RASHER	4	03-40N 126-58E	AK	4200	T3/5NSV	S	AI J	30-1 29	XPG	Anshu M.	2601	S	Davao Gulf	W credits 254 GURNARD but PR shows no such attack 29-31 May.
30/09	267 POMPON	6	33-15N 134-11E	AP	2300	T1/3DUP	S	AIJ	30	C-APK	Shiga M.	742	S	Off Murotosaki	
30/18	363 GUITARRO	1	24-30N 122-30E	AK	9500	T2/3DUP	S	AIJ	30	C-AK	Shisen M.	2201	S	24-32N 123-24E	
31	233 HERRING	8L	48- N 153- E	DE	700	T1/?D	S	AIJW	31	PF	Ishigaki	860	S	W Matsuwa I.	U says attack reported by Japanese prisoner picked up by 220 BARB.
31 J	233 HERRING	8L	48- N 153- E	Unk	Unk	Unk	U	AIJ	31	A-AK	Hokuyo M.	1590	S	W Matsuwa I.	Attack not in SORG.
31/13	220 BARB	8	48-21N 151-20E	AP	9900	T3/3DUP	S	AIJ	31	A-AK	Madras M.	3802	S	W Matsuwa I.	
31/18	220 BARB	8	47-52N 151-02E	AK	1100	T3/3DSR	S	AIJW	31	XAP	Koto M.	1053	S	47-55N 151-42E	

103

Dt/Hr	Submarine	Pt	Position	Tgt	Size	Attack	Cl	So	Date	Type	Name	Tons	Dm	Location	Comments
JUN	1944														
1	233 HERRING	8L	48-00N 153-00E	AK	3100	Unk	S	AIJW	1	XAP	Iwaki M.	3124	S	Matsuwa I.	W lists 2 ships this name, 3124T & 3142T, same date & location of sinking. [Appear to be same ship.]
1	233 HERRING	8L	48-00N 153-00E	APK	4400	Unk	S	AIJ	1	A-AK	Hiburi M.	4366	S	Matsuwa I.	U says HERRING believed sunk here.
1/05	387 PINTADO	1	18-13N 141-19E	AK	5000	T5/6NSR	S	AIJW	1	XAP	Toho M.	4716	S	18-08 141-14E	W misspells sub name Pintano.
1/05	387 PINTADO	1	18-13N 141-19E	AK	10300	T1/ NSR	S								
2/01	285 BALAO	5	05-40N 133-00E	AK	5000	T2/6NUP	D								
2/02	382 PICUDA	2	22-48N 121-24E	AP	10000	T2/4NUP	D								
2/02	382 PICUDA	2	22-48N 121-24E	AK	5000	T1/2NUP	S								
2/04	363 GUITARRO	1	22-30N 121-16E	AO	10500	T1/2TUP	S								
2/23	314 SHARK	1	20-54N 140-17E	AO	10000	T3/4NUP	S	AIJW	2	XAP	Chiyo M.	4700	S	21-00N 140-30E	
2/23	314 SHARK	1	20-54N 140-17E	AK	5600	T1/ NUP	D								
2/23	363 GUITARRO	1	22-34N 121-15E	DD	1200	T1/2NUP	S	AIW J	2	PF	Awaji	940 900	S	Near Yasho I.	
3/16	288 CABRILLA	4	01-33S 118-39E	Mis		GD	S									
3	HMS STOIC	3	Off Penang	2Jk	95	G	S									
4/05	250 FLIER	1	22-55N 136-44E	AK	4000	T2/3NUP	S	AJW I	4	XAP	Hakusan M.	10380 10330	S	SW of Iwo Jima	
4/05	250 FLIER	1	22-55N 136-44E	AK	4000	T1/3NUP	S								
4/10	288 CABRILLA	4	05-20S 117-10E	Mis	100	GD	S									
4/16	314 SHARK	1	19-35N 138-43E	AP	8700	T4/4DUP	S	AIJ	4	A-AP	Katsukawa M.	6886	S	19-45N 138-15E	
?	N 361 GOLET	2L	Unk		Unk	Unk	Unk	U	IW	4	XPkt	Shinko M. #10	72	S	35-47N 154-54E	Attack not in SORG or U, but location is in area assigned to GOLET. [Attribution ?]
5/10	268 PUFFER	4	06-32N 120-40E	AO	9500	T3/3DUP	S	AIW J	5	AOR	Ashizuri	7951 2166	S	06-44N 120-55E	
5/10	268 PUFFER	4	06-32N 120-40E	AO	7300	T1/1DUP	D								

Dt/Hr	Submarine	Pt	Position	Tgt	Size	Attack	Cl	So	Date	Type	Name	Tons	Dm	Location	Comments
JUN	1944														
5/10	268 PUFFER	4	06-32N 120-40E	AO	7300	T3/3DUP	S	AIW J	5	AOG	Takasaki	4465 2500	S	06-44N 120-55E	
5/17	314 SHARK	1	17-37N 140-32E	AK	8500	T3/3DUP	S	AIJ	5	A-AP	Takaoka M.	7006	S	18-40N 140-35E	
5/17	314 SHARK	1	17-37N 140-32E	AK	5000	T3/3DUP	S	AIJW	5	XAP	Tamahime M.	3080	S	18-40N 140-35E	
6/00	387 PINTADO	1	17-15N 141-23E	AK	6300	T4/4NUP	D								
6/11	387 PINTADO	1	16-41N 142-43E	AK	7200	T3/3DUP	S	AIJW	6	XAK	Kashimasan M.	2825	S	16-28N 142-16E	
6/11	387 PINTADO	1	16-41N 142-43E	AK	8500	T3/3DUP	S	AIJ	6	A-AP	Havre M.	5652	S	16-28N 142-16E	
6/21	270 RATON	4	08-58N 109-30E	DD	1200	T2/3NUP	S	AIW J	6	PF	CD 15	810 800	S	C. St. Jacques	PR says target blew up & broke in two. Posit is well east of Cape St. Jacques. [Location in I may be misprint.] misprint.]
6/22	257 HARDER	5	04-30N 119-30E	DD	1700	T2/3NUP	S	AIW J	6	DD	Minazuki Minatsuki	1313 1500	S PS	04-02N 119-18E	
7/12	257 HARDER	5	04-43N 120-00E	DD	1700	T2/3DUP	S	IW J	7	DD	Hayanami	2520 2100	S	S of Tawitawi	
7/23	239 WHALE	8	31-00N 143-55E	AP	10000	T1/3NSR	D	I	8	XAP	Shinroku M.	2857	?U	N Chichi Jima	W lists ship as both XAP & Std AO 2TA.
7/23	239 WHALE	8	31-00N 143-55E	AK	4000	T2/3NSR	D	I	7	XAP	Sugiyama M.	4379	M	31-06N 142-34E	PR says crippled AK later seen towed.
8/02	256 HAKE	5	06-03N 125-57E	DD	1500	T3/6NUP	S	AI J	8	DD	Kazagumo Kazegumo	2077 1900	S	Davao Bay	W misspells sub RAKE & lists DD as Kazekumo.
8/17	269 RASHER	4	03-04N 124-03E	AG	9200	T5/6DUP	S	AIW J	8	AOR	Shioya	7950 4000	S	03-00N 123-15E	
8	HMS SIRDAR	1	N Sumatra	Jk	50	G	D								
8 S	HMS STOIC	3	Off Penang	Cstr	200	G	D								
9/04	193 SWORDFISH	12	26-59N 143-13E	DD	1700	T2/4NUP	S	AIJW	9	DD	Matsukaze	1270	S	NE Chichi Jima	
9/15	243 BREAM	1	02-14N 127-57E	AK	4000	T1/6DUP	D								
9/21	206 GAR	12	24-35N 141-38E	AK	500	GM	D								
9/21	257 HARDER	5	05-42N 120-41E	DD	1700	T2/3NUP	S	AIW J	9	DD	Tanikaze	2033 1900	S	04-55N 119-40E	

Dt/Hr	Submarine	Pt	Position	Tgt	Size	Attack	Cl	So	Date	Type	Name	Tons	Dm	Location	Comments
JUN	1944														
9/21	257 HARDER	5	05-42N 120-41E	DD	1700	T1/1NUP	S								
10/13	310 BATFISH	3	32-38N 131-58E	AK	3500	T1/3DUP	S								
10/17	257 HARDER	5	04-33N 120-07E	DD	1700	T2/3DUP	S								
10	HMS TANTALUS	2	03-05N 099-56E	MV	800	G	S	AIJ	10	A-AK	Hiyoshi M.	536	S	03-00N 099-50E	BSH gives name Hyoshi M.
11/01	272 REDFIN	3	06-02N 120-48E	AO	10000	T1/6NSR	S	AIJW	11	XAO	Asanagi M.	5141	S	06-00N 120-50E	
11/12	220 BARB	8	48-13N 144-21E	Sam		GD	S								
11/13	220 BARB	8	48-11N 144-21E	Sam	100	GD	S								
11/21	255 HADDO	6	07-13N 123-13E	Tra	200	GN	S								
11/21	255 HADDO	6	07-13N 123-13E	Tra	300	GN	S								
11/24	220 BARB	8	46-58N 143-50E	AK	5800	T4/6NSR	S	AIJ	11	Fish	Chihaya M.	1160	S	46-50N 144-05E	Fluckey says 2738T correct.
11/24	220 BARB	8	46-58N 143-50E	AK	9800	T2/3NSR	S	AIJ	11	Fish	Toten M.	3823	S	46-50N 144-05E	
11	HMS SIRDAR	1	N Sumatra	Cstr	500	G	D								
12	HMS STOIC	1	07-54N 098-27E	MV	3500	T2/3	S	AIJ	12	XAP	Kainan M.	1134	S	Phuket, Siam	
13/15	250 FLIER	1	16-00N 119-42E	AO	9500	T2/4DUP	D	A I	13	C-AO	Marifu M.	5135	M S	15-57N 119-42E 16-00N 119-41E	PR says 2 timed hits & breaking-up noises heard. J says sunk 6 Nov 44 by CV a/c at 14-25N 120-30E; A says ship towed to Cavite, broke in half during storm & scrapped. [J attribution ?]
13/20	270 RATON	4	04- S 109-46E	Sam		GN	S								
13/23	220 BARB	8	51-38N 151-20E	AP	10800	T2/2NSR	S	AIJ	13	A-AP	Takashima M.	5633	S	50-53N 151-43E	
13 S	HMS STOIC	3	Off Penang	LC	70	G	S								
14/09	269 RASHER	4	04-31N 122-25E	AK	7000	T2/2DUP	S	AIJ	14	A-AK	Koan M.	3183	S	04-35N 122-23E	
14/09	269 RASHER	4	04-31N 122-25E	AK	4000	T2/2DUP	D								
14/09	269 RASHER	4	04-31N 122-25E	AP	6100	T1/1DUP	D								
14/17	168 NAUTILUS	10	04-28S 126-27E	Sam	100	GD	S								

Dt/Hr	Submarine	Pt	Position	Tgt	Size	Attack	Cl	So	Date	Type	Name	Tons	Dm	Location	Comments
JUN	1944														
14/17	385 BANG	2	23-15N 143-15E	AO	7500	T1/3DUP	D								
15/01	193 SWORDFISH	12	29-30N 141-11E	AK	4800	T3/8NSR	S	AJ I	15	A-AK	Kanseishi M. Amaiko M.	4804	S	29-30N 141-07E	
16/05	282 TUNNY	6	20-10N 121-18E	Tra	100	GT	S								
16/07	256 HAKE	5	06-13N 126-06E	XAV	10000	T2/6DUP	D								
16/09	222 BLUEFISH	5	02-28N 118-09E	AK	3000	T1/3DUP	S	AIJ	16	C-AK	Nanshin M.	1422	S	02-22N 118-14E	
16/17	243 BREAM	1	02-19N 128-40E	AK	4000	T2/6DUP	D	AIJ	16	A-AK	Yuki M.	5704	S	02-23N 128-43E	
16/17	243 BREAM	1	02-19N 128-40E	AK	4000	T1/ DUP	D	I AJ	16	A-AK	Hinode M.	1916	M SA	02-23N 128-43E 01-01N 127-49E	[Attribution ?]
17/10	270 RATON	4	05-48N 113-51E	AK	2500	T1/3DUP	S								
17/11	256 HAKE	5	06-17N 126-17E	AK	5500	T3/4DUP	S	AJW I	17	XAP	Kinshu M.	5591 5606	S	06-10N 126-18E	
17/13	251 FLOUNDER	2	06-58N 127-52E	APK	4000	T4/4DUP	S	AIW J	17	XAG	Nihonkai M. Nipponkai M.	2684	S	06-33N 127-55E	W lists as torpedo recovery ship.
17/14	269 RASHER	4	03-46S 128-05E	AK	5100	T1/2DUP	D								
17	HMS STOIC	3	Off Penang	Jk	30	G	S								
17 S	HMS STOIC	3	Off Penang	Jk	30	Dem	S								
17	HMS TRUCULENT	4	S Malacca Str.	Jk	20	G	S								
18/13	310 BATFISH	3	33-26N 135-34E	AK	2200	T1/2DUP	S								
18/21	283 TINOSA	7	33-45N 128-03E	Sch	400	GN+Burn	S								
18	HMS STORM	4	05-59N 099-10E	MV	1500	T3/4	S	AIJ W	18 8	XPG	Eiko M.	3011	S	05-59N 099-10E	
19/08	218 ALBACORE	9	12-22N 137-04E	CV	29800	T1/6DUP	S	AIW J	19	CV	Taiho	29300 31000	S	12-05N 138-12E	
19/11	244 CAVALLA	1	11-50N 137-57E	CV	29800	T3/6DUP	S	AIW J	19	CV	Shokaku	25675 30000	S	12-00N 137-46E	
20/07	256 HAKE	5	05-34N 125-16E	AP	7500	T2/4DUP	S	AIJ	20	A-AK	Hibi M.	5875	S	05-36N 125-17E	

Dt/Hr	Submarine	Pt	Position	Tgt	Size	Attack	Cl	So	Date	Type	Name	Tons	Dm	Location	Comments
JUN	1944														
21/02	222 BLUEFISH	5	04-04S 116-45E	AK	4000	T2/9NSR	S	AI J	21	A-AK	Kanan M.	3280 3312	S	03-58S 116-35E	
21/06	167 NARWHAL	12	11-12N 121-42E	Mis	200	GT	D								
21 N	HNMS K-XIV	6	01-00S 130-35E	CM	4400	T	D								DNO identifies target as CM Tsugaru; see 227 DARTER 29 Jun. Patrol not in BSH; K-XIV operated from Fremantle under US control for Neth Forces Intelligence Svc.
22/05	167 NARWHAL	12	09-01N 120-58E	AO	7300	T2/4NUR	D	I	22	XAO	Itsukushima M.	10007	M	09-08N 120-55E	
22/13	310 BATFISH	3	34-35N 137-51E	AK	3000	T2/4DUP	S	AI J	22	C-AK	Nagaragawa M.	887 990	S	34-36N 137-56E	J confuses ship with one of 990T sunk by a/c 20 Oct 43.
22/19	283 TINOSA	7	33-43N 127-44E	Sam	100	GT	S								
22/23	250 FLIER	1	13-10N 120-27E	AK	4000	T2/3NSR	D								
22/23	250 FLIER	1	13-10N 120-27E	AK	4000	T2/3NSR	S	I	23	A-AK	Belgium M.	5838	M	13-10N 120-21E	
23/00	250 FLIER	1	13-13N 120-00E	AK	7500	T3/4NSR	S								
23 N	HNMS K-XIV	6	Off Ceram	LC	10	G	S				Note				See note 21 Jun. DNO gives name Dornia Baru PPA 446.
24/00	214 GROUPER	9	34-36N 139-32E	AK	3500	T2/3NSR	S	AIW J	24	XAK	Kumanosan M. Kumanoyama M.	2857	S	34-45N 139-30E	
24/00	214 GROUPER	9	34-36N 139-32E	AK	2000	T1/3NSR	D	A I	30	C-AO	Nanmei M. #6	834	S	Off Omaezaki SC Gozeniwa	[Attribution ?]
24/06	384 PARCHE	2	30-14N 152-33E	PC	300	GD	S								
24/08	272 REDFIN	3	09-57N 125-07E	AP	6100	T2/3DUP	S	AIJ	24	A-AK	Aso M.	3028	S	09-56N 125-06E	
24/12	272 REDFIN	3	09-54N 125-06E	AP	9300	T1/4DUP	D								
24/24	306 TANG	3	32-30N 129-35E	AK	7500	T2/3NSR	S	AIJ	24-5	A-AK	Tamahoko M.	6780	S	32-24N 129-38E	
24/24	306 TANG	3	32-30N 129-35E	AO	10000	T2/3NSR	S	AIJ	24-5	C-AO	Nasusan M.	4399	S	32-24N 129-38E	

Dt/Hr	Submarine	Pt	Position	Tgt	Size	Attack	Cl	So	Date	Type	Name	Tons	Dm	Location	Comments
JUN	1944														
24/24	306 TANG	3	32-30N 129-35E	Same	Same	Same	0	AIJW	24-5	C-AK	Tainan M.	3175	S	32-24N 129-38E	PR says fired at convoy of 6 ships & 12 escorts; AK & AO sink. Some sources say Tainan M & Kennichi M (below) collided and sank in 2nd convoy.
24/24	306 TANG	3	32-30N 129-35E	Same	Same	Same	0	AI J	24-5	A-AK	Kennichi M.	1937	S PS	32-24N 129-38E	See above.
--							-	I	24	A-AK	Tsurushima M.	4645	S	14-15N 119-40E	See 259 JACK 30 Jun.
25/02	241 BASHAW	2	03-36N 127-14E	AP	4400	T1/3NSR	D								
25/02	241 BASHAW	2	03-36N 127-14E	AK	5700	T2/3NSR	S	AJ I	25	A-AK	Yamamiya M.	6440	S H	03-28N 127-06E	
25/03	259 JACK	5	16-07N 119-44E	AO	10000	T1/3NUR	S	AIJW	25	XAO	San Pedro M.	7268	S	16-17N 119-40E	
25/03	259 JACK	5	16-07N 119-44E	AK	7000	T1/3NUR	S								
25/15	168 NAUTILUS	10	04-15S 126-00E	Sam		GD	S								
25	HMS TRUCULENT	4	S Malacca Str.	Jk	20	G	D								
26/23	193 SWORDFISH	12	27-25N 141-55E	Tra	400	GN	D								
26	HMS TRUCULENT	4	03-15N 099-46E	MV	4000	T2/4	D	AI J	26	B-AK	Harugiku M. Harukiku M.	3040	S	03-15N 099-46E	BSH gives name Harukiku M; ship not in W.
27/00	193 SWORDFISH	12	27-10N 141-57E	Tra	400	GN	S								
27/04	304 SEAHORSE	5	21-21N 120-18E	AK	4000	T1/2TUR	S	AIJ	27	C-AO	Medan M.	5135	S	21-10N 120-31E	
27/04	304 SEAHORSE	5	21-21N 120-18E	AK	4000	T1/ TUR	D	I	27	PF	Etorofu	870	H	21-10N 120-31E	
27/04	304 SEAHORSE	5	21-21N 120-18E	AO	10000	T3/4TUR	S	AJ I	28	A-AP	Ussuri M.	6385	SA S	23-34N 119-57E	PR says seen to sink. [Attribution ?; sinking not near attack.]
27/15	264 PARGO	4	06-21N 124-02E	AK	4000	T1/4DUP	D								
27	HMS SEA ROVER	4	Off Penang	Jk	20	Dem	S								
27	HMS TRUCULENT	4	S Malacca Str.	Jk	20	Dem	S								
27. S	HMS CLYDE	1	Andaman Is.	MV		G	D								

Dt/Hr	Submarine	Pt	Position	Tgt	Size	Attack	Cl	So	Date	Type	Name	Tons	Dm	Location	Comments
JUN	1944														
28/06	264 PARGO	4	06-50N 122-41E	AK	6600	T1/3DUP	S	AIJ	28	A-AK	Yamagiku M.	5236	S	06-50N 122-32E	
28/06	264 PARGO	4	06-50N 122-41E	AK	4000	T1/3DUP	D	I	28	PF	CD 10	940	M	06-50N 122-33E	
28/08	315 SEALION	1	34-03N 129-00E	AK	4000	T1/3DUP	S	AIJW	28	XAC	Sansei M.	2386	S	33-53N 129-01E	
28/11	311 ARCHERFISH	3	24-44N 140-20E	DD	1400	T2/4DUP	S	AIW J	28	PF	CD 24	940 800	S	S of Io-Jima	
28/13	206 GAR	12	25-50N 143-05E	AK	900	GD	S								
28	HMS TRUCULENT	4	S Malacca Str.	Jk	20	Dem	S								
29/01	249 FLASHER	3	00-43S 105-31E	AK	7500	T3/3NSR	S	A IJ	29	C-AK	Niho M. Nippo M.	6079	S	00-44N 105-40E	
29/01	249 FLASHER	3	00-43S 105-31E	AP	10000	T2/3NSR	S	I AW	29	AO	Notoro	14050	H HA	Singapore	[Attribution ?]
29/02	215 GROWLER	9	19-09N 120-37E	AO	10000	T3/6NSR	S								
29/02	215 GROWLER	9	19-09N 120-37E	DE	600	T1/ NSR	D	AIJW	29	XAP	Katori M.	1920	S	19-00N 121-42E	
29/07	187 STURGEON	11	27-41N 129-09E	AK	9300	T4/4DUP	S	AIJ	29	A-AK	Toyama M.	7089	S	27-47N 129-05E	
29/14	227 DARTER	3	02-19N 127-57E	CM	4400	T2/6DUP	S	AIW J	29	CM	Tsugaru	4000 4400	S	Morotai I.	
29/15	385 BANG	2	17-13N 118-24E	AO	10000	T3/4DUP	S	I	29	C-AO	Sarawak M.	5135	M	17-13N 118-18E	
29/15	385 BANG	2	17-13N 118-24E	APK	7500	T2/2DUP	S	AIW	29	XAO	Mirii M.	10564	M	17-13N 118-18E	W says laid up at Takao, later sunk.
29/15	385 BANG	2	17-13N 118-24E	AK	6500	T3/4DUP	S								
29	HMS STURDY	1	W coast Siam	Jk	30	Dem	S								
29	HMS TRUCULENT	4	S Malacca Str.	Jk	20	Dem	S								
30/01	306 TANG	3	35-03N 125-08E	AK	5500	T1/1NSR	S	AJ I	30	C-AK	Nikkin M.	5705 5857	S	35-05N 125-00E	
30/02	259 JACK	5	14-25N 119-47E	AK	4000	T1/3NSR	D								
30/02	259 JACK	5	14-25N 119-47E	AK	4000	T2/3NSR	S	AJ I	30 24	A-AK	Tsurushima M.	4645	S	Off Manila Bay 14-15N 119-40E	[J attribution ?; date discrepancy.]

110

Dt/Hr	Submarine	Pt	Position	Tgt	Size	Attack	Cl	So	Date	Type	Name	Tons	Dm	Location	Comments
JUN	1944														
30/02	259 JACK	5	14-25N 119-47E	AK	4000	T2/4NSR	D								
30/03	259 JACK	5	14-25N 119-47E	AK	4000	T2/4NSR	D								
30/04	259 JACK	5	14-25N 119-47E	AK	4000	T3/4NSR	S	AJ I	30	A-AK	Matsukawa M.	3832	S SA	14-25N 119-45E	
30/09	315 SEALION	1	34-28N 125-21E	Sam	100	GD	S								
30/16	390 PLAICE	1	28-22N 141-17E	AK	4000	T2/4DUP	S	AIJ W	30	XAP	Hyakufuku M. Hyakafuku M.	986	S	28-20N 141-23E	
30/16	390 PLAICE	1	28-22N 141-17E	AK	4000	T1/ DUP	S								
30/21	193 SWORDFISH	12	28-02N 153-24E	Tra	100	GN	S								
30	S HMS SPITEFUL	2	NE Sumatra	Smc		G	D								
JUL	1944														
1/12	310 BATFISH	3	31-45N 140-39E	Tra	500	GD	S	IW	1	XPkt	Isuzugawa M #5	226	S	31-26N 141-11E	
1/12	310 BATFISH	3	31-45N 140-39E	YP	300	GD	S	I W	1	XPkt	Kamoi M. Kamo M.	138	S	31-26N 141-11E	
1/15	306 TANG	3	34-27N 123-46E	AK	2000	T1/2DUP	S	AI JW	1	XAO	Takatori M. #1	878	SA S	Mokpo, Korea	I gives date 28 Jun. [J attribution ?]
1/23	306 TANG	3	34-33N 125-12E	AK	4000	T1/2NSR	S	AJ I	1	C-AK	Taiun M. #2 Daiun M. #2	998	S	34-40N 125-25E	
1	234 KINGFISH	5	05-10S 119-20E	--	--	Mine	U	AJ I	1	C-AK	Nikko M.	3098	SM S	05-38S 119-28E	Minefield laid 10 Oct 43; J credits Navy mine. [Attribution ?; mines 8 months old.]
--							-	I	1	A-AK	Yoshino M.	8990	S	19-00N 120-55E	See 280 STEELHEAD & 384 PARCHE 31 Jul.
1	S HMS STRATAGEM	1	Andaman Is.	MV	1100	T1/4	D								BSH evaluates attack unsuccessful.
2/12	311 ARCHERFISH	3	27-08N 142-04E	AP	10000	T4/6DUP	D								
2/12	311 ARCHERFISH	3	27-08N 142-04E	AK	2000	T1/1DUP	D								
2	HMS SPITEFUL	2	NE Sumatra	Jk	70	G	S								
3/10	218 ALBACORE	9	08-10N 136-18E	AK	1000	GD	S								

Dt/Hr	Submarine	Pt	Position	Tgt	Size	Attack	Cl	So	Date	Type	Name	Tons	Dm	Location	Comments
JUL	1944														
3/13	187 STURGEON	11	28-52N 129-56E	APK	9300	T3/4DUP	S	AIJ	3	A-AP	Tairin M.	6862	S	28-53N 129-51E	
3/23	283 TINOSA	7	32-25N 128-46E	AP	10900	T2/2NUP	S	AIJ	3	C-APK	Kamo M.	7954	S	32-25N 128-50E	
3/23	283 TINOSA	7	32-25N 128-46E	AK	7500	T3/4NUP	S	AJ I	3	C-AO	Konsan M. Konzan M.	2733	S	32-42N 128-13E	
3/24	304 SEAHORSE	5	19-28N 115-41E	AK	7500	T2/2NUR	S	AIJ	3-4	A-AK	Gyoyu M.	2232	S	20-21N 115-00E	
3/24	304 SEAHORSE	5	19-28N 115-41E	AK	4000	T3/6NUR	S	AIJ	3-4	C-AK	Nitto M.	2186	S	19-20N 115-50E	
4/04	362 GUAVINA	2	07-34N 133-45E	AK	5800	T3/4NUP	S	AIJW	4	XAP	Tama M.	3052	S	07-50N 133-40E	
4/06	306 TANG	3	35-22N 125-56E	XAV	16000	T2/3DUP	S	AI J	4	C-AK	Asukasan M. Asukazan M.	6886	S	35-22N 125-55E	
4/13	304 SEAHORSE	5	20-20N 114-54E	APK	4000	T3/3DUP	S	AI J	4	C-APK	Kyodo M. #28	1518 1506	S	20-18N 115-02E	
4/13	304 SEAHORSE	5	20-20N 114-54E	APK	7500	T2/3DUP	S								
4/21	306 TANG	3	36-05N 125-48E	AK	7000	T1/2NUR	S	AJ I	4 ?	C-AK	Yamaoka M.	6932	S	W coast Korea	
4	S HMS STRATAGEM	1	Andaman Is.	MV	1900	T1/2	D								BSH evaluates attack unsuccessful.
4	HMS STURDY	1	W coast Siam	2Tug	400	G	S								
4	HMS STURDY	1	W coast Siam	3Ltr	300	G	S								
5/02	390 PLAICE	1	27-43N 141-02E	APK	9500	T2/3NSR	S	AIJW	5	XAN	Kogi M.	857	S	Ototo Jima	
5/15	281 SUNFISH	7	51-35N 156-30E	AK	4000	T1/3DSP	S	AIJ	5	C-APK	Shinmei M.	2577	S	51-28N 156-28E	
5/16	223 BONEFISH	5	00-41N 119-51E	Sch	100	GD	S								
5	HMS SEA ROVER	4	Off Penang	Jk	50	G	S								
5	HMS SEA ROVER	4	Off Penang	Jk	40	Dem	S								
6/00	281 SUNFISH	7	52-12N 154-30E	AK	4000	T1/3TSR	S								
6/03	306 TANG	3	38-40N 123-40E	AK	4000	T2/2TUR	S	AI J	6	C-AK	Dori Go Dori M.	1469	S	38-50N 123-35E	
6/05	315 SEALION	1	29-59N 122-53E	AK	7500	T1/4TUP	S	AIJ	6	C-APK	Setsuzan M.	1922	S	29-55N 122-56E	

Dt/Hr	Submarine	Pt	Position	Tgt	Size	Attack	Cl	So	Date	Type	Name	Tons	Dm	Location	Comments
JUL	1944														
6/09	263 PADDLE	4	03-24N 125-28E	AK	7500	T1/1DUP	D								
6/09	263 PADDLE	4	03-24N 125-28E	DD	1200	T1/2DUP	S	AIW J	6	DD	Hokaze	1215 1300	S	W Sangihe I.	
6/14	383 PAMPANITO	2	34-35N 137-48E	AK	5100	T1/3DUP	D								
6/23	245 COBIA	1	28-25N 151-46E	XAM	400	GM	S	AI W	6	XPkt	Takamiya M IGo Takamiya M.	138	S	28-54N 150-50E	W credits 193 SWORDFISH as probable; PR shows no such attack.
6	HMS PORPOISE	1	Malacca Strait	Jk	10	G	S								
6	HMS STURDY	1	W coast Siam	Jk	50	Dem	S								
6	HMS STURDY	1	W coast Siam	MV	200	G	S								
7/02	261 MINGO	4	13-55N 118-30E	DD	1700	T3/8NUP	S	AIW J	7	DD	Tamanami	2077 2100	S	W of Manila	
7/14	223 BONEFISH	5	02-40N 118-22E	Mis	200	GD	S	AIW	7	XPkt	Ryuei M.	207	S	Tarakan	
7/14	281 SUNFISH	7	47-29N 152-29E	Note	2500	GD	S								PR says sank 13 sampans: 3 100T, 8 200T, 2 300T.
7/14	281 SUNFISH	7	47-29N 152-29E	Pat	500	GD	S								
7/17	305 SKATE	5	47-43N 147-55E	DD	1700	T2/3DUP	S	AIW J	7	DD	Usugumo	2090 1950	S	N of Etorofu	
7/17	305 SKATE	5	47-43N 147-55E	AK	7500	T1/3DUP	D								
7/24	249 FLASHER	3	13-02N 109-26E	AK	4000	T2/4NSR	S	AI J	7	XAP	Koto M. #2 Koto M.	3557	S	13-08N 109-28E	
--							-	AIW	7	SC	Cha 6	135	S	Rabaul	No likely sub attack.
7	HMS STURDY	1	W coast Siam	2Jk	120	Dem	S								
8/07	199 TAUTOG	12	40-56N 141-27E	AK	2000	T2/4DSR	S	AIJ	8	C-AK	Matsu M.	887	S	41-17N 141-30E	
8/18	223 BONEFISH	5	02-41N 118-09E	Mis	300	GT	S	IW	8	XPkt	Moji M.	60	S	02-25N 118-14E	
8/20	280 STEELHEAD	6	18-05N 120-08E	Sam		GN	D								
--							-	I	8	SC	Cha 7	135	L	Rabaul	No likely sub attack.

Dt/Hr	Submarine	Pt	Position	Tgt	Size	Attack	Cl	So	Date	Type	Name	Tons	Dm	Location	Comments
--							-	I	8	SC	Cha 9	135	L	Rabaul	No likely sub attack.
--							-	AI	8	XSC	Kurama M.	233	S	08-00N 114-38E	See 260 LAPON 18 Jul.
9/00	364 HAMMERHEAD	1	19-13N 120-41E	Pat	100	GN	S								
9/11	281 SUNFISH	7	51-17N 155-34E	AK	7500	T2/3DUP	S	AIJ	9	A-AK	Taihei M.	6284	S	51-19N 155-43E	
9/11	281 SUNFISH	7	51-17N 155-34E	AK	6600	T2/3DUP	D								
9/13	199 TAUTOG	12	43-06N 144-08E	Tra	100	GD	S	I	9	Fish	Yawata M.	18	S	SW of Kushiro	
9/15	247 DACE	4	06-22N 126-18E	AP	10000	T2/6DUP	D								
9	HMS SPIRIT	1	N Sumatra	AO	400	G	D								
10/06	223 BONEFISH	5	07-10N 119-12E	Sam	100	GD	S								
10/08	283 TINOSA	7	32-12N 127-00E	Tra	100	GD	S	I	9	Fish	Shosei M. #5	19	S	W of Danjo I.	
10 S	HMS TALLY HO	6	Not given	MV	250	G	D								
11/01	315 SEALION	1	37-30N 124-34E	AK	4000	T1/3NSR	S	AIJ	11	C-AK	Taian M. #2	1034	S	37-31N 124-23E	
11/07	315 SEALION	1	37-24N 124-31E	AK	4100	T1/2DSR	S	AIJ	11	C-AK	Tsukushi M. #2	2417	S	N of Tsingtao	
12/02	308 APOGON	4	19-11N 122-38E	AK	4000	T3/4NUP	D								
12/03	308 APOGON	4	19-11N 122-38E	AK	7500	Ram	D	IW	12	XPkt	Nichiran M. #3	32	S	18-50N 122-40E	PR says rammed during attack, believed by AK. W says sunk by APOGON gunfire, but PR shows no gun attack; I gives location same as 389 PIRANHA attack below. [Attribution ?]
12/05	389 PIRANHA	1	18-33N 122-53E	AP	8700	T2/3TUP	S	AIJ	12	A-AO	Nichiran M.	6503	S	18-50N 122-40E	PR says attacked 6-ship convoy, heard 2 explosions & breaking-up noises; later saw another ship picking up survivors.
12/09	279 SNOOK	6	33-24N 135-45E	AK	6600	T1/4DUP	D								
13/07	245 COBIA	1	27-23N 140-33E	AF	8800	T2/3DUP	S	AIW J	13	XAK	Daiji M. Taishi M.	2813 2800	S	27-27N 140-32E	
14/12	381 SAND LANCE	3	06-00S 121-30E	AK	7500	T2/3DUP	S	AIJW	14	XPG	Taiko M.	2984	S	05-56S 121-34E	
14/12	381 SAND LANCE	3	06-00S 121-30E	AK	4000	T1/3DUP	D								

Dt/Hr	Submarine	Pt	Position	Tgt	Size	Attack	Cl	So	Date	Type	Name	Tons	Dm	Location	Comments
JUL	1944														
15/22	305 SKATE	5	48-08N 148-06E	AK	1500	T1/2NSR	S	A IJW	15	Crab XAP	Miho M.	515	S	48-29N 147-36E	PR says ship identified by prisoner.
16/02	305 SKATE	5	48-12N 148-04E	AO	10100	T1/6NSR	S	A IJW	16	XAP	Niho M. Nippo M.	1942	S	48-29N 147-36E	A says these are same ship; PR says US consul at Vladivostok named ship as 10100T AO Nippon M; W lists Nippo M as both XAP & Std AK 1D.
16/02	305 SKATE	5	48-12N 148-04E	Same	Same	Same	0	I	16	C-AO	Nikkaku M.	1937	S	48-32N 147-35E	A says this is same ship as Niho M. [Attribution ?]
16/08	389 PIRANHA	1	19-26N 120-18E	AO	8700	T2/3DUP	S	AI J	16	A-AP	Seattle M.	5773	S PS	19-17N 120-15E	
16/09	223 BONEFISH	5	10-18N 119-55E	Sam	100	GD	S									
16/17	288 CABRILLA	5	08-15N 122-50E	AP	9900	T2/6DUP	S									
16/23	200 THRESHER	13	18-55N 119-44E	DD	1300	T2/3NSR	S									
16/23	200 THRESHER	13	18-55N 119-44E	AK	7500	T2/3NSR	S									
16/23	200 THRESHER	13	18-55N 119-44E	AK	7500	T2/4NSR	S									
16/24	217 GUARDFISH	8	18-21N 119-43E	AO	10000	T2/3NSR	S									
16/24	217 GUARDFISH	8	18-21N 119-43E	AK	7400	T1/ NSR	S	AJ I	16	A-AK	Jinzan M. Jinsan M.	5215	PS S	19-17N 120-15E	
16/24	217 GUARDFISH	8	18-21N 119-43E	AK	5800	T2/3NSR	S									
16/24	217 GUARDFISH	8	18-21N 119-43E	AK	5800	T1/ NSR	S	AIW J	16	XAP	Mantai M.	5863	S PS	Cape Bojeador	I says location unk.
17/01	217 GUARDFISH	8	18-17N 119-50E	AK	5800	T2/3NSR	S	AJ I	16	C-AK	Hiyama M. Hizan M.	2838	PS S	19-17N 120-15E	
17/01	288 CABRILLA	5	07-40N 122-03E	AO	10000	T2/4NSR	S									
17/01	288 CABRILLA	5	07-40N 122-03E	AK	4000	T2/2NSR	S	AIJ	17	A-AP	Maya M.	3145	S	07-42N 122-05E	
17/02	288 CABRILLA	5	07-40N 122-03E	AK	4000	T1/3NSR	S	I	17	XAP	Natsukawa M.	4739	M	07-42N 122-05E	
17/03	200 THRESHER	13	19-04N 119-26E	AK	7500	T2/2NSR	S	AI J	16-7	C-AK	Sainei M.	4916	S PS	19-17N 120-15E	

Dt/Hr	Submarine	Pt	Position	Tgt	Size	Attack	Cl	So	Date	Type	Name	Tons	Dm	Location	Comments
JUL	1944														
17/03	200 THRESHER	13	19-04N 119-26E	AO	10000	T2/2NSR	S	AI J	16-7	A-AK	Shozan M.	2838	S PS	19-17N 120-15E	
17/03	200 THRESHER	13	19-04N 119-26E	DD	1300	T1/ NSR	S								
17/03	217 GUARDFISH	8	18-10N 119-49E	AK	7500	T2/4NSR	S								
17/03	252 GABILAN	2	33-52N 138-35E	DD	1700	T1/4NUR	S	AIW J	4 17	AM	W 25	648 492	SA S	28-35N 141-04E Sub position	PR says 3 explosions, target never seen, heavy oil slick later. [J attribution ?; date & location do not agree with attack.]
17/22	260 LAPON	5	08-22N 116-45E	AK	4000	T2/4NSR	S	AIJW	17-8	XAGS	Kyodo M. #36	1499	S	W of Borneo	
17	HMS TELEMACHUS	1	05-10N 100-00E	SS	1600	T1/6	S	IW J	17	SS	I-166	1575 1635	S	Near Singapore	
17/24	260 LAPON	5	08-22N 116-45E	AK	4000	T2/4NSR	S	AIW	18	XSC	Kamo M.	234	S	08-00N 114-38E	[W attribution ?; location & target size do not agree with attack.]
18/00	260 LAPON	5	08-22N 116-40E	AK	4000	T2/4NSR	S	W AI	18 8	XSC	Kurama M.	233	S	08-10N 114-38E	[W attribution ?; same as above.]
18/00	390 PLAICE	1	29-22N 139-14E	DD	1400	T3/4NSR	S	A JW	20 18	SC	Ch 50	442 300	S	Chichi Jima	
18/02	245 COBIA	1	29-12N 139-10E	AK	4000	T2/4NSR	S	AIJW	17-8	XAG	Unkai M. #10	851	S	29-15N 139-08E	
18/03	223 BONEFISH	5	11-05N 119-55E	AK	2000	T1/3NSR	S								
18/06	271 RAY	5	05-21S 112-30E	AO	10000	8/22DUP	S	AJ I	18	C-AO	Janbi M. Jambi M.	5244	S	N of Bawean I.	
18/06	274 ROCK	3	22-05N 119-54E	AK	4000	T1/3DUP	D								
18/06	274 ROCK	3	22-05N 119-54E	AP	7500	T2/3DUP	D								
18/06	274 ROCK	3	22-05N 119-54E	AO	10000	T3/4DUP	D								
18/07	245 COBIA	1	28-43N 139-24E	AK	9500	T4/10DUP	S	AIJ	18	A-AK	Nisshu M.	7785	S	28-40N 139-25E	
18/09	276 SAWFISH	7	21-52N 119-47E	AO	9500	T2/9DUP	D								
18/11	307 TILEFISH	2	21-50N 119-55E	DD	1700	T2/7DUP	S	I	18	PF	CD 17	810	H	Near Takao	
18/16	244 CAVALLA	1	16-02N 123-00E	Sam	100	GD		S							

116

Dt/Hr	Submarine	Pt	Position	Tgt	Size	Attack	Cl	So	Date	Type	Name	Tons	Dm	Location	Comments
JUL	1944														
18/18	217 GUARDFISH	8	20-27N 119-11E	AG	9800	T2/3DUP	S								
18	HMS SIRDAR	2	W coast Siam	Jk	100	G	S								
19/06	309 ASPRO	4	02-20S 126-37E	AK	4000	T2/3TUR	S								
19/06	309 ASPRO	4	02-20S 126-37E	AK	4000	T3/4TUR	S								
19/08	217 GUARDFISH	8	20-07N 118-20E	AK	6100	T2/4DUP	S	AI J	19	A-AK	Teiryu M.	6512 6550	S	20-50N 118-27E	I gives tons as 5872.
19/08	217 GUARDFISH	8	20-07N 118-20E	AK	4000	T1/ DUP	D								
19/13	249 FLASHER	3	12-45N 114-20E	CL	5100	T2/8DUP	S	AIW J	19	CL	Oi	5100 5700	S	13-12N 114-52E	
19/15	314 SHARK	2	27-08N 141-47E	AK	4300	T1/4DUP	D								
19/17	199 TAUTOG	12	31-30N 140- E	Tra	200	GD	S	A IW	19- 20	XPkt	Hokuriku M. #1 Hokuryu M. #1	148	S	NE Torishima	PR says survivor gave name Hokuriu M.
20/23	245 COBIA	1	28-06N 141-32E	Pat	600	GN	S	AIW	21	XSC	Yusen M. #3	193	S	28-10N 141-36E	
20/23	245 COBIA	1	28-06N 141-32E	Tra	300	GN	S	IW	21	XSC	Kaio M. #2	62	S	28-10N 141-36E	
20/23	245 COBIA	1	28-06N 141-32E	Tra	200	GN	S								
21/17	274 ROCK	3	20-50N 122-52E	AO	10000	T2/4DUS	D								
21/17	274 ROCK	3	20-50N 122-52E	AP	7500	T1/ DUS	D								
21	HMS SIRDAR	2	W coast Siam	2Cst	750	G	S								
23/24	392 STERLET	1	25-30N 141-41E	AK	700	GN	S								
23	HMS STORM	5	Port Owen Hbr.	Cstr	200	G	S	J	23	AK	Kiso M.	554	S	14-00N 086-50E	BSH claims sinking; A & I say sunk by mine at Rangoon, 15 Dec 43. [May have been salvaged; attribution ?]
23	HMS STORM	5	Port Owen Hbr.	2Pat	400	G	S								
24/12	178 PERMIT	13	09-09N 138-11E	AK	800	T1/3DUP	S								
25/22	224 COD	4	01-46S 125-33E	AK	4000	T1/1NSR	D								

Dt/Hr	Submarine	Pt	Position	Tgt	Size	Attack	Cl	So	Date	Type	Name	Tons	Dm	Location	Comments
JUL	1944														
--							-	A J	25	DD	Samidare	1685 1580	JS	08-10N 134-38E	J credits 310 BATFISH & a/c. See BATFISH 26 Aug. No likely sub attack 25 Jul.
26/02	175 TARPON	11	06-47N 152-07E	Esc	300	GN	D								
26/02	175 TARPON	11	06-47N 152-07E	Esc	300	GN	D								
26/02	175 TARPON	11	06-47N 152-07E	Mis	100	GN	S								
26/02	175 TARPON	11	06-47N 152-07E	Esc	300	GN	D								
26/02	249 FLASHER	3	18-10N 117-56E	AK	8800	T2/3NSR	P	AJ I	26-7	A-AK	Tosan M. Tozan M.	8666	JS	17-58N 118-04E	J credits FLASHER & 291 CREVALLE.
26/02	249 FLASHER	3	18-10N 117-56E	AK	6900	T1/3NSR	S	I	26	XAV	Kiyokawa M.	6863	M	18-15N 118-00E	[Attribution ?; could have been hit by 240 ANGLER or 291 CREVALLE.]
26/02	249 FLASHER	3	18-10N 117-56E	AO	10000	T1/1NSR	S	AI J	26	C-AO	Otorisan M. Otoriyama M.	5280	S	17-56N 118-07E	291 CREVALLE PR says ship exploded from hit by FLASHER.
26/04	240 ANGLER	4	18-30N 117-57E	AK	8800	T2/6NSV	D	I	26	XAV	Kiyokawa M.	6863	M	18-15N 118-00E	PR says i hit seen. [Attribution ?; could have been hit by 249 FLASHER or 291 CREVALLE.]
26/05	291 CREVALLE	4	18-28N 117-59E	AK	7600	T2/5NSV	S	AIJW	26	XAK	Aki M.	11409	S	18-24N 118-02E	PR says target seen to sink.
26/05	291 CREVALLE	4	18-28N 117-59E	AK	9300	T3/4NSV	S	I	26	XAV	Kiyokawa M.	6863	M	18-15N 118-00E	PR says ship hit, took up-angle. [Attribution ?; could be ship hit by 249 FLASHER or 240 ANGLER.]
26/17	276 SAWFISH	7	20-10N 121-50E	SS	1900	T3/4DUP	S	IW J	26	SS	I-29	2198 2212	S	20-10N 121-55E	
27/01	247 DACE	4	05-25N 121-43E	AK	2000	T5/10NSR	S	AIW J	27	XAO	Kyoei M. #2	1192 1157	S	05-25N 121-42E	
27/10	291 CREVALLE	4	18-13N 117-56E	AK	8800	T4/4DUP	P	AJ I	26-7	A-AK	Tosan M. Tozan M.	8666	JS S	17-58N 118-04E	J credits CREVALLE & 249 FLASHER. PR says ship did not appear damaged before attack, photos.
27/15	254 GURNARD	6	01-18S 123-36E	AK	4000	T2/3DUP	D								
27/15	267 POMPON	6	37-18N 142-57E	Tra	300	GD	S								

Dt/Hr	Submarine	Pt	Position	Tgt	Size	Attack	Cl	So	Date	Type	Name	Tons	Dm	Location	Comments
JUL	1944														
28/03	198 TAMBOR	11	40-40N 142-36E	AK	2000	T2/3NSR	D								PR describes as small AK or trawler. Blair says CO thought ship was Russian.
28/10	291 CREVALLE	4	16-18N 119-44E	AK	6700	T2/6DUP	S	AJ I	28	C-APK	Hakubasan M.	6641	S H	16-23N 119-40E	
28/15	309 ASPRO	4	17-33N 120-21E	AP	4000	T3/3DUP	S	AIW J	21 28	XPG	Peking M.	2288	DC S	17-31N 120-23E	PR says ship at anchor, later seen aground & gutted by fire.
29/16	313 PERCH	2	10-46N 127-13E	Tra	100	GD	S	AI W	31	XPkt	Kannon M. I-Go Kannon M.	115	SU	SW Pacific	[Attribution ?, location not specific.
29/17	228 DRUM	10	09-18N 133-20E	Sam		GD	S								
29/17	285 BALAO	6	09-27N 133-19E	Mis	100	GD	S								
30/01	223 BONEFISH	5	06-03N 119-54E	AO	10000	T4/5NSR	S	AIJW	30	XAO	Kokuyo M.	10026	S	06-07N 120-00E	
30/06	364 HAMMERHEAD	1	20-52N 120-47E	APK	8600	T4/6TSR	S								PR says seen sinking by stern.
30/06	364 HAMMERHEAD	1	20-52N 120-47E	AK	6200	T2/4TSR	D								
30/06	364 HAMMERHEAD	1	20-52N 120-47E	AK	6200	T1/ TSR	D								
31/04	280 STEELHEAD	6	18-57N 120-50E	AO	10000	T2/6NSR	D	AJ I	31 1	A-AP	Yoshino M.	8990	JS S	19-05N 120-55E	PR says hits heard, target smoking. 384 PARCHE PR says 2 ships seen burning but AO rejoined convoy. J credits STEELHEAD & 384 PARCHE below.
31/04	280 STEELHEAD	6	18-57N 120-50E	AK	7500	T1/ NSR	D								
31/04	280 STEELHEAD	6	18-57N 120-50E	AK	7500	T0/4NSR	0								PR says 2 hits possible.
31/04	384 PARCHE	2	19-10N 120-58E	AK	4000	T1/3NSR	D								PR says hit probable.
31/04	384 PARCHE	2	19-10N 120-58E	AO	10000	T4/4NSR	S	AIJ	31	C-AO	Koei M.	10238	S	19-00N 122-55E	PR ssys target sank immediately.
31/04	384 PARCHE	2	19-10N 120-58E	AO	10000	T5/6TSR	S	I	31	C-AK	Kokura M. #1	7270	M	19-02N 120-56E	PR says target sank after 2 salvos. [Attribution ?]
31/04	384 PARCHE	2	19-10N 120-58E	APK	4000	T2/2NSR	S	AIJW	30-1	XAP	Manko M.	4471	S	19-00N 120-50E	PR says broke in two & sank.
31/05	384 PARCHE	2	19-10N 120-58E	AP	10000	T3/4TSR	S	AJ I	31 1	A-AP	Yoshino M.	8990	JS S	19-05N 120-55E	J credits PARCHE & 280 STEELHEAD above.

Dt/Hr	Submarine	Pt	Position	Tgt	Size	Attack	Cl	So	Date	Type	Name	Tons	Dm	Location	Comments
JUL	1944														
31/05	280 STEELHEAD	6	18-57N 120-50E	AP	10000	T2/4TSR	S	AIJ	31	A-AP	Fuso M.	8195	S	19-00N 120-55E	PR says target slowed but showed no lights.
31/05	280 STEELHEAD	6	18-57N 120-50E	AK	4000	T2/4TSR	S	AJ I	31	A-AP	Dakar M.	7169	S H	19-08N 120-51E	PR says target down by bow.
31/14	247 DACE	4	06-12N 124-08E	AK	1200	T1/4DUP	S								
31/20	260 LAPON	5	08-22N 116-40E	AO	19400	T2/3NUP	D								
31/20	260 LAPON	5	08-22N 116-40E	AK	4000	T1/3NUP	D								
31/20	260 LAPON	5	08-22N 116-40E	AO	10000	T3/4NUP	S	AIJ	31	C-AO	Tenshin M.	5061	S	08-50N 116-00E	
AUG	1944														
1/11	268 PUFFER	5	05-07N 119-34E	AS	12000	T2/6DUP	S	AI	1	AOG	Sunosaki	4465	M	NE of Borneo	[Attribution ?]
1/13	381 SAND LANCE	3	01-11N 125-05E	AK	4000	T2/4DUP	D	IJW	1	XAE	Seia M.	6659	SA	01-46N 125-32E	PR says 2 hits heard. [Attribution ?]
1	HMS STORM	5	Mergui Arch.	2Cst	550	G	S								
1	HMS STORM	5	Mergui Arch.	Sch	100	G	S								
1	S HMS STORM	5	Mergui Arch.	Cstr	350	G	S								
2/16	199 TAUTOG	12	33-57N 136-20E	AK	2000	T2/3DUP	S	AI J	2	C-AK	Konei M.	1992 1922	S	34-00N 136-17E	
3/02	224 COD	4	01-45S 126-14E	AK	4000	T3/4NUR	S	AIJW	3	XAN	Seiko M.	708	S	01-46S 126-51E	
3/05	223 BONEFISH	5	07-11N 121-52E	AO	7500	T1/4NSR	D								
3	HMS TRUCULENT	4	02-51N 101-15E	--	--	Mine	U	I	3	CM	Hatsutaka	1608	LM	S Klang Strait	Minefield laid in Klang Strait 24 Jun.
4/01	392 STERLET	1	28-11N 141-43E	AK	2000	T3/3NUP	S	AIW	4	XPkt	Miyagi M.	248	S	29-10N 141-05E	PR says ship disintegrated, 30 survivors in water.
4/01	392 STERLET	1	28-11N 141-43E	Esc	300	T0/1NUP	O	AIW	4	XPkt	Zensho M.	99	S	29-10N 141-05E	PR says target believed missed, many US a/c seen attacking shipping. [Attribution ?]
4/04	271 RAY	5	03-59S 117-54E	AP	6400	T3/4NUP	S	AI J	4	A-AK	Koshu M.	2812 2612	S	04-05S 117-40E	
4/10	270 RATON	5	16-01N 119-44E	AO	9200	T1/4DUP	D								

Dt/Hr	Submarine	Pt	Position	Tgt	Size	Attack	Cl	So	Date	Type	Name	Tons	Dm	Location	Comments
AUG	1944														
5/06	245 COBIA	1	27-09N 142-32E	Pkt	500	T1/2DUP	S	AIW	4	XAP	Yayoi M.	495	SA	Chichi Jima	PR says stern blown off; target later strafed by a/c & set afire. [Attribution ?]
5/12	225 CERO	5	05-51N 125-42E	AO	8000	T4/6DUP	S	AW J	5	AO	Tsurumi	14050 6500	S SA	S of Davao	W gives date 5 Aug 42; I says sunk by a/c; A says records support both sub & a/c. PR says target broke in two after hits. [Attribution ?]
5/13	316 BARBEL	1	27-36N 128-54E	AK	4100	T1/4DUP	S	AIJ	5	C-APK	Miyako M.	970	S	Tokunoshima	
5	HMS TERRAPIN	1	W Sumatra	Cstr	150	G	S								
5	HMS TERRAPIN	1	W Sumatra	Cstr	150	G	D								
6/02	269 RASHER	5	14-14N 117-16E	AK	8200	T5/6NUP	S	AIJ	6	A-AK	Shiroganesan M	4739	S	14-10N 117-12E	
6/04	387 PINTADO	2	30-53N 129-47E	AK	6100	T2/6NUP	S	AIJ	6	A-AK	Shonan M.	5401	S	30-55N 129-45E	PR says fired at convoy of 8 ships & 3 escorts.
6/04	387 PINTADO	2	30-53N 129-47E	AK	6300	T2/ NUP	S	I	6	PF	Etorofu	870	M	36-53N 129-45E	See above note. [Attribution ?; latitude discrepancy, but I location could be misprint.]
6/10	309 ASPRO	4	18-19N 120-29E	AK	2000	T1/3DUP	D								
7/04	309 ASPRO	4	17-12N 119-56E	AK	7500	T2/2NUP	S								
7/04	309 ASPRO	4	17-12N 119-56E	AK	4000	T1/2NUP	D								
7/05	392 STERLET	1	28-11N 141-43E	AK	4000	T2/4TUP	S								
7/11	246 CROAKER	1	32-09N 129-54E	CL	5100	T1/4DUP	S	AIW J	7	CL	Nagara	5170 5700	S	32-12N 129-55E	
7/13	268 PUFFER	5	07-50N 122-07E	AK	3200	T1/1DUP	S	AIW	7	XSC	Kyo M. #2	340	S	07-50N 122-00E	
7/14	242 BLUEGILL	2	06-04N 124-22E	AK	4000	T2/5DUP	S	AIW J	7	XAP	Yamatama M. Sanju M.	4642	S	06-05N 124-23E	W gives tons as 46,426 [misprint].
7/18	192 SAILFISH	11	20-09N 121-19E	CM	1200	T1/3DUP	S	I	7	A-AK	Shinten M.	1254	H	20-09N 121-44E	PR saya fired at CM, not AK; saw target blow up.
7/18	192 SAILFISH	11	20-09N 121-19E	Same	Same	Same	0	A I	7	A-AK	Kinshu M.	238	SA S	20-09N 112-44E	Notes by Wilds at NavHistCen give longitude 121-44E, but PR says attacked only 1 ship. [Attribution ?]

Dt/Hr	Submarine	Pt	Position	Tgt	Size	Attack	Cl	So	Date	Type	Name	Tons	Dm	Location	Comments
AUG	1944														
7/21	363 GUITARRO	2	14-51N 119-51E	DD	1700	T3/3NSR	S	AIW J	7	PF	Kusagaki Kusakaki	940 900	S	W of Manila	
7/23	316 BARBEL	1	27-36N 128-30E	AK	19400	T5/10NSR	S								
8/14	213 GREENLING	10	19-50N 119-58E	Tra	100	GD	S								
8/20	363 GUITARRO	2	15-16N 119-57E	AK	700	GN	S								
8/23	392 STERLET	1	28-36N 141-06E	AK	7500	T4/4NUP	S	AIW	9	XSC	Tama M. #6	275	S	W Chichi Jima	W says ship was XAM used as XSC.
9/04	316 BARBEL	1	27-53N 128-49E	AP	8500	T1/4NUP	D	AIJ	9	A-AK	Yagi M.	1937	S	N Okinoshima	
9/04	316 BARBEL	1	27-53N 128-49E	AK	5400	T2/2NUP	S	AIJ	9	C	Boko M.	2333	S	27-56N 128-47E	
9	HMS TRENCHANT	1	W Sumatra	Cstr	200	G	S	I	9	Fish	Hiyoshi M. #3	48	S	Near Padang	I lists as B-Fish; ship not in W.
9	HMS TRENCHANT	1	W Sumatra	ML		G	S								
9	S HMS TRENCHANT	1	W Sumatra	Cstr		G	D								
10/09	287 BOWFIN	6	25-50N 131-12E	AK	1000	T1/3DUP	S								
10/09	287 BOWFIN	6	25-50N 131-12E	AK	1000	T3/3DUP	S	AI	10	C-AK	Seiyo M.	197	S	Minami-Daito	
10/10	363 GUITARRO	2	16-17N 119-46E	CL	6000	T2/3DUP	D								
10/10	363 GUITARRO	2	16-17N 119-46E	AK	4000	T1/1DUP	D	AIJ	10	C-AO	Shinei M.	5135	S	16-15N 119-45E	
10/12	224 COD	4	05-15S 121-14E	AK	2000	T3/4DUP	S	IW	10	XSC	Toseki M.	89	S	S Celebes	
10/13	363 GUITARRO	2	16-18N 119-46E	DD	1700	T2/4DUP	S								
11/00	224 COD	4	05-38S 120-37E	AK	2000	T2/8NUR	S	AI	11	C-AK	Shinsei M. #6	260	S	S of Celebes	
11/17	306 TANG	4	34-12N 136-19E	AK	5400	T1/3DUP	S	AIJ	11	C-AK	Roko M.	3328	S	33-58N 136-19E	
11/17	306 TANG	4	34-12N 136-19E	AK	4000	T2/3DUP	D								
11/18	186 STINGRAY	12	01-33N 126-06E	Tra	100	GT	S								
12/07	268 PUFFER	5	13-17N 120-07E	AO	10000	T2/3DUP	S	AIJ	12	C-AO	Teikon M.	5113	S	13-18N 120-11E	
12/07	268 PUFFER	5	13-17N 120-07E	AK	7500	T2/3DUP	S								

Dt/Hr	Submarine	Pt	Position	Tgt	Size	Attack	Cl	So	Date	Type	Name	Tons	Dm	Location	Comments
AUG	1944														
12/07	268 PUFFER	5	13-17N 120-07E	AO	10000	T1/ DUP P		A IJ	12	XAO	Shinpo M. Shimpo M.	5135	S JS	13-18N 120-11E	I says disabled; W gives name Shinko M., torp by PUFFER & "Bluefin"; J credits PUFFER & 222 BLUEFISH, see 17 Aug. PR says 2 AOs last seen abandoned & drifting.
12/24	267 POMPON	6	50-28N 144-09E	AO	8000	T2/3NSR D									
12/24	267 POMPON	6	50-28N 144-09E	AK	4000	T2/3NSR S		AIJ	12	C-AK	Mayachi M.	2159	S	50-35N 144-02E	
13/02	316 BARBEL	1	28-31N 129-18E	AK	4000	T2/4NSR S		AI	13	B-AG	Koan M.	223	S	Amami Oshima	Ship not in W.
13/10	242 BLUEGILL	2	06-17N 126-10E	AK	4000	T1/3DUP S		AIJW	13	XAP	Kojun M.	1931	S	06-15N 126-45E	
13/10	242 BLUEGILL	2	06-17N 126-10E	DE	500	T1/1DUP S		AIW	13	XSC	Misago M.	154	S	San Augustin	PR says escort hit & blew up.
13/10	242 BLUEGILL	2	06-17N 126-10E	Same	Same	Same	0	A J	13	SC	Ch 12	290 300	S	Sub position	W says Ch 12 lost Aug 44 off Palau Is. [J attribution ?; see above sinking.]
13/12	198 TAMBOR	11	48-56N 149-03E	AK	4000	T2/4DSR S		AIJ	13	C-AK	Toei M.	2324	S	48-35N 149-08E	
13/12	311 ARCHERFISH	4	32-55N 152-43E	Pat	300	GD	D								
13/24	179 PLUNGER	12	08-08N 154-20E	AK	5000	T4/6NSR S									
--							-	A I	13 14	C-AK	Taketsu M.	5949 6000	S SC	Luzon Strait	A says sunk by unk sub. No likely sub attack.
14/01	246 CROAKER	1	37-25N 125-12E	AK	2000	T2/6NSR S		AJW I	14	XPG	Daigen M. #7 Taigen M. #7	1289	S	37-30N 125-50E	
14/01	271 RAY	5	03-52N 112-56E	AO	10000	T3/3NSV S		AIJ	14	C-AK	Zuisho M.	5286	S	03-54N 113-00E	
14/01	271 RAY	5	03-52N 112-56E	AK	7500	T1/3NSV D									
14/02	224 COD	4	04-17S 126-46E	LSM	1000	T3/4NUR S		AI J	14	APD	T 129	890 1000	S	04-04S 126-59E	W says sunk by COLE (DD 155).
14/10	262 MUSKALLUNGE	4	13-13N 120-21E	ODD	800	T1/4DUP S									
14/19	306 TANG	4	33-03N 140-35E	PY	100	GT	D								
--							-	AI J	14 Note	A-AO	Nanshin M. #20	834	S SA	Off Takao 22-37N 120-15E	A says sunk by unk sub; I by marine casualty; J by a/c 12 Oct. No likely sub attack.

Dt/Hr	Submarine	Pt	Position	Tgt	Size	Attack	Cl	So	Date	Type	Name	Tons	Dm	Location	Comments
AUG	1944														
14	HMS STURDY	2	W coast Burma	2Cst	300	G	S								
15/14 242 BLUEGILL		2	02-35S 126-20E	Sch	100	GD	S								
16/22 246 CROAKER		1	36-09N 125-55E	PC	500	T1/1NSR	S	AIW	16	XAM	Taito M.	267	S	36-15N 125-52E	
17/03 246 CROAKER		1	36-38N 126-10E	AO	10000	T2/6NSR	S	A J	17	C-AK	Yamateru M. Sansho M.	6862	S	35-33N 126-10E	PR says seen to sink. I says Yamateru M sunk by mine.
17/19 222 BLUEFISH		6	13-32N 120-23E	AO	10000	T1/1DUP	P	A IJ	12	B-AO	Shinpo M. Shimpo M.	5135	S JS	13-18N 120-11E	J credits BLUEFISH & 268 PUFFER; see 12 Aug. PR says target was AO previously hit by PUFFER, aground, deck torn up forward. I says disabled.
18/02 192 SAILFISH		11	18-40N 116-10E	DD	1500	T2/4NSR	S								
18/04 395 REDFISH		1	20-02N 120-46E	Unk	4000	T1/4NSR	D	AI	18	C-AO	Eiyo M.	8673	M	20-28N 121-04E	
18/05 365 HARDHEAD		1	12-29N 128-49E	CL	5200	10/15NSR	S	IW J	18	CL	Natori	5170 5700	S	NE of Davao	
18/13 271 RAY		5	08-48N 116-58E	AO	10000	T3/4DUP	S	AIJ	18	C-AO	Nansei M.	5878	S	08-39N 116-39E	
18/13 271 RAY		5	08-48N 116-58E	AK	4000	T1/2DUP	D								
18/21 269 RASHER		5	18-16N 120-21E	AO	10000	T2/2NSR	S	J	18	AK	Eishin M.	542	S	Sub position	PR says AO broke up. [J attribution ?; ship does not appear to resemble target.]
18/22 269 RASHER		5	18-09N 120-13E	AP	10000	T3/6NSR	S	AIJW	18-9	XAO	Teiyo M.	9849	S	17-30N 119-30E	PR says target stopped & afire.
18/22 269 RASHER		5	18-09N 120-13E	Unk	4000	T1/ NSR	D								
18/22 269 RASHER		5	18-09N 119-56E	Unk	4000	T1/ NSR	D								
18/22 269 RASHER		5	18-09N 119-56E	CVE	20000	T3/4NSR	S	AIW J	18	CVE	Taiyo Otaka	17830 20000	S	18-10N 120-22E	
18/23 269 RASHER		5	18-09N 119-56E	AK	7500	T3/4NSR	S	AIJW	18-9	XAP	Teia M.	17537	S	18-18N 120-13E	PR say ship stopped, burned & disappeared.
18/23 269 RASHER		5	18-09N 119-56E	Unk	4000	T1/ NSR	D								
18/23 269 RASHER		5	18-09N 119-56E	AP	10000	T2/2NSR	D	AIW	19	XAP	Noshiro M.	7184	M	18-10N 120-00E	PR says last seen low in water, heading for beach.

124

Dt/Hr	Submarine	Pt	Position	Tgt	Size	Attack	Cl	So	Date	Type	Name	Tons	Dm	Location	Comments
AUG	1944														
18	HNMS ZW'RDVISCH	1	04-00N 099-32E	Jk	48	G	S	N			Kim Hup Soen	48			Name from DNO.
19/04 411 SPADEFISH		1	18-48N 119-47E	AP	10000	T2/6NUR	S	AIJW	19	XARL	Tamatsu M.	9589	S	18-12N 120-20E	W lists as landing craft depot ship.
19/05 222 BLUEFISH		6	17-34N 119-23E	AO	10000	T3/5NSR	S	IW J	19	AO	Hayasui	18300 6500	S	NW Luzon	PR says last seen with midships awash, bow & bridge high in air.
19/06 395 REDFISH		1	21-55N 120-19E	AO	10500	T2/4TSR	S								PR says target slowed down with 30 degree port list.
19/07 222 BLUEFISH		6	17-36N 119-38E	AK	19500	T5/7DUP	S	I	19	XAH	Awa M.	11249	L	18-11N 119-58E	PR says 3 hits & flames seen, photos.
19	HNMS ZW'RDVISCH	1	04-30N 098-15E	Jk	50	G	S								Date & size from DNO.
19	HNMS ZW'RDVISCH	1	04-30N 098-15E	Jk	100	G	S								See note above.
21/06 271 RAY		5	13-23N 120-19E	AP	6900	T1/4DUP	D	AIJ	21	C-AO	Taketoyo M.	6964	S	13-23N 120-19E	255 HADDO PR says ship exploded & stopped; 363 GUITARRO PR says burning ship seen.
21/06 255 HADDO		7	13-22N 120-19E	AK	7500	T2/2DUP	S	AI J	21	C-AK	Kinryu M. Kinryo M.	4392	S	13-23N 120-19E	PR says target afire.
21/06 255 HADDO		7	13-22N 120-19E	AK	4000	T3/3DUP	S	AIJ	21	C-AK	Norfolk M.	6576	S	13-23N 120-19E	PR says smoke column seen.
21/06 255 HADDO		7	13-22N 120-19E	AK	7500	T0/1DUP	0	AJ I	Note 21	C-AO	Taiei M.	10045 9929	SA S	11-59N 120-02E 13-30N 120-15E	PR says hit possible. A & J give date 24 Sep. Attribution ?]
21/07 363 GUITARRO		2	13-21N 120-18E	AK	5700	T2/4DUP	S	AIJ	21	C-AK	Uga M.	4433	S	13-20N 120-15E	
21/09 262 MUSKALLUNGE		4	11-43N 109-17E	AK	7500	T1/3DUP	D								
21/09 262 MUSKALLUNGE		4	11-43N 109-17E	AK	10000	T3/3DUP	D	AIJ	21	A-AP	Durban M.	7163	S	11-45N 109-15E	
21	HNMS ZW'RDVISCH	1	04-15N 099-14E	Jk	32	G	S								Date & size from DNO.
22/02 306 TANG		4	34-02N 136-21E	PC	1500	T1/4NSV	S	AI	22	A-AK	Nansatsu M. #2	116	S	Off Mikizaki	
22/04 257 HARDER		6L	14-15N 120-05E	DD	1200	Unk	0								225 HADDO PR says explosion seen, later attacked 2 damaged DDs.
22/04 255 HADDO		7	14-15N 120-05E	DD	1200	T1/3NSV	D								PR says hit DD later sunk below. SORG credits no hits this attack.
22/04 255 HADDO		7	14-15N 120-05E	AP	4000	T1/ NSV	P								PR says fired at DD, stray hit on AK. SORG credits HADDO & 257 HARDER.

Dt/Hr	Submarine	Pt	Position	Tgt	Size	Attack	Cl	So	Date	Type	Name	Tons	Dm	Location	Comments
AUG	1944														
22/06 255 HADDO		7	14-15N 120-05E	DD	1200	T1/2DUP	S	AIW J	22	PF	Sado	870 860	S	W of Manila	PR says this was DD damaged previously.
22/06 257 HARDER		6L	14-15N 120-05E	AP	4000	Unk	P	AIW J	22	PF	Matsuwa	870 860	S	W of Manila	SORG credits HARDER & 255 HADDO with unk AP.
22/07 257 HARDER		6L	14-15N 120-05E	DD	1200	Unk	S	AIW J	22	PF	Hiburi	940 900	S	W of Manila	HARDER believed lost 24 Aug.
22/13 411 SPADEFISH		1	18-48N 120-48E	AO	10500	T2/3DUP	S	AJ I	22	XAO	Hakko M. #2	10023 10000	S H	18-48N 120-46E	W gives name Hakko M.
22/19 387 PINTADO		2	29-44N 125-22E	AO	16800	T2/10TUP	S	AIJW	22	C-AO	Tonan M. #2	19262	S	29-54N 125-17E	W lists ship as XAO, credits 223 BONEFISH; PR shows no such attack.
22/19 387 PINTADO		2	29-44N 125-22E	AO	9800	T1/ TUP	S								
22/19 387 PINTADO		2	29-44N 125-22E	AO	7300	T1/ TUP	S								
22/22 287 BOWFIN		6	29-32N 129-31E	AK	7100	T2/6NSR	S	AIJ	22	A-AK	Tsushima M.	6754	S	29-33N 129-30E	
22/22 287 BOWFIN		6	29-32N 129-31E	AK	6700	T2/ NSR	S								
22/22 287 BOWFIN		6	29-32N 129-31E	DD	1300	T1/ NSR	S								
22/22 287 BOWFIN		6	29-32N 129-31E	AK	6800	T1/4NSR	S								
22/22 287 BOWFIN		6	29-32N 129-31E	DD	1300	T1/ NSR	S								
22	HMS STATESMAN	1	11-40N 092-45E	MV	3000	T1/4	S	AIJ	22	A-AK	Sugi M. #5	1983	S	Port Blair	
22	HMS TALLY HO	7	Malacca Strait	Cstr	300	G	S								
22	HMS TUDOR	1	N Sumatra	Jk	100	G	S								
23/04 396 RONQUIL		1	25-29N 123-15E	Unk	4000	T5/6NSR	D	AJ IW	24	A-AK XAP	Yoshida M. #3 Toyo M. #3	4646 985	S	Sancho Point	Other sources say Toyo M #3 sunk 12 Jun 45 by a/c; I says Yoshida M #3 sunk by a/c at above location. PR says fired at convoy, explosions heard but not seen. [I & W appear to confuse 2 ships.]
23/07 255 HADDO		7	16-06N 119-44E	DD	1300	T1/5DUP	D	AIW J	23	DD	Asakaze	1270	S PS	W of Lingayan	
23/11 306 TANG		4	34-37N 137-50E	AP	10000	T2/3DUP	S	AI J	23	C-AK	Tsukushi M.	1859 8135	S	34-37N 137-51E	J confuses ship with one of same name that survived war.

Dt/Hr	Submarine	Pt	Position	Tgt	Size	Attack	Cl	So	Date	Type	Name	Tons	Dm	Location	Comments
AUG	1944														
23/14 310	BATFISH	4	08-09N 134-38E	DD	1200	T3/3DUP	S	AW J	Note 23	AM	W 22	648 492	SA S	Off Palau	A says sunk by a/c off Palau; W says sunk by mine near Babelthuap, both 11 Nov. PR says Minekaze-cl DD seen to sink. [J attribution ?]
23/20 396	RONQUIL	1	25-07N 124-40E	AK	6700	T1/3TUP	D								
24/04 192	SAILFISH	11	21-29N 121-18E	AK	6500	T2/4NSR	S	AJW I	24	XAP	Toan M.	2110	S	21-23N 121-37E 21-27N 126-12E	W lists ship as both XAP & Std AK 2D.
24/05 192	SAILFISH	11	21-36N 121-19E	AK	4000	T2/8NSR	S								
24/07 183	SEAL	11	42-30N 144-05E	AK	2000	T2/3DSR	S	AIJ	24	C-AK	Tosei M.	531	S	42-30N 143-40E	
24/07 396	RONQUIL	1	25-13N 121-49E	AK	7100	T1/4DUP	S	AJ I	24	C-AK	Fukurei M.	5969	S H	Sankaku I. Sancho Point	
24	HMS TALLY HO	7	Malacca Strait	3Jk	270	G	S								
25/09 382	PICUDA	3	18-46N 120-46E	AK	4000	T1/2DUP	S	AIJ	25	C-AO	Kotoku M.	1943	S	18-41N 120-50E	PR says wreckage & survivors seen after attack.
25/13 395	REDFISH	1	18-33N 120-34E	AP	7500	T2/4DUP	S	AJ I	25	A-AK	Batopaha M. Batupahat M.	5953	S H	18-31N 120-31E	
25/13 395	REDFISH	1	18-33N 120-34E	AK	4000	T1/ DUP	S								
25/16 259	JACK	6	03-21N 120-49E	AK	200	GD	S								
25/16 382	PICUDA	3	18-45N 120-44E	PGE	1500	T0/3DUP	O	AIJW	25	DD	Yunagi	1270	S	NW Luzon	PR says down-the-throat shot believed missed.
25/18 306	TANG	4	33-55N 136-18E	AO	5000	T2/2DUP	S	AI	25	C-AO	Nanko M. #8	834	S	S of Mikizaki	
25/18 306	TANG	4	33-55N 136-18E	PCE	600	T1/1DUP	S								
26/18 310	BATFISH	4	08-30N 134-37E	DD	1700	T2/2TUP	S	AI J	26 Note	DD	Samidare	1685 1580	S JS	N of Palau I.	J credits BATFISH & a/c; see 25 Jul; W says wrecked 18 Aug then torp by BATFISH 25 Aug. PR days DD was stranded on Velasco Reef & under salvage, broke in two when hit.
27/19 363	GUITARRO	2	12-28N 119-57E	AO	2000	GM	S	J I	27	C-AO	Nanshin M. #27	834	S M	12-26N 119-55E	PR says 3 coastal AOs attacked, 1 left afire & sinking by stern. A says Nanshin M #27 ran aground 12 Sep at 12-06N 119-53E. [J attribution ?]

Dt/Hr	Submarine	Pt	Position	Tgt	Size	Attack	Cl	So	Date	Type	Name	Tons	Dm	Location	Comments
AUG	1944														
27/19	363 GUITARRO	2	12-28N 119-57E	Same	Same	Same	0	I	27	C-AO	Nanshin M. #3	834	M	12-26N 119-55E	A says no record of this ship. [Attribution ?]
27/19	363 GUITARRO	2	12-28N 119-57E	Same	Same	Same	0	I	27	C-AO	Nanshin M. #25	834	S	12-26N 119-55E	Same as above.
27/19	363 GUITARRO	2	12-28N 119-57E	Same	Same	Same	0	I W	27	XSC	Nanshin M.	52	M S	12-21N 119-55E	See above. PR noted no escorts with target group. [Attribution ?; sources appear confused as to ships involved.]
27	HMS STURDY	2	En rt Perth	Fish	150	G	S								
28/19	287 BOWFIN	6	25-56N 128-54E	Tra	500	GT	S								
29/02	259 JACK	6	02-07N 122-29E	AK	7500	T2/4NSR	S	AIJ	29	A-AK	Mexico M.	5785	S	02-15N 122-29E	A says owner gives date 21 Aug.
29/04	259 JACK	6	02-03N 122-29E	CM	500	T4/9NSR	S	AIW J	29	AM	W 28	755 492	S	02-15N 123-29E	
30 S	HMS STRONGBOW	1	W coast Siam	MV	1000	T2/15	S								BSH evaluates attack unsuccessful.
31/02	393 QUEENFISH	1	21-21N 121-06E	AK	7500	T2/3NUP	S								PR says hits heard on 2 ships.
31/02	393 QUEENFISH	1	21-21N 121-06E	AO	10000	T2/3NUP	S	AIJ	30-1	C-AO	Chiyoda M.	4700	S	21-24N 121-04E	PR says much debris in water after attack.
31/03	272 REDFIN	4	08-48N 117-54E	AK	200	GN	D								
31/05	315 SEALION	2	21-25N 121-19E	AO	10000	T2/10NSR	S	I	31	C-AO	Rikko M.	9181	H	21-30N 121-19E	J says sunk by marine casualty; I by a/c; both 6 Mar 45. [Attribution ?; see 215 GROWLER & 220 BARB below.]
31/05	215 GROWLER	10	21-29N 121-21E	AO	10000	T3/3TSR	S	I	31	C-AO	Rikko M.	9181	H	21-30N 121-19E	PR says target exploded. [Attribution ?; see 315 SEALION above & 220 BARB below.]
31/05	215 GROWLER	10	21-29N 121-21E	AK	7500	T2/3TSR	D								PR says target listing after hits.
31/05	215 GROWLER	10	21-29N 121-21E	DD	1300	T1/4TSR	S								PR says 1 hit seen, 2 heard. BARB PR says escort blew up after 2 hits about this time.
31/07	220 BARB	9	21-14N 121-22E	AK	7500	T2/3DUP	S	AIJ	30-1	C-AK	Okuni M.	5633	S	20-55N 121-17E	PR says hits seen on 2 ships.
31/07	220 BARB	9	21-14N 121-22E	AO	5000	T1/ DUP	D	I	31	C-AO	Rikko M.	9181	H	21-30N 121-19E	[Attribution ?; see 215 GROWLER & 315 SEALION above.]

Dt/Hr		Submarine	Pt	Position	Tgt	Size	Attack	Cl	So	Date	Type	Name	Tons	Dm	Location	Comments
AUG		1944														
31/07		315 SEALION	2	21-05N 121-26E	DD	2300	T2/3DUP	S	AIJW	31	PF	Shirataka	1345	S	20-55N 121-07E	W says ship was ex-minelayer.
31/07		315 SEALION	2	21-05N 121-26E	AP	10000	T3/3DUP	S								PR says 2 hits heard.
31/16		362 GUAVINA	3	05-53N 124-44E	AK	500	GD	S								
31/16		362 GUAVINA	3	05-53N 124-44E	AK	500	GD	S								
31/18		220 BARB	9	21-04N 121-08E	AK	2000	T3/3DUP	S	AI W	31 21	XAM	Hinode M. #20	281	S	21-21N 121-11E	[Attribution ?; many other sub attacks; W date may be misprint.]
31		HMS TANTALUS	4	Malacca Strait	Jk	30	G	S								
31	S	HMS TANTALUS	4	Malacca Strait	Jk	30	G	D								
SEP		1944														
1/03		386 PILOTFISH	2	30-32N 140-55E	AK	1000	T0/8NSR	O	AI J	1	XAG	Ina M.	853	S SA	30-26N 140-53E 30-26N 140-53E	W says sunk by a/c 1944; A says owners give location 36-26N 140-53E by unk sub. [JANAC attribution ?; owners location may be misprint.]
1		HMS SIRDAR	3	NW Sumatra	Cstr	300	G	S								
2/05		388 PIPEFISH	2	32-11N 139-58E	AGS	2100	T1/4TUP	D								
2/17		217 GUARDFISH	9	29-48N 140-20E	Tra	100	GD	D	I	1	C-AK	Shirakami M.	245	HW	N Chichi Jima	[Attribution ?]
2	S	HMS SIRDAR	3	NW Sumatra	Esc	250	G	D	I	2	XPkt	Kaiyo M. #5	93	S	03-55N 096-20E	
2	S	HMS SIRDAR	3	NW Sumatra	Cstr	300	G	D								
2		HMS STRONGBOW	1	W coast Siam	Cstr	800	T1/1	S	AI	2	A-AK	Toso M. #1	292	S	07-57N 098-49E	A says sunk by gunfire.
2		HMS STRONGBOW	1	W coast Siam	5Jk	100	G	S								
2		HMS STRONGBOW	1	W coast Siam	Ltr	50	G	D								
2	S	HMS STORM	6	Note	3Smc	510	G	S								Patrol was passage Ceylon->Fremantle; not in BSH.
2	S	HMS STORM	6	Note	2Smc	1000	G	D								See above note.
3		HMS STRONGBOW	1	W coast Siam	3Jk	60	G	S								
3		HMS TANTALUS	4	Malacca Strait	2Cst	1400	T2/3	S								

Dt/Hr	Submarine	Pt	Position	Tgt	Size	Attack	Cl	So	Date	Type	Name	Tons	Dm	Location	Comments
SEP	1944														
4/09	220 BARB	9	21-05N 119-34E	Sam	100	GD	S								
4/13	287 BOWFIN	6	31-54N 152-05E	AK	1000	TO/4+GD	S	AI	4	XPkt	Hinode M. #6	245	S	31-55N 152-00E	
4/19	196 SEARAVEN	12	47-03N 151-22E	Tra	100	GD	S								
4	HNMS O-19	6	W Sumatra	Prau	10	G	S								Date & size from DNO; BSH lists this patrol as 1st of 2nd commission.
4	HMS TANTALUS	4	Malacca Strait	Tug	200	G	D								
5/16	218 ALBACORE	10	32-24N 134-15E	AO	5000	T2/3DUP	S	AIJ	5	C-AK	Shingetsu M.	880	S	N Muroto Saki	
5	HMS TANTIVY	5	05-42S 104-58E	AK	4000	T2/7	S	AIJ	5	C-AK	Shiretoko M.	1799	S	05-44S 104-58E	
5	HMS STRONGBOW	1	W coast Siam	Jk		G	S								
5	HMS STRONGBOW	1	W coast Siam	Tug		G	S								
5	HMS STRONGBOW	1	W coast Siam	Ltr		G	S								
6/11	256 HAKE	6	16-19N 119-44E	DD	1500	T1/3DUP	S	I	6	DD	Hibiki	2300	H	8 mi. E Ryukyu	[Attribution ?; sinking not near attack.]
6/16	218 ALBACORE	10	33-29N 135-32E	Pat	2000	T1/4DUP	S	AIW	6	XAM	Eguchi M. #3	198	S	33-27N 135-33E	W credits 235 SHAD; PR shows no such attack.
--							-	AJ I	6	A-AP	Eiji M.	6968	SM S	22-19N 120-30E	No likely sub attack.
6	HNMS O-19	6	03-09S 101-20E	Cstr	200	G	S								See note 4 Sep.
6	HMS STYGIAN	1	W coast Burma	Sch	150	G	S								
7/17	263 PADDLE	5	08-11N 122-40E	AO	5000	T2/4DUP	S	J AI	7	XAO	Eiyo M. #2	5061	JS M	08-12N 122-37E	J credits PADDLE & a/c; A says damaged here & sunk by a/c 12 Sep in Cebu Port; W says sunk by a/c 1944. PR says 2 hits seen.
7/17	263 PADDLE	5	08-11N 122-40E	AK	4000	T2/2DUP	D	AIW J	7	XAP	Shinyo M.	2634 2518	S	08-12N 122-37E	PR says 2 timed hits, breaking-up noises heard. W lists ship as both XAP & Std AK 1C.
8/02	241 BASHAW	3	08-14N 121-47E	AK	7500	T3/6NUP	S	AJ IW	8	XAP	Yanagigawa M. Yanagawa M.	2813	S	08-10N 121-50E	PR describes target as large, modern AK. W lists ship as both XAP & Std 1W (steam ferry).

130

Dt/Hr	Submarine	Pt	Position	Tgt	Size	Attack	Cl	So	Date	Type	Name	Tons	Dm	Location	Comments
SEP	1944														
8/02	241 BASHAW	3	08-14N 121-47E	Same	Same	Same	0	A	8	?	Ryuka M.	?	M	08-19N 121-30E	PR does not mention any other ship. [Attribution ?]
8/19	255 HADDO	7	11-48N 121-10E	Sam	100	GN	S								
8/21	183 SEAL	11	47-18N 148-28E	DD	1700	T2/4NSR	S	I	8	DD	Namikaze	1215	H	N of Staten I.	Japanese records say after part of hull severed, remainder towed to Otaru.
8/21	183 SEAL	11	47-18N 148-28E	AK	4000	T1/ NSR	D								
8/21	183 SEAL	11	47-18N 148-28E	AK	4000	T1/ NSR	S								
8/21	411 SPADEFISH	1	24-46N 123-15E	AK	4000	T1/4NSR	S	AIJ	8	C-AK	Nichiman M.	1922	S	24-45N 123-20E	
8/21	411 SPADEFISH	1	24-46N 123-15E	AK	7500	T2/3NSR	S	AIJ	8	C-AK	Nichian M.	6197	S	24-45N 123-20E	
8/21	411 SPADEFISH	1	24-46N 123-15E	AK	4000	T2/4NSR	D								
8/22	411 SPADEFISH	1	24-39N 123-31E	AK	4000	T2/3NSR	S	AIJW	8	XAP	Shokei M.	2557	S	24-45N 123-20E	
8/22	411 SPADEFISH	1	24-39N 123-31E	AK	4000	T2/7NSR	S	AIJ	8	A-AK	Shinten M.	1254	S	24-45N 123-20E	
8/24	183 SEAL	11	47-40N 148-36E	AK	6900	T2/4NSR	D								
--							-	AI	8-11	C-APK	Usa M.	842	S	22-21N 120-26E	A says torpedoed; I says sunk by sub 11 Sep. No likely sub attack.
								J	13				SA	23-52N 118-56E	
--							-	I	11	C-AK	Nankai M.	842	S	22-21N 120-26E	A says this is same ship as Usa M above.
9/02	393 QUEENFISH	1	19-45N 120-56E	DD	1300	T1/3NUP	S	I	8	TB	Manazuru	600	?	NW Hatoma I.	PR says 1 timed hit heard.
9/02	393 QUEENFISH	1	19-45N 120-56E	AO	10000	T1/ NUP	S	AIJ	9	C-APK	Manshu M.	3053	S	19-45N 120-53E	
9/02	393 QUEENFISH	1	19-45N 120-56E	AP	10000	T3/3NUP	S	AIJW	9	XAP	Toyooka M.	7097	S	19-45N 120-53E	
9/03	183 SEAL	11	47-58N 148-20E	AK	9900	T2/4NUP	D	AIJ	9	A-AK	Shonan M.	5859	S	47-03N 148-18E	
9/11	390 PLAICE	2	27-26N 126-54E	XCL	7100	T1/6DUP	D								
9/12	241 BASHAW	3	08-30N 124-32E	AK	200	GD	S	A	?	XARS	Miho M.	632	M	Zamboanga-Cebu	A says torpedoed in convoy with Shinyo M & others (see attacks 7-8 Sep), sunk at Cebu. PR says inter-island supply ship was strafed by F6Fs & hit by 4" gunfire, burned to waterline & left sinking. [Attribution ?]
								IW	12				SA	Cebu	

Dt/Hr	Submarine	Pt	Position	Tgt	Size	Attack	Cl	So	Date	Type	Name	Tons	Dm	Location	Comments
SEP	1944														
9/16	385 BANG	3	28-53N 137-42E	AK	4000	T2/3DUP	S	AIJW	9	XAP	Tokiwasan M.	1804	S	28-58N 137-45E	
9/16	385 BANG	3	28-55N 137-42E	AO	7600	T2/3DUP	S	AIJ	9	C-AK	Shoryu M.	1916	S	28-58N 137-45E	
9	HMS PORPOISE	1	03-54N 098-42E	--	--	Mine	U	IW J	9	SC	Cha 8	130 100	SM	Belawan	Minefield laid 6-8 Jul; BSH claims sinking.
9	HMS PORPOISE	1	03-54N 098-42E	--	--	Mine	U	IW	9	SC	Cha 9	130	SM	N Sumatra	Minefield laid 6-8 Jul; not in BSH.
10/12	281 SUNFISH	8	33-52N 127-41E	AK	7200	T2/3DUP	S	AIJ	10	C-AO	Chihaya M.	4701	S	33-49N 127-41E	
10/12	281 SUNFISH	8	33-52N 127-41E	AO	7500	T1/ DUP	D								
10/12	281 SUNFISH	8	33-52N 127-41E	AK	6800	T1/2DUP	S								
10	HMS PORPOISE	1	03-54N 098-42E	--	--	Mine	U	J I	10	A-AO	Takekun M. Bukun M.	3029	PM SM	03-54N 098-43E	Minefield laid 8 Jul; BSH claims sinking.
10/24	264 PARGO	5	06-27S 116-48E	AK	4000	T2/7NSR	S	AIJW	10-1	XAN	Hinoki M.	599	S	06-17S 116-27E	See HNMS O-19 below.
10	HNMS O-19	6	05-59S 101-12E	AK	599	G	S	N			Korei M.	599			DNO claims sinking; BSH does not; A says ship is same as Hinoki M, above, sunk by 264 PARGO. [Attribution ?]
11/01	218 ALBACORE	10	32-20N 131-50E	AK	4000	T1/3NUR	S	AW J	11	SC	Cha 165	135 170	S	Sub position	
11/02	230 FINBACK	10	27-37N 140-21E	AO	1000	T1/3NSR	S	AJ I	11	C-AK	Hakuun M. #2 Hakuun M. #20	866	S	27-45N 140-40E	
11/02	230 FINBACK	10	27-37N 140-21E	AK	900	T2/3NSR	S	AJ I	11 10	A-AK	Hassho M. Kaneshige M.	536 522	S	N Chichi Jima	
12/02	215 GROWLER	10	17-54N 114-59E	DD	2300	T1/3NSR	S	AIW J	12	PF	Hirado	870 860	S	E of Hainan I.	I gives name Hirato.
12/02	215 GROWLER	10	17-54N 114-59E	AK	7500	T2/4NSR	S								
12/02	215 GROWLER	10	17-54N 114-59E	AK	7500	T1/ NSR	D								
12/05	315 SEALION	2	18-42N 114-30E	AO	10000	T2/5TUP	S	AJ W	12	XAP	Nankai M. Nankei M.	8416	S	18-15N 114-21E	
12/05	315 SEALION	2	18-42N 114-30E	AP	10000	T1/ TUP	S								

Dt/Hr	Submarine	Pt	Position	Tgt	Size	Attack	Cl	So	Date	Type	Name	Tons	Dm	Location	Comments
SEP	1944														
12/05	315 SEALION	2	18-42N 114-30E	AP	9400	T2/3TUP	S	AIJ	12	C-APK	Rakuyo M.	9418	S	18-32N 114-29E	PR says picked up 54 British & Australian POWs.
12/07	215 GROWLER	10	18-16N 114-40E	DD	1700	T2/6DUP	S	AIW J	12	DD	Shikinami	2090 1950	S	E of Hainan I.	
12/10	388 PIPEFISH	2	33-31N 135-57E	AK	4000	T2/4DUP	S	AIJW	12	XAG	Hakutetsu M #7	1018	S	33-32N 135-55E	
12/14	272 REDFIN	4	05-29S 120-30E	AO	5000	T1/4DUP	D								
12/23	383 PAMPANITO	3	19-18N 111-53E	AP	10500	T3/3NSR	S	AIJ	12	C-APK	Kachidoki M.	10509	S	19-25N 112-23E	
12/23	383 PAMPANITO	3	19-18N 111-53E	AK	6600	T1/2NSR	S	AIJ	12	C-AO	Zuiho M.	5135	S	19-16N 111-51E	
12/23	383 PAMPANITO	3	19-18N 111-53E	AK	6500	T1/2NSR	S								
12/23	383 PAMPANITO	3	19-18N 111-53E	AK	4000	T1/2NSR	D								
13/11	200 THRESHER	14	33-25N 124-20E	AK	5400	T1/4DUP	D								
13/24	281 SUNFISH	8	35-04N 124-49E	AO	10000	T3/3NSR	S	AI J	14 13	A-AK	Etajima M. Etashima M.	6933 6435	S	34-31N 124-46E	
13/24	281 SUNFISH	8	35-04N 124-49E	AO	9500	T2/2NSR	S	I	14	SC	Cha 99	135	H	34-29N 124-48E	
14	HMS SPIRIT	2	N coast Sumatra	3Jk	100	G	S								
15/18	362 GUAVINA	3	05-35N 125-24E	CM	2000	T8/12DUP	S	AJ IW	15 14	APD	T 3	1500	S SC	05-35N 125-20E Sarangani	W says ran aground. PR says target completely destroyed.
16/06	400 SEA DEVIL	1	34-30N 145-23E	SS	1900	T2/4TUP	S	IW J	15	SS	I-364 RO-42	1440 965	S	Missing	RO-42 lost Jun 44; most authorities agree I-364 sunk here.
16/07	235 SHAD	7	34-33N 138-25E	AK	5500	T3/4DUP	S								
16/13	382 PICUDA	3	21-16N 121-29E	AK	4000	T3/4DUP	S	AJ I	16	A-AK	Tokushima M.	5975	S H	21-27N 121-35E	
16/13	382 PICUDA	3	21-16N 121-29E	AK	4000	T1/1DUP	S								
16/13	382 PICUDA	3	21-16N 121-29E	AK	4000	T1/1DUP	S								
16/15	395 REDFISH	1	21-24N 121-17E	AO	10000	T2/4DUP	D	AIJW	16	XAO	Ogura M. #2	7311	S	21-42N 121-14E	
16/23	393 QUEENFISH	1	19-11N 116-21E	AP	10000	T1/4NSR	S								

Dt/Hr	Submarine	Pt	Position	Tgt	Size	Attack	Cl	So	Date	Type	Name	Tons	Dm	Location	Comments
SEP	1944														
16/24 220 BARB		9	19-18N 116-26E	AO	10000	T2/6NSR	S	AIW J	16-7	XAO	Azusa M.	10022 11177	S	19-15N 116-33E	
16/24 220 BARB		9	19-18N 116-26E	CVE	22500	T3/ NSR	S	AIW J	16-7	CVE	Unyo	17830 20000	S	19-24N 116-22E	
16	HMS TRADEWIND	3	Sunda Strait	2Bge	40	Dem	S								
18/02 388 PIPEFISH		2	32-49N 152-22E	AK	2600	T1/8NSR	D	I	18	A-AP	Rokko M.	3038	?	?	I says missing but lists ship again as sunk 5 Oct. PR says believed target not badly damaged. [Attribution ?; location not given.]
18/10 249 FLASHER		4	14-12N 120-02E	AK	7500	T4/5DUP	S	AIJW	18	XPG	Saigon M.	5350	S	14-20N 120-05E	
18/22 200 THRESHER		14	35-05N 124-24E	XAS	11600	T3/4NSR	S	AIJ	18	A-AK	Gyoku M.	6854	S	35-02N 124-24E	
18	HMS TRADEWIND	3	02-53S 101-10E	AK	4500	T2/4	S	AIJ	18	A-AK	Junyo M.	5065	S	02-53S 101-11E	
19/05 235 SHAD		7	33-40N 138-18E	DE	600	T3/4TUP	S	AIW J	19	CL PF	Ioshima	2461 900	S	Hachijo Jima	Ex-Chinese Ning Hai.
19/06 272 REDFIN		4	05-36S 122-16E	Tra	100	GD	S								
19/09 385 BANG		3	24-56N 122-14E	AK	5800	T2/4DUP	D	I	19	PF	CD 30	940	H	24-54N 122-23E	
19/09 385 BANG		3	24-56N 122-14E	AK	5800	T2/4DUP	S	AIJ	19	C-AO	Tosei M. #2	500	S	24-54N 122-23E	
19/09 397 SCAB'RDFISH		1	27-35N 127-07E	AS	5200	T2/4DUP	D	I	19	AS	Jingei	8600	H	NW of Okinawa	
19	HMS SPIRIT	2	N Sumatra	Jk	80	G	S								
19	HMS TRENCHANT	2	E Sumatra	2Jk		Ram	S								
20/12 255 HADDO		7	13-28N 120-15E	DD	1300	T1/4DUP	S								
21/00 385 BANG		3	25-21N 123-58E	AK	4000	T2/6NSR	D								
21/00 385 BANG		3	25-21N 123-58E	AK	4000	T1/ NSR	S								
21/00 385 BANG		3	25-21N 123-58E	AO	10000	T2/4NSR	S								
21/06 382 PICUDA		3	18-43N 120-52E	AK	4000	T2/4DUP	S	AIJW	21	XAP	Awaji M.	1948	S	18-42N 120-50E	
21/06 382 PICUDA		3	18-43N 120-52E	AP	10000	T2/2DUP	D								

Dt/Hr	Submarine	Pt	Position	Tgt	Size	Attack	Cl	So	Date	Type	Name	Tons	Dm	Location	Comments
SEP	1944														
21/09	235 SHAD	7	34-23N 139-43E	PG	800	T1/3DUP	S	AIW	21	XCMc	Fumi M. #2	304	S	34-25N 139-40E	W says XAM used as XCMc.
21/09	395 REDFISH	1	18-36N 120-39E	AP	4000	T2/4DUP	S								
21/09	395 REDFISH	1	18-36N 120-39E	AK	7500	T1/ DUP	S	AIJ	21	A-AP	Mizuho M.	8506	S	18-38N 120-43E	
21/09	395 REDFISH	1	18-36N 120-39E	AO	10500	T2/2DUP	D								
21/22	255 HADDO	7	13-35N 119-06E	CM	1000	T2/6NSR	S	AIJW	21	AGS	Katsuriki	1540	S	SW of Manila	
21/23	196 SEARAVEN	12	49-50N 145-10E	Esc	1000	T1/4NSR	D								
21/24	196 SEARAVEN	12	49-16N 145-29E	AK	4000	T2/4NSR	S	A J	21	A-AK	Rizan M.	4850 4747	S	49-36N 145-30E	I gives date 25 Sep; A says Japanese records give both dates.
22/03	260 LAPON	6	15-22N 119-17E	AK	4000	T1/3NSR	D								
22/04	260 LAPON	6	15-22N 119-17E	AO	10000	T2/3NSR	D	AI J	22	C-AK	Jungen Go Shun Yuan	1610	S	15-28N 118-48E	A says Shun Yuan former Chinese name.
22/10	264 PARGO	5	08-15N 117-06E	AK	5400	T1/4DUP	D								
22/10	264 PARGO	5	08-15N 117-06E	AP	7500	T2/2DUP	D								
23/16	308 APOGON	5	34-58N 155-00E	Tra	400	GD	S								
23/19	307 TILEFISH	3	51-26N 153-57E	Sam	100	GT	S								
23	HMS TRENCHANT	2	05-46N 100-04E	SS	1800	T1/3	S	U	23	SS	U-859	1616	S	Sub position	11 survivors taken prisoner.
23	287 BOWFIN	3	03-36S 116-35E	--	--	Mine	U	I	23	XAP	Hokkai M.	8416	HM	Balikpapan	Minefield laid 29 Jan. [Attribution ?; mines 9 months old.]
24/00	235 SHAD	7	34-43N 139-04E	AK	4000	T1/4NSR	D								
24/08	390 PLAICE	2	29-30N 129-15E	BB	29300	T4/6DUP	D								
24/18	272 REDFIN	4	04-31S 118-26E	Sam		GT	S								
25/19	272 REDFIN	4	01-06S 118-01E	AO	5000	T2/4TUP	S								
25/20	196 SEARAVEN	12	44-40N 146-50E	2Tra	400	GN	S								
25/20	196 SEARAVEN	12	44-40N 146-50E	8Sam	600	GN	S								
25/21	200 THRESHER	14	37-32N 124-33E	AK	4000	T2/2NSR	S	AIJ	25	C-AK	Nissei M.	1468	S	37-00N 124-06E	

135

Dt/Hr	Submarine	Pt	Position	Tgt	Size	Attack	Cl	So	Date	Type	Name	Tons	Dm	Location	Comments
SEP	1944														
25/22 217 GUARDFISH		9	38-30N 124-06E	AO	3100	T1/2NSR	S	AIJ	25		C-AK Miyakawa M. #2	873	S	Off Chinnampo	
25/22 316 BARBEL		2	29-50N 130-06E	AK	4000	T2/6NSR	S	AIJ	25		C-AK Bushu M.	1223	S	29-46N 129-40E	
25/22 316 BARBEL		2	29-50N 130-06E	DE	600	T1/ NSR	S								
25/22 316 BARBEL		2	29-50N 130-06E	AK	4000	T1/4NSR	D								
--							-	W I	25		XPkt Iwaki M.	122	S L	25-10N 125-51E	No likely sub attack.
26/03 200 THRESHER		14	37-13N 123-48E	AO	5000	T2/4NSR	S	AIJ	25-6	C-AK	Koetsu M.	873	S	37-45N 123-37E	
26/07 264 PARGO		5	07-06N 116-00E	ACV	6000	T3/8DUP	S	AIJW	26	CMc	Aotaka	1608	S	07-00N 116-00E	
27/02 390 PLAICE		2	29-26N 128-50E	AP		10000 T3/4NSR	S								
27/02 390 PLAICE		2	29-26N 128-50E	DE	600	T1/ NSR	S	AIW J	27	PF	CD 10	940 800	S	Amami Oshima	
27/03 196 SEARAVEN		12	45-41N 148-38E	AM	500	GN+TO/3	D	AI	26	DD	Momi	1262	M	45-44N 148-41E	PR says CO mistook DD for smaller ship & made gun attack first.
27/05 223 BONEFISH		6	13-48N 119-36E	AO		10000 T1/4NSR	S	I	27	AO	Kamoi	17000	M	SW of Manila	
27/06 308 APOGON		5	46-32N 146-48E	AK	5900	T2/3DSR	S	AIJW	26-7	XAK	Hachirogata M.	1999	S	47-07N 151-25E	
27/07 249 FLASHER		4	15-40N 117-09E	AP	7500	T1/4DUP	S	AIJ	27		A-AP Ural M.	6374	S	15-45N 117-19E	PR says hits on 2 ships heard. [J attribution ?; see 260 LAPON below.]
27/07 249 FLASHER		4	15-40N 117-09E	AK	4000	T1/ DUP	D	I	27		C-AO Tachibana M.	6521	L	W of Luzon	260 LAPON PR says 1 ship seen to explode, another hit. [Attribution ?]
27/12 260 LAPON		6	15-45N 117-48E	AK	9500	T2/3DUP	S	AI	27		A-AP Ural M.	6374	S	15-45N 117-19E	PR says hits seen on 2 overlapping ships, 1 broke in two, later saw cripple on fire & abandoned with bow awash; photo. [J credits 249 FLASHER above; attribution ?]
27/12 260 LAPON		6	15-45N 117-48E	AK	5600	T2/3DUP	S	AJ I	27		C-AO Hokki M.	5599	S H	15-50N 117-41E	See above comments.
--							-	I	27	PF	CD 25	810	M	Takao, Formosa	No likely sub attack.
27	HMS THOROUGH	2	N coast Sumatra	Cstr	300	G	S								

136

Dt/Hr	Submarine	Pt	Position	Tgt	Size	Attack	Cl	So	Date	Type	Name	Tons	Dm	Location	Comments
SEP	1944														
28/05	223 BONEFISH	6	13-16N 120-08E	AO	10000	T2/4NSR	S	AIJ	28	C-AO	Anjo M.	2086 2068	S	13-13N 120-04E	
29/13	305 SKATE	6	27-12N 128-18E	AK	4000	T1/4DUP	S	AIJ	29	A-AK	Ekisan M.	3690	S	27-11N 128-22E	
29/13	305 SKATE	6	27-12N 128-18E	PC		T0/2DUP	O	AIW	29	XAM	Hoei M.	219	S	27-14N 128-21E	PR says torps believed prematures.
30/13	309 ASPRO	5	17-01N 120-25E	AK	7500	T2/6DUP	S								
30 U	294 ESCOLAR	1L	N of Bonin Is.	PG	Unk	G	U								Attack not in SORG; info from U.
OCT	1944														
1/04	412 TREPANG	1	30-32N 138-12E	AO	10000	T1/5NUP	S	AIJW	1	XAF	Takunan M. Takunan	752	S	25-30N 142-30E	PR says 1 hit seen. [J attribution ?; sinking not near attack.]
1/10	185 SNAPPER	11	28-11N 139-30E	AK	4000	T2/4DUP	S	AIWJ	1	XAP	Seian M.	1990 1900	S	28-20N 139-25E	
1/10	185 SNAPPER	11	28-11N 139-30E	DE	600	T0/4DUP	O	AIJW	1	CMc	Ajiro	720	S	28-20N 139-25E	PR says fired at convoy of 2 AKs & 2 escorts, heard explosions & breaking-up noises but believed only 1 ship was hit.
1/11	288 CABRILLA	6	16-15N 119-43E	AP	6900	T3/3DUP	S	AIJW	1	XAO	Kyokuho M.	10059	S	16-11N 119-44E	
1/11	288 CABRILLA	6	16-15N 119-43E	AK	4000	T1/3DUP	S	AIJ	1	C-AO	Zuiyo M.	7385	S	16-11N 119-44E	
1/23	364 HAMMERHEAD	2	06-30N 116-11E	AK	7500	T2/3NSR	S	AIJ	2	C-Ore	Kokusei M.	5396	S	06-30N 116-15E	
1/23	364 HAMMERHEAD	2	06-30N 116-11E	AK	7500	T1/3NSR	S	AJI	2	C-Ore	Hiyori M. Nichiwa M.	5321	S	06-25N 116-13E	
1/24	364 HAMMERHEAD	2	06-30N 116-11E	AK	4000	T1/2NSR	S	IJ	2	C-AK	Higane M.	5320	S	06-30N 116-15E	
1/24	364 HAMMERHEAD	2	06-30N 116-11E	AO	5000	T2/2NSR	D								
2/09	309 ASPRO	5	18-25N 120-32E	AO	5000	T3/4DUP	S	AIJW	2-3	XAK	Azuchisan M.	6886	S	18-30N 120-33E	
2/16	261 MINGO	5	00-59S 117-22E	Tra	300	GD	S								
2/16	261 MINGO	5	00-59S 117-22E	3Tra	600	GD	S								
2/22	391 POMFRET	2	21-00N 121-46E	AK	7500	T2/3NUP	S	AIJ	2	A-AP	Tsuyama M.	6962	S	20-51N 121-31E	
2/22	391 POMFRET	2	21-00N 121-46E	AK	4000	T1/3NUP	D	I	2	A-AP	Macassar M.	4026	L	21-02N 121-36E	I gives name Makassar M.

Dt/Hr	Submarine	Pt	Position	Tgt	Size	Attack	Cl	So	Date	Type	Name	Tons	Dm	Location	Comments
OCT	1944														
3/10	307 TILEFISH	3	45-02N 148-02E	AK	2000	T1/5DUP	S								
3/10	307 TILEFISH	3	45-02N 148-02E	AK	2000	T1/ DUP	S								
3/10	309 ASPRO	5	17-56N 119-52E	AK	5500	T3/4DUP	S								
3/18	200 THRESHER	14	30-49N 153-26E	Tra	200	GT	D	W I	3	XPkt	Nanshin M. #28	83	P L	Northeast area	W credits probable US sub. PR says 4 hits with 5" gun.
4/08	249 FLASHER	4	15-27N 119-49E	AK	4000	T1/3DUP	S	AJ I	4	A-AK	Taibin M. Otoshi M.	6886	S	15-22N 119-51E	
4/08	249 FLASHER	4	15-27N 119-49E	AK	4000	T2/3DUP	S								
4	HMS TALLY HO	8	Malacca Strait	MV	200	G	D								
4	HMS SEA ROVER	6	Flores Sea	Cstr	150	G	D								
4	HMS SEA ROVER	6	Flores Sea	Ltr	80	G	D								
4	HNMS ZW'RDVISCH	2	08-05S 115-29E	AO	500	G	S								
5/13	224 COD	5	13-02N 120-15E	AK	7500	T1/2DUP	D								
5/15	224 COD	5	13-06N 120-15E	AO	10000	T6/8DUP	S	AIJ	5	C-AK	Tatsushiro M.	6886	S	13-02N 120-16E	
--							-	AJ AI	5	A-AP	Rokko M.	3038	SA S	23-09N 119-58E Takao-Keelung	A says records support both versions of loss. No likely sub attack.
6/08	309 ASPRO	5	16-53N 120-18E	AO	10000	T1/3DUP	D								PR describes target as new AO, #525 on stack.
6/14	239 WHALE	9	19-40N 118-05E	AO	10000	T5/6DUP	S	AIJ	6	C-AO	Akane M.	10241	S	19-48N 118-22E	
6/15	239 WHALE	9	19-40N 118-05E	Same	Same	Same	0	AIW	7	XAP	Kinugasa M.	8407	S	19-48N 118-22E	J credits 366 HAWKBILL & 318 BAYA, 7 Oct, but location matches WHALE posit. PR says fired at convoy, heard 5 timed hits & breaking-up noises. [Attribution ?]
6/14	288 CABRILLA	6	17-31N 120-21E	AK	4900	T3/3DUP	S	A I	6	C-AP	Hokurei M.	2407	S M	17-37N 120-19E	PR says 3 hits followed by breaking-up noises. J credits a/c & sub (not identified) 18 Oct at 17-46N 120-25E. [Attribution to CABRILLA appears intended.]

Dt/Hr	Submarine	Pt	Position	Tgt	Size	Attack	Cl	So	Date	Type	Name	Tons	Dm	Location	Comments
OCT	1944														
6/14	288 CABRILLA	6	17-31N 120-21E	AO	9200	T2/3DUP	S	AIJ	6	C-AO	Yamamizu M. #2	5154	S	17-29N 120-21E	
6/18	242 BLUEGILL	3	13-31N 122-30E	AK	1500	T1/1TSV	S								
6/18	304 SEAHORSE	6	19-27N 118-08E	DD	1700	T1/6TUP	S	AW J	6	PF	CD 21	810 800	S	19-45N 118-22E	I says missing, cause unk.
6/22	321 BESUGO	1	30-03N 151-11E	Pat	300	GM	D								
6	HMS TALLY HO	8	04-20N 098-24E	SC	100	G	S	AIW J	6	SC	Cha 2	135 100	S	W of Penang	
6	HMS STATESMAN	2	Mergui Arch.	2Cst	300	G	S								
6	HNMS ZW'RDVISCH	2	Java Sea	SS	1140	T1/6	S	U	5-6	SS	U-168	1247	S	06-20S 111-28E	27 survivors; DNO gives tons as 1144.
7/03	224 COD	5	13-40N 119-25E	AO	15000	T2/4NUR	D	AI	7	AO	Shiretoko	14050	H	13-30N 119-20E	PR says 2 hits; 271 RAY PR confirms.
7/04	258 HOE	6	17-46N 119-40E	AK	7500	T2/4NSR	S	AJ I	7	A-AP	Macassar M. Makassar M.	4026	S	17-30N 119-52E	PR says 2 hits, target seen smoking heavily; J credits 309 ASPRO below. [Attribution ?]
7/04	258 HOE	6	17-46N 119-40E	AK	4000	T1/2NSR	D								
7/05	271 RAY	6	13-02N 119-49E	AO	15000	T3/6TUP	D	AI	7	AO	Shiretoko	14050	H	13-30N 119-20E	PR says AO seen to reach anchorage.
7/05	309 ASPRO	5	17-54N 119-57E	AK	7500	T3/4TUR	S	AJ I	7	A-AP	Macassar M. Makassar M.	4026	S	17-30N 119-52E	PR says hits heard, target settled by stern. See 258 HOE above.
7/06	288 CABRILLA	6	17-50N 119-37E	AK	4900	T3/4DUP	S	AIJW	7	XAP	Shinyo M. #8	1959	S	NW of Luzon	PR says broke in half & sank (PR). W lists ship as both XAP & Std AK 1D.
7/22	318 BAYA	1	14-30N 115-48E	AK	7500	T2/6NUR	S	J	7	XAP	Kinugasa M.	8407		JS Sub position	J credits BAYA & 366 HAWKBILL. Japanese location matches 239 WHALE attack 6 Oct (19-48N 118-22E). PR says 2 timed hits & breaking-up noises heard. [J attribution ?; location not near attack.]
7/22	366 HAWKBILL	1	14-22N 115-46E	AK	7500	T2/9NSV	S	J	7	XAP	Kinugasa M.	8407		JS Sub position	J credits HAWKBILL & 318 BAYA. Japanese location matches 239 WHALE attack 6 Oct (19-48N 118-22E). PR says 2 hits & huge explosion seen. [J attribution ?; location not near attack.]
--							-	I	7	CM	Itsukushima	1970	S	S of Bawean I.	See HNMS ZWAARDVISCH 17 Oct.

139

Dt/Hr	Submarine	Pt	Position	Tgt	Size	Attack	Cl	So	Date	Type	Name	Tons	Dm	Location	Comments
OCT	1944														
8/01	319 BECUNA	1	14-05N 115-38E	AO	5000	T2/4NUP	D	I	8	XAV	Kimikawa M.	6863	H	14-12N 115-53E	
8/04	258 HOE	6	17-43N 119-55E	AK	4000	T1/3NSR	D								PR says last seen smoking entire length.
8/04	258 HOE	6	18-30N 116-15E	AK	4000	T1/3NSR	D								
8/04	258 HOE	6	18-32N 116-13E	Esc	500	T1/1NSR	D	I	8	PF	CD 8	940	H	19-30N 116-38E	
8/04	258 HOE	6	18-32N 116-13E	AK	7500	T2/4NSR	S	AIJ	8	A-AP	Kohoku M.	2576	S	18-40N 116-00E	PR says blew up.
8	HMS STURDY	3	Gulf of Boni	Cstr	300	G	S								
9/02	217 GUARDFISH	9	32-44N 127-03E	DD	1500	T1/4NSR	D								
9/02	276 SAWFISH	8	19-33N 116-38E	AO	9200	T3/10NSR	S	AIJ	9	C-AO	Tachibana M.	6521	S	19-30N 116-38E	
9/07	320 BERGALL	1	11-40N 109-12E	AK	700	T1/3DUP	S								
9/08	263 PADDLE	6	01-20S 117-36E	Sch	100	GD	S								
9/17	319 BECUNA	1	12-45N 118-00E	AO	5000	T2/2DUP	S	I	9	XAO	San Luis M.	7268	M	12-43N 118-05E	PR says last seen with bow sunk, stern still out.
9/17	319 BECUNA	1	12-45N 118-00E	AO	5000	T2/2DUP	S	AI J	9	C-AO	Tokuwa M.	1943	S JS	12-43N 118-05E	J credits BECUNA & 366 HAWKBILL. PR says seen sinking by stern, funnel broken.
9/17	319 BECUNA	1	12-45N 118-00E	AP	7500	T2/3DUP	D								
9/17	319 BECUNA	1	12-45N 118-00E	AK	4000	T1/1DUP	D								
9/18	366 HAWKBILL	1	12-46N 118-02E	AK	4000	T2/4TUP	S	AI J	9	C-AO	Tokuwa M.	1943	S JS	12-43N 118-05E	J credits HAWKBILL & 319 BECUNA. PR says seen with bow straight up.
9/18	366 HAWKBILL	1	12-46N 118-02E	AK	4000	T1/2TUP	D								
9/20	246 CROAKER	2	32-08N 129-51E	AO	10000	T4/4NSR	S	AIJ	9	C-AK	Shinki M.	2211	S	32-14N 129-54E	
9/20	392 STERLET	2	26-17N 128-12E	Sam		GN	S								
9/23	366 HAWKBILL	1	12-21N 118-14E	AK	7500	T1/3NSV	D								
10/11	223 BONEFISH	6	16-20N 119-45E	AK	4000	T2/4DUP	D								
10/11	223 BONEFISH	6	16-20N 119-45E	AK	4000	T1/2DUP	D								

Dt/Hr	Submarine	Pt	Position	Tgt	Size	Attack	Cl	So	Date	Type	Name	Tons	Dm	Location	Comments
OCT	1944														
10/12	401 SEA DOG	1	26-50N 127-30E	Tra		GD	D								
10/13	260 LAPON	6	16-10N 119-44E	AK	5800	T2/3DUP	D	AIJ	10	A-AP	Ejiri M.	6968	S	16-10N 119-45E	
10/13	260 LAPON	6	16-10N 119-44E	DE	500	T1/1DUP	S								
10	HNMS ZW'RDVISCH	2	05-57S 112-29E	Cstr	500	G	S	IW	10	XPkt	Koei M.	19	S	SW Bawean I.	
11/04	263 PADDLE	6	01-34S 117-19E	AK	500	GM	S								
11/04	263 PADDLE	6	01-34S 117-19E	AK	500	GM	S								
11/05	306 TANG	5L	25- N 121- E	AK	7500	T2/3TUP	S	AJ I	10	C-AK	Joshu Go Joshu M.	1658	S SM	25-20N 121-32E Fukueichia	
11/05	412 TREPANG	1	33-18N 137-42E	AO	10000	T3/4TUP	S								
11/09	412 TREPANG	1	33-18N 137-42E	LST	2000	T0/4DUP	0	AIW J	11	APD	T 105	890 1000	S	33-07N 137-38E	PR says torps believed missed, heard 2 end of run explosions. [Possibly hit in earlier attack on AO.]
11/21	306 TANG	5L	25- N 121- E	AK	5800	T1/1NSV	S	AIJ	10-1	C-AK	Oita M.	711	S	SW Fukueichia	
11	HMS SUBTLE	1	Sabang	ML		T1/3	D								
12/01	246 CROAKER	2	32-11N 129-41E	AM	600	T3/3NSR	S								
12/08	192 SAILFISH	12	22-16N 120-26E	Sam		GD	S								
12/09	227 DARTER	4L	08-40N 116-42E	AO	10000	T2/2DUP	D								
12/10	242 BLUEGILL	3	07-53N 122-09E	2Smc	1000	GD	D								
12/14	192 SAILFISH	12	22-23N 120-15E	YTL	100	GD	D								
12/14	271 RAY	6	13-31N 120-19E	AK	5500	T2/4DUP	S	AIJW	12	XAP	Toko M.	4180	S	13-32N 120-21E	
12/21	412 TREPANG	1	33-52N 138-09E	BB	29300	T1/6NSR	D								
12/21	412 TREPANG	1	33-52N 138-09E	DD	2300	T1/ NSR	S	AI	12	DD	Fuyuzuki	2700	M	Off Omaesaki	W gives name Fuyutsuki.
12	HMS STRONGBOW	2	02-50N 100-50E	MV	2000	T1/1	S	AJ	12	AK	Manryo M.	1185	S	Sub position	
13/06	316 BARBEL	2	29-38N 127-27E	AO	10000	T1/4TSR	D								
13/06	316 BARBEL	2	29-38N 127-27E	DD	1500	T2/ TSR	S								

Dt/Hr	Submarine	Pt	Position	Tgt	Size	Attack	Cl	So	Date	Type	Name	Tons	Dm	Location	Comments
OCT	1944														
13/09	320 BERGALL	1	11-52N 109-20E	AK	4000	T2/4DUP	S	AIJ	13	C-AO	Shinshu M.	4182	S	11-53N 109-17E	
13/15	178 PERMIT	14	07-15N 151-45E	Pat	500	T1/2DUP	S									
13	HMS STURDY	3	Gulf of Boni	Cstr	350	G	S	I	13	C	Kosei M.	99	S	W of Celebes	
13	HMS STURDY	3	Gulf of Boni	Cstr	150	Dem	S	Note	13	?	Hansei M.	?	S	04-34S 121-27E	Name from notes by Wilds in NavHistCtr. [Attribution ?]
13	HMS STURDY	3	Gulf of Boni	5Cst	750	Dem	S									
14/01	247 DACE	5	06-05N 115-55E	AP	7500	T1/6NSR	S	AJ I	14	C-AO	Eikyo M.	6948	S H	06-00N 115-55E	
14/01	247 DACE	5	06-05N 115-55E	AO	10000	T1/ NSR	S	AIJ	14	C-AO	Nittetsu M.	5993	S	06-00N 115-55E	
14/01	247 DACE	5	06-05N 115-55E	AK	7500	T2/4NSR	O	I	14	C-Ore	Taizen M.	5396	H	06-00N 115-55E	
14/08	240 ANGLER	5	11-53N 121-39E	AK	4000	T2/4DUP	S	AIJ	14	A-AP	Nanrei M.	2407	S	11-48N 121-40E	
14/11	223 BONEFISH	6	16-12N 119-45E	AK	2000	T1/4DUP	S	AIJ	14	C-AK	Fushimi M.	2546	S	16-17N 119-45E	
14	HMS STURDY	3	Gulf of Boni	Cstr	300	G	S	I	14	B-AG	Comm. Ship 128	230	S	S of Celebes	Ship not in W. [Attribution ?]
15/04	198 TAMBOR	12	29-43N 143-09E	AK	4000	T1/4NSR	S									
15	HMS STURDY	3	Gulf of Boni	3Sch	450	Dem	S									
15	HMS SUBTLE	1	Nicobar Is.	Cstr	500	T1/5	S	Note								BSH claims this was Kaiyo M #2 but location does not agree with Japanese records. See HNMS ZWAARDVISCH below.
15	HNMS ZW'RDVISCH	2	06-30S 111-41E	Cstr	143	G	S	AI N	15	XSC	Kaiyo M. #2 Kaiyo M.	143	S	06-30S 111-35E	BSH says 2000T AK damaged this attack; Neth sources say target misidentified as such, missed by torp, later sunk by gunfire; W says both Kaiyo M #2 & Kaiyo #1, 270T AGOR, sunk by 247 DACE, same date & location; DACE not in area.
16/06	307 TILEFISH	3	48-07N 153-04E	AK	3000	T2/2TUP	S									
16/06	307 TILEFISH	3	48-07N 153-04E	PYc	1000	T1/2DUP	S	AIW	16	XPkt	Kyowa M. #2	108	S	Matsuwa Jima	
16/21	305 SKATE	8	27-49N 130-37E	CL	3200	T1/3NUS	D									

142

Dt/Hr	Submarine	Pt	Position	Tgt	Size	Attack	Cl	So	Date	Type	Name	Tons	Dm	Location	Comments
OCT	1944														
16/22 321 BESUGO		1	32-30N 132-36E	CA	10000	T1/6NSR	D	I	16	DD	Suzutsuki	2700	M	Off Toizaki	
--							-	I A	16	C-AK	Tokkan M. #2	101	S	S of Celebes 06-30S 111-35E	A says sunk by torp, location same as HNMS ZWAARDVISCH attack above. No likely sub attack S of Celebes.
17/05 246 CROAKER		2	33-05N 128-27E	Sam		GN	D								
17/13 307 TILEFISH		3	46-47N 151-44E	AK	5000	T1/5DUP	D								
17	HNMS ZW'RDVISCH	2	05-26S 113-48E	CM	1970	T1/3	S	AJ IW	17 7	CM	Itsukushima	1970	S	05-23S 113-48E E of Bawean I.	Holmes gives name Itsutshima; DNO gives tons as 2330.
17	HNMS ZW'RDVISCH	2	05-26S 113-48E	XCM	1600	T1/2	D	I	17	CM	Wakataka	1608	M	N of Bawean I.	W gives name Wakatake; DNO gives tons as 1990; some sources confuse this ship with Itsukushima, above.
17	HMS STYGIAN	2	Off Penang	2Jk	180	G+Dem	S								
17	HMS STYGIAN	2	Off Penang	Cstr	350	G	S								
18/06 242 BLUEGILL		3	14-06N 119-40E	APK	7500	T2/3DUP	S	AIJ	18	A-AK	Arabia M.	9480	S	14-04N 119-52E	PR says ship hit but not seen to sink.
18/06 242 BLUEGILL		3	14-96N 119-40E	APK	7500	T1/3DUP	D								
18/06 242 BLUEGILL		3	14-06N 119-40E	APK	7500	T1/ DUP	D								SORG shows 800T DE sunk this attack; PR says APK.
18/11 242 BLUEGILL		3	14-06N 119-40E	AK	7500	T2/2DUP	S	AJ I	18	C-AK	Hakushika M. Hakuroku M.	8152	S	14-04N 119-52E	PR says target was previously damaged cripple.
18/11 242 BLUEGILL		3	14-06N 119-40E	AP	4000	T2/4DUP	S	AIJ	18	A-AK	Chinzei M.	1999	S	14-04N 119-52E	
18/20 242 BLUEGILL		3	13-55N 119-20E	AK	7500	T2/3NSR	S								PR says target was another cripple.
18/22 270 RATON		6	12-37N 118-46E	AP	10000	T2/2NSR	S	AJ I	18	A-AK	Shiranesan M.	4739	S H	14-44N 118-00E	[Location appears closer to 242 BLUEGILL attacks above; J attribution ?]
18/22 270 RATON		6	12-37N 118-46E	AK	8200	T1/ NSR	S								
18/22 270 RATON		6	12-37N 118-46E	AK	7500	T2/2NSR	S	AIJ	18	A-AK	Taikai M.	3812	S	12-30N 119-10E	
18/22 270 RATON		6	12-37N 118-46E	AK	7500	T3/4NSR	S								
--							-	J	18	C-AP	Hokurei M.	2407	JS	17-46N 120-25E	J credits a/c & unidentified sub. See 288 CABRILLA 6 Oct.

Dt/Hr	Submarine	Pt	Position	Tgt	Size	Attack	Cl	So	Date	Type	Name	Tons	Dm	Location	Comments
OCT	1944														
18	HMS STYGIAN	2	Off Penang	LC	50	Dem	S								
19/00	270 RATON	6	12-24N 118-42E	DD	1500	T1/4NSR	S								
19/02	270 RATON	6	12-02N 118-52E	AK	5900	T1/6NSR	D								
19/02	270 RATON	6	12-02N 118-52E	AK	5900	T1/ NSR	D								
19/03	198 TAMBOR	12	34-26N 139-52E	DE	1000	T2/4NSR	S								
19 S	HMS STYGIAN	2	Off Penang	Jk	120	G	D								
19	HMS STYGIAN	2	Off Penang	Cstr	200	G	S								
20/01	310 BATFISH	5	06-45S 119-00E	PC	300	T1/1NSR	D								
20/03	364 HAMMERHEAD	2	04-52N 113-24E	AK	7500	T1/4NSR	S	AIJ	20	A-AK	Ugo M.	3684	S	04-45N 113-30E	
20/03	364 HAMMERHEAD	2	04-52N 113-24E	AK	7500	T1/2NSR	S								
20/04	364 HAMMERHEAD	2	04-41N 113-22E	AK	7500	T2/4NSR	S	AIJW	20	XAP	Oyo M.	5458	S	04-45N 113-30E	
20 S	HMS STYGIAN	2	Off Penang	Cstr	800	G	S								
20 S	HMS STYGIAN	2	Off Penang	Smc		G	D								
21	HMS TANTIVY	6	Makassar Strait	Sch	100	G	S	AI	20	C-AK	Otori M.	198	S	Off Balikpapan	
21	HMS TANTIVY	6	Makassar Strait	Sch	100	G	S	AI	20	C-AK	Takasago M. #3	82	S	Kutei Estuary	
21	HMS TANTIVY	6	Makassar Strait	Sch	100	G	S	AI	20	C-AK	Chokyu M. #2	136	S	Kutei Estuary	A says torp by unk sub.
21	HMS TANTIVY	6	Makassar Strait	6Sch	230	G	S								
22/01	194 SEADRAGON	11	21-57N 118-14E	CV	28000	T2/4NSR	D								
22/01	194 SEADRAGON	11	21-57N 118-14E	CL	4000	T1/ NSR	D								
22/07	401 SEA DOG	1	29-20N 129-45E	AK	4000	T1/6DUP	S	AIW J	22	AF	Muroto	8215 4500	S	29-18N 129-44E	
22/07	401 SEA DOG	1	29-20N 129-45E	AK	4000	T1/ DUP	0	AIJW	22	XPG	Tomitsu M.	2933	S	29-18N 129-44E	SORG does not credit sinking; PR says verified by intelligence.
22/08	224 COD	5	16-30N 119-49E	Sam	100	GD	D								

Dt/Hr	Submarine	Pt	Position	Tgt	Size	Attack	Cl	So	Date	Type	Name	Tons	Dm	Location	Comments
OCT	1944														
22	HMS TANTIVY	6	Makassar Strait	SC		Note	S	I	22	C-AK	Comm. Ship 137	200	H	05-47S 119-42E	BSH says ship blew up after hitting floating torpedo. [Ship not in W; attribution ?]
22	HMS TANTIVY	6	Makassar Strait	6Cst	500	G	S								
22	HMS TANTIVY	6	Makassar Strait	Cstr	500	G	D								
23	306 TANG	5L	25- N 122- E	AO	10000	T2/2NSV	S								
23/01	246 CROAKER	2	35-29N 126-05E	AK	2000	T1/4NSR	S	AI J	23	A-AK	Hakuran M. Byakuran M.	887	S	35-30N 126-15E	
23/02	246 CROAKER	2	35-30N 125-56E	Sch	100	GN	D								
23/03	243 BREAM	3	14-06N 119-37E	CA	9000	T3/6NSR	D	AW I	24 23	CA	Aoba	9000	H MA	Manila Bay WSW of Manila	PR says timed explosions seen & heard.
23/04	306 TANG	5L	25- N 122- E	AO	10000	T2/3NSV	S	AJ I	23	A-AK	Toun M.	1915	S H	24-49N 120-26E	
23/04	306 TANG	5L	25- N 122- E	AO	10000	T1/ NSV	S	AJ I	22	A-AK	Tatsuju M.	1944	S H	24-49N 120-26E	
23/04	306 TANG	5L	25- N 122- E	AP	7500	T2/4NSV	S	AIJ	23	A-AP	Wakatake M.	1920	S	24-49N 120-26E	
23/04	306 TANG	5L	25- N 122- E	AP	7500	T2/ NSV	S	A I	24 23	C-AK	Kori Go	1339	S ?U	24-42N 120-21E	
23/06	227 DARTER	4L	09-24N 117-11E	CA	12500	T5/6TUP	S	AW J	23	CA	Atago	13160 12200	S	09-30N 117-13E	I says sunk by a/c.
23/06	227 DARTER	4L	09-24N 117-11E	CA	12500	T4/4TUP	D	I	23	CA	Takao	13160	?A	W of Palawan	
23/06	247 DACE	5	09-28N 117-20E	CA	12500	T4/6NUP	S	AW J	23	CA	Maya	13160 12200	S	09-22N 117-07E	I says sunk by a/c.
23/17	276 SAWFISH	8	18-58N 118-31E	AK	8700	T4/5DUP	S	AIJW	23	XAV	Kimikawa M.	6863	S	18-58N 118-46E	
23/23	276 SAWFISH	8	19-28N 119-22E	AO	10100	T1/5NSR	D								PR says hit heard but target did not slow.
23/24	279 SNOOK	7	19-44N 118-25E	AK	7500	T2/5NSR	S	AI J	24	C-AO	Kikusui M.	3887	S PS	19-46N 118-30E	PR says target afire, stopped & settled.
23	HMS TANTIVY	6	Makassar Strait	Sch	40	G	S								

145

Dt/Hr	Submarine	Pt	Position	Tgt	Size	Attack	Cl	So	Date	Type	Name	Tons	Dm	Location	Comments
OCT	1944														
24/01	367 ICEFISH	1	19-31N 118-10E	AK	4000	T1/4NUS	S	AIJ	24	C-AK	Tenshin M.	4236	S	19-58N 118-33E	[Kokuryu M location looks closer to attack; see 194 SEADRAGON below; J attribution ?]
24/02	279 SNOOK	7	20-54N 118-19E	AK	7500	T2/3NSR	D								PR says 1 hit seen, another heard.
24/02	279 SNOOK	7	20-54N 118-19E		7500	T1/3NSR	S	AI J	24	C-AK	Arisan M.	6886	S PS	20-46N 118-18E	PR says stern disintegrated.
24/03	246 CROAKER	2	33-00N 125-49E	AD	7500	T2/2NSR	D	A I	24	C-APK	Gassan M.	4515	S H	32-56N 125-54E	
24/03	246 CROAKER	2	33-00N 125-49E	AK	4000	T3/4NSR	S	AI J	24	C-AK	Mikage M.	2741 2761	S	32-56N 125-54E	I says cause & location unk.
24/04	246 CROAKER	2	32-58N 125-46E	Unk	4000	T1/4NSR	D	I	24	C-AK	Mikagesan M.	2741	S	32-56N 125-54E	A says this is same ship as Mikage M above. [Listing appears to be duplication.]
24/04	321 BESUGO	1	30-19N 132-49E	DE	700	T1/3NSR	S	I	24	PF	CD 132	940	H	Ashizuri Saki	
24/05	279 SNOOK	7	20-10N 118-17E	AK	7500	T2/5TSR	S	A J	23-4	A-AK	Shinsei M. #1	5863 5878	S PS	20-25N 118-44E	PR says ship sank. [Tenshin M location looks closer to attack; see 367 ICEFISH above; J attribution ?]
24/08	228 DRUM	11	20-27N 118-31E	AK	6700	T3/4DUP	S	AIJ	24	C-AK	Shikisan M.	4725	S	20-09N 118-35E	PR says hits & breaking-up noises heard.
24/11	194 SEADRAGON	11	20-31N 118-32E	AK	5500	T2/4DUP	S	AIW J	24	XAK	Daiten M. Taiten M.	4642 6442	S PS	20-23N 118-47E	PR says breaking-up noises heard.
24/11	234 KINGFISH	9	27-08N 143-13E	AK	2500	T1/4DUP	S	AJ	24	AK	Ikutagawa M.	2220	S	27-15N 143-19E	
24/12	194 SEADRAGON	11	20-33N 118-34E	AK	4000	T3/4DUP	S	AI J	24	C-APK	Kokuryu M.	7369	S PS	19-34N 118-32E	PR says ship sank. [Shinsei M #1 location looks closer to attack; see 279 SNOOK above; J attribution ?]
24/14	194 SEADRAGON	11	20-31N 118-33E	AK	4000	T2/4DUP	S	AIJW	24	XAP	Eiko M.	1843	S	20-35N 118-32E	PR says target broke in two.
24/19	306 TANG	5L	25- N 119- E	AP	10000	T2/2NSV	S								
24/19	306 TANG	5L	25- N 119- E	AP	7500	T2/2NSV	S								
24/19	306 TANG	5L	25- N 119- E	AO	10000	T2/2NSV	S	AJW I	25	XAO	Matsumoto M.	7024	S	25-04N 119-35E 28-07N 119-45E	

Dt/Hr	Submarine	Pt	Position	Tgt	Size	Attack	Cl	So	Date	Type	Name	Tons	Dm	Location	Comments
OCT	1944														
24/19 306 TANG		5L	25- N 119- E	AO	10000	T1/1NSV	S	A IJ	25	C-AK C-AO	Ebara M. Kogen M.	6957 6600	S	25-03N 119-35E 28-07N 119-45E	
24/19 306 TANG		5L	25- N 119- E	DD	1500	T1/ NSV	S								
24/19 306 TANG		5L	25- N 119- E	AP	10000	T2/4NSV	S								TANG lost when hit by own torpedo in this attack.
24 U 314 SHARK		3L	20-41N 118-27E	AK	Unk	Unk	S								Attack not in SORG; U says SHARK believed sunk this date after possible attack on AK.
24 HMS STYGIAN		2	Off Penang	SS		T2/2	S								BSH evaluates explosions as prematures.
25/04 392 STERLET		2	30-15N 129-45E	AO	10000	T3/6NSR	S	A J	25	C-AO	Jinei M.	10241 10500	S	30-15N 129-45E	I gives name Ikutagawa M.
25/04 392 STERLET		2	30-15N 129-45E	AK	7500	T1/ NSR	S								
25/09 183 SEAL		12	50-18N 150-50E	AK	6000	T3/4DUP	S	AIJW	25	XAP	Hakuyo M.	5742	S	50-21N 150-20E	
25/19 232 HALIBUT		10	20-29N 126-36E	CA	10000	T5/6TUP	S	IWA J	25	DD	Akizuki Akitsuki	2700 1900	SA PS	20-29N 126-30E	Galantin believes Hatsuzuki (Hatsusuki) listed by I as missing at Leyte, possibly sunk here. See note below. [J attribution ?]
25/19 232 HALIBUT		10	20-29N 126-36E	Same	Same	Same	0	AW J	25	DD	Yamagumo	1960 1850	SW	Leyte	I lists as missing, attacked by sub. See note above. (Sources disagree on fate of Japanese DDs lost in Leyte battles.) [Attribution ?]
25/21 188 SARGO		12	29-54N 149-06E	XAM	300	GM	D								
25/21 188 SARGO		12	29-54N 149-06E	XAM	300	GM	D								
25/22 368 JALLAO		1	21-33N 127-19E	CL	5200	T3/4NUP	S	AIW J	25	CL	Tama	5100 5700	S JS	E Luzon Str.	J credits JALLAO & a/c; W says torp & sunk after initial damage by a/c.
25 HMS STOIC		5	Java Sea	Cstr	700	G	S								
25 HMS TANTIVY		6	Flores Sea	Cstr	600	G	S	Note	25	Ltr	Lighter #136	?	S	08-08S 117-45E	Name from notes by Wilds in NavHistCtr. [Attribution ?]
25 HMS TANTIVY		6	Flores Sea	Cstr	600	G	S								
25 S HMS TANTIVY		6	Flores Sea	Sch	50	G	S								

Dt/Hr	Submarine	Pt	Position	Tgt	Size	Attack	Cl	So	Date	Type	Name	Tons	Dm	Location	Comments
OCT	1944														
26/02	402 SEA FOX	1	29-05N 127-40E	AK	4000	T3/4NSR	S								
26/04	228 DRUM	11	19-21N 120-50E	AK	4000	T1/3NSR	D	I A	26 Note	A-AK	Tensho M.	4982	?	19-07N 120-42E	PR says 1 torp hit heard. A says Tensho M arrived at Naha, Okinawa 25 Oct. [Attribution ?]
26/04	228 DRUM	11	19-21N 120-50E	AK	7500	T2/3NSR	S	AIJ	26	C-APK	Taisho M.	6886	S	19-30N 120-44E	PR says seen burning and exploding. [Taiyo M location looks closer to attack; see 367 ICEFISH below; J attribution ?]
26/04	228 DRUM	11	19-21N 120-50E	AK	4000	T2/4NSR	S	AIJ	26	C-AK	Taihaku M.	6886	S	19-07N 120-42E	PR says target seen to sink.
26/06	274 ROCK	4	10-18N 117-47E	AO	9200	T3/6DUP	D	J A	26 Note	C-AO	Takasago M. #7	834	S	Sub position Balabac Strait	I says sunk 1 Nov SW of Manila; A says sources credit ROCK but give date 26 Nov & say ship later salvaged in Balabac Str. PR says attacked large AO & 3 SCs. [J attribution ?]
26/07	228 DRUM	11	19-00N 120-45E	AK	6900	T1/3DUP	S	I	26	XAP	Tatsuura M.	6420	M	19-07N 120-42E	PR says seen listing with back broken.
26/07	228 DRUM	11	19-00N 120-45E	AK	5500	T2/3DUP	D								PR says seen burning 5 hours after attack.
26/07	367 ICEFISH	1	19-04N 120-36E	AP	9300	T2/4DUP	S	AIJ	26	C-AK	Taiyo M.	4168	S	19-07N 120-42E	PR says 1 hit seen, breaking-up noises heard. [Tensho M location looks closer; see 228 DRUM above; J attribution ?]
26	287 BOWFIN	3	03-36S 116-35E	--	--	Mine	U	J I	26	C-AK	Seito M.	2219	SM DM	03-12S 116-15E	Minefield laid 29 Jan; J credits Australian mine. [Attribution ?; mines 9 months old.]
26	HMS TANTIVY	6	Flores Sea	Cstr	800	G	D								
27/01	234 KINGFISH	9	25-22N 141-31E	AO	5000	T2/3NUS	S	AIW J	26-7	APD	T 138	890 1000	S	Near Iwo Jima	
27/01	234 KINGFISH	9	25-22N 141-31E	Same	Same	Same	O	AIJ	27	A-AK	Tokai M. #4	537	S	25-26N 141-36E	PR says 3 torps fired by sonar at AO & PC; escort left after depth charging sub.
27/03	279 SNOOK	7	20-34N 120-41E	Unk	2000	T1/3NSR	D								
27/04	312 BURRFISH	4	29-08N 128-45E	AK	7500	T3/6NSR	S								

Dt/Hr	Submarine	Pt	Position	Tgt	Size	Attack	Cl	So	Date	Type	Name	Tons	Dm	Location	Comments
OCT	1944														
27/04	320 BERGALL	1	07-09N 116-40E	XAO	16800	T4/6NSR	S	A IJW	27	XAO	Nichiho M. Nippo M.	10528	S	07-17N 116-45E	PR says 2 large ships, poor visibility, attacked 1. W lists Nichiho M & Nippo M as both XAO & Std AO 1TL.
27/04	320 BERGALL	1	07-09N 116-40E	Same	Same	Same	O	AIW J	27 29	XAO	Itsukushima M.	10007	S SA	07-17N 116-45E 06-45N 116-55E	See above. [Attribution ?]
27/23	225 CERO	6	17- N 119- E	Mis	100	GM	D	IW	29	XPkt	Kyoei M. #3	38		SU Luzon I.	PR says driven ashore.
27/23	225 CERO	6	17- N 119- E	Mis	100	GM	D								
27	HMS TRENCHANT	3	07-54N 098-28E	AK	4900	Dem	S	AIJW	28	XAP	Sumatra M.	984	S	Phuket Harbor	BSH says chariots (swimmer vehicles) attacked ex-Italian Sumatra, 4859T & Volpi, 5292T; being salvaged. The 984T Sumatra M was ex-Dutch Tomori. [Records appear to confuse the 2 ships.]
27	HMS TRENCHANT	3	Phuket harbor	AK	5300	Dem	D								See note above.
29/23	392 STERLET	2	30-04N 132-24E	AK	1000	T0/4+GM	S								PR says 200-ft steel hulled armed ship burned & sank after gun hits.
29 S	HMS SHALIMAR	1	Nicobar Is.	MV	3000	T?/6	U								BSH evaluates attack unsuccessful.
29	HMS STORM	7	Gulf of Boni	2Sch	60	G	S								
30/13	243 BREAM	3	16-03N 119-42E	AP	10000	T2/6DUP	D								
30/16	237 TRIGGER	10	30-14N 132-50E	AO	10000	T4/4DUP	P	AJ I	30	C-AO	Takane M. Korei M.	10021 10000	JS S	30-13N 132-49E	J credits TRIGGER, 182 SALMON & 392 STERLET. PR says target seen hit, stern destroyed.
30/20	182 SALMON	11	30-08N 132-33E	AO	10000	T2/4NUP	P	AJ I	30	C-AO	Takane M. Korei M.	10021 10000	JS S	30-13N 132-49E	J credits SALMON, 237 TRIGGER & 392 STERLET. 236 SILVERSIDES PR confirms hits seen at this time.
30/21	182 SALMON	11	30-08N 132-33E	PF	1000	GN	D	I	30	PF	CD 22	940	L	SE of Toizaki	PR says SALMON badly damaged by depth charges, unable to submerge, fought off PFs with gun.
30/21	182 SALMON	11	30-08N 132-33E	PF	1000	GN	D								Same as above.
30	HMS TERRAPIN	3	Malacca Strait	2Jk	20	G	S								

Dt/Hr	Submarine	Pt	Position	Tgt	Size	Attack	Cl	So	Date	Type	Name	Tons	Dm	Location	Comments
OCT	1944														
30 S	HMS TERRAPIN	3	Malacca Strait	Sch	70	G	S								
31/01	392 STERLET	2	30-09N 132-45E	AO	10000	T4/6NSR	P	AJ I	30	C-AO	Takane M. Korei M.	10021 10000	JS S	30-13N 132-49E	J credits STERLET, 237 TRIGGER & 182 SALMON. PR says AO found dead in water, down by stern.
31/06	252 GABILAN	3	32-50N 134-21E	AK	2200	T1/4TUP	S	AI J	31	Fish YP	Kaiyo M. #6	200 100	S PS	Off Murotosaki	W lists ship as Kaiyo #6, 270T trawler-type AGOR, sunk here.
31/06	386 PILOTFISH	3	28-03N 141-32E	AK	4000	T1/4TUP	D								
31/09	363 GUITARRO	3	15-18N 119-50E	AK	8200	T2/4DUP	S	AIJW	31	XAK	Komei M.	2857	S	15-15N 119-56E	
31/09	363 GUITARRO	3	15-18N 119-50E	AK	7500	T2/2DUP	S	AIJ	31	A-AK	Pacific M.	5872	S	15-15N 119-56E	
31/09	363 GUITARRO	3	15-18N 119-50E	AK	7500	T2/2DUP	S								
31	HMS STOIC	5	Off Surabaya	MV	4000	T3/4	S								
31	HMS STOIC	5	Java Sea	Cstr	150	G	S								
31	HMS STOIC	5	Java Sea	LC		G	S								
NOV	1944														
1/05	403 ATULE	1	20-09N 117-38E	AP	10000	T2/6NSR	S	AIJW	1	XAP	Asama M.	16975	S	20-17N 117-08E	W gives date 1 Jan 44 [may be misprint].
1/08	231 HADDOCK	10	18-40N 113-37E	AK	6800	T1/7NUP	D								
1/08	322 BLACKFIN	1	12-54N 120-10E	AK	4000	T4/6DUP	S	AIJW	1	XAP	Unkai M. #12	2745	S	12-57N 120-12E	271 RAY PR says this hit seen; A lists ship as both XAP & Std AK 1C.
1/08	322 BLACKFIN	1	12-54N 120-10E	Same	Same	Same	0	AIW	1	XAG	Caroline M.	320	S	12-57N 120-12E	W credits BLACKFIN. PR says 1 torp may have hit escort. [Attribution ?; see 271 RAY below.]
1/09	271 RAY	6	13-02N 120-17E	AO	2500	T1/1DUP	S	AI	1	XAG	Caroline M.	320	S	12-57N 120-12E	PR says torp heard to hit, screws stopped. [Attribution ?; see 322 BLACKFIN above.]
1/09	271 RAY	6	13-02N 120-17E	AO	2500	T2/2DUP	S	AI J	1	C-AO	Horai M. #7	834 865	S	12-57N 120-12E	PR says hits seen.
--							-	I	1	C-AO	Takasago M. #7	834	S	SW of Manila	See 274 ROCK 26 Oct.

Dt/Hr	Submarine	Pt	Position	Tgt	Size	Attack	Cl	So	Date	Type	Name	Tons	Dm	Location	Comments
NOV	1944														
1	HMS STORM	7	Gulf of Boni	2Sch	30	G	S								
2/11	317 BARBERO	2	04-30S 118-20E	AP	2700	T1/3DUP	S	AIJ	2	A-AK	Kuramasan M.	1995	S	Makassar Str.	
2/23	391 POMFRET	3	20-20N 121-30E	AK	4900	T1/3NUP	D	AIJW	2-3	XAP	Atlas M.	7347	S	20-33N 121-32E	
2	HMS TANTALUS	5	00-48N 107-43E	MV	3000	T2/2	S	AIJW	2	XAK	Hachijin M.	1918	S	00-50N 107-44E	
2	HMS TANTALUS	5	00-48N 107-43E	Same	Same	Same	0	I	2	PC	Ch 1	400	M	05-00N 107-44E	TANTALUS attacked convoy of 4 MV & several escorts in heavy weather, heard 2 explosions but claimed only 1 ship hit. [Attribution ?; location of damage not near attack, but may be misprint.]
2	HMS TERRAPIN	3	Malacca Strait	Cstr	600	G	S	AI JW	2 30	XAN	Kumano M.	872	S PS	01-30N 103-00E	J & W credit British sub (probable); I says sunk Malacca Strait Nov 44; A attributes to unk sub, location not clear. [Attribution ?]
2	HMS SHALIMAR	1	Car Nicobar	5LC		G	D								
2	HMS STORM	7	Gulf of Boni	7Sch	210	G	S								
3/01	254 GURNARD	7	05-48N 110-05E	AO	5000	T2/3NUP	S	AJ I	3	C-AK	Taimei M.	6923 6600	S	05-53N 111-12E	
3/01	254 GURNARD	7	05-48N 111-05E	AO	5000	T1/3NUP	D								
3/05	391 POMFRET	3	20-19N 121-30E	AK	4900	T2/8NUP	D	AIJ	2-3	A-AK	Hamburg M.	5271	S	20-24N 121-28E	
3/22	387 PINTADO	3	16-48N 117-17E	CV	28000	T2/6NUP	D								
3/22	387 PINTADO	3	16-48N 117-17E	DD	2300	T2/ NUP	S	AIW J	3	DD	Akikaze	1215 1300	S	NW of Manila	
4/14	198 TAMBOR	12	30-05N 138-20E	Pat	200	GD	D								
4/16	192 SAILFISH	12	20-10N 121-43E	DD	800	T2/4DUP	S	I W	4	DD	Harukaze	1523	M HM	Luzon Strait	PR says 1 seen, another heard.
4/16	192 SAILFISH	12	20-10N 121-43E	ODD	800	T1/3DUP	D	I	3	APD	T 111	890	M	19-51N 121-48E	
4/16	243 BREAM	3	16-06N 119-39E	AP	10000	T1/4DUP	P	AIW J	4	XAP	Kagu M.	6806	S JS	15-55N 119-44E	PR says 1 hit heard. J credits BREAM, 271 RAY & 363 GUITARRO (see below); SORG credits BREAM and GUITARRO only; W credits BREAM & RAY only; I gives tons as 8417.

Dt/Hr	Submarine	Pt	Position	Tgt	Size	Attack	Cl	So	Date	Type	Name	Tons	Dm	Location	Comments
NOV	1944														
4/16	363 GUITARRO	3	16-03N 119-43E	AP	10000	T1/4DUP	P	AI J	4	XAP	Kagu M.	6806	S JS	15-55N 119-44E	PR says believed sunk. J credits GUITARRO, 243 BREAM & 271 RAY; SORG credits BREAM & GUITARRO only; W credits BREAM & RAY only; I gives tons as 8417.
4/19	271 RAY	6	15-54N 119-45E	AP	8600	T2/2NSP	S	AIW J	4	XAP	Kagu M.	6806	JS	15-55N 119-44E	PR says seen to sink. J credits RAY, 243 BREAM & 363 GUITARRO; W credits BREAM & RAY only; SORG credits BREAM & GUITARRO; I gives tons as 8417.
4	HMS TERRAPIN	3	03-14N 099-50E	PG	Unk	T2/5	S	AIW J	4	AM	W 5	702 615	S	03-44N 099-50E	W identifies TERRAPIN as minesweeper.
6/05	184 SKIPJACK	10	45-12N 148-56E	AK	3000	T1/4NSR	D								
6/08	363 GUITARRO	3	15-55N 119-45E	CA	12500	T3/9DUP	D	AIW	6	CA	Kumano	12400	D	W of Lingayan	W credits damage to GUITARRO, 243 BREAM & 270 RATON.
6/09	243 BREAM	3	16-01N 119-43E	CA	12500	T2/4DUP	D	AIW	6	CA	Kumano	12400	D	W of Lingayan	PR says 2 Or 3 hits heard. W credits damage to BREAM, 263 GUITARRO & 270 RATON.
6/10	270 RATON	6	16-11N 119-39E	CA	8500	T3/6DUP	D	AIW	6	CA	Kumano	12400	D	W of Lingayan	PR says CA was Mogami class, later aground near Rena Point. W credits damage to RATON, 363 GUITARRO & 243 BREAM.
6/10	271 RAY	6	16-08N 119-43E	CA	14000	T2/4DUP	P	AI	6	CA	Kumano	12400	D	W of Lingayan	PR says CA being towed away, bow missing. A says Kumano was towed to Dasol Bay, Luzon & sunk there by a/c. SORG gives half credit to RAY; W credits damage to 363 GUITARRO, 243 BREAM & 270 RATON.
6/10	231 HADDOCK	10	21-00N 122-22E	AK	3900	T1/4DUP	D								
7/10	322 BLACKFIN	1	11-19N 118-26E	AO	10000	T1/5DUP	D								
7/17	213 GREENLING	11	34-32N 138-33E	AO	5000	T2/4TUP	S	AI J	7	C-AO	Kota M. Kotai M.	971	S	34-34N 138-35E	
7/17	213 GREENLING	11	34-32N 138-33E	AK	4000	T1/ TUP	S	AIJW	7	XAP	Kiri M. #8	945	S	34-34N 138-35E	
7/22	286 BILLFISH	6	29-34N 127-56E	AK	4000	T1/3NSR	D								
7/22	286 BILLFISH	6	29-34N 127-56E	AK	4000	T1/ NSR	D								

Dt/Hr	Submarine	Pt	Position	Tgt	Size	Attack	Cl	So	Date	Type	Name	Tons	Dm	Location	Comments
7/22	286 BILLFISH	6	29-34N 127-56E	AK	4000	T2/4NSR	D								
8/04	365 HARDHEAD	2	13-53N 119-26E	AO	9200	T4/4NUP	S	AIW J	8	XAO	Banei M. Manei M.	5266 5226	S	13-30N 119-25E	
8/07	253 GUNNEL	7	16-10N 118-56E	DE	600	T1/3DUP	S	AIW J	8	TB	Sagi	840 585	S	W of Luzon	
8/10	402 SEA FOX	1	29-05N 127-40E	AK	4000	T2/6DUP	S								
8/21	393 QUEENFISH	2	31-10N 129-39E	AK	4000	T2/4NSR	S	AIJ	8	C-AK	Keijo M.	1051	S	31-10N 129-41E	
8/21	393 QUEENFISH	2	31-10N 129-39E	AK	3000	T1/2NSR	D	AIJW	8	XAK	Hakko M.	1948	S	31-10N 129-41E	
8/21	393 QUEENFISH	2	31-10N 129-39E	Same	Same	Same	0	AIW	8	XSC	Ryusei M.	99	S	31-10N 129-41E	PR says fired at only 2 AKs, does not mention hitting escort. [Attribution ?]
8/22	272 REDFIN	5	13-46N 116-53E	AO	10000	2/12NSR	S	AJ I	8	C-AO	Nichinan M. #2	5226	S H	13-00N 116-48E	
8/24	317 BARBERO	2	14-01N 117-17E	AO	7500	T3/11NSR	S	AIJ	8-9	C-AO	Shimotsu M.	2854	S	14-32N 116-53E	
8	HMS TRADEWIND	4	W coast Burma	5Jk	105	G	S								
9/03	393 QUEENFISH	2	31-17N 129-10E	AP	7500	T3/3NUP	S	AIJW	9	XPG	Chojusan M.	2131	S	31-15N 129-10E	
9/03	393 QUEENFISH	2	31-17N 129-10E	AO	10000	T2/3NUP	S								
9/14	255 HADDO	8	12-27N 120-05E	AO	2000	T1/4DUP	D	AIJW	9	XAO	Hishi M. #2	856	S	12-24N 120-45E	
10/04	220 BARB	10	33-24N 129-04E	AP	10500	T3/6NUR	S	AIJW A	10 17	XAP	Gokoku M.	10438	S	33-31N 129-19E	A says records give both dates.
10/08	251 FLOUNDER	4	07-13S 115-17E	UB	700	T2/4DUP	S	U	9	SS	U-537	1144	S	Sub position	
10/10	213 GREENLING	11	34-30N 138-34E	DD	900	T1/4DUP	S	AIW J	10	PF	P 46	910 820	S	SW of Irosaki	Ex-DD Yugao.
10	HMS TRADEWIND	4	W coast Burma	2Jk	70	G	D								
11/09	393 QUEENFISH	2	32-20N 128-00E	AK	4000	T1/4DUP	D	AIW	11	XAP	Miho M.	4667	M	32-24N 127-58E	W lists ship as both XAP & Std AK 1B.
11	HMS TANTALUS	5	E coast Malaya	Cstr	200	G	S	Note				Palang M.				Name from "Success Book." A says no record.

Dt/Hr	Submarine	Pt	Position	Tgt	Size	Attack	Cl	So	Date	Type	Name	Tons	Dm	Location	Comments
NOV	1944														
12/02 220 BARB		10	31-39N 125-36E	AK	7500	T1/2NSR	S	AIJ	12	A-AK	Naruo M.	4823	S	31-30N 125-57E	PR says last seen with bow under, stern high in air.
12/02 220 BARB		10	31-39N 125-36E	AK	4000	T1/2NSR	S								PR says target down by 30 deg angle.
12/02 220 BARB		10	31-39N 125-36E	AK	4000	T1/2NSR	S								
12/02 220 BARB		10	31-29N 125-36E	AK	7500	T1/2NSR	D								
12/04 220 BARB		10	31-29N 125-36E	AK	4000	T1/3NUP	S	A I	12	C-AK	Gyokuyo M.	5396	H S	31-30N 125-57E	PR says blew up. A says ship was disabled & abandoned; see 411 SPADEFISH 14 Nov.
12/04 220 BARB		10	31-29N 125-36E	AK	2000	T1/ NUP	D								
12/06 265 PETO		7	31-21N 125-33E	AK	4000	T2/4NSR	D								PR says target slowed & dropped back.
12/06 265 PETO		7	31-18N 125-30E	AK	7500	T2/2TSR	S	AI J	12	A-AK	Tatsuaki M.	2746 2766	S	31-24N 125-43E	PR says target blew up and sank. I gives name Tatsusho M.
12/06 265 PETO		7	31-18N 125-30E	AK	7500	T2/4TSR	S								PR says target settled with port list.
12/14 310 BATFISH		5	16-38N 120-18E	AK	4000	T1/2DUP	D								
12/21 272 REDFIN		5	13-00N 118-14E	AK	9000	T1/4NSR	D								
12	HMS SPIRIT	3	Andaman Is.	AO	840	T2/2	D								
12	HMS SPIRIT	3	Andaman Is.	SC		G	D								
12	HMS TRADEWIND	4	W coast Burma	Cstr	400	G	D								
12 S	HMS TRADEWIND	4	W coast Burma	ML		G	S								
13/17 183 SEAL		12	45-35N 148-14E	AK	4000	T1/4DUP	S	AI	13	C-AK	Gassan M.	887	S	45-32N 148-16E	J says sunk 2 Jun 45 by Army a/c. PR says 1 hit & breaking-up noises heard. [Attribution ?]
13/17 286 BILLFISH		6	29-30N 130-02E	Sam	100	GD	S								
13	HMS THOROUGH	3	Malacca Strait	Jk	25	G	S								
14/00 411 SPADEFISH		2	31-04N 123-56E	AK	7500	T4/5NSR	S	AJ I	14 12	C-AK	Gyokuyo M.	5396	S	31-04N 123-56E	PR says target exploded & burned. A says ship was abandoned & drifting after 220 BARB attack 12 Nov.

Dt/Hr	Submarine	Pt	Position	Tgt	Size	Attack	Cl	So	Date	Type	Name	Tons	Dm	Location	Comments
NOV	1944														
14/08 184 SKIPJACK		10	46-40N 151-40E	Sam	300	GD	S								
14/08 220 BARB		10	34-15N 127-54E	3Sch	900	GD	S								
14/12 232 HALIBUT		10	20-56N 121-33E	AK	4000	T2/4DUP	D								
14/21 271 RAY		6	17-46N 117-57E	AK	7500	T4/5NSR	S								
14/21 271 RAY		6	17-46N 117-57E	Esc	1500	T1/1NSR	S	AIW J	14	PF	CD 7	810 800	S	W of Luzon	
14/22 270 RATON		6	17-57N 117-45E	AK	7500	T2/2NSR	S	AIW J	14-5	AF AG	Kurasaki	2371 989	S	17-40N 118-00E	
14/22 270 RATON		6	17-57N 117-45E	AK	7500	T2/2NSR	S	AIJ	14	C-AO	Unkai M. #5	2841	S	17-48N 117-58E	
14/22 316 BARBEL		3	15-04N 112-46E	AK	5400	T2/6NSR	S	AIJW	14	XAP	Misaki M.	4422	S	15-10N 112-40E	
14/23 259 JACK		7	11-20N 109-02E	AK	4000	T2/4NSR	S	AI J	14	C-AK	Hinaga M.	5596 5396	S	11-11N 108-56E	I gives name Nichiei M.
14/23 259 JACK		7	11-20N 109-02E	Unk	4000	T2/4NSR	D	AIJ	15	C-AO	Yuzan M. #2	6859	S	11-16N 108-54E	
14/23 270 RATON		6	17-47N 117-43E	AK	7500	T2/4NSR	S								
14 HMS THOROUGH		3	Malacca Strait	2Cst	1150	G	S								
14 S HMS THOROUGH		3	Malacca Strait	Cstr	350	G	D								
15/00 310 BATFISH		5	18- N 118- E	AK	4000	T2/3NSR	S								
15/00 310 BATFISH		5	18- N 118- E	DE	1000	T1/1NSR	S								
15/02 316 BARBEL		3	15-14N 112-14E	AK	4000	T1/4NSR	S	AIJW	14-5	XAP	Sugiyama M.	4379	S	15-15N 112-10E	
15/12 236 SILVERSIDES		11	30-02N 137-36E	Pat	200	GD	D	W I	15	XPkt	Nachiryu M #12 Hachiryu M #12	97	S M	30-10N 137-23E	W credits 392 STERLET. PRs say both SILVERSIDES & STERLET made hits with 4" & 5" guns; 237 TRIGGER also fired but made no hits.
15/12 392 STERLET		2	30-04N 137-26E	Pat	200	GN	O	W I	15	XPkt	Nachiryu M #12 Hachiryu M #12	97	S M	30-10N 137-23E	W credits STERLET. PRs say both STERLET & 236 SILVERSIDES made hits with 4" & 5" guns; 237 TRIGGER also fired but made no hits.
15/12 393 QUEENFISH		3	33-15N 128-10E	CVE	17000	T2/4DUP	S	AIJW	15	XAPV	Akitsu M.	9186	S	33-17N 128-11E	

Dt/Hr	Submarine	Pt	Position	Tgt	Size	Attack	Cl	So	Date	Type	Name	Tons	Dm	Location	Comments
NOV	1944														
15/20 189 SAURY		11	29-59N 139-44E	Pat	200	TO/4NSV	0	IW	16	XPkt	Kojo M.	91	S	29-59N 139-39E	PR says 2 explosions, but target fired back & left at high speed. [Attribution ?]
15/22 362 GUAVINA		4	12-25N 120-55E	AP	7500	T2/3NSV	P	AI J	14	A-AK	Toyo M. Yutaka M.	2704	SA JS	12-28N 120-50E	J credits GUAVINA & a/c; SORG gives partial credit to GUAVINA. PR says found ship stopped, fires burning on deck.
15/23 220 BARB		10	32-16N 126-38E	CV	29800	T1/5NSR	D								
16/03 397 SCAB'RDFISH		2	28-56N 141-59E	AK	2100	T1/4NSR	S	AIJW	16	XAG	Kisaragi M.	873	S	29-03N 142-12E	
16/06 198 TAMBOR		12	30-35N 140-05E	Pat	200	GT	S	IW	16	XPkt	Taikai M. #3	95	S	30-00N 139-40E	W credits TAMBOR & 189 SAURY. PRs say TAMBOR sank ship & took 2 prisoners; SAURY did not attack; sinking witnessed by 237 TRIGGER.
16/17 396 RONQUIL		2	32-15N 139-53E	Pat	200	GT	S								
16/23 392 STERLET		2	31-28N 139-37E	SCs	100	T1/4NSR	S								
--							-	I	16	C-AK	Asokawa M.	6925	M	Brunei	No likely sub attack.
16	HMS TUDOR	3	W Sumatra	Cstr	150	G	S								
16	HNMS O-19	7	Java Sea	Cstr	150	G	S	N			Kaishin M. #2				Name given by Voss.
17/03 253 GUNNEL		7	16-56N 110-30E	Unk	4000	T3/6NSR	S	AIW J	17	TB	Hiyodori	840 595	S	S of Hainan	
17/04 253 GUNNEL		7	16-56N 110-30E	AO	10000	T2/ NSR	S	AJ AI	17	C-AO	Shunten M.	5623	S SA	16-45N 110-15E 19-22N 113-46E	A says records support both versions. PR says fired at 3 targets, saw 3 hits on one, second blew up; one later seen listing & down by stern.
17/06 253 GUNNEL		7	17-05N 110-42E	AK	4000	T1/7TSR	D								
17/06 312 BURRFISH		4	32-33N 140-10E	Pat	200	GT	P	A IW	17	XAG	Fusa M.	177	S H	32-50N 140-10E	W credits BURRFISH & 396 RONQUIL, says "written off" after damage. PRs show both subs made hits in joint attack.
17/06 396 RONQUIL		2	32-15N 140-00E	Pat	200	GT	P	A IW	17	XAG	Fusa M.	177	S H	32-50N 140-10E	W credits RONQUIL & 312 BURRFISH, says "written off" after damage. PRs show both subs made hits in joint attack; RONQUIL hit by return fire & holed in after torp room.

Dt/Hr	Submarine	Pt	Position	Tgt	Size	Attack	Cl	So	Date	Type	Name	Tons	Dm	Location	Comments
NOV	1944														
17/13	253 GUNNEL	7	17-36N 110-33E	AO	7300	T1/3DUP	D	W	19	XAG	Banshu M. #17	459	S	E of Hainan	PR says fired at 7-ship convoy, heard 1 explosion. [W attribution ?; see 383 PAMPANITO 18 Nov.]
17/18	382 PICUDA	4	33-16N 124-43E	AO	10000	T2/3TUP	S	I	17	C-AO	Awagawa M.	6925	M	33-32N 124-09E	PR says fired at AK, hit AO beyond. [Attribution ?; other subs made many attacks.]
17/18	382 PICUDA	4	33-16N 124-43E	AK	8800	T2/3TUP	S	AJW I	17	XARL	Mayasan M.	9433	S SA	33-17N 124-41E	Table in I says sunk by a/c but symbol on chart indicates sub.
17/22	281 SUNFISH	9	33-31N 124-32E	AK	6700	T2/3NSR	S	AIJ	17	A-AP	Edogawa M.	6968	S	33-30N 124-30E	
17/22	281 SUNFISH	9	33-31N 124-32E	AK	6700	T1/1NSR	S									
17/22	411 SPADEFISH	2	33-02N 123-33E	CVE	20000	T4/6NSR	S	AIW J	17	CVE	Shinyo Jinyo	17500 21000	S	32-59N 123-38E	
17/23	411 SPADEFISH	2	33-02N 123-33E	AO	10000	T1/4NSR	D									
17	HMS TALLY HO	9	Malacca Strait	7Jk	185	G		S							
18/00	411 SPADEFISH	2	33-07N 123-19E	DD	1700	T3/4NSR	S	J	18	SC	Cha 156	135	P	Sub position	W & I say Cha 156 sunk 29 Mar 45 at Takao by a/c; J gives tons as 100e. PR says 3 timed hits on large escort, heavy smoke. [J attribution ?]
18/02	265 PETO	7	33-50N 124-44E	AO	10000	T2/3NSR	S	AJ I	17-8	A-AK	Aisakasan M. Osakasan M.	6923 6600	S	33-30N 124-30E	PR says target blew up & burned, only stern above water, sank later.
18/03	189 SAURY	11	30-50N 141-56E	AO	6000	T1/8NSR	D	I	18	C-AK	Asahi M. #11	100	H	31-40N 141-47E	
18/03	281 SUNFISH	9	33-36N 124-18E	AK	6400	T3/3NSR	S	AIJ	17-8	A-AP	Seisho M.	5463	S	33-35N 124-34E	
18/05	265 PETO	7	33-39N 124-26E	AK	3000	T1/3NSR	S	AIJ	17-8	A-AK	Chinkai M.	2827	S	33-30N 124-30E	PR says ship stopped & sank in 3 minutes.
18/22	383 PAMPANITO	4	19-08N 111-28E	AK	7500	T2/6NSR	S	AI	19	XAF	Banshu M. #17	459	S	19-12N 115-51E	PR says target afire, seen to sink. W credits 253 GUNNEL (see 17 Nov). [Attribution ?]
18/22	383 PAMPANITO	4	19-08N 111-28E	AK	4000	T1/4NSR	D	AIJ	19	C-AK	Shinko M. #1	1200	S	19-06N 111-08E	
18	HMS TALLY HO	9	Malacca Strait	3Jk	135	G		S							
19/05	256 HAKE	7	14-22N 119-38E	CL	5200	T2/6TUP	D	I	19	CL	Isuzu	5170	M	W Corregidor	

Dt/Hr	Submarine	Pt	Position	Tgt	Size	Attack	Cl	So	Date	Type	Name	Tons	Dm	Location	Comments
NOV	1944														
19	HMS STRATAGEM	4L	01-36N 102-53E	MV	2000	T2/4	S	AI J	19	C-AO	Nichinan M.	1945	S PS	01-37N 102-53E	STRATAGEM lost 22 Nov; info provided postwar by survivor.
20/05 403 ATULE		1	21-21N 119-45E	DD	1400	T1/4NSR	S	AW J	19-20	AM	W 38	755 630	S	Takao	I says missing.
20/16 395 REDFISH		2	25-15N 122-23E	Sam	100	GD	S								
20	HMS TALLY HO	9	06-55N 094-15E	Esc	1000	T3/3	S	IW J	19-20	CMc	Ma 4	288 600	S	S Nicobar Is.	BSH gives name M 4.
20	HMS SPARK	1	Mergui Arch.	Sch	150	G	S								
21/03 315 SEALION		3	26-09N 121-23E	BB	30000	T3/6NSR	S	AIW J	21	BB	Kongo	31270 31000	S	NE of Keelung	
21/03 315 SEALION		3	26-09N 121-23E	BB	30000	T1/3NSR	D	AIW J	21	DD	Urakaze	2033 1900	S	NE of Keelung	
21/17 241 BASHAW		4	10-30N 114-59E	AO	5000	T1/1DUP	D	A I	21	A-AK	Gyosan M. Gyozan M.	5698	S	10-30N 115-08E	PR says aimed at AK but thought hit overlapping AO. SubPac ltr says reassessed credit to BASHAW & 251 FLOUNDER; J credits FLOUNDER & 362 GUAVINA (see 23 Nov). [Attribution ?]
21/18 251 FLOUNDER		4	10-39N 115-05E	AK	5000	T3/6TUP	D	AJ I	21	A-AK	Gyosan M. Gyozan M.	5698	JS	10-30N 115-08E	SubPac ltr says reassessed credit to FLOUNDER & 241 BASHAW; J credits FLOUNDER & 362 GUAVINA (see 23 Nov).
21/21 397 SCAB'RDFISH	2		33-28N 141-35E	AO	5000	T2/3NSR	S	AIW	21	XAF	Hokkai M.	407	S	33-20N 142-00E	
21/23 397 SCAB'RDFISH	2		33-35N 141-33E	AK	4000	T1/3NSR	D								
--							-	A I	21	C-AK	Fukuri M.	1398	SC S	Changshan I.	J gives name Fukurei M., sunk by a/c at 38-08N 124-39E; A says ran aground. No likely sub attack.
21	HMS THOROUGH	3	Malacca Strait	Jk	50	G	S								
22/00 397 SCAB'RDFISH	2		33-46N 141-35E	PC	500	T1/3NSR	0	I	21	PF	Oki	870	M	33-20N 142-00E	PR says 1 torp appeared to hit AK or PC.
22/05 321 BESUGO		2	11-40N 119-36E	AO	5000	T1/4TSR	S								
22/06 321 BESUGO		2	11-44N 119-32E	Bge	3000	T1/4DSR	S								

Dt/Hr	Submarine	Pt	Position	Tgt	Size	Attack	Cl	So	Date	Type	Name	Tons	Dm	Location	Comments
NOV	1944														
22/09 395 REDFISH		2	24-14N 122-25E	Sam		GD	S								
22/19 362 GUAVINA		4	10-22N 114-21E	AO	9500	T2/2TUR	S	AIJ	22	A-AK	Dowa M.	1916	S	10-18N 114-15E	
22/24 321 BESUGO		2	11-22N 119-07E	AK	7500	T3/16NSR	D	AIW J	22-3	APD	T 151	890 1000	S	11-22N 119-07E	
22 HMS THOROUGH		3	Malacca Strait	Jk	25	G	S								
23/00 395 REDFISH		2	24-28N 122-43E	AK	4000	T2/4NSR	S								
23/00 395 REDFISH		2	24-27N 122-47E	AK	4000	T1/6NSR	S	AI J	22-3	C-AK	Hozan M.	2552 2345	S PS	24-21N 122-38E	PR says target blew up & sank.
23/01 385 BANG		4	24-24N 122-41E	AK	4000	T2/3NSR	S								
23/01 385 BANG		4	24-24N 122-41E	AK	8400	T2/7NSR	S	AIJ	22-3	C-AK	Sakae M.	2878	PS	24-21N 122-38E	PR says target sank on even keel.
23/01 385 BANG		4	24-24N 122-41E	AK	4000	T1/ NSR	D								PR says hit seen.
23/02 385 BANG		4	24-24N 122-45E	AK	4000	T3/4NSR	S	AI J	22-3	C-AP	Amakusa M.	2345	S PS	24-21N 122-38E	PR says ship sank; may have been damaged previously.
23/03 385 BANG		4	24-12N 122-53E	CM	2000	T2/4NSR	S								PR says hit seen, target disappeared.
23/04 382 PICUDA		4	34-19N 128-05E	AO	10000	T2/10NSR	D								
23/04 382 PICUDA		4	34-19N 128-05E	AK	7500	T1/ NSR	S	AIJ	23	C-AK	Fukuju M.	5293	S	34-14N 128-28E	
23/09 382 PICUDA		4	34-15N 128-58E	AO	9000	T2/4DUP	S	AIJ	23	C-AK	Shuyo M.	6933	S	34-10N 128-58E	
23/09 385 BANG		4	24-20N 122-38E	Sam	100	GD	D								
23/15 362 GUAVINA		4	10-22N 114-22E	AK	7500	T1/3DUP	S	AJ I	21	A-AK	Gyosan M. Gyozan M.	5698	JS S	10-30N 115-08E	PR says target was large AK, stern blown away & rusty, rolled over & sank with bow on reef. [Appears to be attack credited by J to GUAVINA & 251 FLOUNDER (21 Nov).]
25/01 403 ATULE		1	20-12N 121-51E	AP	10000	T1/8NSR	S	AI J	25	C-AK	Manju M. Santos M.	7266	S	20-14N 121-40E	Former XAS originally named Santos Maru; W confuses with XAP of same name sunk 29 Nov 43 by 264 PARGO.
25/01 403 ATULE		1	20-12N 121-51E	DD	1300	T2/ NSR	S	W AI	25	PF	P 38	935	S	N Cape Engano Luzon Strait	Ex-DD Yomogi; W credits ATULE but J credits 391 POMFRET below. PR says target blew up. [W attribution ?]

159

Dt/Hr	Submarine	Pt	Position	Tgt	Size	Attack	Cl	So	Date	Type	Name	Tons	Dm	Location	Comments
NOV	1944														
25/03	244 CAVALLA	3	02-21N 107-20E	DD	2300	T4/4NSR	S	AIW J	25	DD	Shimotsuki	2700 2300	S	Natoena Strait	
25/05	261 MINGO	6	05-30N 113-21E	AO	10000	T3/6NSR	S	AIJ	25	A-AP	Manila M.	9486	S	05-45N 113-15E	
25/05	261 MINGO	6	05-30N 113-21E	PCE	1500	T1/4NUP	D								
25/05	391 POMFRET	3	20-18N 121-34E	DD	1300	T1/3NSR	S	AI J	25	PF	P 38	935 820	S	Luzon Strait	Ex-DD Yomogi; W credits 403 ATULE above. PR says attacked 5-ship hunter/killer group, target disintegrated. [J attribution ?]
25/05	391 POMFRET	3	20-18N 121-34E	DD	1300	T1/3NSR	S	AIJW	25	XAP	Shoho M.	1358	S	20-20N 121-40E	See above. PR says pip disappeared from radar after hit.
25/10	206 GAR	14	13-47N 119-30E	AK	1000	GD	S								
25/19	255 HADDO	8	14-01N 119-20E	Unk	4000	T1/4TUR	S	AI	25	PF	Shimushu	860	M	14-00N 119-25E	
25/21	365 HARDHEAD	2	14-22N 119-57E	AK	7500	T1/1NUP	D								
25/21	365 HARDHEAD	2	14-22N 119-57E	PC	600	T1/4NUP	S	AIW J	25	PF	CD 38	940 800	S	W of Manila	
25	HMS STURDY	4	SE Borneo	Cstr	350	G	S								
26/15	264 PARGO	6	04-55N 114-06E	AO	10000	T4/4DUP	S	AIJW	26	XAO	Yuho M.	5226	S	04-54N 114-07E	W lists ship as both XAO & Std AO 1TM.
--							-	A	26	C-AO	Takasago M. #7	834	S	Balabac Strait	See 274 ROCK 26 Oct. No likely sub attack 26 Nov.
26	HMS STURDY	4	SE Borneo	2Jk	180	G	S								
26	HMS SUPREME	1	Andaman Is.	2Jk	100	G	S								
27/04	403 ATULE	1	20-20N 121-48E	AK	4000	T4/4NSV	S								
27	HMS SUPREME	1	Andaman Is.	Jk	30	G	S								
28/14	362 GUAVINA	4	12-52N 109-29E	AK	4000	T2/3DUP	S								
28	HMS STYGIAN	3	Sabang	Cstr	200	G	S								
28	HMS SPARK	1	Mergui Arch.	Sch	35	Dem	S								

Dt/Hr	Submarine	Pt	Position	Tgt	Size	Attack	Cl	So	Date	Type	Name	Tons	Dm	Location	Comments
NOV	1944														
28	HMS STRONGBOW	3	W Sumatra	Tug	150	G	S								
28	HMS STRONGBOW	3	W Sumatra	Ltr	100	G	S								
29/03	311 ARCHERFISH	5	32- N 137- E	CV	28000	T6/6NUP	S	AIW J	29	CV	Shinano	64800 59000	S	Shionomisaki	
29/10	397 SCAB'RDFISH	2	34-44N 141-01E	SS	1500	T1/2DUP	S	IW J	28	SS	I-365	1440 1470	S	Sub position	PR says I-365 identified by survivor.
29/12	411 SPADEFISH	2	37-17N 125-11E	AK	4000	T2/4DUP	S	AJ I	29 ?	C-AK	Daiboshi M. #6 Taisei M. #6	3925	S	W coast Korea	
29	HMS STURDY	4	Macassar Str.	2Lug	160	G	S								
29	HMS SUPREME	1	Andaman Is.	3Jk	200	G	S								
30/14	281 SUNFISH	9	38-06N 124-39E	AP	4000	T1/5DUP	S	AIJ	30	C-AK	Dairen M.	3748	S	38-07N 124-37E	
30	HMS STRONGBOW	3	W Sumatra	3Jk	140	G	S								
--							-	JW AI	30 2?	XAN B-Aux	Kumano M.	872	PS S	01-30N 103-00E Malacca Strait	J & W credit British sub but do not give name. No likely sub attack 30 Nov. See HMS TERRAPIN 2 Nov.
DEC	1944														
1	HMS STURDY	4	Macassar Str.	Cstr	300	G	S								
1 S	HMS SUPREME	1	Andaman Is.	Jk		G	D								
2/04	258 HOE	7	06-32S 111-49E	AO	1500	T2/7NSV	D								
2/04	400 SEA DEVIL	2	30-51N 128-45E	AO	10000	T2/2NUP	S	AJ I	2	C-AO	Akigawa M. Akikawa M.	6859 6800	S	30-24N 128-17E	
2/04	400 SEA DEVIL	2	30-51N 128-45E	AK	7500	T1/4NUP	S	AIJ	2	C-APK	Hawaii M.	9467	S	30-24N 128-17E	Also see I listing 8 Jan 45.
2	HMS STURDY	4	Macassar Str.	Aux	300	G	S	I	2	C	Comm. Ship 142	200	S	04-08N 119-33E	Ship not in W. [Attribution ?]
3/04	196 SEARAVEN	13	19-06N 112-03E	AP	11600	T3/4NSR	S								
3/04	399 SEA CAT	1	18-37N 111-33E	AO	10000	T2/2NSR	S								
3/05	196 SEARAVEN	13	18-42N 111-54E	AO	9200	T3/4NSR	S								

Dt/Hr	Submarine	Pt	Position	Tgt	Size	Attack	Cl	So	Date	Type	Name	Tons	Dm	Location	Comments
DEC	1944														
3/05	388 PIPEFISH	3	18-36N 111-54E	AK	4000	T1/3TSR	D	AIW J	3	PF	CD 64	940 800	S	E of Hainan I.	
3/06	383 PAMPANITO	4	18-25N 111-30E	AO	10000	T1/4TUP	D	I	3	A-AO	Seishin M.	5239	L	18-24N 111-25E	
3/22	196 SEARAVEN	13	17-48N 111-20E	AO	10000	T0/1NSR	P								SORG credits SEARAVEN & 399 SEA CAT. PR says torp missed & exploded at end of run.
4/01	399 SEA CAT	1	17-40N 110-42E	AO	10000	T2/4NSR	P								SORG credits SEA CAT & 196 SEARAVEN above. PR says AO was damaged by SEARAVEN, listed & settled after this attack.
4/13	249 FLASHER	5	13-12N 116-37E	DD	1700	T6/10DUP	S	AIW J	4-5	DD	Kishinami	2077 2100	S	NW Palawan I.	PR shows 2 separate attacks; not sure whether 1 or 2 DDs were involved.
4/13	249 FLASHER	5	13-12N 116-37E	Same	Same	Same	0	J	4	DD	Iwanami	2100	S	Sub position	No such ship listed in W. [J attribution ?; appears to be duplicate of Kishinami above.]
4/19	249 FLASHER	5	13-12N 116-37E	AO	10000	T1/1NSR	S	AIJW	4-5	C-AO	Hakko M.	10022	S	13-12N 116-39E	
4	HMS SHALIMAR	2	Malacca Strait	Jk	20	G	S								
5/06	394 RAZORBACK	2	19-50N 121-10E	DD	1400	T3/6TUP	D								
5	HMS SHALIMAR	2	Malacca Strait	3Jk	100	G	S								
5	HMS STURDY	4	Macassar Str.	Jk	40	G	S								
6/20	255 HADDO	8	14-43N 119-39E	AO	4000	T2/6NSR	S	I	6	XAO	Kyoei M. #3	1189	M	14-40N 119-35E	W lists ship as both XAO & Std AO 1TS; I gives tons as 1178.
6/21	412 TREPANG	2	18-54N 120-49E	AK	7500	T3/6NSR	S	AIJW	6-7	XAG	Banshu M. #31	748	S	W Dalupiri I.	PR says 2 AKs hit, both disappeared from radar.
6/21	412 TREPANG	2	18-54N 120-49E	AK	7500	T2/ NSR	S	I	7	C-AK	Yamakuni M.	500	H	Pasaleng	See above note. [Attribution ?]
6/21	412 TREPANG	2	18-54N 120-49E	AO	10000	T2/4NSR	S	AIJ	6-7	C-AK	Jinyo M.	6862	S	W Dalupiri I.	PR says target burned, dropped back & sank.
6/22	255 HADDO	8	14-43N 119-39E	AK	1000	T1/1NSR	S								

Dt/Hr	Submarine	Pt	Position	Tgt	Size	Attack	Cl	So	Date	Type	Name	Tons	Dm	Location	Comments
DEC	1944														
6/22	398 SEGUNDO	2	18-57N 120-58E	AP	10000	T2/6NSR	P	AI J	6-7	C-AK	Kenjo M.	6933	S JS	W Dalupiri I.	PR says target was whaler-type AO, saw 1 hit & timed another. J credits SEGUNDO & 394 RAZORBACK below.
6/23	398 SEGUNDO	2	18-51N 121-07E	AK	7700	T1/ NSR	S	AJ I	7		C-AK Yasukuni M.	5794	JS H	W Dalupiri I.	PR says fired at 7500T AK (below), saw closer ship blow up. J credits SEGUNDO & a/c.
6/23	398 SEGUNDO	2	18-51N 121-07E	AK	7500	T4/6NSR	S	I J	6		A-AK Shinto M.	1215	SA PA	18-52N 120-57E 22-35N 120-30E	PR says hits seen & timed on center ship of 3. [Attribution ?; A & I say sunk or heavily damaged at Takao 12 Oct.]
6/23	412 TREPANG	2	18-59N 121-05E	AP	10000	T5/12NSR	S	AI J	6-7		A-AK Fukuyo M.	5463	S PS	19-15N 121-13E	PR says target burned & sank stern first.
6	S HMS SHALIMAR	2	Malacca Strait	Cstr	100	G		D	I	6		C-AO Shinbun M.	25	H	04-25N 098-20E	[Attribution ?]
7/00	394 RAZORBACK	2	18-48N 121-30E	AP	10000	T4/8NUP	P	AI J	6-7		C-AK Kenjo M.	6933	S JS	W Dalupiri I.	J credits RAZORBACK & 398 SEGUNDO. PR says target had been damaged previously, burned & apparently sank; SEGUNDO PR says still burning 45 minutes later; see attack 6 Dec.
7	HMS SEA ROVER	7	Off Surabaya	Cstr	200	G		S							
7	HMS STYGIAN	3	Malacca Strait	Cstr	300	G		S							
7	HMS STYGIAN	3	Malacca Strait	LC	40	G		S							
8/00	263 PADDLE	7	04-03N 111-31E	AO	10000	T4/6NSR	S	AI J	8		C-AO Shoei M.	2854	S JS	03-50N 111-30E	PR says target burned and sank. J credits PADDLE & 364 HAMMERHEAD. PRs indicate subs fired almost simultaneously.
8/00	263 PADDLE	7	04-03N 111-31E	ODD	800	T1/4NSR	S									
8/00	364 HAMMERHEAD	3	04-14N 111-30E	AO	10000	T2/9NSR	S	AI J	8		C-AO Shoei M.	2854	S JS	03-50N 111-30E	PR says target burned & sank, oil fire on surface. J credits HAMMERHEAD & 263 PADDLE. PRs indicate subs fired almost simultaneously.
--							-	I	8	?	Sumiwa M.	?	S	W of Manila	No likely sub attack.
9/01	400 SEA DEVIL	2	31-43N 129-04E	CV	29800	T2/4NUR	D	AI	9	CV	Junyo	24140	M	SW of Homozaki	395 REDFISH PR says hits seen & CV dropped back.

Dt/Hr	Submarine	Pt	Position	Tgt	Size	Attack	Cl	So	Date	Type	Name	Tons	Dm	Location	Comments
DEC	1944														
9/01	400 SEA DEVIL	2	31-43N 129-04E	Unk	4000	T1/ NUR	D								
9/02	390 PLAICE	3	31-57N 129-01E	DD	2300	T4/7NSR	D	I	9	DE	Maki	1262	M	Onajima Lt.	
9/03	395 REDFISH	2	32-13N 129-13E	CV	29800	T2/12NSR	D	AIW	9	CV	Junyo	24140	M	SW of Homozaki	PR says hit again after hits by 400 SEA DEVIL. Japanese records list ship as constructive total loss.
10	HMS PORPOISE	3	Malacca Strait	Jk	10	Dem	S								
10	HMS SHALIMAR	2	Malacca Strait	2Jk	220	G	S								
11/05	405 SEA OWL	1	33-48N 128-20E	DD	1300	T2/2NSV	S	AIW	11	SC	Cha 76	135	S	Tsushima> Goto	
12/24	387 PINTADO	3	20-34N 118-45E	AK	7500	T2/3NSR	S	IW J	13	APD	T 104	890 1900	S	SE of Takao Sub position	PR says 2 targets blew up & disappeared. A says sunk by a/c 15 Dec off San Fernando, P.I. [J attribution ?]
12/24	387 PINTADO	3	20-34N 118-45E	AK	4000	T1/3NSR	S	AIW J	12-3	APD	T 12	1500 1900	S	SE of Takao	
12-14	HMS SUBTLE	2	Malacca Strait	3Jk		Dem	S									Exact dates not given.
13/03	387 PINTADO	3	20-07N 118-56E	AK	7500	T1/10NSV	S								
13/20	320 BERGALL	2	08-10N 105-31E	CA	12500	T2/3NSR	S	I	13	CA	Myoko	13380	M	Cape Camau	Towed to Singapore & never repaired.
13/20	320 BERGALL	2	08-10N 105-31E	CA	11500	T1/3NSR	D								
14/07	324 BLENNY	1	16-27N 119-43E	Mis	300	GD	S	IW	14	XPkt	Taisho M. #5	47		SU SE Pacific	[Attribution ?; location not definite.]
14/22	324 BLENNY	1	15-46N 119-45E	DE	800	T2/3NSR	S	AIW J	14	PF	CD 28	940 800	S	Hermana Mayor	
14 S	HMS SHALIMAR	2	Malacca Strait	Cstr	1200	T1/4	S	AIW	14	XAM	Choun M. #7	163	S	Off Belawan	BSH evaluates attack unsuccessful. [Attribution ?]
14	HMS SPITEFUL	5	Macassar Str.	Cstr	200	G	S								
15/19	366 HAWKBILL	2	16- N 117-39E	DD	1000	T3/3NSR	S	AIW J	15	DD	Momo	1262 760	S	NW of Manila	
15/21	366 HAWKBILL	2	16- N 117-39E	DD	1000	T1/13NSR	D								
15	HMS SHALIMAR	2	Malacca Strait	Tug	40	G	S								

Dt/Hr	Submarine	Pt	Position	Tgt	Size	Attack	Cl	So	Date	Type	Name	Tons	Dm	Location	Comments
DEC	1944														
15	HMS SHALIMAR	2	Malacca Strait	2Ltr	300	G	S								
16/03 230	FINBACK	11	27-35N 141-35E	AK	5000	T2/3NSR	S	AI JW	16	XAP	Jusan M. I-Go Jusan M.	2111	S	27-24N 141-44E	I gives name Juzan M I-Go.
16	HMS STOIC	6	05-45S 104-43E	MV	3000	T1/4	S	AIJ W	16	XPG	Shoei M.	1986	S	W Sunda Strait	W credits HMS TALLY HO; no such attack listed.
17-29	HMS THULE	2	N Malacca Str.	13Jk	360	G	S								Exact dates not given.
17-29	HMS THULE	2	N Malacca Str.	2Ltr		G	S								Exact dates not given.
17+ S	HMS THULE	2	N Malacca Str.	5Sam		G	S								"Success Book" gives dates 17-29 Dec only.
19/16 395	REDFISH	2	28-59N 124-03E	CV	28000	T2/5DUP	S	AIW J	19	CV	Unryu	17150 18500	S	NW Miyako Jima	
19/21 308	APOGON	6	49-33N 149-40E	AO	6500	T1/1NSR	D								
--							-	AI J	19	A-AK	Hiroshi M. #3	940	SA S	44-56N 147-39E	J credits unk sub. No likely sub attack. [J attribution ?]
21/01 315	SEALION	4	17-48N 114-09E	AK	15800	T6/9NSR	S	AIW J	20	AF	Mamiya	15820 7000	S	18-10N 115-30E	
21/18 405	SEA OWL	1	32-21N 128-54E	XPC	300	T1/1TUS	S								
21	HMS TRENCHANT	4	Malacca Strait	2LC	100	G	S								
22/05 249	FLASHER	5	15-04N 109-06E	AO	10000	T2/3NSR	S	AIJW	22	XAO	Omurosan M.	9204	S	15-07N 109-05E	
22/05 249	FLASHER	5	15-04N 109-06E	AO	10000	T2/3NSR	S	AIJ	22	C-AO	Otowasan M.	9204	S	15-07N 109-05E	
22/05 249	FLASHER	5	15-04N 109-06E	AO	10000	T2/4NSR	S	AIJ	22	C-AO	Arita M.	10238	S	15-07N 109-05E	
22/11 307	TILEFISH	4	34-33N 138-02E	CA	9000	T3/8DUP	S	AIW J	22	TB	Chidori	600 527	S	W of Omaezaki	
22	HMS TERRAPIN	4	Malacca Strait	Cstr	900	G	P	A I	20	C-AO	Yaei M. #6 Iyasaka M. #6	834	S	01-18S 104-34E	Joint attack with HMS TRENCHANT; "Success Book" identifies target as Sakura M (see 364 HAMMERHEAD 10 Jul 45); sinking not claimed in BSH; J says Yaei M #6 sunk by marine casualty. [Attribution ?]

Dt/Hr	Submarine	Pt	Position	Tgt	Size	Attack	Cl	So	Date	Type	Name	Tons	Dm	Location	Comments
DEC	1944														
22	HMS TRENCHANT	4	Malacca Strait	Cstr	900	G	P	A I	20	C-AO	Yaei M. #6 Iyasaka M. #6	834	S	01-19S 104-34E	See above note.
22	HMS TUDOR	4	W coast Burma	Sch	70	G	S								
23/10	324 BLENNY	1	16-50N 120-18E	AP	10000	T5/6DUP	S	AIJ	23	C-AO	Kenzui M.	4156	S	San Fernando	
23/22	239 WHALE	10	29-04N 129-45E	2Tra	200	GN	S								
23/22	239 WHALE	10	29-04N 129-45E	2Sam	200	GN	S								
24/00	317 BARBERO	2	02-45N 110-53E	AO	7500	T1/2NSR	S	AIW	24	PC	Ch 30	442	S	02-42N 111-05E	
24/00	317 BARBERO	2	02-45N 110-53E	AO	5000	T1/4NSR	D								
24/23	317 BARBERO	2	01-10N 108-20E	AK	4000	T3/4NUP	S	AIJ	25	XAP	Junpo M.	4277	S	00-51N 108-18E	
24	HMS TUDOR	4	W coast Burma	2Jk	95	G	S								
25	HMS SIRDAR	5	Off Surabaya	Cstr	350	G	S								
--							-	I	25	C-AO	Yuzan M. #2	6859	D	SE C. Batalan	I gives tons as 6930; ship of same name listed as sunk 15 Nov; A says these are the same ship; see 259 JACK 14 Nov. No likely sub attack 25 Dec.
25	HMS TRENCHANT	4	Malacca Strait	Tra		G	P								Joint attack with HMS TERRAPIN.
25	HMS TERRAPIN	4	Malacca Strait	Tra		G	P								Joint attack with HMS TRENCHANT.
25	HMS TRENCHANT	4	Malacca Strait	Cstr	200	G	P	AIW	25	XAM	Reisui M.	219	S	03-19N 099-45E	Joint attack with HMS TERRAPIN.
25	HMS TERRAPIN	4	Malacca Strait	Cstr	200	G	P	AIW	25	XAM	Reisui M.	219	S	03-19N 099-45E	Joint attack with HMS TRENCHANT.
25	HMS TRENCHANT	4	Malacca Strait	3Cst		G	D								Joint attack with HMS TERRAPIN.
25	HMS TERRAPIN	4	Malacca Strait	3Cst		G	D								Joint attack with HMS TRENCHANT.
25	HMS TUDOR	4	W coast Burma	2Jk	85	G	S								
26	HMS TERRAPIN	4	Malacca Strait	CMc		T1/5	S								
27/14	324 BLENNY	1	17-16N 120-24E	AK	4000	T1/2DUP	D								
27	HMS TUDOR	4	W coast Burma	Sch	45	G	S								

Dt/Hr	Submarine	Pt	Position	Tgt	Size	Attack	Cl	So	Date	Type	Name	Tons	Dm	Location	Comments
DEC	1944														
28/12 247 DACE		6	12-39N 109-30E	AK	4000	T1/4DUP	D								
28/12 247 DACE		6	12-39N 109-30E	AK	4000	T1/2DUP	S	AIW J	28	AF	Nozaki	640 1000	S	Off C. Varella	
28	HMS THULE	2	N Malacca Str.	SS		T1/3	S								BSH evaluates explosion as premature.
29/21 366 HAWKBILL		2	05-35S 113-29E	Mis	300	GN		S	Note 29		Ltr	Lighter #130	250	S	05-29S 113-08E	Identification from notes by Wilds in NavHistCtr. [Attribution ?]
29	HMS STATESMAN	4	NE Sumatra	Jk	50	G	S								
29	HMS SEASCOUT	1	Nicobar Is.	2Cst	1000	G	D								
29 S	HMS TERRAPIN	4	Malacca Strait	Jk	70	G	S								
29	HMS TRENCHANT	4	Malacca Strait	2Jk	40	G	S								
29	HMS THOROUGH	4	W coast Siam	2Jk	120	Dem	S								
29	HMS TUDOR	4	W coast Burma	Jk	100	G	S								
30/13 394 RAZORBACK		2	21-00N 121-24E	AO	7500	T2/6DSP	S								
30/14 394 RAZORBACK		2	21-00N 121-24E	ODD	800	T2/6DUP	S	AIJW	30	DD	Kuretake	820	S	Bashi Channel	
30/20 394 RAZORBACK		2	21-36N 121-12E	AK	4000	T2/6NUP	D								
30/20 394 RAZORBACK		2	21-36N 121-12E	AK	7500	T3/4NUP	S								
30	HMS TERRAPIN	4	Malacca Strait	2Jk	40	Dem	S								
30 S	HMS TRENCHANT	4	Malacca Strait	Jk	50	G	S								
31	HMS SHAKESPEARE	1	11-40N 093-15E	MV	1000	T5/6		S	AIJ	31	C-AK	Unryu M.	2515	S	E Port Blair	See listing of same ship 31 Jan 45.
31	HMS TRENCHANT	4	Malacca Strait	2Jk	50	G	S								
JAN	1945														
1/10 393 QUEENFISH		3	25-11N 135-15E	Mis	300	GD	P								SORG credits QUEENFISH, 382 PICUDA & 220 BARB; PRs say QUEENFISH & PICUDA hit target & left it burning, finally sunk by BARB. burning; it was finally sunk by BARB (PR).

Dt/Hr	Submarine	Pt	Position	Tgt	Size	Attack	Cl	So	Date	Type	Name	Tons	Dm	Location	Comments
JAN	1945														
1/11	382 PICUDA	5	25-00N 135-15E	Tra	300	GD	P								SORG credits PICUDA, 393 QUEENFISH & 220 BARB; PRs say PICUDA & QUEENFISH hit target & left it afire, finally sunk by BARB.
1/14	220 BARB	11	25-15N 135-21E	Mis	300	GD	P								SORG credits BARB, 393 QUEENFISH & 382 PICUDA; PRs say QUEENFISH & PICUDA hit target & left it afire, finally sunk by BARB.
1	HMS TRADEWIND	4	12-26N 098-38E	--	--	Mine	U	J	1	AK	Kyokko M.	593	SM	12-26N 098-38E	Minefield laid 30 Oct 44. BSH claims sinking.
1	HMS STATESMAN	4	NE Sumatra	4Ltr	400	G	S								
1	S HMS STATESMAN	4	NE Sumatra	2Ltr	50	G	D								
1	HMS THOROUGH	4	W coast Siam	Jk	120	G	D								
2/07	309 ASPRO	6	22-42N 119-14E	AK	7500	T1/3TUP	D	J AIW	3 3-5	LS	Shinshu M.	8170 8160	JS SA	21-57N 119-44E	J credits ASPRO & a/c; A & W say sunk 5 Jan by TF38; I says heavily damaged by a/c 3 Jan.
2/07	319 BECUNA	2	05-50S 113-12E	Mis	300	GD	S								
2/13	319 BECUNA	2	06-09S 113-33E	Trk	800	GD	S								
2/20	285 BALAO	7	38-45N 122-56E	Sch	700	T1/1NSR	S								
3/21	234 KINGFISH	10	30-29N 142-03E	AK	5500	T2/3NSR	S	AJ I	3	C-AK	Yaei M. Iyasaka M.	1941	S	30-21N 142-13E	
3/21	234 KINGFISH	10	30-29N 142-03E	AO	10000	T3/9NSR	S	AIJ	3	C-AK	Shibazono M.	1831	S	30-21N 142-13E	
3/21	234 KINGFISH	10	30-29N 142-03E	Same	Same	Same	O	AI J	5	A-AK	Shoto M.	572	S SU	29-35N 141-07E Off Bonin Is.	A says sunk by unk sub. PR says fired only at AK & AO in heavy seas, but noted small ships in convoy. [Attribution ?]
4/17	268 PUFFER	6	27-13N 128-23E	Smc	500	T1/3DUP	S								
5/20	244 CAVALLA	3	05-00S 112-16E	AK	2000	T1/3NSR	S	AIJW	5	XAN	Kanko M.	909	S	05-00S 112-20E	
5/20	244 CAVALLA	3	05-00S 112-16E	AO	2000	T1/ NSR	S	AIJW	5	XAN	Shunsen M.	971	S	05-00S 112-20E	
5/24	309 ASPRO	6	21-57N 119-44E	AO	8000	T2/4NSR	S								

Dt/Hr	Submarine	Pt	Position	Tgt	Size	Attack	Cl	So	Date	Type	Name	Tons	Dm	Location	Comments
JAN	1945														
6/01	407 SEA ROBIN	1	19-41N 111-25E	AK	4000	T2/3NSR	S	AIJW	6	XAO	Tarakan M.	5135	S	19-45N 111-25E	W lists ship as both XAO & Std AO 1TM.
6/20	321 BESUGO	3	06-57N 102-57E	AO	10000	T3/6NSR	S	AIJW	6-7	XAO	Nichiei M.	10020	S	04-30N 103-30E	
7/10	382 PICUDA	5	25-38N 121-08E	AO	10000	T2/4DUP	S	AI	7	A-AO	Munakata M.	10045	H	25-44N 121-14E	I & J say finally sunk by a/c at Keelung 21 Jan. 220 BARB PR says ship seen to blow up at this time.
7/11	413 SPOT	1	31-20N 123-04E	2Tra	200	GD	S								
--							-	IW	7	XPkt	Nichiei M. #2	78	S	South Seas	Location not specific enough to correlate with sub attack.
8/02	285 BALAO	7	34-28N 122-39E	AO	10500	T8/16NUR	S	AIJ	7-8	C-AK	Daigo M.	5244	S	SW Korea	
8/17	220 BARB	11	24-55N 120-26E	AP	10000	T1/3DUP	S								PR says target stern seen at 30 degree angle. Note: Attributions in this & next 10 entries are based on sequence of hits given by A for the confused wolf-pack attack on convoy MO-TA-30.
8/17	220 BARB	11	24-55N 120-26E	AK	9200	T1/ DUP	P								SORG credits BARB & 382 PICUDA; J attributes Anyo M to this attack (see PICUDA below).
8/17	220 BARB	11	24-55N 120-26E	AE	7500	T2/3DUP	S	A J	8	C-AK	Tatsuyo M. Shinyo M.	6892 5892	S	24-50N 120-35E	PR describes target as engines aft; 393 QUEENFISH PR says AE blew up at this time; A says Tatsuyo M (correct name) was loaded with munitions; I says Shinyo M, 6600T, sunk by a/c this date SW of Taipeh; J attributes Sanyo M to this attack (see below).
8/19	393 QUEENFISH	3	24-51N 120-30E	AK		T0/10	0	J AI	8	C-AO	Hikoshima M.	2854	JS	24-37N 120-30E ?C W Formosa	J credits QUEENFISH, 220 BARB & 382 PICUDA; A says this ship evaded 26 torpedoes but while doing so ran aground at Tunghsiao Bay & was abandoned.
8/20	382 PICUDA	5	24-41N 120-40E	AK	7600	T1/3NSR	P	AI	8	A-AK	Anyo M.	9256	JS	24-34N 120-37E	SORG credits PICUDA & 220 BARB; J credits BARB only; A says Anyo M was hit by 3 torps, broke in two & sank. BARB PR says 2 explosions heard at this time, claimed 2 hits (see below). [Attribution ?]

Dt/Hr	Submarine	Pt	Position	Tgt	Size	Attack	Cl	So	Date	Type	Name	Tons	Dm	Location	Comments
JAN	1945														
8/20	382 PICUDA	5	24-41N 120-40E	AK	9200	T1/3NSR	P	J AI	8	C-AO	Hikoshima M.	2854		JS 24-37N 120-30E ?C W Formosa	SORG credits PICUDA & 220 BARB; J credits PICUDA, BARB & 393 QUEENFISH; A says this ship evaded 26 torps but while doing so ran aground in Tunghsiao Bay & was abandoned.
8/20	220 BARB	11	24-37N 120-31E	AK	7500	T2/3DUP	S	AIJ	8	A-AK	Anyo M.	9256	S	24-34N 120-37E	J credits Anyo M to earlier BARB attack. PR says target disappeared after being hit. See 382 PICUDA attack above for possible hit on this ship.
8/20	220 BARB	11	24-37N 120-31E	AK	7600	T1/ NSR	P	AJ I	8-9	C-AO	Sanyo M.	2854	PS SA	24-42N 120-46E W Formosa	SORG credits BARB & 382 PICUDA; J credits earlier BARB attack; A says Sanyo M hit by 1 of 4 torps & beached, broke in two & sank 9 Jan. PR says target believed to be AK or AO; PICUDA PR says BARB's torps were heard & target was seen to explode.
8/21	220 BARB	11	24-31N 120-28E	AE	7500	T3/3NSR	S	J AI	8	C-AO	Hikoshima M.	2854		JS 24-37N 120-30E ?C W Formosa	J credits BARB, 382 PICUDA & 393 QUEENFISH; A says this ship evaded 26 torps but while doing so ran aground at Tunghsiao Bay & was abandoned. PR says Japanese appeared to be shooting at a/c.
8/22	393 QUEENFISH	3	24-25N 120-28E	AO	10000	T2/4NSR	S	AI JW	8 21	XAO	Manju M.	6516	H SA	24-27N 120-32E 22-37N 120-15E	PR says target stopped & settled; 382 PICUDA & 220 BARB PRs say explosions seen & heard at this time. A says ship hit by 3 torps & beached.
8/22	393 QUEENFISH	3	24-25N 120-29E	Same	Same	Same	0	A I	8	A-AK	Meiho M.	2857	D ?C	?	A says ship hit by 1 torp in same attack as Manju M, then beached; J says sunk by a/c 28 Mar at 25-00N 121-00E; I says sunk by sub 28 Mar off Shinchiku. [Attribution ?]
8/23	389 PIRANHA	3	30-27N 130-09E	Unk	4000	T1/3NSR	D								
8/23	389 PIRANHA	3	30-27N 130-09E	Unk	4000	T1/3NSR	D								
8	HMS STOIC	3	05-57N 100-14E	--	-	Mine	U	I	8	A-AK	Malay M.	4556	L	05-58N 100-05E	Minefield laid 3 Jun 44. [Attribution ?]
--							-	IW	8	XPkt	Kisei M.	91	S	Sunda Strait	W credits 244 CAVALLA (possible); no such attack or other likely sub attack.

Dt/Hr	Submarine	Pt	Position	Tgt	Size	Attack	Cl	So	Date	Type	Name	Tons	Dm	Location	Comments
JAN	1945														
--							-	I	8	C-APK	Hawaii M.	9467	S	Formosa Strait	I, A & J list this ship sunk 2 Dec 44; see 400 SEA DEVIL that date. [This I entry appears incorrect.]
9	HNMS O-19	8	Bantam Bay	AK	Unk	T1/3	S	AIJW	9	XAG	Shinko M. #1	935	S	03-41S 111-54E	BSH gives date 7 Jan; DNO shows CO as Van Karnebeek; both give name Shinko M.
--							-	I	9	PC	Ch 5	309	?	03-41N 111-54E	A says Ch 5 badly damaged 18 Aug 43 & out of action for rest of war. No likely sub attack.
10/02	268 PUFFER	6	27-01N 126-34E	AO	9200	T2/3NSR	S								
10/02	268 PUFFER	6	27-01N 126-34E	AK	7500	T1/ NSR	S								
10/04	268 PUFFER	6	27-01N 126-34E	AK	4000	T1/2NSR	D								
10/04	268 PUFFER	6	27-01N 126-34E	DD	1700	T1/2NSR	D	I	10	PF	CD 30	940	H	W of Okinawa	
10/04	268 PUFFER	6	27-01N 126-34E	DD	1700	T2/2NSR	S	AIW J	10	PF	CD 42	940 800	S	W of Okinawa	
10/14	268 PUFFER	6	26-49N 127-15E	AK	3600	T1/3DUP	D								
10	HMS STRONGBOW	4	S Malacca Str.	Jk	40	G	S								
11/09	413 SPOT	1	29-48N 123-05E	AK	1200	GD	S								
11/17	190 SPEARFISH	12	23-47N 139-49E	Sam	100	GD	S								
13/13	413 SPOT	1	29-55N 123-00E	AM	300	GD	S								
13/13	413 SPOT	1	29-55N 123-00E	AM	400	GD	S								
14/13	245 COBIA	3	05-51N 103-16E	CM	700	T1/5DUP	S	AW IJ	14	CMc	Yurijima Yurishima	750 720	S	SE coast Malay	
14/15	413 SPOT	1	29-58N 123-02E	2Tra	100	GD	S								
--							-	AI	15	C-AK	Yayoi M.	875	S	Off Inchon	No likely sub attack.
15	HMS PORPOISE	4L	05-20N 100-08E	--	--	Mine	U	IW	15	XAM	Kyo M. #1	340	SM	05-18N 100-20E	Minefield laid 9 Jan in Penang approaches; this sinking not claimed in BSH. [Attribution ?]
16	HMS STYGIAN	4	S Malacca Str.	Jk	100	G	S	Note	16		#2115				Name from "Success Book."

Dt/Hr	Submarine	Pt	Position	Tgt	Size	Attack	Cl	So	Date	Type	Name	Tons	Dm	Location	Comments
JAN	1945														
16 S	HMS STYGIAN	4	S Malacca Str.	2Jk	60	G	S								
17/14	199 TAUTOG	13	31-09N 130-29E	APD	1500	T2/4DSP	S	AIJW	17	APD	T 15	1500	S	31-06N 130-34E	
--							-	I	17	SC	Cha 179	135	S	SW Kaimon Mt.	W says surrendered at end of war. No likely sub attack.
17	HMS SHALIMAR	3	S Malacca Str.	4LC	200	G	D								
17	HMS STYGIAN	4	S Malacca Str.	AO	500	G	S								
17	HMS STYGIAN	4	S Malacca Str.	Jk	20	G	S								
18	HMS SHALIMAR	3	S Malacca Str.	4Jk	240	G	S								
19/01	413 SPOT	1	39-07N 122-51E	AK	3200	T1/4NSR	S	AI	19	C-AK	Usa M.	184	S	39-09N 122-52E	
19/06	413 SPOT	1	38-55N 123-55E	AO	5000	T2/9TSR	S								
19/18	384 PARCHE	4	28-26N 129-30E	AO	8500	T1/6TUP	D								
19/18	384 PARCHE	4	28-26N 129-30E	AK	2000	T1/4TUP	D								
19	HMS SUPREME	2	Andaman Is.	Cstr	500	G	D	I	19	XAN	Agata M.	302	H	S of Ross I.	
20/07	413 SPOT	1	34-45N 124-10E	AK	800	GD	S	A I	20	Fish	Tokiwa M.	221 1203	S	34-50N 124-07E	J & A say 1203T Tokiwa Maru sunk by a/c 13 Dec 43. [I appears to confuse two ships.]
20/24	199 TAUTOG	13	33-37N 128-40E	AK	1900	T2/3NSR	S	AIJW	20-1	XAG	Shuri M.	1857	S	33-45N 128-43E	W lists ship as torpedo recovery vessel.
--							-	I	20	AM	W 34	755	?	02-36N 104-34E	No likely sub attack.
20 S	HMS SHALIMAR	3	S Malacca Str.	2Cst	200	G	D								
20	HMS SUPREME	2	Andaman Is.	Cstr	150	G	D								
21/17	199 TAUTOG	13	33-33N 129-33E	AO	5000	T3/7DUP	S	I	21	C-AO	Zuiun M.	10000	H	33-31N 129-31E	
--							-	AJ I	22	C-AK	Hikosan M.	2073	SA S	Off Okinawa	No likely sub attack.
22	HMS SPIRIT	4	W Java Sea	Q		Dem	S								
22	HMS SPIRIT	4	W Java Sea	Cstr	600	G	S								

Dt/Hr	Submarine	Pt	Position	Tgt	Size	Attack	Cl	So	Date	Type	Name	Tons	Dm	Location	Comments
JAN	1945														
22	HMS STYGIAN	4	S Malacca Str.	3Jk	50	G	S								
22	HMS SUPREME	2	Andaman Is.	Cstr	150	G	D								
22	HMS THRASHER	1	W coast Burma	4Jk	75	G	S								
Note	HMS SUBTLE	3	Malacca Strait	4Jk	70	Dem	S								Attacks made between 22 Jan & 11 Feb, exact dates not given.
23/02	221 BLACKFISH	10	21-35N 114-37E	Sch	100	GM	D								
23/04	220 BARB	11	27-04N 120-27E	AK	7500	T3/4NSR	D								PR says attacked 30 ships in Namquan harbor; most those hit bottomed in shallow water, this target seen to settle.
23/04	220 BARB	11	27-04N 120-27E	AK	4000	T1/ NSR	D								PR says hit but not observed closely.
23/04	220 BARB	11	27-04N 120-27E	AE	7500	T1/4NSR	S	AIJ	23	A-AK	Taikyo M.	5244	S	27-25N 120-16E	PR says large AE blew up & sank.
23/04	220 BARB	11	27-04N 120-27E	AK	7500	T1/ NSR	S								PR says hit & afire.
23/04	220 BARB	11	27-04N 120-27E	AE	4000	T1/ NSR	S								PR says side of ship blew out, ship sank.
23/04	220 BARB	11	27-04N 120-27E	AK	7500	T1/ NSR	D								PR says hit, large smoke cloud seen.
23/12	408 SENNET	1	30-00N 141-00E	Pat	500	T1/1DUS	S	I	23	XPkt	Kainan M. #7	84	S	30-00N 120-16E	W credits 220 BARB at 27N 120-16E by gunfire, but BARB PR does not mention such an attack. [Attribution ?; longitude not close but may be misprint.]
23/18	408 SENNET	1	30-25N 141-05E	Pat	500	GT	D								
23	HMS TRENCHANT	2	04-11N 098-25E	--	--	Mine	U	A IJ	23	C-AO	Hozan M. I-go Hozan M. #1	? 868	SM	04-08N 098-15E N of Sumatra	Minefield laid 16 Sep 44. BSH claims sinking Hozan Maru, 896T; I says sunk by a/c N of Sumatra.
23	HMS TRENCHANT	2	04-11N 098-25E	--	--	Mine	U	J	23	AK	Nikkaku M.	1946	SM	04-08N 098-15E	Minefield laid 16 Sep 44. BSH claims sinking.
23 S	HMS THRASHER	1	W coast Burma	Jk	60	G	D								
24/06	322 BLACKFIN	2	06-00N 103-48E	AO	10000	T2/6TSR	D	I	24	C-AO	Sarawak M.	5135	M	E coast Malay	PR says hit aft. [Attribution ?]

Dt/Hr	Submarine	Pt	Position	Tgt	Size	Attack	Cl	So	Date	Type	Name	Tons	Dm	Location	Comments
JAN	1945														
24/05	322 BLACKFIN	2	06-00N 103-48E	DD	1500	T1/2TSR	S	AIW J	24	DD	Shigure	1685 1580	S	E coast Malay	
24/07	321 BESUGO	3	06-08N 103-34E	AO	5000	T2/6DUP	D	I	24	C-AO	Sarawak M.	5135	M	E coast Malay	PR says hit in stern; 365 HARDHEAD PR says hit seen in bow. [Attribution ?]
24/20	403 ATULE	2	36-47N 123-59E	AK	6700	T3/6NUP	S	AIJ	24	C-AK	Taiman M. #1	6888	S	36-42N 123-43E	
25/14	236 SILVERSIDES	12	31-18N 130-08E	AK	6800	T2/4DUP	D	AIJ	25	A-AK	Malay M.	4556	S	31-19N 130-05E	
--							-	A I	25	SC	Cha 90	135	H S	Tsurukui Saki	W says surrendered at end of war. No likely sub attack.
--							-	W	25	SC	Cha 91	130	S	NW of Kyushu	No likely sub attack. A says no record of this sinking.
26/14	199 TAUTOG	13	29-25N 136-25E	Tra	100	GD	S	I	26	Sail	Naga M. #11	43	S	30-00N 136-20E	PR says wooden trawler with nets out.
26	247 DACE	6	13-36N 109-18E	--	--	Mine	U	J I	26	C-AK	Tamon M. #15	6925	SM	13-34N 109-17E Coast of Annam	Minefield laid 16 Dec 44. J credits USN mine.
27/04	320 BERGALL	3	08-35S 115-40E	PC	200	T1/1NUS	S	J	27	AMc	Wa 102	175	S	Sub position	A & W say surrendered at end of war. PR says fired CUTY, surfaced, sighted wreckage & picked up 2 prisoners who identified ship as sub chaser 102. Wa 102 was ex-Dutch Fakfak. [J attribution ?; identity of ship uncertain.]
27	HMS SHALIMAR	3	S Malacca Str.	Cstr	250	G	S								
27	HMS THRASHER	1	W coast Burma	3Jk	180	G	S								
28/02	411 SPADEFISH	3	33-56N 123-06E	AK	7500	T3/3NUP	S	AJW I	28	XAP	Sanuki M.	7158 9246	S	33-55N 122-55E	W lists as former XAV, 7189T, rerated XAP Aug 42.
28/02	411 SPADEFISH	3	33-56N 123-06E	AK	7500	T1/4NUP	D	AIW J	28	PF	Kume	940 900	S	33-54N 122-55E	
28	HMS THRASHER	1	W coast Burma	3Jk	100	G	S								
29/06	220 BARB	11	25-08N 119-39E	AK	7500	T2/4TSR	D								
29/06	382 PICUDA	5	25-33N 120-54E	AP	7500	T1/3NSR	D								
29/06	382 PICUDA	5	25-33N 120-54E	AK	7500	T2/3NSR	D								

Dt/Hr	Submarine	Pt	Position	Tgt	Size	Attack	Cl	So	Date	Type	Name	Tons	Dm	Location	Comments
JAN	1945														
29/06	382 PICUDA	5	25-33N 120-54E	AK	4000	T3/4NSR	S	AIJ	29	A-AK	Clyde M.	5497	S	25-20N 121-06E	
30/05	221 BLACKFISH	10	21-37N 115-54E	Sam	100	GM	S								
30/05	221 BLACKFISH	10	21-37N 115-54E	Sam	200	GM	D								
30/05	320 BERGALL	3	08-26S 115-40E	AM	700	T1/1TUS	S	I	1 Feb	AF	Arasaki	920	DM	W of Soerabaja	PR says target seen to sink. [Attribution ?]
30/08	410 THREADFIN	1	33-30N 135-31E	AK	2000	T1/6DUP	S	AIJ	30	C-AK	Issei M.	1864	S	33-30N 135-34E	
30/08	410 THREADFIN	1	33-29N 135-31E	PC	200	T0/1DUS	0	A IW	Note	XPkt	Nanshin M. #26	81	SA S	SW Mikomoto Lt 30-05N 135-15E	W credits THREADFIN possible; A gives date 17 Feb; I & W say 1 Feb. PR says attacked with homing torp, results unk. [Attribution ?] See 287 BOWFIN 17 Feb.
30	HMS TANTALUS	6	S China Sea	Cstr	120	G	S								
31/04	264 PARGO	7	10-59N 109-06E	DD	2500	T1/6NUP	S	I	31	PF	Manju	870	M	11-51N 109-12E	
31/04	327 BOARFISH	1	14-55N 109-01E	AK	6500	T1/2NUP	S	AIJ	30-1	C-AO	Enki M.	6968	S	14-56N 109-00E	
31/04	327 BOARFISH	1	14-55N 109-01E	AP	6600	T1/2NUP	P	AI J	31	C-AK	Daietsu M. Taietsu M.	6890	S JS	14-56N 109-00E	J credits BOARFISH & a/c; SORG gives partial credit to BOARFISH. PR says target last seen heading for shore, later heard distant bombs.
31/04	411 SPADEFISH	3	34-13N 123-28E	Mis	500	T1/6NUP	S								
--							-	I	31	C-AK	Unryu M.	2515	S	Off Port Blair	I gives tons as 2333, lists 2515T ship of same name sunk 31 Dec 44; see HMS SHAKESPEARE that date; A says these are same ship. No likely sub attack. [Listing in I appears incorrect.]
31 S	HMS SHALIMAR	3	S Malacca Str.	Cstr	250	G	D								
31	HMS TANTALUS	6	S China Sea	Lug	50	G	S								
FEB	1945														
1/23	221 BLACKFISH	10	21-58N 115-39E	3Sam	200	GM	S								
1/23	221 BLACKFISH	10	21-58N 115-39E	8Sam	400	GM	D								
1	HMS SPARK	2	W Java Sea	Cstr	500	G	S								

Dt/Hr	Submarine	Pt	Position	Tgt	Size	Attack	Cl	So	Date	Type	Name	Tons	Dm	Location	Comments
FEB	1945														
1	HMS SPARK	2	W Java Sea	Ltr		G	S								
1	HMS SPARK	2	W Java Sea	Tug	150	G	S								
1	HMS SPARK	2	W Java Sea	Cstr	500	G	D								
1	HMS TANTALUS	6	S China Sea	Tug	50	G	S								
1	HMS TANTALUS	6	S China Sea	3Ltr	300	G	S								
2/01	321 BESUGO	3	04-32N 104-30E	DD	1000	T1/4NUP	S	AW J	2	PF	CD 144	940 800	S	04-11N 104-35E	I says sunk by mine.
2/23	365 HARDHEAD	3	05-40N 103-17E	AO	2500	T2/4NSR	S	AI J	11 2	C-AO	Nanshin M. #19	834	S	04-00N 103-30E	PR says target broke in two & sank. See HMS TRADEWIND 11 Feb. [J attribution ?; discrepancy in date and location.]
3	HMS TANTIVY	8	Panjang harbor	Tug	100	G	S								
3	HMS TANTIVY	8	Panjang Harbor	2Cst	200	G	S								
4/16	411 SPADEFISH	3	37-18N 125-22E	AK	4400	T2/4DUP	S	AIJ	4	C-AK	Tairai M.	4273	S	37-15N 125-17E	
4/18	310 BATFISH	6	21-00N 119-50E	LBV	200	GD	D								
6/12	411 SPADEFISH	3	38-44N 121-23E	AK	4000	T1/3DUP	S	AIJ W	6	C-APK XPG	Shohei M.	1092	S	38-47N 121-28E	
6/21	383 PAMPANITO	5	06-29N 106-12E	AK	7500	T2/6NSR	S	A IJ	6	C-AO	Engen M.	6890 6968	S	06-31N 106-12E	I gives location 06-22N 101-00E [may be misprint].
6	HMS STATESMAN	5	Malacca Strait	2Jk	80	G	S								
7/03	362 GUAVINA	5	07-03N 106-05E	AO	10000	T2/3NUP	S	AI J	7	C-AK	Taigyo M.	6892	S	06-56N 106-20E Sub position	PR says 2 hits seen, heard breaking-up noises & sighted oil & debris. I gives longitude 109-20N [may be misprint].
7/03	362 GUAVINA	5	07-03N 106-05E	AK	4000	T1/3NUP	D								
7/07	396 RONQUIL	3	31-48N 140-10E	AO	10100	T1/3TUP	S	I	7	A-AK	Kuretake M.	1924	M	31-46N 140-07E	
7/09	320 BERGALL	3	11-56N 109-18E	AO	10000	T1/6DUP	D	AIW J	7	PF	CD 53	810 800	S	11-55N 109-20E	PR says convoy of 2 AOs & 4 escorts, does not mention hitting escort. W credits 321 BESUGO; no such attack reported.

Dt/Hr	Submarine	Pt	Position	Tgt	Size	Attack	Cl	So	Date	Type	Name	Tons	Dm	Location	Comments
FEB	1945														
7/09	320 BERGALL	3	11-56N 109-18E	AO	10000	T2/ DUP	D	I	7	C-AO	Toho M.	10238	M	11-55N 109-20E	
7/09	384 PARCHE	4	29-09N 129-45E	AK	2000	T1/4DUP	S	AJ	6-7	A-AK	Okinoyama M.	984	S	S China Sea	
7/23	383 PAMPANITO	5	07-04N 104-46E	AO	5000	T2/7NSR	S	AIJW	8	XPG	Eifuku M.	3520	S	07-05S 104-50E	
7	S HMS SUBTLE	3	Malacca Strait	Cstr	400	T3/6	D									BSH evaluates attack unsuccessful.
7	HNMS ZW'RDVISCH	4	Java Sea	MV	5000	T1/3	U									BSH says CO fired at DD & may have hit MV; DNO does not claim damage.
9/00	310 BATFISH	6	18-56N 121-34E	SS	1500	T1/3NSR	S	J	9	SS	I-41	2212	S	Sub position	I says I-41 (2230T) given up 2 Dec 44. RO-115, given up 21 Feb, possibly sunk here but most authorities credit surface ships 31 Jan. [J attribution ?]
9	271 RAY	3	10-18N 107-50E	--	--	Mine	U	I	9	PF	CD 61	810	MM	C. St. Jacques	Minefield laid 22 Feb 44. [Attribution ?; mines 11 months old.]
10/13	264 PARGO	7	12-51N 109-20E	AO	10000	T4/6DUP	S									
--							-	A. I	9 10	C-AK	Waka M.	2036	SC M	Po-Hai	A says sank after striking pack ice.
11/22	310 BATFISH	6	18-53N 121-47E	SS	1500	T3/4NUR	S	IJW	11	SS	RO-112	525	S	Luzon Strait	
11	HMS TRADEWIND	6	S China Sea	AK	834	Unk	S	Note	11	AK	Nanshin M.	834	S	China Sea	BSH claims this sinking, but it is not mentioned in PR summary. See 365 HARDHEAD 2 Feb & 271 RAY 20 Jun. [Attribution ?]
12	366 HAWKBILL	3	09- S 116- E	2LC	100	G	S									
12/03	366 HAWKBILL	3	09-20S 115-47E	Smc	300	T1/1NUS	S									
13/05	310 BATFISH	6	19-10N 121-25E	SS	1500	T1/3NUR	S	IJW	12	SS	RO-113	525	S	Luzon Strait	
13/06	231 HADDOCK	11	30-05N 136-31E	Mis	300	GD	P	IW	13	XPkt	Kotoshiro M #8	109	S	30-00N 136-30E	SORG credits HADDOCK, 371 LAGARTO & 408 SENNET. PR claims only damage.
13/07	371 LAGARTO	1	30-16N 136-21E	Mis	300	GT	P	I	13	B-Pkt	Showa M. #3	76	S	30-00N 136-30E	SORG credits LAGARTO, 231 HADDOCK & 408 SENNET. PR says made hits. Ship not in W.

Dt/Hr	Submarine	Pt	Position	Tgt	Size	Attack	Cl	So	Date	Type	Name	Tons	Dm	Location	Comments
FEB	1945														
13/07	408 SENNET	2	30-04N 136-25E	Mis	300	GD	P	I	13	B-Pkt	Showa M. #3	76	S	30-00N 136-30E	SORG credits SENNET, 231 HADDOCK & 371 LAGARTO. PR says made hits.
13/06	231 HADDOCK	11	30-05N 136-31E	Mis	300	GD	P	I	13	B-Pkt	Showa M. #3	76	S	30-00N 136-30E	SORG credits HADDOCK, 371 LAGARTO & 408 SENNET. PR says HADDOCK sank this target.
13/07	371 LAGARTO	1	30-16N 136-21E	Mis	300	GT	P	IW	13	XPkt	Kotoshiro M #8	109	S	30-00N 136-30E	SORG credits LAGARTO, 231 HADDOCK & 408 SENNET. PR says made hits.
13/07	408 SENNET	2	30-04N 136-25E	Mis	300	GD	P	IW	13	XPkt	Kotoshiro M #8	109	S	30-00N 136-30E	SORG credits SENNET, 231 HADDOCK & 371 LAGARTO. PR says SENNET sank this target.
13/12	320 BERGALL	3	15-34N 110-50E	BB	32000	T1/6DUP	D								
13	HMS THOROUGH	5	W coast Burma	Jk	20	G	S								
14/00	366 HAWKBILL	3	09-25N 115-39E	Smc	300	T1/2NUS	S	AIW J	15 14	SC	Cha 114	130 100	? S	08-45N 108-28E Sub position	W says ex-Dutch ship, surrendered at end of war. [J attribution ?]
14/06	366 HAWKBILL	3	09-20N 115-38E	PC	300	T1/1NUS	S	AW J	Note 14	SC	Cha 4	135 100	Unk S	Sub position	A & W say surrendered at end of war. [J attribution ?]
14/06	231 HADDOCK	11	30-19N 135-17E	Mis	300	T0/1TUS	0	W I	14	XPkt	Kanno M. #3	98	H LM	29-50N 135-31E	W credits HADDOCK gunfire. PR says believed missed with CUTY, did not make gun attack. [Attribution ?]
14/07	371 LAGARTO	1	30-21N 134-44E	Mis	200	GD	S	W I	14	XPkt	Kanno M. #3	98	H LM	29-50N 135-31E	PR says made hits. See 231 HADDOCK & 408 SENNET.
14/07	408 SENNET	2	30-05N 135-33E	Mis	200	GD	D	W I	14	XPkt	Kanno M. #3	98	H LM	29-50N 135-31E	PR says made hits. See 231 HADDOCK & 371 LAGARTO.
14/07	371 LAGARTO	1	30-21N 134-44E	Mis	100	GD	D								PR says made hits.
14/07	408 SENNET	2	30-05N 135-33E	Mis	100	GD	D								PR says made hits, same target as 371 LAGARTO.
14/21	212 GATO	11	34-48N 125-28E	DE	600	T2/4NSR	S	AIW J	14	PF	CD 9	810 800	S	32-43N 125-37E	
14/23	311 ARCHERFISH	6	20-37N 127-33E	SS	1100	T1/8NSR	S								
14	HMS THOROUGH	5	W coast Burma	Jk	80	G	S								

Dt/Hr	Submarine	Pt	Position	Tgt	Size	Attack	Cl	So	Date	Type	Name	Tons	Dm	Location	Comments
FEB	1945														
14	HMS THOROUGH	5	W coast Burma	Cstr	100	G	S								
15	HMS THOROUGH	5	W coast Burma	Jk	30	G	S								
16	366 HAWKBILL	3	09- S 116- E	Smc	300	T1/1	S								
16/00 287 BOWFIN		7	33-53N 139-45E	DD	1400	T1/3NSR	S	AIW J	17	PF	CD 56	940 750	S	33-52N 139-42E	
16/05 269 RASHER		6	26-55N 121-03E	Unk	4000	T1/6NUR	D								
16/06 408 SENNET		2	32-10N 135-54E	DD	1800	T2/3DUR	S	AW IJ	16	CMc	Naryu Nariu	720	S	Izu Peninsula Yomeiwa	
16	HMS THOROUGH	5	W coast Burma	Jk	20	G	S								
16	HMS THOROUGH	5	W coast Burma	2Jk	60	G	S								
17/12 287 BOWFIN		7	33-11N 140-46E	Mis	200	GD	P	A	17	XPkt	Nanshin M. #26	81		SA Mikomoto Lt.	PR says target was abandoned & afire, probably from air attack. SORG gives partial credit to BOWFIN. See 410 THREADFIN 30 Jan. [Attribution ?]
17	HMS STATESMAN	5	Malacca Strait	Tra	150	G	S								
17	HMS STATESMAN	5	Malacca Strait	3Cst	1100	G	S								
17	HMS STATESMAN	5	Malacca Strait	2Cst	800	G	D								
18/00 363 GUITARRO		4	15-12N 108-54E	AK	7500	T3/3NSR	D								
18	HMS THOROUGH	5	W coast Burma	5Jk	135	G	S								
18 S HMS THOROUGH		5	W coast Burma	Jk	30	G	D								
19/19 399 SEA CAT		2	33-36N 127-40E	Mis	300	GT	D								
20/02 264 PARGO		7	12-48N 109-38E	DD	2300	T1/4NSR	S	AIW J	20	DD	Nokaze	1215 1300	S	12-27N 109-40E	
20/02 366 HAWKBILL		3	00-42S 106-18E	AK	7500	T4/6NSR	S	AJ I	20	C-AK	Daizen M. Taizen M.	5396 5376	S M	00-49N 106-05E	
20/02 366 HAWKBILL		3	00-42S 106-18E	AK	4000	T2/ NSR	S								

Dt/Hr	Submarine	Pt	Position	Tgt	Size	Attack	Cl	So	Date	Type	Name	Tons	Dm	Location	Comments
FEB	1945														
20/07	362 GUAVINA	5	11-17N 109-00E	AO	10000	T3/4DUP	S	AJ I	20	C-AO	Eiyo M.	8673	S M	11-22N 109-02E	
20	HMS STATESMAN	5	Malacca Strait	AO	900	G	S								
20	HMS STATESMAN	5	Malacca Strait	2Cst	500	G	D								
20	HMS STATESMAN	5	Malacca Strait	Tug		G	D								
20	HMS STATESMAN	5	Malacca Strait	2Ltr		G	D								
21/03	212 GATO	11	35-24N 125-23E	AK	4100	T1/3NSR	S	AJ I	20-1 19	C-AK	Tairiku M.	2325	S	Yellow Sea	
21/20	241 BASHAW	5	20-24N 111-33E	Smc	200	T1/3NSR	S								
21/20	241 BASHAW	5	20-24N 111-33E	Smc	200	GN	P								SORG credits BASHAW & 249 FLASHER. PR says made hits.
21/20	249 FLASHER	6	20-23N 111-31E	Smc	200	GN	P								SORG credits FLASHER & 241 BASHAW. PR says both subs made hits, target capsized, 2 survivors picked up.
22/09	319 BECUNA	3	11-28N 109-06E	AO	7500	T1/6DUP	S	AIJ	22	C-AO	Nichiyoku M.	1945	S	11-30N 109-06E	
23/10	364 HAMMERHEAD	4	12-39N 109-29E	DE	800	T2/4DUP	S	AIW J	23	PF	Yaku	940 900	S	12-44N 109-29E	
23	HMS SEASCOUT	2	Malacca Strait	2Jk	35	G	S								
23	HMS THOROUGH	5	W coast Burma	LC		G	S								
23	HMS THOROUGH	5	W coast Burma	Cstr	100	G	S								
23	HMS THOROUGH	5	W coast Burma	Jk	30	G	S								
23	HMS THOROUGH	5	W coast Burma	Ltr	300	G	S								
24/10	404 SPIKEFISH	2	29-05N 127-25E	AK	5000	T3/6DUP	D								
24/11	371 LAGARTO	1	32-40N 132-33E	SS	700	T1/4DUP	S	J W	24	SS	RO-49 I-371	965 1440	S PS	Sub position	RO-49 believed sunk 4-5 Apr; W & others believe I-371 sunk here, but I says given up 12 Jan. [J attribution ?; see below.]

180

Dt/Hr	Submarine	Pt	Position	Tgt	Size	Attack	Cl	So	Date	Type	Name	Tons	Dm	Location	Comments
FEB	1945														
24/11	371 LAGARTO	1	32-40N 132-33E	Same	Same	Same	O	AIJ	24	C-AK	Tatsumomo M.	880	S	32-42N 132-34E	PR identified target as sub conning tower with forward antenna raised. [If LAGARTO sank this ship, credit for I-371 is unlikely.]
24/14	412 TREPANG	3	33-58N 136-18E	AK	2300	T1/3DUP	D	AIJ	24	C-AK	Uzuki M. Usuki M.	875	S	NNE Mikizaki	
24	HMS TERRAPIN	5	Malacca Strait	4Cst	800	G	P								Joint with HMS TRENCHANT. (Sources not clear whether following attacks were joint or separate.)
24	HMS TRENCHANT	5	Malacca Strait	4Cst	800	G	P								Joint with HMS TERRAPIN. (Sources not clear whether following attacks were joint or separate.)
24	HMS TERRAPIN	5	Malacca Strait	Cstr		G	S								
24	HMS TRENCHANT	5	Malacca Strait	Cstr	100	G	S								
24	HMS TRENCHANT	5	Malacca Strait	2Ltr	20	G	S								
24	HMS TRENCHANT	5	Malacca Strait	Jk	100	G	S								
24	HMS THOROUGH	5	W coast Burma	3Jk	70	G	S								
25/02	258 HOE	8	17-08N 110-02E	DD	2300	T1/4NUP	S	AIWJ	25	PF	Shonan	940 900	S	17-52N 110-05E	
25/04	409 PIPER	1	33-56N 138-38E	Unk	2000	T1/3NSR	S	AIW	25	XPkt	Hosen M. #3 Hosho M. #3	111	S	34-06N 138-22E	
25/21	249 FLASHER	6	20-04N 111-21E	AK	2000	T3/3NUP	S	AIJ	25	C-AK	Koho M.	850	S	20-01N 111-19E	
--							-	WI	25	XPkt	Koki M.	80	SW S	31-00N 143-00E	W gives tons as 74, sinking by US DD. No likely sub attack.
25	HMS TRENCHANT	5	Malacca Strait	Cstr	100	T1/4	S								
26/18	245 COBIA	4	06-07S 114-06E	2Mis	600	GD	S								
26/23	324 BLENNY	2	11-57N 109-18E	AO	10000	T2/4NUP	D								
26/23	324 BLENNY	2	11-57N 109-18E	AO	10000	T1/1NUP	S	AIJ	26-7	C-AO	Amato M.	10238	S	11-56N 109-18E	
26/23	324 BLENNY	2	11-57N 109-18E	AO	10000	T1/4NUP	D								

Dt/Hr	Submarine	Pt	Position	Tgt	Size	Attack	Cl	So	Date	Type	Name	Tons	Dm	Location	Comments
FEB	1945														
26	HMS SEASCOUT	2	Malacca Strait	2Jk	20	G	S								
27/08	249 FLASHER	6	19-28N 111-18E	2Mis	100	GD	P								SORG credits FLASHER & 241 BASHAW. PR says both made hits.
27/09	241 BASHAW	5	19-25N 111-21E	2Mis	100	GD	P								SORG credits BASHAW & 249 FLASHER. PR says both made hits.
27/09	397 SCAB'RDFISH	3	25-45N 123-20E	Lug	100	GD	D	AIW	27	XPkt	Kikaku M. #6	137	S	NE of Keelung	
27/10	389 PIRANHA	4	22-15N 120-17E	Sam	100	GD	S								
28/08	307 TILEFISH	5	29-04N 129-39E	Mis	100	GD	S								
28/09	241 BASHAW	5	20-01N 111-25E	Smc	300	GD	D								
28/09	241 BASHAW	5	20-01N 111-25E	Mis	100	GD	D								
--							-	I	28	?	Nanshin M. #12	5381	S	19-00N 111-15E	No likely sub attack.
28	HMS SEASCOUT	2	Malacca Strait	2Jk	35	G	S								
28	HMS THOROUGH	5	W coast Burma	2Jk	100	G	S								
MAR	1945														
1/17	390 PLAICE	4	24-40N 124-02E	AK	4400	T1/4DUP	D								
1/20	392 STERLET	3	34-11N 139-44E	AK	5000	T3/6NSR	S	AIJ	1	A-AK	Tateyama M.	1148	S	34-10N 139-38E	
--							-	AJ I	1	C-AK	Eijo M.	6862	SC S	36-53N 122-26E	A says ran aground. No likely sub attack.
--							-	I	1	C-AK	Manryo M.	1945	S	SW Pacific Area	Location not specific enough to identify attack.
1	HMS SUPREME	3	E Sumatra	Jk	10	Dem	S								
1	HMS TERRAPIN	5	Malacca Strait	2Jk	80	G	S								
2/07	287 BOWFIN	7	33-50N 139-22E	AK	1200	T1/1TUS	S	AIW	1-2	XPkt	Chokai M.	135	S	34-16N 139-39E	
2	HMS TERRAPIN	5	Malacca Strait	Jk	70	G	S								
2	S HMS CLYDE	5	W Sumatra	Jk	30	S	S								

Dt/Hr	Submarine	Pt	Position	Tgt	Size	Attack	Cl	So	Date	Type	Name	Tons	Dm	Location	Comments
MAR	1945														
3/05	412 TREPANG	3	34-05N 139-54E	AK	6100	T2/4NSR	S	AIJW	3	XPG	Nissho M. #2	1386	S	Miyake-Jima	
3/20	407 SEA ROBIN	2	06-29S 112-48E	AK	3400	T1/7NSR	S	AIW J	3	XAP	Suiten M.	1805 2500	D S	Malang, Java	PR says 3 survivors identified ship as "Sea Tan" Maru. W says ran aground after being hit; I gives tons as 1508.
4/02	318 BAYA	3	12-52N 109-30E	AO	5000	T2/6NUR	S	AIJ	4	C-AO	Palembang M.	5236	S	C. Varella FIC	
4/02	318 BAYA	3	12-52N 109-30E	AK	7500	T2/ NUR	S								
--							-	I	4	C-AK	Daiai M.	6919	?	Tokyo->Muroran	I says missing. No likely sub attack.
4/08	287 BOWFIN	7	31-55N 141-21E	Mis	300	GD	D								
4/09	307 TILEFISH	5	28-43N 130-20E	Tra	20	GD	S	Note			Siko M.				PR says survivor gave name Siko M; A says this is merely a slang expression. [Attribution ?]
4	HMS TRENCHANT	5	04-04N 110-35E	SC	290	G	P	AIW J	4	PC	Ch 8	309 290		JS 04-04N 100-35E	Joint attack with HMS TERRAPIN. BSH identifies as Ch 5.
4	HMS TERRAPIN	5	04-04N 110-35E	SC	290	G	P	AIW J	4	PC	Ch 8	309 290		JS 04-04N 100-35E	Joint attack with HMS TRENCHANT. BSH gives name Ch 5.
4	HMS CLYDE	5	W Sumatra	Tra	50	G	D	AIW	4	XSC	Kiku M.	233	S	04-08N 096-07E	W credits HMS SELENE; no such attack in BSH.
4	HMS SUPREME	3	E Sumatra	Jk	30	G	S								
4	S HMS SEASCOUT	2	Malacca Strait	Sam	30	G	S								
5/01	407 SEA ROBIN	2	05-56S 113-46E	APK	7200	T3/3NUR	S	AIJ W	5	XPG	Manyo M. Man-Yo M.	2904	S	05-50S 113-46E	
5/05	407 SEA ROBIN	2	05-42S 114-02E	AK	2500	T1/3NUR	S	AIJ	5	C-AK	Shoyu M.	855	S	05-23S 114-06E	
5/05	407 SEA ROBIN	2	05-42S 114-02E	AK	2000	T1/6TUR	S	AIJW	5	XAN	Nagara M.	855	S	05-23S 114-03E	
5/06	231 HADDOCK	11	32- N 132- E	Mis	300	T1/1TUS	D								
5/10	241 BASHAW	5	16-46N 108-41E	AO	10000	T2/6DSR	D	I AJ	10	A-AO	Seishin M.	5239	S SA	16-01N 108-10E	PR says target stopped, also saw possible hit on more distant ship. [Attribution ?]
5/15	394 RAZORBACK	3	31-51N 127-27E	2Mis	200	GD	S								

Dt/Hr	Submarine	Pt	Position	Tgt	Size	Attack	Cl	So	Date	Type	Name	Tons	Dm	Location	Comments
MAR	1945														
5/16	307 TILEFISH	5	29-36N 129-45E	DE	600	T2/2DUP	S	AIW J	5	AM	W 15	800 492	S	Akuseki I.	W says beached & abandoned.
5/19	241 BASHAW	5	16-46N 108-41E	AO	10000	T3/8NSP	S	AIJW	5	XAO	Ryoei M.	10016	S	16-47N 108-41E	PR says target was ship's bow sticking out of sea. [May have been ship torpedoed earlier.] W lists ship as both XAO & Std AO 1TL.
5/21	392 STERLET	3	34-56N 140-15E	AO	10000	T5/6NSR	S								
--							-	AIW	5	XSC	Yusen M. #11	245	S	Okino Erabu I.	W credits 285 BALAO (possible); PR shows no such attack. No likely sub attack.
5	HMS SEASCOUT	2	Malacca Strait	Jk	40	G	S								
5	HMS STURDY	6	E Java Sea	2LC	100	G	S								
5	HMS SUPREME	3	E Sumatra	Jk	10	G	S								
6/10	241 BASHAW	5	16-18N 108-32E	Smc	300	GD	S	I	5	?	Ryoei M. #66	?	?	Tourane>Hainan	[Attribution ?; location not specific.]
6/12	394 RAZORBACK	3	33-50N 128-00E	Sch	100	GD	S								
6/21	399 SEA CAT	2	33-45N 127-26E	AK	2000	T1/6NSR	S								
6	HMS SEADOG	1	Andaman Is.	Cstr	500	G	D								
6	HMS SUPREME	3	E Sumatra	Jk	35	G	S								
6	HMS SUPREME	3	E Sumatra	Jk	15	G	D								
--							-	I	7	C-AK	Enkei M.	6892	L	20-24N 128-20E	No likely sub attack.
7	HMS SEASCOUT	2	Ulee Lhoe Hbr.	2Cst	250	T4/4	D								
8	HMS SCYTHIAN	1	Mergui Arch.	3Jk	65	G	S								
9/09	394 RAZORBACK	3	29-40N 133-28E	Sch	100	GD	S								
9/11	412 TREPANG	3	33-26N 139-41E	PC	400	T0/1DUS	0	AW I	14	XPkt	Kaiko M.	139	S	35-40N 141-00E SW Inubozaki	W credits 412 TREPANG; A credits gunfire by unk sub. PR says CUTY apparently missed. [Attribution ?; sinking not near attack.]

Dt/Hr	Submarine	Pt	Position	Tgt	Size	Attack	Cl	So	Date	Type	Name	Tons	Dm	Location	Comments
MAR	1945														
9/12	412 TREPANG	3	33-26N 139-41E	PC	400	TO/1DUS	O	AIW	17	XPkt	Tsukiyura M.	115	S	30-00N 137-30E	W credits TREPANG. [Attribution ?; sinking not near attack.]
9	HMS TRENCHANT	5	Malacca Strait	Tug	30	G	S								
9	HMS TRENCHANT	5	Malacca Strait	Ltr	30	G	S								
10	369 KETE	2L	29-31N 127-55E	AK	4000	Unk	S	AIJW	10	XAP	Keizan M.	2116	S	29-48N 128-02E	
10	369 KETE	2L	29-31N 127-55E	AK	4000	Unk	S	AIJ	10	A-AK	Sanka M.	2495	S	29-48N 128-02E	
10	369 KETE	2L	29-31N 127-55E	AK	4000	Unk	S	AJ I	10	A-AK	Dokan M.	2270 2990	S	29-25N 127-30E	
10	N 369 KETE	2L	29-31N 127-55E	Same	Same	Same	O	I	10	PF	CD 44	940	?	29-48N 128-02E	Attack not in SORG or U. CD 44 not sunk here. [Attribution ?]
--							-	AJ I	10	A-AO	Seishin M.	5239	SA S	16-01N 108-10E	No likely sub attack.
--							-	A J	10 Note	A-AK	Ryusho M.	2863	S SA	Camranh Bay 14-15N 109-10E	A says sunk by unk sub; I says lightly damaged by marine casualty Dec 44 at 14-27N 109-07E; J says sunk by a/c 12 Jan. No likely sub attack.
							-	A I	10 4	C-AK	Daiai M.	6919	S ?	Off Kamaishi Tokyo->Muroran	A says owners report sunk by unk sub, other source says by a/c. No likely sub attack.
10	HMS SUPREME	3	E Sumatra	Cstr	150	G	S								
11/04	398 SEGUNDO	3	34-29N 127-55E	AK	4000	T2/4NSR	S	AIJ	11	C-AK	Shori M.	3087	S	34-25N 127-54E	
--							-	AJW I	11	C-Tra	Koko M.	1520	SM S	31-22N 121-38E	No likely sub attack.
12/07	326 BLUEBACK	2	13-17N 109-58E	Mis	100	GD	S								
13/18	243 BREAM	5	05-35S 114-11E	Mis	100	GD	S								SORG misprints longitude 141-11E.
13/18	243 BREAM	5	05-35S 114-11E	Mis	100	GD	D								See above.
14/14	243 BREAM	5	05-41S 114-03E	AK	2500	T1/4DUP	S	IW	14	XSC	Keihin M.	76	S	05-50S 114-02E	W credits 407 SEA ROBIN; no such attack reported.
14	HMS SCYTHIAN	1	Mergui Arch.	3Jk	65	G	S								

Dt/Hr		Submarine	Pt	Position	Tgt	Size	Attack	Cl	So	Date	Type	Name	Tons	Dm	Location	Comments
MAR		1945													
14		HMS SUBTLE	4	Malacca Strait	3Jk	90	G	S								
14	S	HMS SUBTLE	4	Malacca Strait	4Jk	120	G	D								
14		HMS SPIRIT	5	W Java Sea	Cstr	300	G	S								
15		HMS SCYTHIAN	1	Mergui Arch.	2Jk	40	G	S								
16/23		413 SPOT	2	25-48N 119-53E	AK	7500	T1/8NSR	S	A IJ	26 17	A-APK	Ikomasan M.	3173	S JS	25-52N 120-18E	J credits SPOT & CV a/c. PR says target left down by bow, afire & abandoned.
16		HMS THRASHER	2	W coast Siam	Jk	15	G	S								
16		HMS TORBAY	1	W coast Siam	Cstr		G	D								
17/02		413 SPOT	2	25-34N 120-01E	Unk	4000	T1/2NSR	S	AIJ	17	A-AK	Nanking M.	3005	S	25-28N 120-10E	
17/03		315 SEALION	5	05-18N 103-23E	AO	7300	T1/4NSR	S	A J	17	AO	Samui	1458	S	Off Trengganu	Siamese Navy ship, not listed in W.
17/06		413 SPOT	3	25-44N 120-13E	AM	500	GD	D								
18/03		414 SPRINGER	1	26-38N 127-12E	DD	1500	T3/7NUR	S	AJ IW	18	APD	T 18	1500	PS ?U	27-00N 127-15E	I says missing.
18/03		414 SPRINGER	1	26-38N 127-12E	Same	Same	Same	O	I	18	AM	W 17	707	L	Mutsure Jima	PR says additional explosion heard, no damage claimed. [Attribution ?]
18/06		285 BALAO	8	35-00N 123-51E	Tra	200	GD	S	A Note	19	Tra	Daito M. #2 Daito M. #3	188	S	35-20N 124-00E	PR says survivor gave name Daito M #3.
18	U	237 TRIGGER	12L	28-05N 126-44E	AK	4000	Unk	S	AIJ	18	A-AK	Tsukushi M. #3	1012	PS	28-15N 126-50E	Attack not in SORG; info from U.
18	U	237 TRIGGER	12L	28-05N 126-44E	AK	4000	Unk	D								Same as above.
18		HMS THRASHER	2	W coast Siam	Jk	20	G	S								
19/02		285 BALAO	8	33-09N 122-08E	AP	9800	T3/4NSR	S	AIJW	19	XAP	Hakozaki M.	10413	S	33-07N 122-05E	
19/02		285 BALAO	8	33-09N 122-08E	DE	1000		D								
19/02		285 BALAO	8	33-09N 122-08E	AP	7500	T1/4NSR	S	AI W	19	XAP	Tatsuharu M.	6345	H S	33-07N 122-05E	W lists as XCL rerated XAP Aug 42, beached W of Shanghai, salvaged 1946.
19/17		285 BALAO	8	34-11N 123-01E	Tra	200	GD	S	AI	19	Fish	Daito M. #1	156	S	35-20N 124-00E	

Dt/Hr	Submarine	Pt	Position	Tgt	Size	Attack	Cl	So	Date	Type	Name	Tons	Dm	Location	Comments
MAR	1945														
19/17	285 BALAO	8	34-11N 123-01E	3Tra	300	GD	S								
19/19	222 BLUEFISH	7	32-10N 137-57E	XAM	200	GT	D								
19	HMS SELENE	2	NE Sumatra	Jk	40	G	D								
19	HMS THRASHER	2	W coast Siam	3Jk	110	G	S								
20/00	318 BAYA	3	11-55N 109-18E	DD	1000	T1/3NUR	S	AIJW	21	XAN	Kainan M.	525	S	12-00N 109-17E	
20/15	324 BLENNY	2	11-18N 108-56E	AK	4000	T1/4DUP	S	AIJ	20	C-AO	Nanshin M. #21	834	S	11-18N 108-57E	
20/15	324 BLENNY	2	11-18N 108-56E	AK	7500	T1/ DUP	S	AIJ	20	C-AO	Hosen M.	1039	S	11-17N 108-58E	
20/15	324 BLENNY	2	11-18N 108-56E	AK	4000	T1/ DUP	S	AJ I	20	Fish	Yamakuni M. Yamaguchi M.	500	S	11-18N 108-57E	
21	HMS SUBTLE	4	Malacca Strait	Jk	30	G	S								
22/08	326 BLUEBACK	2	13-06N 109-39E	Mis	100	GD	S								
22/20	313 PERCH	5	01-06S 117-19E	AO	300	GN	S								
22	HMS SELENE	2	NE Sumatra	3Jk	60	G	S								
23/17	411 SPADEFISH	4	29-31N 127-41E	AK	6700	T2/4DUP	S	AIJW	23	XAP	Doryo M.	2274	S	29-24N 127-31E	
24	237 TRIGGER		12L 28-05N 126-44E	AK	4000	Unk	S								
24	237 TRIGGER		12L 28-05N 126-44E	AK	4000	Unk	D								
24	HMS STYGIAN	5	N of Bali	Cstr	200	G	S								
25/14	420 TIRANTE	1	31-08N 130-30E	AK	3100	T1/3DUP	S	AIJW	25	XAN	Fuji M.	703	S	31-09N 130-31E	
25 S	HMS RORQUAL	3	W Sumatra	Jk	25	G	S								
26/09	285 BALAO	8	35-14N 123-44E	AK	2300	GD	S	AJ I	26	A-AF	Shinto M. #1	884 1933	S	35-17N 123-13E	I confuses ship with 1933T one of same name sunk 19 Feb 44.
27/04	274 ROCK	6	11-43N 109-24E	DE	600	T1/6NSR	S								
27 J	237 TRIGGER		12L 30-40N 127-50E	Unk	Unk	Unk	S	AJW I	27	ARC	Odate	1564	PS SA	SW of Ibusaki	Attack not in SORG. U says TRIGGER lost 26-28 Mar near 31N 132E.

Dt/Hr	Submarine	Pt	Position	Tgt	Size	Attack	Cl	So	Date	Type	Name	Tons	Dm	Location	Comments
MAR	1945														
27	HMS PORPOISE	1	03-54N 098-42E	--	--	Mine	U	W J	27	CMc	Ma 1	215 500		SM NE of Belawan 03-52N 098-45E	Minefield laid 8 Jul 44; BSH claims sinking.
27	HMS RORQUAL	3	W Sumatra	Cstr	560	G	S								
27	HMS RORQUAL	3	W Sumatra	Cstr	350	G	S								
27	HMS RORQUAL	3	W Sumatra	Cstr	500	G	D								
27	HMS STYGIAN	5	Java Sea	CM	1500	T1/1	D	I	27	CM	Wakataka	1608	H	S Kangean I.	W gives name Wakatake.
28/10	242 BLUEGILL	5	12-38N 109-30E	DD	1500	T1/1DUS	D								
28/13	420 TIRANTE	1	32-15N 129-55E	AK	2700	T1/3DUP	S	AJ I	28	C-AK	Nase M. Naze M.	1218	S	32-14N 129-56E	
28/16	410 THREADFIN	2	31-50N 131-44E	DE	600	T1/6DUP	D	AI J	Note 28	PF	Mikura	940 900	S	31-45N 131-45E	A says records list sinking as 2, 20, or 28 Mar; I says missing 2 Mar, cause & location unk; W says missing 2 May. No likely sub attacks on dates other than 28 Mar.
28/18	417 TENCH	1	34-44N 122-46E	Tra	100	GD	S								
28/18	417 TENCH	1	34-44N 122-46E	Tra	200	GD	S								
28/23	410 THREADFIN	2	32-08N 132-22E	3Lug	100	GM	D								
28/23	410 THREADFIN	2	32-08N 132-22E	2Tra	200	GM	D								
--							-	AJ I	28	A-AK	Meiho M.	2859	SA S	25-00N 121-00E	See 220 BARB 8 Jan.
28	HMS THULE	4	W coast Siam	2Jk	10	G	S								
29/04	242 BLUEGILL	5	12-39N 109-28E	XAO	5700	T2/2NSP	S	AJW I	28	A-AO	Honan M.	5542 5518	S	12-40N 109-27E	
29/05	364 HAMMERHEAD	5	14-39N 109-16E	DD	1800	T1/3TUP	S	AIW J	29	PF	CD 84	940 1000	S	14-44N 109-16E	
29/05	364 HAMMERHEAD	5	14-39N 109-16E	DE	800	T1/3TUP	D	AIW J	29	PF	CD 18	940 1000	SA ?	14-44N 109-16E 14-30N 109-15E	I says missing. PR says fired at convoy with 5-7 escorts. [Attribution ?]
29/05	364 HAMMERHEAD	5	14-39N 109-16E	Same	Same	Same	0	AI JW	29- 30	PF	CD 130	940 1000	? SA	14-44N 109-16E 14-39N 109-16E	I says missing. [Attribution ?]

188

Dt/Hr	Submarine	Pt	Position	Tgt	Size	Attack	Cl	So	Date	Type	Name	Tons	Dm	Location	Comments
MAR	1945														
29	HMS SPARK	3	Flores Sea	Cstr	600	G	S								
30/04	420 TIRANTE	1	31-11N 130-09E	Lug	100	GM	S	I W	30	XPkt	Eikichi M.	19	S SA	Off Kagoshima	PR says left afire & sinking, abandoned by crew.
30/16	326 BLUEBACK	2	13-41N 109-34E	3Mis	200	GD	S								
31/22	396 RONQUIL	4	29-10N 135-06E	Mis	100	T1/1NUS	D								
--							-	AJ I	Note 31	A-AK	Hokutai M.	5220	SA S	07-30N 134-30E Off Palau	J & A say sunk by Navy a/c 30 Mar 44. No likely sub attack. [Listing in I appears incorrect.]
31	HMS SPARK	3	Flores Sea	Cstr	600	G	S								
APR	1945														
1/13	402 SEA FOX	3	25-25N 120-16E	AK	4000	T1/6DSR	D								
1/16	411 SPADEFISH	4	34-23N 128-08E	Sch	100	T1/1DUP	S								
1/23	393 QUEENFISH	4	25-25N 120-07E	APK	12000	T4/4NSR	S	AIW J	1	XAH	Awa M.	11249 11600	S	24-41N 119-12E	Awa Maru claimed by Japan to be AH.
--							-	I	1	Fish	Awa M.	92	S	Off Formosa	No likely sub attack.
1	HMS THULE	4	W coast Siam	Jk		G	S								
2/08	400 SEA DEVIL	3	34-18N 124-04E	AK	4000	T2/3NSR	S	AIJ	2	C-AK	Taijo M.	6866	S	34-02N 124-00E	
2/08	400 SEA DEVIL	3	34-18N 124-04E	AK	4000	T1/ NSR	S	AIJ	2	B-AG	Edogawa M.	1972	S	34-02N 124-00E	Ship not in W.
2/08	400 SEA DEVIL	3	34-18N 124-04E	AK	4000	T2/3NSR	S	AIJ	2	A-AK	Nisshin M.	1179	S	34-02N 124-00E	
2/10	400 SEA DEVIL	3	34-18N 124-04E	Pat	800	T2/3NSR	S	AIW	8	XSC	Tama M.	396	S	E Sohukusan I.	W credits SEA DEVIL. [Attribution ?; see 420 TIRANTE 7 Apr.]
2/10	400 SEA DEVIL	3	34-20N 124-10E	Pat	800	T1/3NSR	S								
2/11	400 SEA DEVIL	3	34-18N 124-09E	AK	4000	T2/3NSR	S	I	5	C-AK	Yamaji M.	6800	L	34-07N 129-38E	[Attribution ?; location not near attack but may be misprint.]
2	HMS STYGIAN	5	Java Sea	Cstr	300	G	S								
2	HMS THOROUGH	6	Nicobar Is.	PGM		G	S								

Dt/Hr	Submarine	Pt	Position	Tgt	Size	Attack	Cl	So	Date	Type	Name	Tons	Dm	Location	Comments
APR	1945														
2	S HMS RORQUAL	3	W Sumatra	2Jk	20	Dem	S								
3/20	417 TENCH	1	31-50N 124-06E	AK	4000	T2/6NSR	S								
3	HMS THOROUGH	6	Andaman Is.	Cstr	600	T2/5	D								
3	HMS THULE	4	W coast Siam	2Jk	10	G	S								
4/02	252 GABILAN	5	05-56S 118-45E	Mis		GM	S								
4/12	282 TUNNY	8	29-27N 146-42E	Sam	200	GD	S								
--							-	AI J	5	XAN	Shinto M. #2	540	S SU	Naha Harbor Off Okinawa	W says sunk by shore artillery. No likely sub attack.
--							-	J AI	5	C-AK	Tokai M. #2	839	SA S	22-42N 115-28E Pinghai Wan	A says sunk by torp. No likely sub attack.
5	HMS STATESMAN	6	Malacca Strait	7LC	210	G+Dem	S								
6/00	365 HARDHEAD	4	09-37N 102-48E	AO	10000	T6/14NSR	S	AIJ	6	C-AK	Araosan M.	6886	S	09-18N 102-50E	
6/16	321 BESUGO	4	08-30S 119-14E	PG	1200	T2/6DUP	S	AIW J	6	AM	W 12	750 630	S	Saniri harbor	
6	HMS STATESMAN	6	Malacca Strait	4Jk	180	G	S								
6	S HMS STATESMAN	6	Malacca Strait	2Jk	80	G	S								
6	HMS THOROUGH	6	Andaman Is.	3LC		G	S								
7/05	252 GABILAN	5	07-40S 118-14E	CL	5200	T1/5TUP	D	AIW J	7	CL	Isuzu	5170 5700	S JS	Soembawa I.	J credits GABILAN & 328 CHARR. PR says target only damaged in this attack.
7/07	328 CHARR	2	07-38S 118-09E	CL	5200	T3/5DUP	S	AIW J	7	CL	Isuzu	5170 5700	S JS	Soembawa I.	J credits CHARR & 252 GABILAN. PR says target was down by bow but making 10 knots when hit.
7/14	411 SPADEFISH	4	36-01N 124-52E	Sam	200	GD	S								PR says 3-masted junk boarded, took prisoner & burned.
7/19	420 TIRANTE	1	34-35N 125-20E	AO	2800	T2/2DUP	S	AI	8	XSC	Tama M.	396	S	E Sohukusan I.	W credits 400 SEA DEVIL attack of 2 Apr. PR says target seen to sink. [Location closer to TIRANTE position; attribution ?]

Dt/Hr	Submarine	Pt	Position	Tgt	Size	Attack	Cl	So	Date	Type	Name	Tons	Dm	Location	Comments
APR	1945														
7	HMS STATESMAN	6	Malacca Strait	Jk	80	G	S								
8/09	407 SEA ROBIN	2	17-28N 109-13E	Mis	100	GD	S								
8/10	407 SEA ROBIN	2	17-29N 109-09E	Tra	700	GD	S								
8/20	411 SPADEFISH	4	37-21N 125-08E	AK	6800	1/10NSR	D	AI J	8	C-AK	Ritsu Go Lee Tung	1834 1853	S	37-27N 125-00E	A says Lee Tung was original Chinese name.
8	HMS STATESMAN	6	Malacca Strait	Jk	50	G	S								
8	HMS STYGIAN	5	Java Sea	2TB		T1/5	U								
9/09	291 CREVALLE	6	32-30N 128-25E	Tra	200	GD	D								
9/09	291 CREVALLE	6	32-30N 128-25E	SCs	100	T1/1DUS	S								
9/10	420 TIRANTE	1	36-50N 123-55E	AP	5100	T3/3DUR	S	AIJ	9	A-AO	Nikko M.	5057	S	36-46N 123-36E	
9/11	420 TIRANTE	1	36-50N 123-55E	PF	1500	T1/1DUS	S	I	9	PF	CD 102	940	M	36-46N 123-46E	
9/13	384 PARCHE	5	39-06N 141-57E	DD	1200	T1/3DUP	S	AIW J	9	AM	W 3	702 615	S	39-07N 141-57E	
9/15	281 SUNFISH	11	39-27N 142-05E	AK	8000	T1/4DUP	D								
9/19	304 SEAHORSE	7	33-20N 127-36E	Sam	100	GN	S								
10/10	328 CHARR	2	04-58S 113-32E	AK	500	GD	S								
10/22	291 CREVALLE	6	33-37N 129-12E	CM	1000	T2/3NSR	S	I	10	PF	Ikuna	940	M	SW of Iki I.	
10	HNMS O-19	9	05-25S 106-39E	AO	700	G	S	A J	10	C-AO	Hosei M.	676 696	S	05-05S 106-07E	I identifies as Hojyo M, 896T; A says same ship as Hosei M.
10	HMS STATESMAN	6	Malacca Strait	Sch	300	G	S								
10 S	HMS STATESMAN	6	Malacca Strait	Jk	50	G	S								
10	HMS STYGIAN	5	Java Sea	2Cst	400	G	S								
10	HMS THOROUGH	6	W Sumatra	Cstr	900	G	S								
11/05	384 PARCHE	5	38-53N 142-05E	AK	800	GD	S	AW I	15	XAM	Togo M.	302 362	S	Todogasaki	PR says target blew up from 20mm & 40mm hits. W credits 225 CERO, but PR says sub did not leave Guam until 13 Apr.

191

Dt/Hr	Submarine	Pt	Position	Tgt	Size	Attack	Cl	So	Date	Type	Name	Tons	Dm	Location	Comments
APR	1945														
11/23	411 SPADEFISH	4	37-11N 125-14E	PC	400	TO/3NSR	O	AIW	11	XAM	Hinode M. #17	235	S	37-13N 125-11E	PR says possible dud hit; identification of ship confirmed by intelligence.
11	HMS STATESMAN	6	Malacca Strait	3Ltr	210	G	S								
12/00	236 SILVERSIDES	13	32-03N 132-05E	AK	2000	T1/7NSR	S	AIW	12	XSC	Shiratori M.	269	S	30-45N 131-50E	PR says burned & sank.
12/20	384 PARCHE	5	38-37N 141-58E	AK	3200	T1/3NSR	S								
12	HMS STYGIAN	5	08-05S 115-06E	SC	200	T3/4+G	S	AIW J	12-3	AMc	Wa 104	175 215	S	N coast Bali	W lists as ex-Dutch Djember, total loss; I says heavy damage.
12	HMS STYGIAN	5	08-05S 115-06E	Cstr	200	Same	S	I	12	SC	Cha 104	75	H	N coast Bali	W lists as ex-Dutch Gedeh, surrendered at end of war.
12	HMS STYGIAN	5	08-05S 115-06E	Cstr	300	Same	S	AIW	15	SC	Cha 114	130	H	09-05S 115-45E	W credits 366 HAWKBILL; no such attack. [Attribution ?]
12	HMS STYGIAN	5	Bewleleng Rds	Cstr	200	G	S								
12 S	HMS THULE	4	W coast Siam	3Jk	30	G	D								
13/11	384 PARCHE	5	38-36N 141-41E	Tra	200	GD	D	AIW	15	XAM	Misago M. #1	265	S	Todogasaki	W credits 225 CERO. PR says sub did not leave Guam until 13 Apr, made no such attack.
13/13	384 PARCHE	5	38-27N 142-13E	Tra	200	GD	D	AW I	15	XPkt	Kosho M. #2	302 133	S	Todogasaki	See note above.
14/04	420 TIRANTE	1	33-25N 126-15E	AO	10000	T2/2NSR	S	AW IJ	14	XAP	Jusan M. Juzan M.	3943	S	W Quelpart I.	
14/04	420 TIRANTE	1	33-25N 126-15E	PF	1500	T2/2NSR	S	AIW J	14	PF	CD 31	810 800	S	W Quelpart I.	
14/04	420 TIRANTE	1	33-25N 126-15E	PF	1500	T1/1NSR	S	AIW J	14	PF	Nomi	940 900	S	W Quelpart I.	
14/07	252 GABILAN	5	05-19S 117-06E	AK	2800	T2/4DUP	S	A J	14	C-AK	Kako Go Kako M.	762	S	Near Rima I.	I says sunk by a/c. PR says 2 hits seen, breaking-up noises heard.
14/07	413 SPOT	2	29-46N 124-11E	2Tra	200	GD	S								
14/22	252 GABILAN	5	05-02S 118-13E	AK	2000	T3/4NUR	S								
14/22	252 GABILAN	5	05-02S 118-13E	AK	2000	T1/ NUR	S								

Dt/Hr	Submarine	Pt	Position	Tgt	Size	Attack	Cl	So	Date	Type	Name	Tons	Dm	Location	Comments
APR	1945														
14	HNMS O-24	11	W Sumatra	Fish	40	G	S	N			Note				DNO gives name Goenoeng Telang.
15	HMS STATESMAN	6	Malacca Strait	Jk	120	G	S								
16/09	281 SUNFISH	11	39-36N 142-05E	PG	1200	T2/3DUP	S	AIW J	16	PF	CD 73	810 800	S	39-35N 142-06E	
16/09	281 SUNFISH	11	39-36N 142-05E	AK	4000	T2/3DUP	S	AIW J	16	XAP	Manryu M.	1630 1620	S	39-35N 142-06E	
16/15	401 SEA DOG	3	33-24N 139-31E	AK	6700	T2/4DUP	S	AI J	16	C-AK	Toko M.	530 6850	S	33-31N 139-36E	[J tons ?; A says no record of 6850T ship.]
16/18	291 CREVALLE	6	33-41N 126-56E	Mis	200	T1/1DUS	S								
17/11	224 COD	6	31-51N 124-51E	AO	2000	GD	S								
17/11	224 COD	6	31-51N 124-51E	AT	2000	GD	S								
18/05	405 SEA OWL	2	19-17N 166-35E	SS	2800	T1/3TUP	S	I J	? 17	SS	RO-56	960 889	S	Near Okinawa Sub position	I says RO-56 given up 15 Apr; most authorities believe sunk by US DDs E of Okinawa 8-9 Apr. Some sources believe RO-46 may have been sunk or I-372 fired at but not damaged by this attack. [J attribution ?]
18/18	288 CABRILLA	7	41-50N 143-35E	AK	2900	T1/4DUP	D								
19/01	281 SUNFISH	11	42-22N 142-16E	AK	4000	T2/6NSR	S	AIJW	19	XPG	Kaiho M.	1093	S	42-12N 142-21E	W lists ship as ex-AO Tsurigisaki.
19/02	281 SUNFISH	11	42-23N 142-13E	AK	4000	T3/11NSR	S	AIJ	19	A-AK	Taisei M.	1948	S	42-09N 142-30E	
19/07	408 SENNET	3	33-35N 135-23E	AK	5200	T1/3DUP	S	AIJ	19	C-AK	Hagane M.	1901	S	33-35N 135-23E	
19/09	225 CERO	7	31-08N 136-59E	Pat	200	T1/2DUP	S	IW	19	XPkt	Isuzu M. #3	74	S	30-42N 136-42E	
19/09	408 SENNET	3	33-32N 135-23E	Esc	500	T1/1DUS	S	AIW	19	SC	Cha 97	135	S	33-35N 135-23E	
19/15	236 SILVERSIDES	13	32-57N 145-03E	Mis	400	GD	D	W I	19	XPkt	Kairyu M.	180	S M	30-00N 145-00E	PR says only 2 positive gun hits made. [Attribution ?; location not near attack.]
19/17	421 TRUTTA	1	37-52N 122-24E	Mis	400	GD	S	I	19	C	Kaiyo M.	?	S	37-58N 122-13E	PR says 2 small freighters attacked, 1 afire & settling, no sign of life; other damaged but escaped.

Dt/Hr	Submarine	Pt	Position	Tgt	Size	Attack	Cl	So	Date	Type	Name	Tons	Dm	Location	Comments
APR	1945														
19/17 421	TRUTTA	1	37-52N 122-24E	Mis	400	GD	D	I	19	Fish	Kinshu M.	75	L	37-58N 122-13E	See above. [Attribution ?]
19/17 421	TRUTTA	1	37-52N 122-24E	Same	Same	Same	O	I	19	Fish	Mitsuyama M.	75	H	37-58N 122-13E	See above. PR says 2 sampans with the freighter were not damaged. [Attribution ?]
20	HMS TRADEWIND	7	Gulf of Siam	2Jk	50	G	S								
20	HMS TRADEWIND	7	Gulf of Siam	Tug	25	G	S								
22/09 384	PARCHE	5	39-30N 142-04E	AO	3200	T2/3DUP	D								
22/09 384	PARCHE	5	39-30N 142-04E	AO	3200	T1/3DUP	D								
22/12 365	HARDHEAD	4	10-25N 099-24E	Mis	200	GD	S								
22/12 365	HARDHEAD	4	10-25N 099-24E	Mis	100	GD	S								
22/17 225	CERO	7	31-38N 139-00E	Pat	100	GD	S	AIW	22		XPkt Amiji M.	107	S	30-50N 138-30E	
22/17 225	CERO	7	31-38N 139-00E	Pat	200	GD	D								
22	HNMS O-19	9	05-29S 107-00E	CA	10000	T1/4	U								DNO identifies target as Haguro; other sources as Ashigara.
23/13 321	BESUGO	4	04-57S 112-52E	UB	700	T1/6DUP	S	U	23	SS	U-183	1144	S	Sub position	
25/01 224	COD	6	25-53N 121-08E	AM	1000	T1/8NUP	S	A J	25	AM	W 41	755 492	S	Sub position	W says W 41 beached 4 Jan. PR says oil slick seen, many men in water, picked up 1 prisoner.
25	HMS SEASCOUT	3	Off Sumbawa	Cstr		G	S								
25	HNMS ZW'RDVISCH	5	Surabaya	Prau	40	Dem	S	N				Nomura				Name given in DNO.
25	HNMS ZW'RDVISCH	5	Surabaya	Prau	30	Dem	S	N				Albania				Name given in DNO.
26	HMS SLEUTH	1	04-50S 115-40E	AMc	215	G	P	AW J	Note 26	AMc	Wa 3	222 215	SA S	Soerabaya Hbr Sub position	BSH says joint attack with HMS SOLENT; A & W say sunk by a/c 24 Jul. [J attribution ?]
26	HMS SOLENT	1	04-50S 115-40E	AMc	215	G	P	AW J	Note 26	AMc	Wa 3	222 215	SA S	Soerabaya Hbr Sub position	BSH says joint attack with HMS SLEUTH; A & W say sunk by a/c 24 Jul. [J attribution ?]
26	HMS SOLENT	1	E Java Sea	LC		G	S								

Dt/Hr	Submarine	Pt	Position	Tgt	Size	Attack	Cl	So	Date	Type	Name	Tons	Dm	Location	Comments
APR	**1945**														
28/06	382 PICUDA	6	34-15N 124-08E	DD	800	T1/1DUS	D								
28/07	408 SENNET	3	33-58N 136-17E	ARC	3000	T2/5DUP	S	AIW J	28	ARC	Hatsushima	1564 2000	S	SSE Mikizaki	I gives name Hashima.
28/07	412 TREPANG	4	32-24N 128-40E	AP	4000	T1/6DUP	S	AIW J	28	APD	T 146	890 1000	S	32-32N 128-46E	
28/09	414 SPRINGER	2	32-35N 128-52E	DD	2300	T2/6DUR	S	AIW J	28	PC	Ch 17	460 440	S	32-25N 128-46E	
--							-	AJ I	28	C-AO	Takasago M. #8	834	SA S	10-49N 106-41E SE of Singora	No likely sub attack.
28	HMS SOLENT	1	E Java Sea	Cstr		G	P								Joint with HMS SLEUTH.
28	HMS SLEUTH	1	E Java Sea	Cstr		G	P								Joint with HMS SOLENT.
29/00	321 BESUGO	4	05-45S 107-30E	Sch	800	GM	S	IW	29	XPkt	Otome M.	199	S	SE of Borneo	
29/04	269 RASHER	7	33-45N 139-20E	Trk	100	GM	S								
29/04	269 RASHER	7	33-45N 139-20E	Trk	100	GM	D								
29/09	225 CERO	7	39-15N 141-58E	AO	5000	T1/4DUP	S	AIJ	29	C-AK	Taishu M.	6925	S	E of Kamaishi	
29/18	243 BREAM	6	04-11S 111-17E	AO	10000	T2/4TUR	S	AIJW	28-9	XAG	Teishu M.	1230	S	Banderjamasin	W lists as minesweeper mother ship.
29	HMS TRADEWIND	7	06-48N 101-36E	AO	1200	T1/4	S	AIJ	28	C-AO	Takasago M.	1116	S	06-48N 101-37E	
30/22	412 TREPANG	4	34-21N 123-58E	AK	6700	T3/10NSR	S	AIJW	30	XAP	Miho M.	4667	S	34-28N 129-43E	W lists ship as both XAP & Std AK 1B.
30	363 GUITARRO	5	01-00S 104-30E	--	--	Mine	U	AJ I	30	A-AO	Yuno M.	2345	SM S	00-58S 104-31E Southern area	J credits British mine; location is fairly close to minefield laid by HNMS 0-19 13 Apr at 01-56S 105-04E. GUITARRO minefield laid 20 Apr is closer to sinking. [Attribution ?]
MAY	**1945**														
1/06	287 BOWFIN	8	41-06N 144-28E	AK	4300	T2/4TUP	S	AIJW	1	XPG	Chowa M.	2719	S	41-02N 144-36E	
1/09	408 SENNET	3	33-58N 136-17E	DD	2000	T0/6DUS	0	I W	1	PF	CD 50	940	H	Off Wakayama 34-15N 135-05E	PR says 5 torpedoes missed, 6th was CUTY, no results given.
1/12	298 LIONFISH	1	35-28N 124-05E	Sch	100	GD	S								

Dt/Hr	Submarine	Pt	Position	Tgt	Size	Attack	Cl	So	Date	Type	Name	Tons	Dm	Location	Comments
MAY	1945														
1	HMS STATESMAN	7	Malacca Strait	Smc		Dem	S								
2/06	412 TREPANG	4	35-48N 124-41E	Sam	100	GT	D								
2/22	270 RATON	7	37-22N 123-43E	AO	6000	T3/4NSR	S	AIJ	2		C-AK	Toryu M.	1992	S	37-24N 123-50E	
2/23	414 SPRINGER	2	33-58N 122-58E	DE	800	T3/4NSR	S	AW IJ	2	PF	Oka Ojika	940 1000	S	33-56N 122-49E	Ojika was former name.
2	HMS SOLENT	1	E Java Sea	Cstr		G	P									Joint with HMS SLEUTH.
2	HMS SLEUTH	1	E Java Sea	Cstr		G	P									Joint with HMS SOLENT.
3/23	414 SPRINGER	2	34-38N 124-15E	DD	1200	T3/6NSR	S	AIW J	3-5	PF	CD 25	810 1000	S	33-56N 122-49E	I says missing. PR says target capsized & sank.
4/00	412 TREPANG	4	34-16N 123-37E	DE	900	T2/4NSR	S	AIW J	4-5	AM	W 20	755 492	S	33-56N 122-49E	I says missing.
4/13	225 CERO	7	39-28N 142-04E	AK	2000	T1/2DUP	S	AIJ	4		C-AK	Shinpen M.	884	S	Todogasaki Lt.	
5	HMS STATESMAN	7	Malacca Strait	2Jk	50	Dem	S									
5	HMS SCYTHIAN	3	Malacca Strait	Smc		G	S									
6/05	364 HAMMERHEAD	6	08-15N 102-15E	AO	2800	T2/8NSR	S	AIW J	6	XAO	Kinrei M.	867 850	S	08-15N 102-00E	PR says target blew up. A gives date 8 Apr [may be misprint], same location; no likely sub attack 8 Apr.
7	363 GUITARRO	5	01-00S 104-30E	--	--	Mine	U	I	7	AF	Hayasaki	920	?M	01-00S 104-30E	Minefield laid 20 Apr. [Attribution ?]
7	HMS SUPREME	4	Gulf of Siam	2Cst	600	G	S									
7	HMS SUPREME	4	Gulf of Siam	Jk	50	G	S									
8/04	287 BOWFIN	8	39-38N 142-08E	AK	4000	T1/7TSR	D									
8/04	287 BOWFIN	8	39-38N 142-08E	AO	5000	T2/3TSR	S	AIJ	8		Fish Daito M. #3	880	S	ESE Todogasaki		
8-31	HMS SIBYL	1	Malacca Strait	5Jk		G+Dem	S									Exact dates not given.
9 S	HMS STATESMAN	7	Malacca Strait	Jk	50	Dem	S									
10 N	HNMS K-XIV	8	Java Sea	Prau	10	G	S									Patrol not in BSH; K-XIV under US operational control for Neth Forces Intelligence Svc.

Dt/Hr	Submarine	Pt	Position	Tgt	Size	Attack	Cl	So	Date	Type	Name	Tons	Dm	Location	Comments
MAY	1945														
11/12	406 SEA POACHER	3	47-08N 152-08E	Tra	500	T1/6DUR	S								
11	HMS RORQUAL	4	W Java Sea	Cstr	700	G	S								
12/08	270 RATON	7	37-25N 123-42E	AK	4100	T1/4DUP	S	AIJ	12	C-AK	Rekizan M.	1311	S	37-25N 124-00E	
13/04	318 BAYA	4	06-31S 111-19E	AK	7500	T3/6NSR	S	A J	13	AO	Yosei M.	2594 2500	S	Unknown Sub position	PR says target seen to sink.
13/04	318 BAYA	4	06-31S 111-19E	CM	1500	T2/2NSR	S	W	13	XPkt	Shosei M. #15	43	S	07-05S 114-13E	See HMS TRUMP below. [W attribution ?; sinking not near attack but may be misprint.]
13/04	318 BAYA	4	06-31S 111-19E	AK	4000	T2/2NSR	S								
13/05	390 PLAICE	5	45-30N 147-04E	Trk	400	GT		S	AIW	15	XPkt	Nisshin M.	111	SC	SW Uruppu I.	All Japanese sources say wrecked. PR says target was 370T steel sea truck which returned fire.
13/06	390 PLAICE	5	45-30N 147-04E	3Trk	900	GT	S								
13/07	390 PLAICE	5	45-30N 147-04E	2Lug	200	GD	D								
13/14	225 CERO	7	39-07N 141-57E	AK	2000	T1/3DUP	S	AI J	13	C-AK	Shinnan M.	1025	S	36-06N 141-57E Sub position	PR says target sank by stern. [Location in I may be misprint.]
13	HMS TRUMP	2	Sapudi Strait	Tra		G		D	IW	13	XPkt	Shosei M. #15	43	S	07-05S 114-13E	W credits 318 BAYA, but PR does not show such an attack (see above).
14/12	381 SAND LANCE	4	42-10N 143-30E	AK	2000	T1/4DUP	S	AIW	14	XAM	Yoshino M.	220	S	ENE C. Erimo	
15/00	364 HAMMERHEAD	6	09-21N 102-25E	AK	5700	T2/3NSR	S	AJW I	15	XAP	Tottori M.	5978	S	09-58N 101-05E 04-49N 103-31E	[I location may be misprint.]
15/08	406 SEA POACHER	3	45-35N 149-12E	Lug	100	GD		S	AI	15	A	Ume M. #56	100	S	45-29N 149-01E	PR describes target as motor-sailer.
15/08	406 SEA POACHER	3	45-35N 149-12E	Lug	100	GD		S	I	15	A-Ms	Fukuun M.	22	SC	45-29N 149-01E	PR says several gun hits.
15/08	406 SEA POACHER	3	45-35N 149-12E	2Lug	200	GD	D									PR says attacked 4 small fishing vessels or cargo luggers, left 2 gutted & afire.
15/21	235 SHAD	10	33-42N 126-37E	AO	2800	T1/4NSR	S	I	15	C-AK	Mako M.	1398	DU	34-16N 126-44E	PR says target seen to sink.
15 S	HMS CLYDE	7	W coast Siam	Jk	10	G	S								

Dt/Hr	Submarine	Pt	Position	Tgt	Size	Attack	Cl	So	Date	Type	Name	Tons	Dm	Location	Comments
MAY 1945															
15	HMS TIPTOE	2	Sumbawa	Cstr		G	S								
16/07 270 RATON		7	37-39N 124-11E	AP	4400	T2/3DUP	S	AIJ	16	C-AK	Eiju M.	2456	S	Yellow Sea	
16/09 366 HAWKBILL		4	04-52N 103-28E	CM	2000	T3/9DUP	S	AIW J	16	CMc	Hatsutaka	1608 1500	S	04-49N 103-31E	
17/22 235 SHAD		10	35-41N 126-17E	AK	7500	T1/4NSR	S	AI J	17-8	C-AK	Chozan M. Chosan M.	3938	S	35-42N 126-13E	
17	HMS TERRAPIN	6	W Java Sea	Sch	70	G	S								
17	HMS TERRAPIN	6	W Java Sea	Lug	20	G	D								
17	HMS TIPTOE	2	Sumbawa	Cstr		G	S								
18/08 320 BERGALL		5	06-53S 115-13E	Smc	100	GD	D								
18/19 390 PLAICE		5	44-33N 146-09E	Lug	100	GD	D								
18	HMS PORPOISE	4L	05-20N 100-08E	--	--	Mine	U	I	18	SC	Cha 57	130	LM	S Penang	Minefield laid 9 Jan. [Attribution ?]
18	HMS SEADOG	2	N Sumatra	MV	300	T1/3	S								
19/14 285 BALAO		9	38-09N 124-40E	Sam	100	T1/3DUP	S								
19/15 271 RAY		7	37-24N 125-05E	Trk	400	GD	S								
19	HMS SCYTHIAN	3	Malacca Strait	Jk		G	S								
20/05 271 RAY		7	38-10N 124-31E	Pat	800	GD	S								
20/13 329 CHUB		2	06-19S 116-05E	AK	600	T1/1DUS	S								
20/24 225 CERO		7	38-06N 142-24E	Tra	500	T1/2NUR	S	AI	20	C-Wh	Seki M. #5	377	S	ESE Kinkazan	
20 S	HMS SEADOG	2	N Sumatra	Sch	50	G	S								
21/02 329 CHUB		2	06-15S 116-01E	AM	600	T1/5NUS	S	AIW J	21	AM	W 34	755 492	S	06-18S 116-04E	
21/21 326 BLUEBACK		3	06-03S 112-21E	PC	300	GM	D								
23/15 271 RAY		7	38-10N 124-31E	Pat		GD	S								
23/15 271 RAY		7	38-10N 124-31E	3Sch	1000	GD	S								

Dt/Hr	Submarine	Pt	Position	Tgt	Size	Attack	Cl	So	Date	Type	Name	Tons	Dm	Location	Comments
MAY	1945														
24/08	271 RAY	7	38-10N 124-31E	2Sch	700	GD	S								
25/00	324 BLENNY	3	06-00S 107-34E	SC	200	T2/3NSV	S	I	25	B-Pkt	Kairyu M.	81	S	06-41S 109-27E	Ship not in W.
25/05	271 RAY	7	38-29N 123-03E	Sch	400	GD	S								
25/21	271 RAY	7	38-46N 122-49E	Sch	300	GM	S	I	25	?	Tsuki M.	57	?	Off Moji City	
25	HMS TRENCHANT	6	06-23S 110-55E	AM	300	G	S	AIW J	25	AMc	Wa 105	175 200	S	06-21S 110-57E	W lists ship as ex-Dutch Grissee.
25	HMS THOROUGH	7	06-45S 112-31E	MV	1900	T1/5	S	J	25	AK	Nittei M.	1000	S	06-45S 112-31E	[Atribution ?]
25	HMS TRUMP	2	Sapudi Strait	Jk		G	S								
26/05	271 RAY	7	38-53N 122-54E	Sch	400	GD	S								
26/06	271 RAY	7	38-55N 122-53E	Sch	300	GD	S								
26/07	271 RAY	7	38-57N 122-53E	Sch	400	GD	S								
26/12	286 BILLFISH	7	33-18N 126-20E	AK	2700	T1/4DUP	S	AIJ	26	C-AK	Kotobuki M. #7	991	S	Off Nagasaki	
27/03	271 RAY	7	38-16N 123-51E	Sch	300	GN	S								
27/05	271 RAY	7	38-16N 123-51E	Sch	400	GT	S								
27/05	419 TIGRONE	2	29-24N 141-01E	Mis	100	GN	S	IW	27	XPkt	Yawata M. #3	19	S	Off Torishima	
27/11	417 TENCH	2	42-54N 144-18E	Tra	100	GD	S	AI	27	C-AK	Kinei M.	?	S	S Kushiro Lt.	
27/15	409 PIPER	2	46-46N 151-22E	Unk	2000	T2/4DSR	S								
27/22	271 RAY	7	37-38N 124-43E	Sch	300	GN	S								
28/05	271 RAY	7	38-19N 124-01E	Sch	400	GT	S								
28/06	271 RAY	7	38-21N 123-58E	Sch	400	GD	S	AI	28	C-AK	Biko M.	144	S	NW Changshan	
28/07	271 RAY	7	38-32N 124-04E	Trk	200	GD	S								
28/20	326 BLUEBACK	3	06-14S 110-32E	SC	100	GM	D								PR says same target as 372 LAMPREY.
28/20	372 LAMPREY	2	06-14S 110-41E	Esc	600	GN	D								PR says same target as 326 BLUEBACK.
28	HMS TRUMP	2	Sapudi Strait	Cstr		G	S								

Dt/Hr	Submarine	Pt	Position	Tgt	Size	Attack	Cl	So	Date	Type	Name	Tons	Dm	Location	Comments
MAY	1945														
29/13	327 BOARFISH	3	05-48S 105-58E	AO	10000	T1/4DUP	D								
29/14	398 SEGUNDO	4	37-08N 125-24E	7Sch	700	GD	S								
29/21	366 HAWKBILL	4	10-05N 099-34E	Smc	400	GM	S								
29/22	392 STERLET	4	46-36N 144-22E	AK	4000	T2/3NSR	S	AIJ	29	A-AK	Kuretake M.	1924	S	46-46N 144-16E	
29/22	392 STERLET	4	46-36N 144-22E	AK	5000	T2/3NSR	D	AJ I	29	A-AK	Tenryo M. Tenrei M.	2231	S	46-46N 144-16E	
30/00	324 BLENNY	3	03-40S 114-16E	Lug	100	GN	S								
30/01	320 BERGALL	5	10-44N 099-30E	5Bge	400	GM	S								
30/01	320 BERGALL	5	10-44N 099-30E	2Tug	100	GM	S								
30/15	271 RAY	7	38-03N 124-06E	Mis	200	GD	S								
30/15	324 BLENNY	3	04-09S 114-16E	AK	500	T1/5DUP	S	J	30	AK	Hokoku M.	520	S	Sub position	PR says 12 survivors identified ship, ex-Chinese Li Liang.
30/17	245 COBIA	5	10-12N 099-14E	Sam	100	GD	S								
30/18	417 TENCH	2	41-19N 141-35E	Mis	100	GD	S								
30/19	332 BULLHEAD	2	06-52N 101-40E	Sch	100	GT	S								
30/21	246 CROAKER	5	05-09S 112-36E	AO	2800	T1/6NSR	S								
30/21	246 CROAKER	5	05-09S 112-36E	PC	200	T1/3NSR	S								
30/22	246 CROAKER	5	04-52S 112-34E	AO	2800	T1/7NSR	S								
31/22	398 SEGUNDO	4	36-37N 125-30E	AK	1300	T1/2NSR	S								
JUN	1945														
1	HMS TIPTOE	2	04-53S 115-48E	MV	1000	T1/2	S	J A	1	AK	Tobi M.	982	S SA	Sub position	BSH claims this sinking.
1	HMS TRUMP	2	Bewleleng Rds	Cstr		G	S								
2/03	417 TENCH	2	41-22N 141-28E	AO	6500	T1/4NSR	S	AIJ	2	C-AK	Mikamisan M.	861	S	SE Shiriyasaki	
2/09	326 BLUEBACK	3	05-51S 105-54E	AK	4000	T1/3DUP	D								

200

Dt/Hr	Submarine	Pt	Position	Tgt	Size	Attack	Cl	So	Date	Type	Name	Tons	Dm	Location	Comments
JUN	1945														
2/09	326 BLUEBACK	3	05-51S 105-54E	PC	300	T1/1D	S								
2/10	326 BLUEBACK	3	05-51S 105-54E	PC	300	T1/1DUS	D								
--							-	J	2	APK	Eika M.	1248	S	20-30N 107-57E	J credits 198 TAMBOR, but date should be 2 Jun 43. [J attribution misprint.]
2	HMS TRIDENT	2	Malacca Strait	Jk	15	Dem	S								
3/01	398 SEGUNDO	4	36-41N 125-23E	AK	600	GM	S	I	2	?	Anto M. #319	?	H	37-13N 125-45E	PR says 4-masted sailing ship, left with deck awash & 3 masts down.
3/06	326 BLUEBACK	3	05-39S 106-47E	Lug	100	GD	S	I	3	?	Fishing Boat	?	?	05-41S 106-37E	
3/06	326 BLUEBACK	3	05-39S 106-47E	Sam		GD	S								
3	HMS THOROUGH	7	Pulo Tengol	2Cst	900	G	S								
4/15	286 BILLFISH	7	38-32N 124-45E	AK	4000	T2/4DUP	S	AIJ	4	C-AK	Taiu M.	2220	S	Taidonkang	
4/15	286 BILLFISH	7	38-30N 124-44E	3Sch	1100	GD	S								
4/21	417 TENCH	2	40-54N 141-29E	AK	4000	T1/4NSR	S	AJW I	4	XAP	Ryujin M.	517 495	S	Near Hachinohe	W lists ship as both XAP & Std AK 1F, 495T.
5	HMS THOROUGH	7	Pulo Tengol	Cstr	120	G	S								
5	HMS TRUMP	2	Bali	AO		T1/6+G	D								
7/01	235 SHAD	10	33-28N 127-34E	Mis	100	GN	D								
7/04	398 SEGUNDO	4	37-42N 124-02E	AK	600	GT	S								
7/06	417 TENCH	2	42-41N 143-53E	Pat	200	GD	S	AIW	7	XPkt	Hanshin M.	92	S	42-35N 143-59E	
7/18	399 SEA CAT	3	37-03N 124-01E	Sch	400	T1/1D	S								
7/20	235 SHAD	10	34-00N 126-45E	AK	3200	T2/4NUP	S	AIJ	7	A-AK	Azusa M.	1370	S	33-55N 126-50E	
8/03	245 COBIA	5	08-56N 105-37E	AO	10000	T2/6NSR	S	J	8	AO	Nanshin M. #22	834	S	Sub position	[Attribution ?; no info in other sources.]
8/03	245 COBIA	5	08-56N 105-37E	AO	5000	T3/3NSR	S	AW J	8	AP	Hakusa	6000 3841	S	Off Cape Camau	W lists as ex-AGS converted to AR & then to AP.
8/06	420 TIRANTE	2	32-17N 129-56E	AK	800	T2/3NUP	S								

Dt/Hr	Submarine	Pt	Position	Tgt	Size	Attack	Cl	So	Date	Type	Name	Tons	Dm	Location	Comments
JUN	1945														
8/10	247 DACE	7	44-20N 146-39E	Trk	300	GD	S								
8/10	247 DACE	7	44-20N 146-39E	Lug	100	GD	S								
8/12	263 PADDLE	8	33-40N 126-27E	2Pat	100	GD	S								
8	HMS TRENCHANT	6	01-59S 104-57E	CA	12700	T5/12	S	AIW J	8	CA	Ashigara	13380 12700	S	N Bangka I.	
9/00	398 SEGUNDO	4	39-08N 123-10E	2Mis	600	GN	S								
9/05	405 SEA OWL	3	34-18N 127-18E	DD	2300	T1/6TUP	S	AIW J	9	PF	CD 41	810 800	S	Tsushima Str.	
9/11	417 TENCH	2	41-52N 141-08E	AK	2000	T2/3DUP	S	AIW J	9	XAP	Shinroku M. Kamishika M.	2857	S	41-49N 141-11E	W lists Shinroku M as both XAP & Std AO 2TA.
9/15	283 TINOSA	11	37-32N 129-10E	AK	2300	T1/3DUR	S	AIJ	9		C-AK Wakatama M.	2211	S	37-27N 129-25E	
9/20	401 SEA DOG	4	38-13N 138-43E	AK	2500	T1/1TUP	S	AIJ	9		C-AK Sagawa M.	1186	S	38-10N 138-50E	
9/21	401 SEA DOG	4	38-11N 138-45E	AO	10500	T2/5NSR	S	AIJ	9		C-AK Shoyo M.	2211	S	38-10N 138-50E	
9/22	291 CREVALLE	7	40-54N 139-48E	AK	2300	T2/2NSR	S	AIJ	9		C-AK Hokuto M.	2215	S	40-57N 139-45E	
9	N HNMS K-XIV	9	Java Sea	Prau	10	G	S								See note 10 May.
9	N HNMS K-XIV	9	Java Sea	Prau	10	G	S								See note 10 May.
10/02	411 SPADEFISH	5	43-21N 140-41E	AK	4000	T3/3NSR	S	AJ I	10		C-AK Daigen M. #2 Taigen M. #2	1999	S	43-23N 140-39E	
10/03	411 SPADEFISH	5	42-24N 140-33E	AK	4000	T2/3NSR	S	AIJ	10-1		C-AK Unkai M. #8	1293	S	43-55N 141-13E	
10/03	411 SPADEFISH	5	43-28N 140-28E	AK	4000	T2/3NUP	S	AIJ	10		C-AK Jintsu M.	985	S	Near Kamoizaki	
10/12	305 SKATE	7	37-29N 137-25E	SS	1500	T2/4DUP	S	AIJW	9-10	SS	I-122	1142	S	37-28N 137-26E	
10/13	229 FLYING FISH	12	41-40N 129-52E	Trk	900	T1/3DUP	S	AIJ	10		A-AK Taga M.	2220	S	41-42N 129-54E	
10/13	247 DACE	7	47-25N 149-05E	AK	4000	T2/2DUP	S	AIJ	10		C-AK Hakuyo M.	1391	S	47-21N 149-07E	
10/13	291 CREVALLE	7	40-44N 139-48E	AK	2300	T2/3DUP	S	AIJ	10		A-AK Daiki M.	2217	S	Off Otosezaki	
10/13	417 TENCH	2	41-10N 141-29E	AO	2800	T1/2DUP	S	AIJ	10		C-AO Shoei M. #6	834	S	41-18N 141-31E	

Dt/Hr	Submarine	Pt	Position	Tgt	Size	Attack	Cl	So	Date	Type	Name	Tons	Dm	Location	Comments
JUN	1945														
10/14	247 DACE	7	47-25N 149-05E	PF	1500	T1/1DUS	D								
10/21	283 TINOSA	11	39-08N 129-43E	AK	4000	T0/4TUR	D								PR says dud torp hit heard.
10/22	396 RONQUIL	5	37-29N 123-43E	AK	4000	T1/3NSR	S								
11/00	398 SEGUNDO	4	37-11N 123-23E	AP	10000	T3/4NSR	S	AI J	11-2	C-AK	Fukui M. #2	1591 1578	SA S	37-13N 123-20E	I gives location 37-14N 137-18E. PR says target not seen, heard and felt 3 hits. [J attribution ?]
11/02	229 FLYING FISH	10	41-47N 131-44E	AK	2000	T1/3NSR	S	AJ I	11	A-AK	Meisei M. Myojo M.	1893	S	41-47N 130-38E	
11/03	287 BOWFIN	9	39-24N 128-59E	AK	4000	T1/4NSR	S	AIJ	11	C-AK	Shinyo M. #3	1898	S	Off Wonsan	
11/04	291 CREVALLE	7	40-43N 139-51E	AK	2300	T2/2TUR	S	IW J	11	XPG	Hakusan M. #5 Hakusan M.	2211	S	40-47N 140-03E	
--							-	I	11	?	Kimi M.	?	S	W Aomori-ken	No likely sub attack.
11/10	323 CAIMAN	3	01-00N 108-54E	2Sch	100	GD	S								
11/11	420 TIRANTE	4	32-37N 129-45E	AK	2300	T2/3DUP	S	AIJ	11	C-AK	Hakuju M.	2220	S	32-39N 129-43E	
11/16	401 SEA DOG	4	40-28N 139-47E	AK	4000	T1/1DUP	S	AIJ	11	C-AK	Kofuku M.	753	S	40-24N 139-45E	
12/03	411 SPADEFISH	5	44-11N 140-31E	Sam	100	GT	S								
12/08	401 SEA DOG	4	40-09N 139-43E	AK	6000	T1/3DUP	S	AIJ	12	C-AK	Shinsen M.	887	S	40-11N 139-46E	
12/08	401 SEA DOG	4	40-09N 139-43E	Same	Same	Same	0	I	12	C-AK	Kaiwa M.	1045	H	41-23N 139-49E	PR says 1 of 4 AKs in convoy hit and sunk, others left area. [Attribution ?]
--							-	I	12	?	Shinsen M.	?	S	Nyudozaki	Appears duplicate of 401 SEA DOG attack above.]
12/08	411 SPADEFISH	5	44-58N 141-05E	Tra	200	GD	S								
12/09	305 SKATE	7	37-08N 136-42E	AK	4000	T2/10DUP	D								
12/09	305 SKATE	7	37-08N 136-42E	AK	1000	T1/ DUP	S	AIJ	12	C-AK	Yozan M.	1227	S	37-08N 136-43E	
12/09	305 SKATE	7	37-08N 136-42E	AO	1000	T1/ DUP	S	AIJ	12	C-AK	Zuiko M.	887	S	37-08N 136-43E	
12/09	305 SKATE	7	37-08N 136-42E	AK	4000	T4/ DUP	S	AIJ	12	C-AK	Kenjo M.	3142	S	37-08N 136-43E	

Dt/Hr	Submarine	Pt	Position	Tgt	Size	Attack	Cl	So	Date	Type	Name	Tons	Dm	Location	Comments
JUN	1945														
12/11	417 TENCH	2	39-17N 144-07E	Tra	100	GD	S								
12/12	411 SPADEFISH	5	44-50N 141-18E	Tra	300	GD	S	AIW	12	XPkt	Daido M.	69	S	Rishiri I.	
12/12	411 SPADEFISH	5	44-50N 141-18E	Tra	100	GD	S								
12/13	417 TENCH	2	39-17N 143-30E	Tra		GD	S								
12/14	283 TINOSA	11	37-47N 129-10E	AK	1500	GD	S	AIJ	12	C-AK	Keito M.	873	S	37-30N 129-20E	
13 J	223 BONEFISH	8L	Unk	AP	Unk	Unk	U	AI J	13	AK	Oshikasan M. Oshikayama M.	6892	S PS	38-30N 136-58E	Attack not in SORG. I gives name Ojikasan M, sunk as above. 282 TUNNY PR says many Japanese sighted on rafts, probably from ship sunk by BONEFISH.
? U	223 BONEFISH	8L	Unk	AK	Unk	Unk	U								Attack not in SORG; U says BONEFISH 16 Jun reported sinking large AP & medium AK, dates not specified; BONEFISH believed sunk 18 Jun at 37-18N 137-25E.
13/02	411 SPADEFISH	5	45-44N 140-48E	AK	4000	T2/2NSR	S	Note 13		AK	Transbalt	10000	S	Sub position	Soviet AK. PR says ship showed no lights & was not on designated route; CO fired on radar bearing & did not identify target. Name given in Blair.
13/04	291 CREVALLE	7	42-36N 139-46E	2Smc	100	GD	S								PR describes as cargo luggers, 75T & 25T.
13/07	255 HADDO	9	32-30N 126-56E	PF	700	T1/3DUR	S								
13/09	287 BOWFIN	9	39-13N 128-08E	AK	2300	T1/3DUP	S	AIJ	13	C-AK	Akiura M.	887	S	39-06N 128-06E	
13/16	405 SEA OWL	3	35-37N 125-36E	Sch	300	GD	S								
13/17	305 SKATE	.7	37-20N 134-28E	AK	1200	T1/2DUP	S	AI	14	C-AK	Sanjin M.	2560	S	Japan Sea	
--							-	A I	13	C-AK	Koun M.	1665	SM ?	Macao Off Canton	No likely sub attack.
14/03	329 CHUB	2	04-41S 106-22E	Unk	1500	T1/5NSR	S								
14/07	411 SPADEFISH	5	47-03N 142-01E	AK	5400	T2/2DUP	S	AIJ	14	C-AK	Seizan M.	2018	S	47-03N 142-01E	
14/08	389 PIRANHA	5	40-49N 141-28E	Pat	500	GD	D								

Dt/Hr	Submarine	Pt	Position	Tgt	Size	Attack	Cl	So	Date	Type	Name	Tons	Dm	Location	Comments
JUN	1945														
14/14 400 SEA DEVIL		4	37-38N 123-34E	AK	2300	T2/4DUP	S	AIJW	14	XAP	Wakamiyasan M.	2211	S	37-35N 123-30E	W lists ship as both XAP & Std AK 2D.
14/22 287 BOWFIN		9	39-14N 128-22E	Sch		GN	D								
14	HMS STYGIAN	6	Banka Strait	Cstr	500	G	D								
15/06 229 FLYING FISH		12	41-50N 129-55E	7Sch	200	GD	S								
15/06 229 FLYING FISH		12	41-50N 129-55E	2Mis	100	GD	D								
15/06 401 SEA DOG		4	39-53N 139-40E	AK	2500	T1/1DUP	S	AI J	15	C-AK	Koan M.	661 884	S	39-57N 139-40E	
15/07 229 FLYING FISH		12	41-50N 129-25E	3Sch	100	GD	S								
16/08 389 PIRANHA		5	41-57N 140-56E	AO	7500	T1/5DUP	S	A I	16	C-AK	Eiso M. Eisaku M.	6890	S H	41-55N 141-13E 42-03N 140-55E	
16/09 389 PIRANHA		5	41-59N 140-56E	SCs	100	T1/1DUS	S								
16/15 217 GUARDFISH		12	38-23N 145-00E	Tra	100	GD	S								
16	HMS TACITURN	1	Off Surabaya	SC		G	S	AIW	16	SC	Cha 105	130	S	N of Soerabaja	W credits 365 HARDHEAD, lists Cha 105 as ex-Dutch. No US sub attacks in area.
16	HMS TACITURN	1	Surabaya	SS		G	S	N			Note ex-K-XVIII			06-48S 112-47E	K-XVIII scuttled at Surabaya; Neth sources say raised by Japanese & used as air warning picket hulk in Madoera Strait.
16	HMS TACITURN	1	Surabaya	Hulk		T2/2	S								Hulk of passenger ship being towed.
16	HMS TRIDENT	2	W Sumatra	LC		G	D								
17/02 411 SPADEFISH		5	42-38N 139-49E	AK	4000	T1/2NSR	S	AIJ W	17	XCM CM	Eijo M. Eijo	2274 5200	S	42-43N 139-57E	
17/11 389 PIRANHA		5	42-07N 141-36E	Lug	100	GD	S								
17	HMS TACITURN	1	Surabaya	Sch		Dem	S								
17	HMS THOROUGH	7	Off Surabaya	Tra	150	G	S								
17	HMS THOROUGH	7	Off Surabaya	Sch	120	Dem	S								

Dt/Hr	Submarine	Pt	Position	Tgt	Size	Attack	Cl	So	Date	Type	Name	Tons	Dm	Location	Comments
JUN	1945														
18/07 283 TINOSA		11	38-25N 128-34E	AK	2000	TO/5DSR	O	I	19	?	Wakae M.	?	S	37-27N 129-20E	PR says fired in fog, thought torps hit rocks. [Attribution ?]
18/08 332 BULLHEAD		2	05-53S 106-02E	AK	700	GD	S								
18/10 335 DENTUDA		1	31-55N 126-48E	XPC	200	GD	D	W I	18	XPkt	Heiwa M.	88	S L	30-45N 126-00E	PR says left smoking from 2 5" hits.
18/10 335 DENTUDA		1	31-55N 126-48E	XPC	200	GD	D	W I	18	XPkt	Reiko M.	88	S L	30-45N 126-00E	PR says left smoking from 1 5" hit.
18/23 308 APOGON		7	50-30N 155-01E	AK	4000	T2/2NSR	S	AIW J	18	XAP	Hakuai M.	2636 2614	S PS	50-23N 155-06E	PR says fired at convoy of 4 ships & 2 escorts; 2 targets disappeared.
18/23 308 APOGON		7	50-30N 155-01E	AK	4000	T1/1NSR	S								
18/23 308 APOGON		7	50-30N 155-01E	Esc	600	T1/3NSR	S	I W	26	XPkt	Kusunoki M. #2	?	S	N of Chishima SW 49-40N 155-30E	[Attribution ?]
18/23 308 APOGON		7	50-30N 155-01E	AK	4000	T3/3NSR	S								
18	HMS TRIDENT	2	W Sumatra	LC		G	S								
19/02 334 CABEZON		1	50-39N 154-38E	AK	4000	T3/3NSR	S	AJ I	18-9	C-AK	Zaosan M.	2631 1631	PS S	50-23N 155-06E	PR says hits seen, target exploded.
19/06 401 SEA DOG		4	43-12N 140-19E	AK	4000	T1/2DUP	S	AJ I	19	A-AK	Kokai M. Kobai M.	1272	S	43-15N 140-18E	
19/06 401 SEA DOG		4	43-12N 140-19E	AK	4000	TO/3DUP	O	AI	19	C-AK	Shinei M. #3	958	S	42-47N 140-08E	PR says 1 of 3 AKs seen to sink, possible hit on 2nd. A credits 400 SEA DEVIL (possible); no such attack.
19/06 401 SEA DOG		4	43-12N 140-19E	Same	Same	Same	O	I	19	?	Naga M.	?	H	Ezan Misaki	See above. [Attribution ?]
19/13 332 BULLHEAD		2	05-56S 106-00E	AK	700	GD	S								
19/14 332 BULLHEAD		2	05-56S 106-00E	AK	700	GD	D								
19/14 332 BULLHEAD		2	05-56S 106-00E	2Smc	600	GD	D								
? J 223 BONEFISH		8L	Unk	Unk	Unk	Unk	U	AI J	19	C-AK	Konzan M.	5488	S PS	Matsunami Noto	Attack not in SORG. U says BONEFISH believed sunk 18 Jun at 37-18N 137-25E.
20/00 370 KRAKEN		3	05-56S 106-00E	AK	700	GM	S								

Dt/Hr	Submarine	Pt	Position	Tgt	Size	Attack	Cl	So	Date	Type	Name	Tons	Dm	Location	Comments
JUN	1945														
20/00	370 KRAKEN	3	05-56S 106-00E	Smc	300	GM	D								
20/07	283 TINOSA	11	35-39N 130-29E	AK	4600	T3/3DUP	S	AIJ	19-20	C-AK	Kaisei M.	880	S	Off Zenzaki	
20/19	283 TINOSA	11	36-04N 130-26E	AK	3700	T2/4DUP	S	AIJ	20	A-AK	Taito M.	2726	S	36-00N 130-40E	
20	271 RAY	3	10-18N 107-50E	--	--	Mine	U	I	20	C-AO	Nanshin M.	834	SM	C. St. Jacques	Minefield laid 22 Feb 44. [Attribution ?; mines 16 months old.] See HMS TRADEWIND 11 Feb.
21/03	220 BARB	12	44-39N 146-42E	2Lug	200	GT	S								
21/06	389 PIRANHA	5	39-28N 142-10E	Sam	100	GD	S	I	21	C-AK	Shirogane M.	122	H	S Todogasaki	
21/09	400 SEA DEVIL	4	37-20N 123-40E	3Tra	200	GD	S								
21/13	384 PARCHE	6	41-19N 141-28E	AK	2700	T1/4DUP	S	AIJ	21	C-AK	Hizen M.	947	S	41-20N 141-29E	
22/01	291 CREVALLE	7	43-23N 139-47E	DD	1500	T1/2NUR	S	I	22	PF	Kasado	870	H	43-20N 139-32E	
22/08	389 PIRANHA	5	39-32N 142-11E	PG	1200	T1/1DUS	S	I	22	PF	CD 196	940	M	39-31N 142-39E	
22/09	389 PIRANHA	5	39-32N 142-11E	Pat	500	T1/1DUS	S								
22/14	384 PARCHE	6	42-08N 140-58E	Lug	100	GD	S	I	22	?	Fishing Boat	?	S	42-10N 140-56E	
22/14	384 PARCHE	6	42-08N 140-58E	Lug	100	GD	S								
22/14	384 PARCHE	6	42-08N 140-58E	Trk	200	GD	D								
22/19	420 TIRANTE	2	37-54N 125-34E	Smc	100	GD	S								PR says 4-masted sailing junk.
22/23	370 KRAKEN	3	05-51S 104-28E	AO	1600	T1/3NSV	S								
22/23	370 KRAKEN	3	05-51S 104-28E	AK	700	T1/2NSV	S								
22	HMS VIVID	1	Malacca Strait	Jk	30	Dem	S								
22	HMS THRASHER	5	W coast Siam	3Jk	100	G	S								
23/01	365 HARDHEAD	5	05-50S 114-18E	CMc	800	T1/4NUR	S	AIWJ	23	SC	Cha 113	179 200	S	Near Madoera	W says Cha 113 ex-Neth minesweeper "A".
23/02	365 HARDHEAD	5	05-43S 114-21E	AK	1000	GM	S	JI	23	AG	Shuttle Bt 833 Comm. Ship 833	200 ?	S L	05-44S 114-16E	PR says target burned & sank. Ship not in W. [Attribution ?]

Dt/Hr	Submarine	Pt	Position	Tgt	Size	Attack	Cl	So	Date	Type	Name	Tons	Dm	Location	Comments
JUN	1945														
23/03	365 HARDHEAD	5	05-39S 114-19E	SC	100	GM	S	AIW J	23	SC	Cha 42	135 100	S	Near Madoera	
23/04	220 BARB	12	47-21N 143-06E	Tra	100	GT	S								PR says target sank, 1 prisoner taken.
23/05	389 PIRANHA	5	39-01N 142-01E	Tra	100	GT	S								
23/08	389 PIRANHA	5	39-09N 142-10E	Pat	200	GD	S								
23/09	384 PARCHE	6	41-54N 142-58E	3Tra	200	GD	S								
23/22	420 TIRANTE	2	37-54N 125-34E	Smc	100	Burn	S	Note	23	Jk	Antung M. #293	132	S		PR says 4-masted sailing junk, identified from papers.
23/23	370 KRAKEN	3	05-51S 104-28E	2Esc	700	GM	D								
24/03	420 TIRANTE	2	38-36N 124-40E	Smc	100	Burn	S	Note	24	Jk	Antung M. #284	132	S		PR says 4-masted sailing junk, identified from papers.
24/03	420 TIRANTE	2	38-36N 124-40E	Smc	200	Burn	S								PR says 2-masted junk.
24/03	420 TIRANTE	2	38-36N 124-40E	Smc	200	Burn	S								PR says 4-masted junk.
24/03	420 TIRANTE	2	38-36N 124-40E	Smc	200	Burn	S								PR says 4-masted junk.
24/05	420 TIRANTE	2	38-36N 124-40E	Smc	200	GD	S								PR says sailing junk.
24	HMS SELENE	3	Gulf of Siam	Jk	100	G	S								
24	HMS SELENE	3	Gulf of Siam	2Cst	1600	G	S								
24	HMS STATESMAN	8	N Sumatra	AS	900	G	D	Note	24	AS	Komahashi	1125	D	Sub position	"Success Book" gives name Komobashi; W lists Komahashi as ex-AS, sunk 28 Jul at Owase, salvaged 1947. [Attribution ?]
24?	HMS TORBAY	4	Malacca Strait	Cstr		G	S	I	24	?	Motor Sailboat ?		?	SSW of Sabang	Date of attack not given. [Attribution ?]
25/19	332 BULLHEAD	2	08-26S 115-47E	Smc	300	GN	S								
25/20	365 HARDHEAD	5	08-19S 115-39E	Sch	100	GN	S								
25/22	420 TIRANTE	2	37-53N 123-34E	Smc	100	Burn	S								PR says 3-masted sailing junk, 132T.

Dt/Hr	Submarine	Pt	Position	Tgt	Size	Attack	Cl	So	Date	Type	Name	Tons	Dm	Location	Comments
JUN	1945														
25	HMS SELENE	3	Gulf of Siam	Sch	200	G	S								
26/02	420 TIRANTE	2	38-32N 124-10E	Smc	100	Burn	S								PR says 4-masted sailing junk.
26/04	420 TIRANTE	2	38-32N 124-10E	Lug	100	GN	S								PR says 90T engine-aft lugger.
26/10	384 PARCHE	6	39-25N 142-04E	AK	4000	T2/3DUP	S	AIJW	26	XPG	Kamitsu M.	2721	S	S Todogasaki	
26/10	384 PARCHE	6	39-25N 142-04E	AK	7500	T2/3DUP	D	A I	26	C-AK	Eikan M.	6903	S L	39-26N 142-05E	
26/11	384 PARCHE	6	39-24N 142-04E	SCs	200	T1/1DUS	D								
--							-	AI J	26	C-AK	Kisei Go Kisei M.	749	SA	34-43N 127-15E	I says sunk by sub, E tip Shantung Peninsula. No likely sub attack.
--							-	I W	26	C XPkt	Kusunoki M. #2	?	S SW	N of Chishima 49-40N 155-30E	
26	HMS STATESMAN	8	N Sumatra	Jk	20	G	S								
27/01	263 PADDLE	8	37-27N 123-47E	Pat	100	GM	S								
27/02	326 BLUEBACK	3	07-25S 116-00E	AM	600	T2/7NUP	S	AIW J	27	PC	Ch 2	400 300	S	07-30S 116-15E	
28	HMS SOLENT	2	N Banka Strait	LC		G	S								
28	HMS SOLENT	2	N Banka Strait	LC		G	D								
30/01	318 BAYA	5	06-30S 117-08E	SCs	200	GM	P								SORG credits BAYA & 336 CAPITAINE (see 2 Jul). PR says 2 5" hits.
30/01	318 BAYA	5	06-30S 117-08E	2Trk	800	GM	D								
30/06	412 TREPANG	5	33-20N 139-03E	AK	600	GD	S								
30 J	371 LAGARTO	2L	15-00N 115-00E	AK	Unk	Unk	U	AI J	30	A-AK	Hokushin M.	5819	S PS	S China Sea Sub position	Attack not in SORG. LAGARTO lost 4 May at 07-55N 102-00E. [J attribution impossible.] No likely sub attack.
ca 30	HMS TORBAY	4	Malacca Strait	2Jk		Dem	S								Exact dates not given.
JUL	1945														
1/12	255 HADDO	9	38-08N 124-38E	AK	4000	T2/2DSR	S	AIJ	1	C-AK	Taiun M. #1	2220	S	Near Changshan	

Dt/Hr	Submarine	Pt	Position	Tgt	Size	Attack	Cl	So	Date	Type	Name	Tons	Dm	Location	Comments
JUL	1945														
1/12	255 HADDO	9	38-08N 124-38E	AK	4000	T2/2DSR	S	AIJ	1	C-AK	Taiun M. #1	2220	S	Near Changshan	
1/12	255 HADDO	9	38-08N 124-38E	AK	4000	T1/2DSR	S	AIJ	1	C-AK	Konri M.	3106	S	Near Changshan	
1/12	255 HADDO	9	38-08N 124-38E	AK	4000	T2/2DSR	S								
1/12	255 HADDO	9	38-08N 124-38E	AK	4000	T2/2DSR	S								
1/12	255 HADDO	9	38-08N 124-38E	Esc	1200	T1/1DSV	S	AIW J	1	PF	CD 72	940 800	S	Changshan	
1/13	421 TRUTTA	2	36-30N 125-50E	8Sch	2300	GD	S								
1/14	384 PARCHE	6	42-20N 142-08E	3Tra	100	GD	S								
1/16	280 STEELHEAD	7	33-23N 135-47E	2Smc	100	GD	S								
1/16	280 STEELHEAD	7	33-23N 135-47E	Smc	100	GD	D								
1	HMS SEASCOUT	4	Gulf of Siam	Tug	100	G	S								
1	HMS SEASCOUT	4	Gulf of Siam	5Bge	500	G	S								
1	HMS SEASCOUT	4	Gulf of Siam	Cstr	800	G	S								
1	S HMS SUPREME	5	Gulf of Siam	SC	170	G	D								
2/03	308 APOGON	7	49-28N 154-19E	SCs	100	GN	S	I	2	SC	Cha 58	135	?	49-20N 154-22E	PR says hit, not seen to sink. W says Cha 58 surrendered at end of war.
2/03	308 APOGON	7	49-28N 154-19E	SCs	100	GN	D	I	2	SC	Cha 65	135	?	49-20N 154-22E	PR says hit, not seen to sink. W says Cha 65 surrendered at end of war.
2/04	424 QUILLBACK	1	31-13N 133-22E	Mis		GN	S								
2/07	220 BARB	12	48-30N 144-38E	3Sam	200	GD	S								PR says burned during shore bombardment.
2/08	263 PADDLE	8	38-28N 124-18E	2Pat	100	GD	S								
2/11	263 PADDLE	8	38-40N 124-03E	3Sch	600	GD	S								
2/17	255 HADDO	9	38-02N 124-41E	2Smc	600	GD	S								
2/17	336 CAPITAINE	1	06-30S 116-24E	SCs	200	GD	P								SORG credits CAPITAINE & 318 BAYA (see 30 Jun.) PR says target found damaged & abandoned.

Dt/Hr	Submarine	Pt	Position	Tgt	Size	Attack	Cl	So	Date	Type	Name	Tons	Dm	Location	Comments
JUL	1945														
2	HMS SELENE	3	Gulf of Siam	Cstr	500	G	S								
3/01	338 CARP	1	33-18N 136-23E	PC	300	T1/1NUS	S								
3/10	255 HADDO	9	38- N 121- E	Tra	100	Burn	S								
3/12	220 BARB	12	48-25N 143-54E	AK	1000	T1/1DUS	S								PR says charts recovered, debris & survivors in water.
3	HMS SELENE	3	Gulf of Siam	Cstr	400	G	D								
4/06	393 QUEENFISH	5	34-59N 124-16E	Smc	400	GD	S								
4/07	420 TIRANTE	2	37-15N 123-19E	Pat	200	GD	S	Note			Koshe M.				Name from PR.
4/07	420 TIRANTE	2	37-15N 123-19E	Pat	200	GD	S	Note			Mashuye M.				Name from PR.
5/11	220 BARB	12	46-04N 142-14E	AK	7500	T1/5DUP	S	AIJ	5	C-AK	Sapporo M. #11	2820	S	46-06N 142-16E	
5/13	268 PUFFER	8	08-10S 115- E	5Mis	100	GD	S								
5/13	373 LIZARDFISH	2	08-10S 114-50E	SCs	100	T1/1DUP	S	AIW J	5	SC	Cha 37	135 100	S	N coast Bali	
5/14	373 LIZARDFISH	2	08-10S 114-50E	Trk	300	GD	S								
5/14	373 LIZARDFISH	2	08-10S 114-50E	4Mis		GD	S								
5/15	268 PUFFER	8	08-04S 115-05E	2Mis	200	GD	S								
5/18	268 PUFFER	8	08-08S 115-05E	Smc	200	T1/2DUP	S								
5/19	365 HARDHEAD	5	07-01S 115-00E	Smc	300	GT	S								
6/20	365 HARDHEAD	5	08-19S 115-38E	Lug	200	GN	S								
6/20	421 TRUTTA	2	37-37N 125-04E	AT	100	GD	S								
6/20	421 TRUTTA	2	37-37N 125-04E	3Sch	900	GD	S								
7/14	412 TREPANG	5	41-21N 141-28E	AK	2000	T2/3DUP	S	AIJ	6-7	C-AK	Koun M. #2	606	S	41-16N 141-29E	
7	HMS SEASCOUT	4	Gulf of Siam	Sch	100	G	S								
8/09	420 TIRANTE	2	38-49N 121-28E	AK	2600	T3/3DSP	S	AIJ	8	C-APK	Saitsu M.	1037	S	38-48N 121-25E	

Dt/Hr	Submarine	Pt	Position	Tgt	Size	Attack	Cl	So	Date	Type	Name	Tons	Dm	Location	Comments
JUL	1945														
8/20	421 TRUTTA	2	38-11N 124-41E	5Sch	1500	GT	S								
8/21	220 BARB	12	47-27N 142-47E	Lug	100	GT	S								PR says left sinking by stern.
8/21	407 SEA ROBIN	3	33-50N 126-42E	PC	500	T1/1NUR	S	AIW	8	SC	Cha 85	135	S	Quelpart I.	
8/22	222 BLUEFISH	9	02-13N 105-03E	PC	300	T2/4NSR	S	AIW J	9	SC	Cha 50	130 100	S	02-20N 105-05E	
8/24	412 TREPANG	5	41-35N 142-24E	DD	1000	T3/4NUR	S								
9/17	326 BLUEBACK	3	05-37S 106-42E	Lug		GD	S								
9/17	413 SPOT	3	38-18N 124-03E	2Smc	300	GD	S								
9	HMS SEASCOUT	4	Gulf of Siam	3Jk	400	G	S								
10/04	407 SEA ROBIN	3	33-39N 126-40E	AK	4000	T4/4NSV	S	AIJ	10	A-AK	Sakishima M.	1224	S	Quelpart I.	
10/05	298 LIONFISH	2	32-45N 131-46E	SS	1400	T2/5TUP	S								
10/05	364 HAMMERHEAD	7	09-38N 101-31E	AK	900	T1/1TUS	S	J	10	AK	Sakura M.	900	S	Sub position	[J attribution ?; not confirmed by other source.]
10/05	364 HAMMERHEAD	7	09-38N 101-31E	PC	200	T1/1TUS	S	AJ	10	C-AO	Nanmei M. #5	834	S	09-22N 101-41E	
10/11	476 RUNNER	1	39-20N 142-07E	AM	600	T3/5DSP	S	AIW J	10	AM	W 27	755 630	S	39-36N 142-02E	
10/11	220 BARB	12	44-13N 145-23E	AK	800	T0/3DUP	0	AI J	15 14	C-AK	Toyu M.	1256	S SA	Off Nemuro 43-17N 145-29E	PR says attacked 2 coastal AKs, torps went straight but no explosions heard. [Attribution ?; sinking 4-5 days after attack.]
10/23	300 MORAY	1	38-11N 142-15E	AK	600	T1/5NSR	S	A I	10	Wh	Fumi M. #6 Fumi M. #5	361 384	SA S	E of Kinkazan	W says Fumi M #5 was XSC, surrendered at end of war. [Attribution ?]
ca 10	HMS SIBYL	2	S Malacca Str.	11Sm		G	S								Exact dates not given.
11/01	234 KINGFISH	12	38-03N 142-29E	Tra	200	T0/7NSR	0	I	10	Fish	Inari M.	68	?	Off Maedate	PR says torps believed missed, heard 300 MORAY's torps shortly before firing second salvo (PR). SORG gives incorrect date 10 Jul (misprint in PR).

Dt/Hr	Submarine	Pt	Position	Tgt	Size	Attack	Cl	So	Date	Type	Name	Tons	Dm	Location	Comments
JUL	1945														
11/09	220 BARB	12	44-03N 146-30E	Sam		GD	S	Note 15	?		Seiho M. #15	91	S	Off Hokkaido	PR says target was diesel sampan. Identification from notes by Wilds in NavHistCtr. [Attribution ?]
11/16	324 BLENNY	4	08-40S 114-23E	Trk	300	GD	S								
11/23	330 BRILL	3	06-46N 101-42E	AK	1000	T1/11NSR	D								
12/02	335 DENTUDA	1	26-06N 119-45E	AK	4000	T2/3NSV	S								
12	HMS SUPREME	5	Gulf of Siam	Lug	60	G	S								
13	HMS TRENCHANT	7	Gulf of Boni	Sch	15	G	S								
14/15	410 THREADFIN	3	38-37N 120-54E	Sch	200	GD	S								
14/15	412 TREPANG	5	38-43N 141-53E	Lug	100	GD	S								
14	HMS SUPREME	5	Gulf of Siam	Tug	90	G	S								
14	HMS SUPREME	5	Gulf of Siam	Ltr		G	S								
14	HMS THULE	6	Java Sea	Cstr	150	G	D								
15/02	222 BLUEFISH	9	05-44N 110-06E	SS	1500	T2/4NSR	S	IJW	14	SS	I-351	2650	S	S China Sea	PR says 1 survivor picked up.
15/13	410 THREADFIN	3	39-24N 123-44E	AK	4000	T1/1DSR	D								
15/13	410 THREADFIN	3	39-30N 123-41E	Sch	300	GD	S								
15/15	333 BUMPER	2	06-39N 101-41E	Sch	200	GD	S								
15/18	326 BLUEBACK	3	03-47S 109-13E	Sch	100	GD	S								
--							-	AJI	15	Fish	Taisho M. #1	606	SA	Off Ofuyo ? Hokkaido	J gives location 42N 140E. No likely sub attack.
15	HMS SUPREME	5	Gulf of Siam	3Cst	1300	G	S								
15	HMS TRENCHANT	7	NE Lombok Str.	SC	150	G	S								
15	HMS TRENCHANT	7	NE Lombok Str.	Tug	200	G	S								
15	HMS TRENCHANT	7	NE Lombok Str.	LC	10	G	S								

Dt/Hr	Submarine	Pt	Position	Tgt	Size	Attack	Cl	So	Date	Type	Name	Tons	Dm	Location	Comments
JUL	1945														
	1945														
16/03	318 BAYA	5	05-48S 115-53E	TB	600	T1/2NUR	S	AIW J	16	TB	Kari	840 595	S	05-30S 116-10E	
16/05	324 BLENNY	4	05-26S 110-33E	XPG	2000	T4/12NSR	S	W	16	PG	Nankai	2400	S	W of Soerabaja	[Attribution ?]
16/07	324 BLENNY	4	06-51S 110-50E	Pat	500	GD	D								
16/10	410 THREADFIN	3	39-45N 123-20E	Smc	300	GD	S								
16/11	324 BLENNY	4	05-25N 110-33E	Mis		GD	S								
16	HMS VIGOROUS	1	N Sumatra	Cstr	150	G	D								
17/09	366 HAWKBILL	5	05- N 104- E	Smc	100	GD	S								
17/10	333 BUMPER	2	10-54N 099-31E	AO	800	T2/3DUP	S								
17	HMS THULE	6	N coast Java	Cstr	150	G	S								
18/12	220 BARB	12	46-04N 142-16E	PF	1000	T1/2DUP	S	AIW J	18	PF	CD 112	940 800	S	46-06N 142-16E	
18/17	338 CARP	1	44-24N 146-59E	2Trk	1000	GD	S								
18/17	338 CARP	1	44-24N 146-59E	4Trk	2000	GD	D								
--							-	AI	18		C-AK	Tenyu M.	169	S	N of Honshu	Location not specific, but no likely sub attack.
19/10	222 BLUEFISH	9	00-04S 105-08E	Mis	200	GD	S								
19/10	373 LIZARDFISH	2	05-55S 105-48E	3Trk	800	GD	S								
19	HMS THULE	6	N coast Java	Cstr	100	G	S								
20/05	333 BUMPER	2	08-08N 103-40E	AO	1200	T1/3NSR	S	AJW	19-20	XAO	Kyoei M. #3	1189	S	Gulf of Siam	W lists ship as both XAO & Std AO 1TS.
20/05	333 BUMPER	2	08-08N 103-40E	Same	Same	Same	0	IW	20	XPkt	Kyoraku M. #3	38	S	Gulf of Siam	W credits BUMPER. PR does not mention attack. [Attribution ?]
20/19	373 LIZARDFISH	2	05-41S 106-37E	Mis		Burn	S								
20/20	366 HAWKBILL	5	04-29N 103-29E	Smc		Burn	S								

Dt/Hr	Submarine	Pt	Position	Tgt	Size	Attack	Cl	So	Date	Type	Name	Tons	Dm	Location	Comments
JUL	1945														
20/21 366 HAWKBILL		5	04-30N 103-28E	AK	600	GM	S								
20/23 406 SEA POACHER		4	37-29N 141-06E	2Trk	500	GM	S								
20/23 410 THREADFIN		3	35-01N 125-42E	AK	4000	T2/5NSR	S	AIW J	18 20	AM	W 39	755 630	SU S	E of Soan I. Sub position	PR says wreckage, survivors in water. I says missing. [J attribution ?; date discrepancy & sub was W of Soan I.]
20	HMS THULE	6	N coast Java	Cstr	150	G	S								
21/13 224 COD		7	05-22N 103-16E	Smc	100	GD	S								
21/14 366 HAWKBILL		5	05- N 103- E	2Smc		GD	S								
21/23 407 SEA ROBIN		3	33-51N 126-32E	AK	500	GM	S								
21/23 407 SEA ROBIN		3	33-51N 126-32E	AK	500	GM	S								
21/23 410 THREADFIN		3	33-54N 126-38E	2Mis	400	GM	S								
22/23 407 SEA ROBIN		3	33-54N 126-30E	Lug	100	GM	S								
22/24 406 SEA POACHER		4	37-16N 141-04E	Trk	200	GN	S	AW I	23		XPkt Kiri M. #2	334 250	S	Unozaki-> Shioyazaki	W misspells sub name Sea Pacher.
23/03 407 SEA ROBIN		3	33-46N 126-30E	Lug		GN	S								
23/03 365 HARDHEAD		6	08-10S 115-29E	PC	300	GM	S	AIW J	23	SC	Cha 117	145 200	S	N coast Bali	W lists ship as ex-Neth Bantam.
23/12 324 BLENNY		4	04-44N 103-29E	Sam		GD	S								SORG gives latitude 04-44S [misprint]. PR says Chinese junk, burned & sunk.
23/12 324 BLENNY		4	04-47N 103-26E	Trk	300	GD	S								
23	HMS TUDOR	7	W Java Sea	Cstr	150	G	S								
23 S	HMS STUBBORN	1	E Java Sea	Smc		G	D								
24/01 406 SEA POACHER		4	37-10N 141-05E	XPC	300	GM	S								
24/08 324 BLENNY		4	04-32N 103-30E	Sam		GD	S								
24/12 331 BUGARA		3	10-12N 100-05E	Sch	100	GD	S								

Dt/Hr	Submarine	Pt	Position	Tgt	Size	Attack	Cl	So	Date	Type	Name	Tons	Dm	Location	Comments
JUL	1945														
24/12	331 BUGARA	3	10-02N 100-08E	Smc	100	GD	S								
24/14	329 CHUB	3	07-46S 114-24E	AT	100	GD	S								
24/19	331 BUGARA	3	09-16N 100-09E	2Smc		GT	S								
24	HMS SEADOG	4	Malacca Strait	Jk	50	G	S								
25/06	309 ASPRO	7	34-57N 140-04E	AT	500	GD	S								
25/07	265 PETO	10	34-23N 137-25E	Sam	100	GD	S								
25/07	324 BLENNY	4	05-50N 102-47E	Sam		GD	S								
25/08	324 BLENNY	4	05-48N 103-14E	Sam		GD	S								
25/10	220 BARB	12	49-04N 143-49E	Sam	100	GD	S								PR says boarded sampan, took 1 prisoner.
25/12	331 BUGARA	3	07-06N 101-23E	Sch	100	GD	S								
24/14	220 BARB	12	48-53N 144-19E	5Sam	200	GD	S								
25/17	331 BUGARA	3	06-41N 101-51E	2Smc	100	GD	S								
25/17	331 BUGARA	3	06-41N 101-51E	2Sch	200	GD	S								
25/19	224 COD	7	04-43N 103-33E	Smc	100	GT	S								
25/19	331 BUGARA	3	06-52N 101-46E	Smc		GT	S								
25	HMS STUBBORN	1	07-07S 115-40E	DD	1250	T2/4	S	AIW J	25	PF	P 2	1215 750	S	07-06S 115-42E	Ex-DD Nadakaze.
25	HMS THRASHER	6	N Malacca Str.	Jk	20	G	S								
26/01	331 BUGARA	3	06-51N 102-08E	Smc		GN	S								
26/03	338 CARP	1	45-10N 148-26E	AK	4000	T1/2NSR	S								
26/03	406 SEA POACHER	4	42-06N 142-50E	Trk	300	GM	S								
26/04	338 CARP	1	45-11N 148-27E	CM	1200	T1/1TSR	S								
26/04	418 THORNBACK	1	39-43N 142-03E	Pat	100	T1/1NUS	S								
26/07	331 BUGARA	3	06-52N 101-42E	Smc	100	GD	S								

Dt/Hr	Submarine	Pt	Position	Tgt	Size	Attack	Cl	So	Date	Type	Name	Tons	Dm	Location	Comments
26/07	391 POMFRET	6	33-47N 126-50E	Smc	100	GD	S								
26/08	391 POMFRET	6	33-47N 126-50E	Sch	100	GD	S								
26/12	224 COD	7	05-08N 103-35E	Smc	100	GD	S								
26/14	331 BUGARA	3	06-19N 102-17E	Trk	100	GD	S								
26/15	220 BARB	12	44-20N 146-01E	35Sm	700	GD	S								PR sats burned in shipyard bombarded & set afire.
26/15	331 BUGARA	3	06-14N 102-20E	Sch	100	GD	S								
26/15	331 BUGARA	3	06-19N 102-24E	Sch	200	GD	S								
26/17	220 BARB	12	44-21N 145-52E	Tra	100	GD	S								PR says burned, rammed & sunk, 2 prisoners taken.
26/20	224 COD	7	04-32N 103-33E	2Sam	100	GN	S								
26	HMS SEADOG	4	Malacca Strait	Jk	95	Dem	S								
27/03	224 COD	7	05-15N 103-16E	3Smc	300	GM	S								
27/05	224 COD	7	05-18N 103-39E	Sam	100	GT	S								
27/05	324 BLENNY	4	05-13N 103-14E	3Smc	300	GM	S								
27/13	331 BUGARA	3	09-11N 100-03E	2Sch	100	GD	S								
27/15	406 SEA POACHER	4	42-14N 143-26E	Lug	100	GD	S								
27/20	331 BUGARA	3	10-14N 099-43E	Sch	200	GN	S								
27/21	266 POGY	10	37-00N 134-02E	AK	7500	T2/4TSR	S	AIJ	27	C-AK	Chikuzen M.	2448	S	SW Kyogasaki	
27	HMS SEADOG	4	Malacca Strait	LST	1200	G	P								Joint with HMS SHALIMAR.
27	HMS SHALIMAR	4	S Malacca Str.	LST	1200	G	P								Joint with HMS SEA DOG.
27	HMS SEADOG	4	Malacca Strait	Jk	30	Dem	S								
27	HMS STUBBORN	1	E Java Sea	Smc	10	G	S								
27	HMS THRASHER	6	N Malacca Str.	4Cst	350	G	S								

Dt/Hr	Submarine	Pt	Position	Tgt	Size	Attack	Cl	So	Date	Type	Name	Tons	Dm	Location	Comments
JUL	1945														
27	HMS THRASHER	6	N Malacca Str.	Jk	40	G	S								
27	HMS TUDOR	7	W Java Sea	Cstr	250	G	D								
28/00	365 HARDHEAD	6	08-09S 115-25E	AK	1500	GM	S								
28/01	408 SENNET	4	40-17N 139-50E	AK	7500	T3/5NSV	S	AIJ	28	C-AK	Hagikawa M.	2995	S	W Noshiro Hbr.	
28/04	408 SENNET	4	39-53N 139-43E	AK	2000	T1/3TUP	S	AIJ	28	C-AK	Unkai M. #15	1205	S	39-49N 139-47E	
28/04	408 SENNET	4	39-53N 139-43E	AK	7500	T2/3TUP	S	AIJ	28	C-AK	Hakuei M.	2863	S	39-49N 139-47E	
28/12	331 BUGARA	3	11-50N 100-00E	3Smc	200	GD	S								
28/20	331 BUGARA	3	11-50N 100-00E	2Sch	400	GD	S								
28	HMS TUDOR	7	W Java Sea	2Cst	500	G	S								
28	HMS STUBBORN	1	E Java Sea	Jk	70	Note	S								Officer left on junk 27 Jul; junk found aground next morning, no trace of officer.
29/07	331 BUGARA	3	10-32N 099-59E	Sch	200	GD	S								
29/10	224 COD	7	04-29N 103-34E	2Smc	200	GD	S								
29/10	224 COD	7	04-29N 103-34E	Smc		Burn	S								
29/12	224 COD	7	04-29N 103-34E	4Sam	200	GD	S								
29/12	331 BUGARA	3	10-06N 099-22E	AG	400	GD	S								
29/12	331 BUGARA	3	10-07N 099-19E	Smc	100	GD	S								
29/13	331 BUGARA	3	10-02N 099-22E	Sch	100	GD	S								
29	HMS SEADOG	4	Malacca Strait	Jk	80	Dem	S								
29 S	HMS TUDOR	7	W Java Sea	Cstr	250	G	S								
29	HNMS O-21	5	NW coast Java	Cstr	100	G	D								
29	HNMS O-21	5	NW coast Java	Cstr	500	G	D								
30/06	224 COD	7	04-43N 103-31E	Smc	100	GD	S								
30/08	331 BUGARA	3	08-11N 100-53E	Smc		GD	S								

218

Dt/Hr	Submarine	Pt	Position	Tgt	Size	Attack	Cl	So	Date	Type	Name	Tons	Dm	Location	Comments
JUL	1945														
30/08	373 LIZARDFISH	2	05-25N 103-31E	Smc		Burn	S								
30/10	408 SENNET	4	42-36N 139-49E	AK	7500	T2/3DUP	S	AIJ	30	C-AK	Yuzan M.	6039	S	42-37N 139-49E	
30/11	331 BUGARA	3	07-47N 100-29E	Sch		GD	S								
30/11	338 CARP	1	45-07N 148-13E	2Lug	200	GD	S								
30/11	338 CARP	1	45-07N 148-13E	2Lug	200	GD	D								
30/14	417 TENCH	3	34-57N 124-59E	Smc	100	GD	S								
30/19	331 BUGARA	3	06-54N 101-33E	Trk	100	GT	S								
30/20	224 COD	7	04-35N 103-31E	Smc	100	GN	S								
30/24	324 BLENNY	4	04-35N 103-30E	Sam		GN	S								
30/24	324 BLENNY	4	04-35N 103-30E	Sch		GN	S								
30	HMS STUBBORN	1	Bewleleng Rds	LC		G	D								
31/02	324 BLENNY	4	04-35N 103-30E	Sam		GN	S								
31	331 BUGARA	3	07- N 101- E	5Smc	100	GD	S								
31	224 COD	7	04-30N 103-30E	6Smc	700	GD	S								
31/11	338 CARP	1	45-11N 148-15E	AK	3000	T3/3DSP	S								
31/12	338 CARP	1	45-11N 148-15E	Pat	100	T1/1DUS	S								
31/15	418 THORNBACK	1	38-53N 141-35E	Pat	100	GD	D	IW	31	PC	Ch 42	442	M	38-24N 141-15E	
31/22	324 BLENNY	4	05-58N 102-34E	Smc		GN	S								
--							-	I	?	C-AK	Hino M. #8	250	?	Kammon Str.	Insufficient info to identify attack; date not given.
31	HNMS O-21	5	NW coast Java	Smc	10	G	S								
31	HMS XE-3	1	Singapore	CA		Expl	D	I	30	CA	Takao	13400	M	Singapore	XE-3 towed by HMS STYGIAN.
31	HMS XE-1	1	Singapore	CA		Expl	D	I	30	CA	Takao	13400	M	Singapore	XE-1 towed by HMS SPARK.
31	HMS TIPTOE	3	Sunda Strait	Cstr		G	D								

219

Dt/Hr	Submarine	Pt	Position	Tgt	Size	Attack	Cl	So	Date	Type	Name	Tons	Dm	Location	Comments
JUL	1945														
--							-	W	?	SC	Cha 59	130	S	Off Singapore	Insufficient info to identify attack; date not given.
AUG	1945														
1/07	324 BLENNY	4	05-35N 102-57E	2Smc		GD	S								
1/17	324 BLENNY	4	04-37N 103-30E	Sam		GD	S								
1/18	224 COD	7	04-21N 103-22E	Smc	100	GT	S								
1	HMS SEADOG	4	Malacca Strait	Lug	100	G	P								Joint with HMS SHALIMAR.
1	HMS SHALIMAR	4	S Malacca Str.	Lug	100	G	P								Joint with HMS SEA DOG.
1	HMS SHALIMAR	4	S Malacca Str.	Jk	20	Dem	S								
1	HMS THOROUGH	8	Bewleleng Rds	Cstr	200	G	S								
1	HMS THOROUGH	8	Bewleleng Rds	LC		G	D								
1	HMS THOROUGH	8	Bewleleng Rds	Sch	100	G	S								
1	HMS TACITURN	2	N of Bali	2Sch		Dem	S								
2/02	331 BUGARA	3	06-40N 101-51E	Sch	200	GN	S								
2/06	266 POGY	10	37-31N 135-45E	AO	10000	T1/5TUR	D								
2/11	331 BUGARA	3	06-30N 102-30E	2Smc		GD	S								
2/11	331 BUGARA	3	06-30N 102-30E	3Sch	400	GD	S								
2/14	394 RAZORBACK	5	44-37N 146-55E	6Trk	1700	GD	S								
2/14	394 RAZORBACK	5	44-37N 146-55E	Trk	200	GD	D								
2/14	394 RAZORBACK	5	44-37N 146-55E	Esc	200	GD	D								
2/19	271 RAY	8	06-45N 101-39E	Smc		GT	S								
2	HMS SEADOG	4	S Malacca Str.	Tug	20	G	P								Joint with HMS SHALIMAR.
2	HMS SHALIMAR	4	S Malacca Str.	Tug	20	G	P								Joint with HMS SEA DOG.
2	HMS SEADOG	4	S Malacca Str.	Ltr	75	G	P								Joint with HMS SHALIMAR.

Dt/Hr	Submarine	Pt	Position	Tgt	Size	Attack	Cl	So	Date	Type	Name	Tons	Dm	Location	Comments
AUG	1945														
2	HMS SHALIMAR	4	S Malacca Str.	Ltr	75	G	P								Joint with HMS SEA DOG.
2	HMS THOROUGH	8	Bewleleng Rds	Sch	120	G	S								
2	HMS TIPTOE	3	Off Batavia	2Cst		G	P								Joint with HMS TRUMP
2	HMS TRUMP	3	Off Batavia	2Cst		G	P								Joint with HMS TIPTOE.
3/08	331 BUGARA	3	06-59N 101-36E	Trk	100	GD	S								
3/08	331 BUGARA	3	06-59N 101-36E	Smc	100	GD	S								
3/13	212 GATO	13	39-06N 142-02E	PF	800	T1/1DUS	S	AI	3	PC	Ch 42	442		SA Onagawa Wan	Chart in I shows sub attack; W says sunk 10 Aug by a/c. PR says attacked 2 ships, heard screws stop & breaking-up noises, only 1 sighted later. [Attribution ?]
3/18	271 RAY	8	09-51N 099-15E	3Smc		GD	S								
3/19	324 BLENNY	4	04-52N 103-26E	Smc		GD	S								
3/19	324 BLENNY	4	04-52N 103-26E	Sam	100	GD	S								
3	HMS SHALIMAR	4	S Malacca Str.	Tug	10	G	S								
3	HMS SHALIMAR	4	S Malacca Str.	Ltr	50	G	S								
3	HMS TRUMP	3	Off Batavia	AK	6000	T2/5	S								Target seen to burn and sink.
3	HMS TIPTOE	3	Off Batavia	AK	4000	T1/4	S								Target seen to sink.
3-23	HMS SPUR	1	S Malacca Str.	11Jk		G+Dem	S								Exact dates not given.
4/07	331 BUGARA	3	10-02N 099-16E	2Smc	400	GD	S								
4/08	324 BLENNY	4	05-40N 102-52E	Smc		GD	S								
4/08	331 BUGARA	3	09-59N 099-17E	Sch	400	GD	S								
4/10	271 RAY	8	10-52N 099-28E	3Smc		GD	S								
4/21	271 RAY	8	11-12N 099-36E	2Smc	200	GN	S								
4/23	.324 BLENNY	4	05-05N 103-23E	Smc		Dem	S								

Dt/Hr	Submarine	Pt	Position	Tgt	Size	Attack	Cl	So	Date	Type	Name	Tons	Dm	Location	Comments
AUG	1945														
4	HMS THOROUGH	8	Bewleleng Rds	Cstr	80	G	S								
5/01	324 BLENNY	4	05-01N 103-23E	2Smc	200	GN	S								
5/02	234 KINGFISH	12	50-43N 156-38E	Pat	100	GN	S								
5/02	234 KINGFISH	12	50-43N 156-38E	Sam	100	GN	S								
5/02	324 BLENNY	4	05-00N 103-26E	Smc	100	GN	S								
5/04	271 RAY	8	11-29N 099-39E	2Smc	200	GN	S								
5/05	324 BLENNY	4	04-55N 103-25E	2Smc		GN	S								
5/06	331 BUGARA	3	10-11N 099-22E	Sch	200	GD	S								
5/06	331 BUGARA	3	10-11N 099-22E	Smc	100	GD	S								
5/07	266 POGY	10	39-52N 138-52E	AO	5000	T2/2DUP	S	AIJ	5	C-AK	Kotohirasan M.	2220	S	39-40N 138-35E	
5/10	324 BLENNY	4	05-10N 103-49E	2Smc	100	GD	S								
5/11	286 BILLFISH	8	38-51N 121-39E	AK	4000	T3/4DUP	S	AIJ	5	C-AK	Kori M.	1091	S	38-51N 121-39E	
5/12	333 BUMPER	2	01-36S 105-24E	Mis	100	GD	S								
5/12	333 BUMPER	2	01-36S 105-24E	Tug	100	GD	S								
5/12	333 BUMPER	2	01-36S 105-24E	Lug	100	GD	S								
5/13	331 BUGARA	3	10-53N 099-31E	Smc		GD	S								
5/17	324 BLENNY	4	04-42N 103-30E	3Smc	100	GD	S								
5/18	329 CHUB	3	07-46S 114-24E	AT	700	T1/1TSV	S								
5/18	329 CHUB	3	07-46S 114-24E	Mis	100	GT	S								
5/18	329 CHUB	3	07-46S 114-24E	AT	200	GT	S								
5/19	331 BUGARA	3	10-42N 099-24E	Sch	100	GT	S								
5	HMS SEADOG	4	S Malacca Str.	Cstr	250	G	P								Joint with HMS SHALIMAR.
5	HMS SHALIMAR	4	S Malacca Str.	Cstr	250	G	P								Joint with HMS SEA DOG.

Dt/Hr	Submarine	Pt	Position	Tgt	Size	Attack	Cl	So	Date	Type	Name	Tons	Dm	Location	Comments
AUG	1945														
5	HMS SEADOG	4	Malacca Strait	Jk	120	Dem	S								
5	HMS SHALIMAR	4	S Malacca Str.	3Jk	40	Dem	S								
5-15	HMS SOLENT	3	Gulf of Siam	15Jk		G	P								Joint with HMS SLEUTH; exact dates not given.
5-15	HMS SLEUTH	3	Gulf of Siam	15Jk		G	P								Joint with HMS SOLENT; exact dates not given.
6/02	324 BLENNY	4	04-43N 103-33E	Sam		GN	S								
6/07	331 BUGARA	3	08-39N 100-20E	Smc	100	GD	S								
6/14	417 TENCH	3	36-07N 125-59E	4Sch	400	GD	S								
6/14	417 TENCH	3	36-07N 125-59E	5Sch	500	GD	D								
6/14	417 TENCH	3	36-07N 125-59E	Trk	100	GD	D								
6/14	417 TENCH	3	36-07N 125-59E	Mis		GD	D								
6/19	331 BUGARA	3	06-51N 101-44E	2Smc		GT	S								
6/19	331 BUGARA	3	06-51N 101-44E	Sch	100	GT	S								
6/21	324 BLENNY	4	04-34N 103-30E	Smc		GN	S								
6/22	331 BUGARA	3	06-42N 101-57E	Smc	100	GN	S								
6/23	324 BLENNY	4	04-32N 103-31E	2Smc		GN	S								
7/09	286 BILLFISH	8	38-48N 121-23E	AK	1200	T1/2DUP	S								
7/12	331 BUGARA	3	07-10N 101-33E	2Smc		GD	S								
7/17	367 ICEFISH	5	00-16S 106-45E	Lug		GD	S								
7	324 BLENNY	4	04-33N 102-37E	4Smc	200	GN	S								
7	271 RAY	8	1-05N 099-28E	10Sm	600	GD	S								
7	271 RAY	8	1-05N 099-28E	7Smc	200	Burn	S								
7	271 RAY	8	1-05N 099-28E	7Sch	1700	GD	S								

Dt/Hr	Submarine	Pt	Position	Tgt	Size	Attack	Cl	So	Date	Type	Name	Tons	Dm	Location	Comments
AUG	1945														
7	HMS SHALIMAR	4	S Malacca Str.	Cstr	150	G	S								
8/06	372 LAMPREY	3	01- N 101- E	Smc		GD	S								
8/08	324 BLENNY	4	05-14N 103-17E	9Smc	200	GD	S								
8/08	324 BLENNY	4	05-14N 103-17E	Sch		GD	S								
8/15	262 MUSKALLUNGE	7	46-41N 151-43E	2Trk	400	GD	D								
8/15	264 PARGO	8	41-23N 131-25E	AK	5200	T3/6DUP	S	AIJ	8		C-AK Rashin M.	5455	S	41-15N 131-19E	
8/15	264 PARGO	8	41-23N 131-25E	AK	2000	T1/ DUP	D								
8/15	264 PARGO	8	41-23N 131-25E	AK	2000	T1/ DUP	D								
8/20	391 POMFRET	6	32-01N 129-02E	Smc	100	GT	S								
8/23	324 BLENNY	4	06-00N 102-31E	2Smc	200	GN	S								
9/07	324 BLENNY	4	05-22N 103-10E	2Smc	200	GD	S								
9/07	324 BLENNY	4	05-22N 103-10E	Trk	300	GD	S								
9/12	329 CHUB	3	07-52S 114-28E	SC	200	GD	S								
9/15	417 TENCH	3	38-48N 121-01E	AT	300	T1/2DSR	S								
9/15	417 TENCH	3	38-48N 121-01E	Smc	400	T1/1DSR	S								
9/15	417 TENCH	3	38-48N 121-01E	Smc	400	T1/2DSR	S								
9	HMS TIPTOE	3	N Sunda Strait	AO		G	P								Joint with HMS TRUMP.
9	HMS TRUMP	3	N Sunda Strait	AO		G	P								Joint with HMS TIPTOE.
10/05	337 CARBONERO	2	04-38N 103-30E	Sch	100	GN	S								
10/05	337 CARBONERO	2	04-38N 103-30E	Sam		GN	S								
10/07	324 BLENNY	4	05-38N 102-49E	Smc		GD	S								
10/08	324 BLENNY	4	05-38N 102-49E	AT	300	GD	S								
10/08	324 BLENNY	4	05-38N 102-49E	4Mis	600	GD	S								

Dt/Hr	Submarine	Pt	Position	Tgt	Size	Attack	Cl	So	Date	Type	Name	Tons	Dm	Location	Comments
AUG	1945														
10/13	323 CAIMAN	4	05-58S 114-10E	Sch		GD	S								
10/22	337 CARBONERO	2	05-45N 102-42E	Sch	100	GN	S								
--							-	AJ I	10	C-AK	Taishun M. Daishun M.	2857	SA S	41-26N 129-49E Chongjin	J says sunk by Army mine, A says sunk by a/c. No likely sub attack.
11/02	264 PARGO	8	41-17N 139-04E	AK	2000	T2/4NSR	S								
11/02	368 JALLAO	4	38-03N 133-12E	AK	4000	T3/8NUP	S	AIJ	11	C-AK	Teihoku M.	5794	S	38-06N 130-20E	
11/04	324 BLENNY	4	05-01N 102-32E	Smc		GN	S								
11/05	404 SPIKEFISH	4	28-37N 124-13E	Trk	300	GT	S								
11/09	324 BLENNY	4	06-38N 102-06E	Smc	100	GD	S								
11/09	391 POMFRET	6	32-46N 128-44E	Trk	100	GD	S								
11/11	324 BLENNY	4	06-38N 102-12E	Smc	200	Demo	S								
11/12	329 CHUB	3	08-34S 115-46E	Trk	200	GD	S								
11/12	329 CHUB	3	08-34S 115-46E	Pat	100	GD	D								
11/20	409 PIPER	3	31-52N 129-49E	2Mis		GT	S								
11/22	337 CARBONERO	2	05-36N 102-53E	Sam		GN	S								
12/02	337 CARBONERO	2	05-36N 102-53E	Smc	100	GN	S								
12/09	423 TORSK	2	36-15N 133-27E	AK	1500	T1/2DUP	S								
12/15	475 ARGONAUT	1	34-22N 125-33E	Smc		GD	S								
12/20	372 LAMPREY	3	06- S 108- E	Smc		Burn	S								
12	HMS THOROUGH	8	Bewleleng Rds	Sch	120	G	S	Note			Palange				Name from "Success Book."
13/01	403 ATULE	4	42-11N 142-14E	PF	800	T1/6NSR	S	AI J	13	PF	CD 6	940 800	S	42-16N 142-12E	W says CD 4 sunk here, CD 6 surrendered at end of war. [J attribution ?]
13/01	403 ATULE	4	42-11N 142-14E	PF	800	T2/ NSR	D	I	13	PF	CD 16	940	L	42-16N 142-12E	
13/04	337 CARBONERO	2	05-06N 103-21E	Sch	100	GN	S								

Dt/Hr	Submarine	Pt	Position	Tgt	Size	Attack	Cl	So	Date	Type	Name	Tons	Dm	Location	Comments
AUG	1945														
13/15	423 TORSK	2	36-16N 136-03E	AK	1500	T1/3DUP	S	AIJ	13	C-AK	Kaiho M.	873	S	36-17N 136-09E	
13/23	391 POMFRET	6	33-48N 126-50E	Smc	100	GN	S								
13/24	337 CARBONERO	2	05-50N 102-41E	Sch	100	GN	S								
14/03	337 CARBONERO	2	06-04N 102-36E	Smc	100	GN	S								
14/04	404 SPIKEFISH	4	29-02N 123-53E	SS	1500	T2/6TUR	S	IJW	13-4	SS	I-373	1660	S	E China Sea	
14/11	423 TORSK	2	35-42N 134-52E	PF	1500	T1/1DUP	S	AIW J	14	PF	CD 47	810 800	S	35-41N 134-38E	
14/12	423 TORSK	2	35-42N 134-52E	PF	1500	T2/2DUS	S	AIW J	14	PF	CD 13	810 800	S	35-41N 134-38E	
14/15	285 BALAO	10	39-12N 141-36E	Pat	100	GD	S								
14/15	285 BALAO	10	39-12N 141-36E	Pat	100	GD	D								
14	HMS STATESMAN	9	Malacca Strait	5Jk	190	G+Dem	S								
15	HMS SEASCOUT	5	Gulf of Siam	APc	300	G	S								
15	HMS SOLENT	3	Gulf of Siam	Pat	100	G	S								
18	HMS STATESMAN	9	Malacca Strait	Cstr		T	S								Target described as derelict.

.
.
.
.
.
.
.
.
.

Bibliography

MAJOR DATA SOURCES

Allan, Roger W. "A Dictionary of Japanese Naval and Merchant Vessels Sunk during World War II." Unpublished manuscript, provided by the author. (Referred to as Allan or A.)

Japanese Naval and Merchant Shipping Losses during World War II by All Causes. Joint Army-Navy Assessment Committee. Washington, D.C.: U.S. Government Printing Office, 1947. (Referred to as JANAC or J.)

Jentschura, Hansgeorg; Jung, Dieter; and Mickel, Peter. Warships of the Imperial Japanese Navy, 1869-1945. Translated by Antony Preston and J. D. Brown. Annapolis, Md.: Naval Institute Press, 1982. (Referred to as WIJN or W.)

The Imperial Japanese Navy in World War II. Military History Section, General Headquarters, U.S. Army, Far East Command, 1952. (Referred to as IJN or I.)

Naval Staff History Second World War, Submarines, Vol. 3, Operations in Far Eastern Waters. Historical Section, Admiralty. London, 1956. (Referred to as BSH.)

"U.S. Submarine Attacks Listed by Date and Hour of Attack." Office of Strategic Planning, ComSubsPac (sic) (Commander Submarines, Pacific). Unpublished report on file at Naval Historical Center, Washington, DC. (Referred to as SORG.)

De Nederlandse Onderzeedienst 1906-1966. Royal Netherlands Submarine Service. Den Haag: AD M.C. Stok-Zuid-Hollandsche Uitgevers Maatschappij, 1966. (Referred to as DNO.)

OTHER SOURCES OF DATA ON U.S. SUBMARINE ATTACKS

Blair, Clay, Jr. Silent Victory. Philadelphia: Lippincott, 1975.

Holmes, J. Undersea Victory. Garden

City, N.Y.: Doubleday, 1966.

Roscoe, Theodore, United States Submarine Operations in World War II. Annapolis, Md.: U.S. Naval Institute, 1949.

The Offensive Minelaying Campaign against Japan. Naval Analysis Division, 1946. Reprint. Washington, D.C.: Department of the Navy, Headquarters Naval Material Command, 1969.

United States Submarine Losses, World War II. Naval History Division, Office of Chief of Naval Operations. Washington, D.C.: U.S. Government Printing Office, 1963. (Referred to as USSL or U.)

Hervieux, Pierre; Sainte Adresse, France. Personal correspondence.

Rohwer, Jürgen; Stuttgart, Germany. Personal correspondence.

OTHER SOURCES OF DATA ON BRITISH SUBMARINE ATTACKS

Mars, Alastair. British Submarines at War, 1939-1945. Annapolis, Md.: Naval Institute Press, 1971.

Roskill, Stephen W. The War at Sea, 1939-1045. 3 vols. in 4. Her Majesty's Stationery Office, 1954-61.

"Success Book." Handwritten notebook listing results of attacks by British submarines. The Royal Naval Submarine Museum, Gosport, England.

OTHER SOURCES OF DATA ON NETHERLANDS SUBMARINE ATTACKS

Kroese, A. The Dutch Navy at War. London: George Allen & Unwin, 1945.

Stöve, G. W. "Queen's Navy at War," U.S. Naval Institute Proceedings, March 1950, pp. 288-301.

Spek, John D.; Zoetermeer, Netherlands. Personal correspondence.

Sweerstra, Dirk; Leeuwarden, Netherlands. Personal correspondence.

Von Münching, L. L.; Wassenaar, Netherlands.   Personal correspondence.

Voss, Maurice; Welkenraedt, Belgium.   Per-
    sonal correspondence.

OTHER SOURCES OF DATA ON JAPANESE SHIP
LOSSES

Bagnasco, Erminio.   Submarines of World
    War II.   Annapolis, Md.: Naval In-
    stitute Press, 1977.

Carpenter, Dorr, and Polmar, Norman.   Sub-
    marines of the Imperial Japanese Navy.
    Annapolis, Md.: Naval Institute
    Press, 1986.

Dull, Paul S.   A Battle History of the Im-
    perial Japanese Navy (1941-1945).   An-
    napolis, Md.: Naval Institute Press,
    1978.

Miller, Vernon J.   Analysis of Japanese
    Submarine Losses to Allied Submarines.
    Bennington, Vt.: Weapons and Warfare
    Publications, 1984.

Appendix A

The main data tables list some ships
that have been evaluated as the victims of
submarine-laid mines. The list cannot be
considered definitive in this regard, however, because of the difficulty of assess-
ing the true effectiveness of U.S. and
Allied minelaying efforts. The table that
follows gives the dates, locations, and
other particulars of the minefields
planted by U.S. and Allied submarines.
U.S. submarines were not equipped with
special mine laying features but carried
mines that had to be discharged from the
torpedo tubes. Two mines could be carried
in place of each spare torpedo, but usually mixed loads were carried. In such
cases the submarines would preferably go
directly to the location of the minefield;
after getting rid of the mines (which were
disliked by most U.S. submariners) the
boat would proceed on a regular combat
patrol.

Most of the Allied submarines operating in the Far East laid mines in the way
just described, but two British boats, the
PORPOISE and RORQUAL, and the Dutch O-19,
were fitted with special external mine
tubes which permitted them to carry much
larger loads of mines.

As previously noted, damage inflicted
by mines cannot easily be attributed to
specific submarines or other agents.
Casualties may have occurred days or
months after the field was laid, although
the Japanese would be expected to attempt
to sweep a field as soon as it was discovered. Also, any unswept mines would
tend to lose their effectiveness as they
aged. Aircraft mines were laid in many of
the areas mined by U.S. submarines, but
the locations of the air drops were necessarily less precise than those of the submarine plants. If the Japanese records
fail to include accurate positions for

230

ship losses in mined areas (which is often the case), attribution of a particular casualty to a specific minefield is essentially guesswork.

The Japanese laid many protective mine fields outside their ports and anchorages, and these resulted in many frightening encounters by U.S. and Allied submarines. Indeed, several U.S. boats are presumed to have been lost to enemy mines, as were a number of Japanese vessels that strayed from the narrow swept channels. Finally, there was the menace of floating mines, usually ones that broke loose from their moorings and drifted far from their original site. U.S. submarines encountered many of these when running on the surface in daylight and tried to sink them with deck gun or small arms fire. It is quite possible that some otherwise inexplicable cases of ship sinkings or damage could have been caused by these wandering death traps.

In 1946 the United States Strategic Bombing Survey, in The Offensive Minelaying Campaign against Japan, (see bibliography for reference) made the first official assessment of the U.S. mining effort and concluded that 27 ships were sunk and another 27 damaged by mines laid by U.S. submarines. Unfortunately, the individual Japanese ships assessed as lost are not identified in the published report, and I have been able to correlate only a few with the postwar Japanese data sources used for this compilation. From a cursory investigation of Strategic Bombing Survey source documents in the National Archives, I have concluded that the above figures were based on wartime intelligence reports that lack postwar corroboration or have since been demonstrated to be inaccurate.

JANAC, published a year later than the Strategic Bombing Survey, attributes only five ships totaling 18,553 tons to U.S. submarine mines. These ships are identified as the following:

Unknown Maru*	4,000	20 Dec 42
Fukken Maru	2,558	29 Dec 42
Teikin Maru	1,972	27 Jul 43
Nikko Maru	3,098	1 Jul 44
Tamon M. #15	6,925	26 Jan 45

*This ship has since been identified by IJN as Mitsuki M., 3,893 tons.

JANAC also includes six ships attributed to British mines that can be correlated to specific submarine-laid minefields, and one (Yuno Maru) that appears more likely to have been sunk by a mine laid by the USS GUITARRO (SS-363). The British Naval Staff History claims the six ships in JANAC plus a seventh that JANAC attributes to Japanese mines, as follows (estimated tonnage indicated by "e"):

Kasumi Maru*	1,400	12 May 44
Cha 8	100e	9 Sep 44
Takekun Maru	3,029	10 Sep 44
Kyokko Maru	593	1 Jan 45
Hozan M. #1	868	23 Jan 45
Nikkaku M.	1,946	23 Jan 45
Ma 1	500e	27 Mar 45

*JANAC-Japanese mine

The above data are indicative of the weakness of official assessments made soon after the war. Unfortunately, IJN and later Japanese data sources do not add much to the record, mainly because locations given are not specific enough to pinpoint the minefields, but also because some losses appear to be misattributed to submarines or marine casualties. Several possible additions to the list of submarine mining victims are included in the main data tables, but a definitive evaluation would require a detailed study of both Japanese and U.S. records and is beyond the scope of this compilation.

Mo/Yr	Date	Submarine	Pt	Commander	Position	Mines	Comments
Oct 42	16	200 THRESHER	5	Millican	12-50N 100-44E	32 Mk 12	Bangkok approaches. 2 prematures.
Oct 42	20	206 GAR	4	McGregor, D.	12-35N 100-45E	32 Mk 12	Bangkok approaches. 4 prematures.
Oct 42	25	239 WHALE	1	Azer	33-46N 135-10E	24 Mk 10-1	Kii Suido. 1 floater.
Oct 42	29	210 GRENADIER	4	Carr	20-38N 107-04E	32 Mk 12	Haiphong. 1 premature.
Nov 42	2	199 TAUTOG	4	Willingham	11-10N 108-47E	32 Mk 12	S of Cape Padaran, FIC. 3 prematures.
Nov 42	2	198 TAMBOR	4	Ambruster	20-04N 109-18E	32 Mk 12	Hainan Strait off Lamka Point Lt. 1 premature.
Dec 42	14-17	281 SUNFISH	1	Peterson	34-28N 137-20E	24 Mk 12	Iseno Umi Bay, Nagoya.
Dec 42	17	228 DRUM	4	McMahon	32-47N 132-10E	24 Mk 10-1	Bungo Suido
Dec 42	20	237 TRIGGER	3	Benson	35-45N 140-55E	19 Mk 12	Inubo Saki
Mar 43	7	199 TAUTOG	6	Sieglaff	02-10S 116-40E	24 Mk 12	Tanjong Aru, SE coast Borneo
Apr 43	7	202 TROUT	8	Ramage	02-00N 109-15E	23 Mk 12	Subi Kechil (Ketjil) I., Api Passage
Apr 43	19	278 SCORPION	1	Wylie	36-05N 140-45E	22 Note	Inubo Saki. 12 Mk 12, 10 Mk 10-1.
Apr 43	20	275 RUNNER	2	Fenno	22-15N 115-15E	32 Mk 12	Hong Kong
Apr 43	21-22	186 STINGRAY	7	Earle	28-10N 121-55E	22 Mk 12	Wenchow Bay. 2 plants close together.
Apr 43	30	279 SNOOK	1	Triebel	30-21N 122-30E	24 Mk 12	Saddle I., off Shanghai
May 43	12	280 STEELHEAD	1	Whelchel	42-07N 143-21E	8 Mk 12	Erimo Saki. (First part of plant.)
May 43	30	280 STEELHEAD	1	Whelchel	41-57N 143-19E	4 Mk 12	Erimo Saki. (Second part of plant.)
Jun 43	4	236 SILVERSIDES	5	Burlingame	02-36S 150-34E	24 Mk 10-1	Steffen Strait, Kavieng. 2 floaters.
Jun 43	8	182 SALMON	6	Nicholas		None	Blair lists as mine plant. This is incorrect; ship conducted a different special mission.
Oct 43	10	234 KINGFISH	5	Lowrance	05-10S 119-20E	11 Mk 12	Cape Pepe, Makassar Strait, off Celebes
Dec 43	13	267 POMPON	3	Hawk	08-50N 106-05E	11 Mk 12	Pulo Condore
Dec 43	18	288 CABRILLA	2	Hammond	10-30N 103-14E	11 Mk 12	Saracen Bay, coast of Cambodia
Jan 44	3	222 BLUEFISH	3	Porter	04-50N 103-35E	11 Mk 12	Pulo Tenggol, E coast Malaya
Jan 44	4	269 RASHER	2	Laughon	09-00N 106-40E	11 Mk 12	Pulo Condore

233

Mo/Yr	Date	Submarine	Pt	Commander	Position	Mines	Comments
Jan 44	14-15	291 CREVALLE	2	Munson	10-33N 108-01E	11 Mk 12	Kega Point, E of Saigon. Strategic Bombing Survey gives date as 19 Jan.
Jan 44	29	287 BOWFIN	3	Griffith	03-36S 116-35E	11 Mk 12	Sebuko I., SE coast Borneo
Feb 44	22	271 RAY	3	Harral	10-18N 107-50E	11 Mk 12	Kega Point, near Saigon
Mar 44	14	HMS TRESPASSER	4	Favell	03-28N 099-29E	12	Malacca Str., Outer Mati Bank
Mar 44	19	HMS TAURUS	4	Wingfield	02-50N 100-36E	12	Malacca Str., Aroa Is.
Apr 44	18	HMS TAURUS	5	Wingfield	05-03N 100-12E	12	Malacca Str., Penang approaches.
Apr 44	22	272 REDFIN	3	Austin		None	Roscoe says laid mines off Sarawak; this is incorrect.
May 44	13	HMS SURF	3	Lambert	06-35N 099-33E	8	Malacca Str., Pulo Terutau
May 44	14	HMS TALLY HO	5	Bennington	03-41N 099-04E	12	Malacca Str., Benja Shoal
May 44	16	HMS TACTICIAN	6	Collett	06-29N 099-53E	12	Malacca Str., Pulo Terutau
May 44	18	HMS SEA ROVER	3	Angell	04-03N 100-36E	8	Malacca Str., Sembilan Is.
Jun 44	2	HMS TANTALUS	2	MacKenzie	04-08N 100-35E	12	Malacca Str., Sembilan Is.
Jun 44	3	HMS STOIC	3	Marriott	05-57N 100-14E	8	Malacca Str., Langkawi
Jun 44	4	HMS TEMPLAR	7	Ridgeway	04-19N 100-29E	12	Malacca Str., Sembilan Is.
Jun 44	7	HMS TANTIVY	3	Rimington	04-01N 100-37E	12	Malacca Str., Sembilan Is.
Jun 44	14	HMS SURF	4	Lambert	06-31N 099-34E	8	Malacca Str., Pulo Terutau
Jun 44	24	HMS TRUCULENT	4	Alexander	02-51N 101-15E	12	Malacca Str., South Klang Strait
Jul 44	6-8	HMS PORPOISE	1	Marsham	03-54N 098-42E	56	Malacca Str., Deli River, Sumatra.
Aug 44	19	272 REDFIN	4	Austin	02-00N 109-15E	11 Mk 12	Api Passage, Sarawak
Sep 44	14-15	264 PARGO	5	Bell	02-39N 108-58E	11 Mk 12	Koti Passage, Natuna Is.
Sep 44	16	HMS TRENCHANT	2	Hezlet	04-11N 098-25E	12	Malacca Str., Aru Bay, Sumatra.
Sep 44	24	HMS TUDOR	2	Porter	07-28N 099-04E	10	W coast Siam
Oct 44	30	HMS TRADEWIND	4	Maydon	12-26N 098-38E	12	Mergui Arch.
Nov 44	6	254 GURNÁRD	7	Hyde	02-08N 109-40E	11 Mk 12	Tanjong Datoe

Mo/Yr	Date	Submarine	Pt	Commander	Position	Mines	Comments
Nov 44	19	HMS THOROUGH	3	Hopkins	03-20N 099-38E	12	Malacca Str., Outer Mati Bank
Dec 44	9	HMS PORPOISE	3	Turner	05-17N 100-07E	50	Malacca Str., Penang approaches
Dec 44	16	247 DACE	6	Cole, O.R.	13-36N 109-18E	11 Mk 12	Pulo Gambir I. 2 prematures.
Dec 44	16	HMS THULE	2	Mars	06-44N 099-42E	12	Malacca Str., Pulo Terutau
Dec 44	23	HMS THOROUGH	4	Hopkins	06-48N 099-39E	12	Malacca Str., Pulo Terutau
Dec 44	--	320 BERGALL	2	Hyde		None	Blair lists as mine plant, but ship did not complete the mission (PR).
Jan 45	3	HMS RORQUAL	1	Oakley	07-45N 098-17E	50	W coast Siam, Salang I. (first part of plant)
Jan 45	3	HMS RORQUAL	1	Oakley	08-13N 098-16E	12	W coast Siam, Salang I. (second part of plant)
Jan 45	3	HNMS O-19	3	Dri. v. Hooff	05-50S 106-16E	40	W Java Sea, Batavia approaches
Jan 45	9	HMS PORPOISE	4L	Turner	05-20N 100-08E	62	Malacca Str., Penang approaches
Jan 45	17	HMS RORQUAL	2	Oakley	11-52N 093-02E	50	Andaman Is., Nancowry Strait (first part of plant)
Jan 45	23	HMS RORQUAL	2	Oakley	11-47N 093-05E	12	Andaman Is., S of Neill I. (second part of plant)
Apr 45	2	365 HARDHEAD	4	Greenup	08-22N 105-01E	23 Mk 12	Pulo Obi
Apr 45	13	HNMS O-19	4	Dri. v. Hooff	01-56S 105-04E	40	E coast Sumatra, North Banka Strait
Apr 45	14-15	328 CHARR	2	Boyle	08-25N 104-37E	23 Mk 12	Pulo Obi
Apr 45	20	363 GUITARRO	5	Dabney	01-00S 104-30E	23 Mk 12	Berhala Strait, NE coast Sumatra
May 45	8-9	243 BREAM	6	McCallum	08-18N 104-49E	23 Mk 12	Pulo Obi
May 45	10	HMS RORQUAL	4	Oakley	05-11S 106-05E	12	W Java Sea, Sumatra Channel (first part of plant)
May 45	10	HMS RORQUAL	4	Oakley	05-47S 106-35E	44	W Java Sea, Batavia approaches (second part of plant)

.

.

.

.

.

Appendix B

COMMANDING OFFICERS OF U.S. SUBMARINES
WITH ATTACKS LISTED IN THE DATA TABLES

SUBMARINE	PAT	COMMANDER
078 R-1	2A	Grant, James D.
133 S-28	7	Sisler, Vincent A., Jr.
135 S-30	7-8	Stevenson, William A.
136 S-31	5	Sellars, Robert F.
137 S-32	5-7	Schmidt, Maximilian G.
138 S-33	7	Stevens, Clyde B., Jr.
139 S-34	6	Keating, Robert A., Jr.
140 S-35	6	Monroe, Henry S.
141 S-36	1	McKnight, John R.
142 S-37	3	Dempsey, James C.
	5	Reynolds, James R.
	6	Baskett, Thomas S.
143 S-38	1	Chapple, Wreford G.
	4-7	Munson, Henry G.
144 S-39	1-3	Coe, James W.
145 S-40	5	Lucker, Nicholas, Jr.
146 S-41	2	Holley, George M., Jr.
	4-6	Hartman, Irvin S.
153 S-42	1	Kirk, Oliver G.
	4-5	Nauman, Harley K.
155 S-44	1-3	Moore, John R.
	4	Whitaker, Reuben T.
157 S-46	4	Crawford, Earl R.
158 S-47	3	Davis, James W.
	4	Haylor, Frank E.
166 ARGONAUT	3	*Pierce, John R.
167 NARWHAL	1-3	Wilkins, Charles W.

SUBMARINE	PAT	COMMANDER
	6-10	Latta, Frank D.
	11-12	Titus, Jack C.
168 NAUTILUS	1-4	Brockman, William H., Jr.
	8	Irvin, William D.
	10	Sharp, George A.
169 DOLPHIN	2	Rutter, Royal L.
170 CACHALOT	2	Lewis, George A.
171 CUTTLEFISH	3	Marshall, Elliot E.
172 PORPOISE	2-5	McKnight, John R.
	6	Bennett, Carter L.
173 PIKE	7-8	McGregor, Louis D.
175 TARPON	6-9	Wogan, Thomas L.
	11	Filippone, Saverio
176 PERH	1	Hurt, David A.
177 PICKEREL	2-5	Bacon, Barton E., Jr.
	6-7	*Alston, Augustus H.
178 PERMIT	5-9	Chapple, Wreford G.
	10-11	Bennett, Carter L.
	12	Scherer, Donald A.
179 PLUNGER	1-4	White, David C.
	5-10	Bass, Raymond H.
	12	Fahy, Edward J.
180 POLLACK	1-3	Moseley, Stanley P.
	5-6	Palmer, Robie E.
	7-10	Lewellen, Bafford E.
181 POMPANO	1-2	Parks, Lewis E.
	3-7	*Thomas, Willis M.
182 SALMON	1-5	McKinney, Eugene B.
	6-9	Nicholas, Nicholas J.
	11	Nauman, Harley K.
183 SEAL	1-5	Hurd, Kenneth C.

*Lost on patrol

SUBMARINE	PAT	COMMANDER
	6	Dodge, Harry B.
	11-12	Turner, John H.
184 SKIPJACK	3-5	Coe, James W.
	7	Stoner, Howard F.
	9	Molumphy, George G.
	10	Andrews, Richard S.
185 SNAPPER	2	Stone, Hamilton L.
	7-8	Clementson, Merrill K.
	9-11	Walker, William W.
186 STINGRAY	2	Lamb, Raymond S.
	4-5	Moore, Raymond J.
	7	Earle, Otis J.
	10-11	Loomis, Sam C., Jr.
187 STURGEON	2-4	Wright, William L.
	5-7	Pieczentkowski, Herman A.
	9-11	Murphy, Charlton L., Jr.
188 SARGO	5	Gregory, Richard V.
	6-7	Carmick, Edward S.
	9-12	Garnett, Philip W.
189 SAURY	4	Mewhinney, Leonard S.
	6-7	Dropp, Anthony H.
	11	Waugh, Richard A.
190 SPEARFISH	3-6	Dempsey, James C.
	7	Sharp, George A.
	8-11	Williams, Joseph W., Jr.
	12	Cole, Cyrus C.
191 SCULPIN	1-8	Chappell, Lucius H.
192 SAILFISH	1-2	Mumma, Morton C., Jr.
	3-5	Voge, Richard G.
	7-8	Moore, John R.
	10-12	Ward, Robert E. M.

SUBMARINE	PAT	COMMANDER
193 SWORDFISH	1-6	Smith, Chester C.
	7	Lewis, Jack H.
	8	Parker, Frank M.
	10	Hensel, Karl G.
	11-12	*Montross, Edmund K.
194 SEADRAGON	1-5	Ferrall, William E.
	6-9	Rutter, Royal L.
	10-11	Ashley, James H., Jr.
196 SEARAVEN	2	Aylward, Theodore C.
	5-6	Cassedy, Hiram
	9-12	Dry, Melvin H.
	13	Berthrong, Raymond
197 SEAWOLF	1-7	Warder, Frederick B.
	8-12	Gross, Royce L.
198 TAMBOR	2	Murphy, John W., Jr.
	3-6	Ambruster, Stephen H.
	7-10	Kefauver, Russell
	11-12	Germershausen, William J.
199 TAUTOG	2-4	Willingham, Joseph H.
	5-10	Sieglaff, William B.
	11-3	Baskett, Thomas S.
200 THRESHER	2-3	Anderson, William L.
	4-7	Millican, William J.
	9-10	Hull, Harry
	11-13	MacMillan, Duncan C.
	14	Middleton, John R., Jr.
201 TRITON	1-2	Lent, Willis A.
	3-5	Kirkpatrick, Charles C.
	6	*MacKenzie, George K., Jr.
202 TROUT	2-3	Fenno, Frank W.

*Lost on patrol

SUBMARINE	PAT	COMMANDER	SUBMARINE	PAT	COMMANDER
	5-8	Ramage, Lawson P.		2-3	McGregor, Rob R.
	9-11	*Clark, Albert H.		7	Hottel, Martin P.
203 TUNA	1-2	DeTar, John L.		9	Wahlig, Frederick H.
	5-8	Holtz, Arnold H.	215 GROWLER	1-4	*Gilmore, Howard W.
	9-10	Hardin, James T.		5-8	Schade, Arnold F.
206 GAR	1-2	McGregor, Donald		9-10	*Oakley, Thomas B.
	5-8	Quirk, Philip D.	216 GRUNION	1	*Abele, Mannert L.
	9-12	Lautrup, George W., Jr.	217 GUARDFISH	1-3	Klakring, Thomas B.
	14	Ferrara, Maurice		5-9	Ward, Norvell G.
207 GRAMPUS	1	Hutchinson, Edward S.		12	Hammond, Douglas T.
	4-6	*Craig, John R.	218 ALBACORE	1-3	Lake, Richard C.
208 GRAYBACK	1	Saunders, Willard A.		5-7	Hagberg, Oscar E.
	4-7	Stephan, Edward C.		8-10	Blanchard, James W.
	8-10	*Moore, John A.	219 AMBERJACK	1-3	*Bole, John A.
209 GRAYLING	2-3	Olsen, Eliot	220 BARB	2A-7	Waterman, John R.
	4-7	Lee, John E.		8-12	Fluckey, Eugene B.
	8	*Brinker, Robert M.	221 BLACKFISH	1A-8	Davidson, John F.
210 GRENADIER	1	Joyce, Allen R.		10	Sellars, Robert F.
	2	Lent, Willis A.	222 BLUEFISH	1-3	Porter, George E., Jr.
	3-4	Carr, Bruce L.		4-7	Henderson, Charles M.
	5	*Fitzgerald, John A.		9	Forbes, George W., Jr.
211 GUDGEON	1-2	Grenfell, Elton W.	223 BONEFISH	1-4	Hogan, Thomas W.
	4-5	Stovall, William S., Jr.		5-8	*Edge, Lawrence L.
	7-11	Post, William S., Jr.	224 COD	1-3	Dempsey, James C.
212 GATO	2	Myers, William G.		4-6	Adkins, James A.
	4-8	Foley, Robert J.		7	Westbrook, Edwin M.
	11	Farrell, Richard M.	225 CERO	1	White, David C.
	13	Holden, Richard		3-6	Dissette, Edward F.
213 GREENLING	1-4	Bruton, Henry C.		7	Berthrong, Raymond
	6-8	Grant, James D.	226 CORVINA	1	*Rooney, Roderick S.
	10-11	Gerwick, John D.	227 DARTER	1-2	Stovall, William S., Jr.
214 GROUPER	1	Duke, Claren E.		3-4	McClintock, David H.
			228 DRUM	1-3	Rice, Robert H.

*Lost on patrol

SUBMARINE	PAT	COMMANDER	SUBMARINE	PAT	COMMANDER
	4-7	McMahon, Bernard F.		6-8	Dornin, Robert E.
	8	Williamson, Delbert F.		9-10	Harlfinger, Frederick J., II
	10-11	Rindskopf, Maurice H.		12	*Connole, David R.
229 FLYING FISH	1-5	Donaho, Glynn R.	238 WAHOO	1-2	Kennedy, Marvin G.
	6-7	Watkins, Frank T.		3-7	*Morton, Dudley W.
	8-12	Risser, Robert D.	239 WHALE	1-2	Azer, John B.
230 FINBACK	1-3	Hull, Jesse L.		3-6	Burrows, Albert C.
	4-8	Tyree, John A., Jr.		7-10	Grady, James B.
	10-11	Williams, Robert R., Jr.	240 ANGLER	1-3	Olsen, Robert I.
				4-5	Hess, Frank G.
231 HADDOCK	1-3	Taylor, Arthur H.	241 BASHAW	1-4	Nichols, Richard E.
	4-7	Davenport, Roy M.		5	Simpson, H. S.
	8-10	Roach, John P.	242 BLUEGILL	1-5	Barr, Eric L., Jr.
	11	Brockman, William H., Jr.	243 BREAM	1-3	Chapple, Wreford G.
				5-6	McCallum, James L.
232 HALIBUT	3-5	Ross, Philip H.	244 CAVALLA	1-3	Kossler, Herman J.
	6-10	Galantin, Ignatius J.	245 COBIA	1-5	Becker, Albert L.
233 HERRING	1A,6	Johnson, Raymond W.	246 CROAKER	1-2	Lee, John E.
	3A	Corbus, John		5	Thomas, William B.
	7-8	*Zabriskie, David J.	247 DACE	1	Enright, Joseph F.
234 KINGFISH	1-5	Lowrance, Vernon L.		2-5	Claggett, Bladen D.
	6	Jukes, Herbert L.		6-7	Cole, Otis R., Jr.
	9-10	Harper, Talbot E.	249 FLASHER	1-4	Whitaker, Reuben T.
	12	Keegan, Thomas D.		5-6	Grider, George W.
235 SHAD	2A-6	MacGregor, Edgar J., III	250 FLIER	1	Crowley, John D.
	7	Julihn, Lawrence V.	251 FLOUNDER	2-4	Stevens, James E.
	10	Mehlop, Donald L.	252 GABILAN	2-3	Wheland, Karl R.
236 SILVERSIDES	1-5	Burlingame, Creed C.		5	Parham, William B.
	6-11	Coye, John S., Jr.	253 GUNNEL	2-3	McCain, John S., Jr.
	12	Nichols, John C.		7	O'Neil, Guy E., Jr.
237 TRIGGER	2-5	Benson, Roy S.	254 GURNARD	2-6	Andrews, Charles H.
				7	Gage, Norman D.
			255 HADDO	5-7	Nimitz, Chester W.

*Lost on patrol

SUBMARINE	PAT	COMMANDER	SUBMARINE	PAT	COMMANDER
	8-9	Lynch, Frank C.		2-5	Selby, Frank G.
256 HAKE	3-5	Broach, John C.		6-8	Dwyer, Carl R.
	6-7	Haylor, Frank E.	269 RASHER	1	Hutchinson, Edward S.
257 HARDER	1-6	*Dealey, Samuel D.		2-4	Laughon, Willard R.
258 HOE	1-6	McCrea, Victor B.		5	Munson, Henry G.
	7-8	Refo, Miles P., III		6	Adams, Benjamin E., Jr.
259 JACK	1-4	Dykers, Thomas M.			
	5-6	Krapf, Arthur E.		7	Nace, Charles D.
	7	Fuhrman, Albert S.	270 RATON	1-4	Davis, James W.
260 LAPON	1	Kirk, Oliver G.		5-7	Shea, Maurice W.
	2-5	Stone, Lowell T.	271 RAY	1-4	Harral, Brooks J.
	6	Baer, Donald G.		5-8	Kinsella, William T.
261 MINGO	1-2	Lynch, Ralph C., Jr.	272 REDFIN	1	King, Robert D.
	4	Staley, Joseph J.		2-5	Austin, Marshall H.
	5-6	Madison, John R.	273 ROBALO	1	Ambruster, Stephen H.
262				2	*Kimmel, Manning M.
MUSKALLUNGE	1	Saunders, Willard A.	274 ROCK	3-4	Flachsenhar, John J.
	2-4	Russillo, Michael P.		6	Keating, Robert A., Jr.
	7	Lawrence, William H.			
263 PADDLE	1-2	Rice, Robert H.	275 RUNNER	1-2	Fenno, Frank W.
	3-5	Nowell, Byron H.		3	*Bourland, John H.
	6-8	Fitz-Patrick, Joseph P.	276 SAWFISH	1-5	Sands, Eugene T.
				6-8	Banister, Alan B.
264 PARGO	1-4	Eddy, Ian C.	277 SCAMP	1-6	Ebert, Walter G.
	5-8	Bell, David B.		7	*Hollingsworth, John C.
265 PETO	2-4	Nelson, William T.			
	5	Van Leunen, Paul, Jr.	278 SCORPION	1-2	Wylie, William N.
	7-10	Caldwell, Robert H.		3	*Schmidt, Maximilian G
266 POGY	1-3	Wales, George H.			
	4-6	Metcalf, Ralph M.	279 SNOOK	1-5	Triebel, Charles O.
	10	Bowers, John M.		6-7	Browne, George H.
267 POMPON	1-3	Hawk, Earl C.	280 STEELHEAD	1-6	Whelchel, David L.
	6	Gimber, Stephen H.		7	Byrnes, Robert B.
268 PUFFER	1	Jensen, Marvin J.	281 SUNFISH	1-4	Peterson, Richard W.

*Lost on patrol

SUBMARINE	PAT	COMMANDER	SUBMARINE	PAT	COMMANDER
	6-9	Shelby, Edward E.		6	Wilkins, Charles W.
	11	Reed, John W.		7	Greer, Harry H., Jr.
282 TUNNY	1-6	Scott, John A.	305 SKATE	2	McKinney, Eugene B.
	8	Pierce, George E.		3-5	Gruner, William P.
283 TINOSA	1-4	Daspit, Lawrence R.		6-8	Lynch, Richard B.
	5-7	Weiss, Donald F.	306 TANG	1-5	O'Kane, Richard H.
	11	Latham, Richard C.	307 TILEFISH	1-4	Keithly, Roger M.
284 TULLIBEE	1-4	*Brindupke, Charles F.		5	Schlech, Walter F., Jr.
285 BALAO	2	Crane, Richard H.			
	3-4	Cole, Cyrus C.	308 APOGON	1-4	Schoeni, Walter P.
	5-7	DeArellano, Marion R.		5-7	House, Arthur C.
	8-10	Worthington, Robert K.	309 ASPRO	1-6	Stevenson, Henry C.
286 BILLFISH	1-2	Lucas, Frederick C.		7	Ashley, James H., Jr.
	3-6	Turner, Vernon C.	310 BATFISH	1	Merrill, Wayne R.
	7-8	Farley, L. C., Jr.		3-6	Fyfe, John K.
287 BOWFIN	1	Willingham, Joseph H.	311 ARCHERFISH	1	Kehl, George W.
	2-4	Griffith, Walter T.		3-4	Wright, William H.
	5-6	Corbus, John		5-6	Enright, Joseph F.
	7-9	Tyree, Alexander K.	312 BURRFISH	2-4	Perkins, William B., Jr.
288 CABRILLA	1-2	Hammond, Douglas T.	313 PERCH	1-5	Hills, Blish C.
	4-6	Thompson, William C., Jr.	314 SHARK	1-3	*Blakely, Edward N.
	7	Lauerman, Henry C.	315 SEALION	1-3	Reich, Eli T.
289 CAPELIN	1-2	*Marshall, Elliot E.		4-5	Putman, Charles F.
291 CREVALLE	1-2	Munson, Henry G.	316 BARBEL	1-3	Keating, Robert A., Jr.
	3-4	Walker, Francis D., Jr.	317 BARBERO	2	Hartman, Irvin S.
	6-7	Steinmetz, Everett H.	318 BAYA	1	Holtz, Arnold H.
294 ESCOLAR	1	*Millican, William J.		3-5	Jarvis, Benjamin C.
298 LIONFISH	1	Spruance, Edward D.	319 BECUNA	1-3	Sturr, Henry D.
	2	Ganyard, Bricker M.	320 BERGALL	1-5	Hyde, John M.
300 MORAY	1	Barrows, Frank L.	321 BESUGO	1-3	Wogan, Thomas L.
304 SEAHORSE	1	McGregor, Donald		4	Miller, Herman E.
	2-5	Cutter, Slade D.	322 BLACKFIN	1	Laird, George H., Jr.

*Lost on patrol

SUBMARINE	PAT	COMMANDER		SUBMARINE	PAT	COMMANDER
	2	Kitch, William L.		367 ICEFISH	1-5	Peterson, Richard W.
323 CAIMAN	3-4	Fey, William L., Jr.		368 JALLAO	1-4	Icenhower, Joseph B.
324 BLENNY	1-4	Hazzard, William H.		369 KETE	2	*Ackerman, Edward
326 BLUEBACK	2-3	Clementson, Merrill K.		370 KRAKEN	3	Henry, Thomas H.
327 BOARFISH	1	Gross, Royce L.		371 LAGARTO	1-2	*Latta, Frank D.
	3	Blonts, Edward C., Jr.		372 LAMPREY	2-3	McDonald, Lucien B.
328 CHARR	2	Boyle, Francis D.		373 LIZARDFISH	2	Butler, Ovid M.
329 CHUB	2-3	Rhymes, Cassius D., Jr.		381 SAND LANCE	1-4	Garrison, Malcolm E.
				382 PICUDA	1-2	Raborn, Albert L.
330 BRILL	3	Dodge, Harry B.			3	Donaho, Glynn R.
331 BUGARA	3	Schade, Arnold F.			4-6	Shepard, Evan T.
332 BULLHEAD	2	Griffith, Walter T.		383 PAMPANITO	1-3	Summers, Paul E.
333 BUMPER	2	Williams, Joseph W., Jr.			4-5	Fenno, Frank W.
334 CABEZON	1	Lautrup, George W., Jr.		384 PARCHE	1-2	Ramage, Lawson P.
					4-6	McCrory, Woodrow W.
335 DENTUDA	1	McCain, John S., Jr.		385 BANG	1-4	Gallaher, Anton R.
336 CAPITAINE	1	Friedrick, Ernest S.		386 PILOTFISH	2	Close, Robert H.
337 CARBONERO	2	Murphy, Charlton L., Jr.			3	Schnable, Allan G.
				387 PINTADO	1-3	Clarey, Bernard A.
338 CARP	1	Hunnicutt, James L.		388 PIPEFISH	2-3	Deragon, William N.
361 GOLET	2	*Clark, James S.		389 PIRANHA	1-3	Ruble, Harold E.
362 GUAVINA	1-4	Tiedeman, Carl			4-5	Irvine, Donald G.
	5	Lockwood, Ralph H.		390 PLAICE	1-3	Stevens, Clyde B., Jr.
363 GUITARRO	1-3	Haskins, Enrique D.			5	Andrews, Richard S.
	4-5	Dabney, Thomas B.		391 POMFRET	2	Acker, Frank C.
364 HAMMERHEAD	1-3	Martin, John C.			3-6	Hess, John B.
	4	Laird, George H., Jr.		392 STERLET	1-2	Robbins, Orme C.
	5-7	Smith, Frank M.			3-4	Lewis, Hugh H.
365 HARDHEAD	1	McMaster, Fitzhugh		393 QUEENFISH	1-4	Loughlin, Charles E.
	2-5	Greenup, Francis A.			5	Shamer, Frank N.
	6	Haines, John L.		394 RAZORBACK	2-5	Brown, Charles D.
366 HAWKBILL	1-5	Scanland, Francis W., Jr.		395 REDFISH	1-2	McGregor, Louis D.
				396 RONQUIL	1-2	Monroe, Henry S.
					3-5	Lander, Robert B.

*Lost on patrol

SUBMARINE	PAT	COMMANDER
397		
SCABBARDFISH	1-3	Gunn, Frederick A.
398 SEGUNDO	2-4	Fulp, James D.
399 SEA CAT	1	McGregor, Rob R.
	2-3	Bowers, Richard H.
400 SEA DEVIL	1-3	Styles, Ralph C.
	4	McGivern, Charles F.
401 SEA DOG	1	Lowrance, Vernon L.
	3-4	Hydeman, Earl T.
402 SEA FOX	1-3	Klinker, Roy C.
403 ATULE	1-4	Maurer, John H.
404 SPIKEFISH	2	Nicholas, Nicholas J.
	4	Managhan, Robert R.
405 SEA OWL	1-2	Bennett, Carter L.
	3	Hall, Warren C., Jr.
406		
SEA POACHER	3-4	Leigh, Charles F.
407 SEA ROBIN	1-3	Stimson, Paul C.
408 SENNET	1-3	Porter, George E., Jr.
	4	Clark, Charles R.
409 PIPER	1-2	McMahon, Bernard F.
	3	Beach, Edward L.
410 THREADFIN	1-3	Foote, John J.
411 SPADEFISH	1-3	Underwood, Gordon W.
	4-5	Germershausen, William J.
412 TREPANG	1-2	Davenport, Roy M.
	3-5	Faust, Allen R.
413 SPOT	1-2	Post, William S., Jr.
	3	Seymour, Jack M.
414 SPRINGER	1-2	Kefauver, Russell
417 TENCH	1	Sieglaff, William B.
	2-3	Baskett, Thomas S.
418 THORNBACK	1	Abrahamson, Ernest P.

SUBMARINE	PAT	COMMANDER
419 TIGRONE	2	Cassedy, Hiram
420 TIRANTE	1-4	Street, George L., III
421 TRUTTA	1	Smith, Arthur C.
	2	Hoskins, Frank P.
423 TORSK	2	Lewellen, Bafford E.
424 QUILLBACK	1	Nicholson, Richard P.
475 ARGONAUT	1	Schmidt, John S.
476 RUNNER	1	Bass, Raymond H.

COMMANDING OFFICERS OF BRITISH SUBMARINES WITH ATTACKS LISTED IN THE DATA TABLES

SUBMARINE	PAT	COMMANDER
HMS CLYDE	1	Brookes, R. S.
	5-7	Bull, R. H.
HMS PORPOISE	1	Marsham, H. A. L.
	3-4	*Turner, H. B.
HMS RORQUAL	3-4	Oakley, J. P. H.
HMS SCYTHIAN	1-3	Thode, C. P.
HMS SEA ROVER	1-7	Angell, J. P.
HMS SEADOG	1-4	Hobson, E. A.
HMS SEASCOUT	1-5	Kelly, J. W.
HMS SELENE	2-3	Newton, H. R. B.
HMS SHAKESPEARE	1	Swanston, D.
HMS SHALIMAR	1-4	Meeke, W. G.
HMS SIBYL	1-2	Murray, H. R.
HMS SIRDAR	1-5	Spender, J. A.
HMS SLEUTH	1-3	Martin, K. H.
HMS SOLENT	1-3	Martin, J. D.
HMS SPARK	1-3	Kent, D. G.
HMS SPIRIT	1-2,	
	4-5	Langridge, A. W.
	3	Catlow, A. A.
HMS SPITEFUL	2-5	Sherwood, F. H.

*Lost on patrol

SUBMARINE	PAT	COMMANDER	SUBMARINE	PAT	COMMANDER
HMS SPUR	1	Beale, P. S.	HMS THULE	2-6	Mars, A. C. G.
HMS STATESMAN	1-7,		HMS TIPTOE	2-3	Jay, R. L.
	9	Bulkeley, R. G. P.	HMS TORBAY	1-4	Norman, C. P.
	8	Seaburne-May, R. M.	HMS TRADEWIND	3-4	Maydon, S. L. C.
HMS STOIC	1-6	Marriott, P. B.		6-7	Nash, J.
HMS STONEHENGE	1	*Verschoyle-Campbell,	HMS TRENCHANT	1-7	Hezlet, A. R.
		D. S. McN.	HMS TRESPASSER	1-3	Favell, R. M.
HMS STORM	1-7	Young, E. P.	HMS TRIDENT	1	Newstead, P. E.
HMS STRATAGEM	1-4	*Pelly, C. R.		2	Profit, A. R.
HMS STRONGBOW	1-4	Troup, J. A. R.	HMS TRUANT	2-4	Haggard, H. A. V.
HMS STUBBORN	1	Davies, A. G.	HMS TRUCULENT	1-4	Alexander, R. L.
HMS STURDY	1-4	Anderson, W. St. G.	HMS TRUMP	2-3	Catlow, A. A.
	6	Wicker, F. A.	HMS TRUSTY	1-8	Balston, E. F.
HMS STYGIAN	1-6	Clarabut, G. S.	HMS TUDOR	1-7	Porter, S. A.
HMS SUBTLE	1-4	Andrew, B. J. B.	HMS VIGOROUS	1	Wood, N. R.
HMS SUPREME	1-5	Barlow, T. E.	HMS VIVID	1	Varley, J. C.
HMS SURF	1	Lambert, D.	HMS XE-1	1	Smart, J. E.
HMS TACITURN	1-2	Stanley, E. T.	HMS XE-3	1	Fraser, I. E.
HMS TACTICIAN	4-6	Collett, A. F.			
HMS TALLY HO	1-9	Bennington, L. W. A.			
HMS TANTALUS	1-2,				
	5-6	MacKenzie, H. S.			
	4	Nash, J.			
HMS TANTIVY	2	Rimington, M. G.	HNMS K-XII	1	Coumou, H. C. J.
	5-8	May, P. H.	HNMS K-XIV	2	#Van Well Groeneveld,
HMS TAURUS	1-5	Wingfield, M. R. G.			C. A. J.
HMS TELEMACHUS	1	King, W. D. A.		6	Drijfhout van
HMS TEMPLAR	4	Beckley, D. J.			Hooff, J. F.
	7	Ridgeway, D. J.		8-9	Smith, J.
HMS TERRAPIN	1	Martin, D. S. R.	HNMS K-XV	2-6	Van Boetzelaer, C. W.
	3-6	Brunner, R. H. H.			Th. Baron
HMS THOROUGH	2-4	Hopkins, J. G.	HNMS K-XVI	2	*Jarman, L. J.
	5-8	Chandler, A. G.	HNMS K-XVIII	1	#Van Well Groeneveld,
HMS THRASHER	1-6	Ainslie, M. F. R.			C. A. J.
			HNMS O-16	1	*Bussemaker, A. J.

**COMMANDING OFFICERS OF DUTCH SUBMARINES
WITH ATTACKS LISTED IN THE DATA TABLES**

*Lost on patrol

SUBMARINE	PAT	COMMANDER
HNMS O-19	2	Bach Kolling, H. F.
	6-7	Van Karnebeek, A.
	8-9	Drijfhout van Hooff, J. F.
HNMS O-21	1-2	Van Dulm, J. F.
	5	Kroesen, F. J.
HNMS O-23	1-3	Valkenburg, A. M.
HNMS O-24	4-8	De Vries, W. J.
	11	De Jong, P. J. S.
HNMS ZWAARDVISCH	1-4	Goossens, H. A. W.
	5	Van Dapperen, J.

Van Well Groeneveld is believed to have been killed by an explosion during the evacuation of the submarine base at Soerabaya.

Index

This computer-generated index provides a convenient cross-reference between ship names and the corresponding chronological entry in the main data tables. Three peculiarities should be noted. (1) All entries for a given ship name are listed immediately below that name. (2) Alternate spellings of some names or alternate identifications of the ships in question appear out of alphabetical order under the preferred name. In such cases, no entry appears in the "Mo/Yr" and "Dt/Hr" columns of the index. Alternate names are repeated in their proper alphabetical places only where necessary to provide an effective cross-reference; where the spellings are closely alike, the alternates are not repeated. (3) Ships whose names consist of letters and numbers (e.g., CD 10 etc.) are sorted according to the first digit of the number so that all numbers starting with 1 appear before those starting with 2, etc. Names that appear only in the "Comments" column are shown in the index with "C" in the "Dt/Hr" column.

Index

NAME	MO/YR	DT/HR
A	Jun 45	23 C
Aden M.	May 44	6/13
Africa M.	Oct 42	20
Agano	Feb 44	16/18
Agata M.	Jan 45	19
Aikoku M.	Jul 43	15/08
Aisakasan M.	Nov 44	18/02
Osakasan M.		
Ajiro	Oct 44	1/10
Akagisan M.	Jan 43	2/05
Akama M.	Sep 43	3 J
Akane M.	May 44	8/05
	Oct 44	6/14
Akashi M.	Sep 43	28/23
Akashisan M.	Mar 44	3/00
Akatsuki M.	May 43	28/19
Akebono M.	Jan 43	13/09
	Jun 43	9/02
	Jan 44	3/03
Aki M.	Feb 44	27
	Jul 44	26/05
Akigawa M.	Dec 44	2/04
Akikawa M.		
Akigumo	Apr 44	11/17
Akikawa M.	Apr 44	27/01
Akigawa M.		
Akikaze	Nov 44	3/22
Akita M.	Jan 42	10
Akitsu M.	Nov 44	15/12
Akiura M.	Feb 44	28/23
	Jun 45	13/09
Akizuki	Jan 43	19/24

NAME	MO/YR	DT/HR
	Oct 44	25/19
Albania	Apr 45	25
Amagi M.	May 44	2
Amagiri	Apr 44	23
Amagisan M.	Feb 42	14
Amaho M.	Apr 43	17/10
Amaiko M.	Jun 44	15/01
Amakasu M. #1	Dec 42	24/09
Amakusu M. #1		
Amakusa M.	Nov 44	23/02
Amari M.	Feb 43	10/10
Amato M.	Feb 45	26/23
Amatsukaze	Jan 44	16/19
Amatsusan M.	May 44	7/01
Tenshinzan M.		
America M.	Mar 44	6/06
Amiji M.	Apr 45	22/17
Amoy M.	Aug 43	--
Anbo M.	May 44	13/21
Anjo M.	Sep 44	28/05
Anshu M.	May 44	30/01
Anto M. #319	Jun 45	3/01
Antung M. #284	Jun 45	24/03
Antung M. #293	Jun 45	23/22
Anyo M.	Jan 45	8/20
	Jan 45	8/20
Anzan M.	Jul 43	3/10
	Jul 43	7/14
	Mar 44	16/02
Aoba	Oct 44	23/03
Aobasan M.	Jul 42	9
	May 44	7/18

NAME	MO/YR	DT/HR	NAME	MO/YR	DT/HR
Aotaka	Sep 44	26/07		Jan 44	10/12
Arabia M.	Oct 44	18/06	Asukasan M.	Jul 44	4/06
Araosan M.	Apr 45	6/00	Asukazan M.		
Arare	Jul 42	5	Atago	Oct 44	23/06
Arasaki	Jan 45	30/05	Ataka M.	Aug 43	23/12
Aratama M.	Mar 44	18/14	Atlantic M.	Jul 43	4/01
	Apr 44	8/02		Mar 44	30/18
Argun M.	Sep 43	21/21	Atlas M.	Aug 43	1/07
Ariake M.	Feb 44	3/03		Nov 44	2/23
Arima M.	Apr 43	3/13	Atsuta M.	May 42	30
Arisan M.	Oct 44	24/02	Atsutasan M.	Dec 41	16
Arita M.	Dec 44	22/05	Awa M.	May 44	13/21
Asahi	May 42	25	Anbo M.		
Asahi M. #11	Nov 44	18/03		Aug 44	19/07
Asahisan M.	Mar 42	7		Apr 45	1/23
	May 42	22		Apr 45	--
Asakaze	Aug 44	23/07	Awagawa M.	Nov 44	17/18
Asama M.	Jan 43	21/23	Awaji	Jun 44	2/23
	Feb 44	24 U	Awaji M.	Sep 44	21/06
	Nov 44	1/05	Awata M.	Oct 43	22/04
Asanagi	May 44	22/04	Ayata M.	Dec 41	12 C
Asanagi M.	Feb 44	19/19	Ayato M.		
	Jun 44	11/01	Azuchisan M.	Oct 44	2/09
Ashigara	Jun 45	8	Azuma M.	Dec 43	3/21
	Apr 45	22 C	Azusa M.	Sep 44	16/24
Ashizuri	Jun 44	5/10		Jun 45	7/20
Aso M.	May 43	9/12	Baikal M.	Mar 42	11
	Jun 44	24/08	Bandai M.	Feb 43	21
Asokawa M.	Nov 44	--	Bandoeng M.	Dec 42	17
Asosan M.	Dec 41	12	Banei M.	Nov 44	8/04
	Apr 44	27/03	Manei M.		
	May 44	2/07	Banei M. #2	May 44	12/07
Asuka M.	May 43	19/12	Bangame M. #3	Mar 44	--

NAME	MO/YR	DT/HR	NAME	MO/YR	DT/HR
Bangkok M.	May 43	20/15	Bushu M.	Sep 44	25/22
Banshu M. #17	Nov 44	17/13	Buyo M.	Jan 43	26/11
	Nov 44	18/22	Byakuran M.	Oct 44	23/01
Banshu M. #2	Dec 42	25/03	Calcutta M.	May 42	1
Banshu M. #31	Dec 44	6/21	Campomanes	Dec 42	26 N
			Canton M.	Jul 43	2/05
Banshu M. #33	Jul 43	6/22	Caroline M.	Nov 44	1/08
Banshu M. #5	Apr 43	19/11		Nov 44	1/09
Banshu M. #7	Jul 43	2/14	CD 10	Jun 44	28/06
Bantam	Jul 45	23 C		Sep 44	27/02
Batopaha M.	Aug 44	25/13	CD 102	Apr 45	9/11
Batupahat M.			CD 112	Jul 45	18/12
Belgium M.	Jun 44	22/23	CD 13	Aug 45	14/12
Belorussia	Mar 44	3/06	CD 130	Mar 45	29/05
Bella Russa			CD 132	Oct 44	24/04
Bengal M.	Mar 44	24/23	CD 144	Feb 45	2/01
Bifuku M.	Aug 42	8	CD 15	Jun 44	6/21
Biko M.	May 45	28/06	CD 16	Aug 45	13/01
Bisaku M.	Apr 44	9/17	CD 17	Jul 44	18/11
Bisan M.	May 44	14/06	CD 18	Mar 45	29/05
Bizen M.	May 44	24/01	CD 196	Jun 45	22/08
Boko M.	Aug 44	9/04	CD 21	Oct 44	6/18
Bokuei M.	Jan 44	3/18	CD 22	Oct 44	30/21
Bokuyo M.	May 44	21/09	CD 24	Jun 44	28/11
Boston M.	Nov 42	16	CD 25	Sep 44	--
Brazil M.	Aug 42	5		May 45	3/23
Brasil M.			CD 28	Dec 44	14/22
Buenos Aires M.	Apr 43	24/13	CD 30	Sep 44	19/09
Bugen M.	Mar 43	22/06		Jan 45	10/04
Bujun M.	May 42	8	CD 31	Apr 45	14/04
Bukun M.	Sep 44	10	CD 38	Nov 44	25/21
Burma M.	Jun 42	12	CD 4	Aug 45	13 C
Busho M.	Jan 44	26/22	CD 41	Jun 45	9/05

NAME	MO/YR	DT/HR	NAME	MO/YR	DT/HR
CD 42	Jan 45	10/04		Mar 45	4
CD 44	Mar 45	10 N	Cha 104	Apr 45	12
CD 47	Aug 45	14/11	Cha 105	Jun 45	16
CD 50	May 45	1/09	Cha 109	Aug 43	19/14
CD 53	Feb 45	7/09	Cha 113	Jun 45	23/01
CD 56	Feb 45	16/00	Cha 114	Feb 45	14/00
CD 6	Aug 45	13/01		Apr 45	12
CD 61	Feb 45	9	Cha 117	Jul 45	23/03
CD 64	Dec 44	3/05	Cha 156	Nov 44	18/00
CD 7	Nov 44	14/21	Cha 165	Sep 44	11/01
CD 72	Jul 45	1/12	Cha 179	Jan 45	--
CD 73	Apr 45	16/09	Cha 2	Oct 44	6
CD 8	Oct 44	8/04	Cha 29	Feb 44	22
CD 84	Mar 45	29/05	Cha 30	Nov 43	4/11
CD 9	Feb 45	14/21	Cha 37	Jul 45	5/13
Ceylon M.	Feb 44	27	Cha 4	Feb 45	14/06
Ch 1	Nov 44	2	Cha 42	Jun 45	23/03
Ch 12	Aug 44	13/10	Cha 50	Jul 45	8/22
Ch 13	Apr 43	3 J	Cha 52	Feb 44	--
	Sep 43	--	Cha 57	May 45	18
Ch 17	Apr 45	28/09	Cha 58	Jul 45	2/03
Ch 2	Jun 45	27/02	Cha 59	Jul 45	--
Ch 20	Nov 43	12/19	Cha 6	Jul 44	--
	Nov 43	14	Cha 61	Jan 44	--
Ch 25	Jul 42	15	Cha 65	Jul 45	2/03
Ch 27	Jul 42	15	Cha 7	Jul 44	--
Ch 30	Dec 44	24/00	Cha 76	Dec 44	11/05
Ch 42	Jul 45	31/15	Cha 8	Sep 44	9
	Aug 45	3/13	Cha 85	Jul 45	8/21
Ch 5	Jan 45	--	Cha 9	Jul 44	--
Ch 50	Jul 44	18/00		Sep 44	9
Ch 54	Mar 44	25/00	Cha 90	Jan 45	--
Ch 8	Mar 45	4	Cha 91	Jan 45	--

NAME	MO/YR	DT/HR	NAME	MO/YR	DT/HR
Cha 97	Apr 45	19/09	Chosa M.	Aug 43	20
Cha 99	Sep 44	13/24	Chosen M.	Jan 44	24/02
Chicago M.	Oct 43	15/01	Choun M.	Jan 44	--
Chichibu M.	Mar 42	13			
Chidori	Dec 44	22/11	Choun M. #7	Dec 44	14 S
Chifuku M.	Jan 43	16/10	Chowa M.	Sep 43	18/17
Chihaya M.	Nov 43	2/04		May 45	1/06
	Jun 44	11/24	Choyo M.	Dec 42	28/22
	Sep 44	10/12	Chozan M.	May 45	17/22
Chikugo M.	Nov 42	3	Chosan M.		
Chikuzen M.	Jul 45	27/21	Chuwa M.	Feb 42	9
Chinkai M.	Nov 44	18/05	Chuyo	Dec 43	4/10
Chinzei M.	Oct 44	18/11	Clyde M.	Mar 43	6/16
Chita M.	Sep 42	4		Jan 45	29/06
Chiyo M.	May 44	26/23	Columbia M.	Nov 42	18
	Jun 44	2/23		Nov 43	30/17
Chiyoda M.	Aug 44	31/02	Comm. Ship 128	Oct 44	14
Chiyoda M. #15	Feb 44	--	Comm. Ship 137	Oct 44	22
Chiyoda M. #5			Comm. Ship 142	Dec 44	2
Choan M. #2	Mar 43	20/14	Comm. Ship 833	Jun 45	23/02
	May 44	10/06	Daiai M.	Mar 45	--
Choi M.	May 44	11/23		Mar 45	--
Chojo M.	Feb 44	16/00	Daiboshi M. #6	Nov 44	29/12
Chojusan M.	Nov 44	9/03	Taisei M. #6		
Chokai M.	Mar 45	2/07	Daido M.	Dec 43	4/18
	May 44	28		Jun 45	12/12
Choko M.	Mar 42	30	Daietsu M.	Jan 45	31/04
	Oct 42	21	Taietsu M.		
	Feb 44	12	Daifuku M.	May 43	5/23
	Feb 44	25/07	Taifuku M.		
Choko M. #2	Jan 44	12/19	Daigen M. #2	Jun 45	10/02
Choko M.			Taigen M. #2		
Chokyu M. #2	Oct 44	21	Daigen M. #3	Feb 44	26/19

NAME	MO/YR	DT/HR	NAME	MO/YR	DT/HR
Taigen M. #3			Dori M.		
Daigen M. #6	Feb 44	21	Dornia Baru	Jun 44	23 C
Taigen M. #6			Doryo M.	Mar 45	23/17
Daigen M. #7	Aug 44	14/01	Dowa M.	Nov 44	22/19
Taigen M. #7			Durban M.	Aug 44	21/09
Daigo M.	Jan 45	8/02	Ebara M.	Oct 44	24/19
Daiji M.	Jul 44	13/07	Kogen M.		
Taishi M.			Ebisu M. #5	Apr 43	30/10
Daiju M.	Apr 44	23/07	Ebon M.	Jan 43	--
Daiki M.	Jun 45	10/13	Echizen M.	Feb 44	24/22
Dainichi M.	Oct 43	8/01	Edo M.	Aug 43	13/23
Dairen M.	Nov 44	30/14	Edogawa M.	Nov 44	17/22
	Feb 44	27/03		Apr 45	2/08
Daishin M.	Sep 43	22/06	Eguchi M. #3	Sep 44	6/16
Daishu M.	Nov 43	22/03	Ehime M.	Nov 43	2/09
Daishun M.	Aug 45	--	Eifuku M.	Aug 42	31
Taishu M.				Jan 43	21/08
Daiten M.	Oct 44	24/11		Feb 44	18
Taiten M.				Feb 45	7/23
Daito M. #1	Mar 45	19/17	Eifuku M. #15	Aug 42	--
Daito M. #2	Mar 45	18/06	Eiji M.	Sep 44	--
Daito M. #3			Eijo M.	Mar 45	--
Daito M. #3	May 45	8/04		Jun 45	17/02
Daiun M. #2	Jul 44	1/23	Eiju M.	May 45	16/07
Daizen M.	Feb 45	20/02	Eika M.	Jun 43	2/03
Taizen M.				Jun 45	--
Dakar M.	Jul 44	31/05	Eikan M.	Jun 45	26/10
Delagoa M.	Nov 43	2/02	Eikichi M.	Mar 45	30/04
Delhi M.	Jan 44	16/00	Eiko M.	Jun 44	18
Denmark M.	Jan 44	16/18		Oct 44	24/14
Djember	Apr 45	12 C	Eikyo M.	Oct 44	14/01
Dokan M.	Mar 45	10	Eiryu M.	May 44	4/16
Dori Go	Jul 44	6/03	Eishin M.	Aug 44	18/21

NAME	MO/YR	DT/HR	NAME	MO/YR	DT/HR
Eisho M.	May 43	29/10	Fujikawa M.	Sep 43	12/04
Eiso M.	Jun 45	16/08		Mar 44	30/03
Eisaku M.			Fukkai M.	Dec 43	13/08
Eiyo M.	Jun 43	22	Fukken M.	Dec 42	29
	Aug 44	18/04	Fukko M.	May 44	17/21
	Feb 45	20/07	Fukuei M.	Apr 43	7 J
Eiyo M. #2	Sep 44	7/17	Fukuei M. #2	Jan 43	26/12
Eizan M.	Jan 42	18	Fukui M. #2	Jun 45	11/00
	Nov 43	21/23	Fukuju M.	Nov 44	23/04
Ejiri M.	Oct 44	10/13	Fukurei M.	Dec 43	13/08
Ekisan M.	Sep 44	29/13		Aug 44	24/07
Engen M.	Feb 45	6/21		Nov 44	21 C
England M.	May 43	17/18	Fukuri M.	Nov 44	--
Enkei M.	Mar 45	--	Fukusei M.	Mar 44	28/24
Enki M.	Jan 45	31/04	Fukushu M.	Mar 42	11
Erie M.	Jan 44	11/13	Fukuun M.	May 45	15/08
Erii M.			Fukuyama M.	Aug 42	4
Erimo	Mar 42	4		Feb 44	22/24
Esutoru M.	Aug 43	9	Fukuyo M.	Jan 42	23
Etajima M.	Sep 44	13/24		Dec 44	6/23
Etashima M.			Fumi M. #2	Sep 44	21/09
Etorofu	Jun 44	27/04	Fumi M. #6	Jul 45	10/23
	Aug 44	6/04	Fumi M. #5		
ex-K-XVIII	Jun 45	16	Fusa M.	Nov 44	17/06
Extractor	Page xx			Nov 44	17/06
Fakfak	Jan 45	27 C	Fusei M.	Sep 43	2/01
Fishing Boat	Jun 45	3/06	Fushimi M.	Feb 43	1/23
	Jun 45	22/14		May 44	3/12
Florida M.	Mar 43	15/22		Oct 44	14/11
France M.	Nov 42	6/13	Fushimi M. #3	Jan 44	7/22
Fuji M.	Oct 43	27/00	Fuso M.	Jul 44	31/05
	Oct 43	27/06	Fuyo	Dec 43	20/08
	Mar 45	25/14	Fuyutsuki	Oct 44	12 C

NAME	MO/YR	DT/HR	NAME	MO/YR	DT/HR
Fuyuzuki	Oct 44	12/21	Gyozan M.		
Ganges M.	May 42	28		Nov 44	21/18
Ganjitsu M. #1	Jan 43	14/12		Nov 44	23/15
Gassan M.	Oct 44	24/03	Gyoten M.	Feb 44	17/04
	Nov 44	13/17	Gyoyu M.	Jul 44	3/24
Gedeh	Apr 45	12 C	H 4	Jan 44	12/19
Genbu M.	Apr 44	27/05	Hachian M.	Dec 42	30/03
Gembu M.			Kanayama M.		
Genei M. #1	May 43	2/08	Hachigen M.	Aug 42	14
Genoa M.	Jun 43	11/10	Hachijin M.	Nov 44	2
Genyo M.	Jan 43	19/11	Hachimanzan M.	Oct 42	9
Genzan M.	Dec 42	16	Yawatasan M.		
Getsuyo M.	Jan 44	11/04	Hachirogata M.	Sep 44	27/06
Gifu M.	Nov 42	2	Hachiryu M. #12	Nov 44	15/12
Ginyo M.	Dec 43	17/04	Haferland-go	Dec 43	22/21
Gio Hokuan	Apr 44	22 C	Hagane M.	Apr 45	19/07
Gisho M.	Apr 43	--	Hagikawa M.	Jul 45	28/01
Goenoeng Telang	Apr 45	14 C	Hague M.	Oct 42	8
Gokoku M.	Dec 42	18/21	Haguro	Apr 45	22 C
	Dec 43	27/24	Hakaze	Jan 43	23/18
	Nov 44	10/04	Hakkai M.	May 43	5/19
Goshu M.	Oct 43	21/02	Hakko M.	Jan 44	4/21
Goyo M.	May 42	16		Nov 44	8/21
	Feb 44	3/03		Dec 44	4/19
Grissee	May 45	25 C		Aug 44	22 C
Gyoku M.	Sep 43	22/00	Hakko M. #2	Aug 44	22/13
	Sep 44	18/22	Hakodate M.	Jul 42	16
Gyokurei M.	Dec 43	18/22	Hakonesan M.	Oct 42	17
Gyokusan M.	Dec 42	12/24	Hakozaki M.	May 43	30/01
Gyokuzan M.				May 43	30
Gyokuyo M.	Nov 44	12/04		Dec 43	14/04
	Nov 44	14/00		Mar 45	19/02
Gyosan M.	Nov 44	21/17	Hakuai M.	Jun 45	18/23

NAME	MO/YR	DT/HR	NAME	MO/YR	DT/HR
Hakubasan M.	Jul 44	28/10	Hassho M.	Sep 44	11/02
Hakuei M.	Jul 45	28/04	Hasshu M.	Jan 43	22/23
Hakuju M.	Jun 45	11/11	Kaneshige M.		
Hakuran M.	Oct 44	23/01	Hasshu M.	Feb 44	22/03
Byakuran M.			Hatsushima	Apr 45	28/07
Hakusa	Jun 45	8/03	Hatsusuki	Oct 44	25 C
Hakusan M.	Jun 44	4/05	Hatsuzuki		
Hakusan M. #5	Jun 45	11/04	Hatsutaka	Aug 44	3
Hakusan M.				May 45	16/09
Hakushika M.	Oct 44	18/11	Havre M.	Jun 44	6/11
Hakuroku M.			Hawaii M.	Apr 44	27/12
Hakutetsu M. #7	Sep 44	12/10		Dec 44	2/04
Hakutetsu M. 13	Sep 43	8/14		Jan 45	--
Hakutetsu M. 30	Sep 43	22/18	Hayamoto	Aug 42	23 C
Hakuun M. #2	Sep 44	11/02	Hayanami	Jun 44	7/12
Hakuun M. #20			Hayasaki	Feb 43	7/02
Hakuyo M.	Mar 44	20/02		May 45	7
Shirataka M.			Hayasui	Aug 44	19/05
	Oct 44	25/09	Hayataka M.	Dec 41	23
	Jun 45	10/13	Hayatomo	Aug 42	23
Haltenbank	Feb 43	19 C		Oct 43	9/06
Hamburg M.	Nov 44	3/05	Hayo M.	Dec 41	22
Hankow M.	Oct 43	9 J	Heijo M.	Jan 42	5
Kanko M.				Sep 43	4/04
Hansei M.	Oct 44	13	Heinan M.	Dec 42	8/12
Hanshin M.	Jun 45	7/06	Heiwa M.	Dec 43	24/03
Harbin M.	Jan 42	10		Jun 45	18/10
Harugiku M.	Jun 44	26	Heiyo M.	Jan 43	17/18
Harukiku M.			Hibari M.	Feb 43	19/21
Harukaze	Nov 44	4/16	Hibi M.	Jun 44	20/07
Harusame	Jan 43	24/15	Hibiki	Sep 44	6/11
Hashidate	May 44	22/18	Hiburi	Aug 44	22/07
Hashima	Apr 45	28 C	Hiburi M.	Jun 44	1

NAME	MO/YR	DT/HR	NAME	MO/YR	DT/HR
Hidaka M.	Aug 43	13/06	Nissho M.		
	Jan 44	20/05	Hiyama M.	Jul 44	17/01
Hide M.	Jun 43	11/01		Jul 42	12
Hinode M.			Hizan M.		
Hie M.	Nov 43	17/15	Hiyo	Oct 42	22
	Dec 41	23		Jun 43	10/20
Higane M.	Oct 44	1/24	Hiyodori	Nov 44	17/03
Hikade M.	Aug 43	13	Hiyori M.	Oct 44	1/23
Hikosan M.	Jan 45	--	Nichiwa M.		
Hikoshima M.	Jan 45	8/19	Hiyoshi M.	Dec 41	23
	Jan 45	8/20	Hie M.		
	Jan 45	8/21		Dec 43	4/01
Himeno M.	Dec 43	5/07		Jun 44	10
Hinaga M.	Nov 44	14/23	Hiyoshi M. #3	Aug 44	9
Hino M. #1	Apr 44	16/02	Hizen M.	Jun 45	21/13
Hino M. #3	Dec 42	7/21	Hoei M.	Sep 44	29/13
Hino M. #5	Oct 43	--	Hoeisan M.	Feb 43	11/14
Hino M. #8	Jul 45	--	Hoeizan M.		
Hinode M.	Jun 44	16/17	Hojyo M.	Aug 45	10 C
	Jun 43	11/01			
Hinode M. #17	Apr 45	11/23	Hokaze	Jul 43	1/19
Hinode M. #20	Aug 44	31/18		Jul 44	6/09
Hinode M. #6	Sep 44	4/13	Hokkai M.	Dec 41	23
Hinoki M.	Sep 44	10/24		Nov 42	12
Hirado	Sep 44	12/02		Sep 44	23
Hirato				Nov 44	21/21
Hirashima	Jul 43	27/12	Hokki M.	Sep 44	27/12
Hiro M.	Jan 44	31/22	Hokko M.	Nov 43	28/12
Hiroshi M. #3	Dec 44	--		Nov 43	19/06
Hirotama M.	Feb 43	14/08	Hoko M.	Mar 44	20/02
Hisashima M.	Mar 43	8/18	Hokko M.		
Hishi M. #2	Nov 44	9/14	Hokoku M.	May 45	30/15
Hiteru M.	Dec 42	30/23	Hokuan I-Go	Apr 44	22

NAME	MO/YR	DT/HR	NAME	MO/YR	DT/HR
Hokuan			Hosen M.	Mar 45	20/15
Hokuan M.	Feb 44	14/04	Hosen M. #3	Feb 45	25/04
Hokuko M.	Nov 43	19/06	Hoshi M. #2	Feb 44	15/11
Hokko M.			Hosho M. #3		
Hokurei M.	Oct 44	6/14	Hoyo M.	Dec 42	--
	Oct 44	--		Nov 43	6/02
Hokuriki M.	Mar 44	18 C	Hozan M.	Mar 43	21/07
Hokuriku M.	Mar 44	18/00		Nov 44	23/00
Hokuroku M.			Hozan M. I-go	Jan 45	23
Hokuriku M. #1	Jul 44	19/17	Hozan M. #1		
Hokuriu M.			Hyakufuku M.	Jun 44	30/16
Hokuryu M. #1			Hyakafuku M.		
Hokusei M.	Sep 43	21 N	Hyoshi M.	Jun 44	10 C
	Oct 43	--	Hyuga M.	Feb 43	16
Hokushin M.	Jun 45	30 J	I-122	Jun 45	10/12
Hokusho M.	Sep 43	5/09	I-166	Jul 44	17
	Sep 43	11/08	I-168	Jul 43	27/18
Hokusui M.	Jan 43	26	I-24		
Hokutai M.	Mar 45	--	I-174	Apr 44	20/10
Hokuto M.	Mar 43	4/07	RO-45		
Hokutu M.			I-18	Jan 43	3/00
	Jun 45	9/22	I-182	Sep 43	9/14
Hokuyo M.	May 44	31 J	I-183	Apr 44	29/01
Holland M.	Oct 42	17	I-28	May 42	17/07
Honan M.	Apr 44	9/02	I-29	Jul 44	26/17
	Mar 45	29/04	I-34	Nov 43	13
Hong Kong M.	Jun 43	19 N	I-351	Jul 45	15/02
Horai M.	Jan 44	10/10	I-364	Sep 44	16/06
Horai M. #7	Nov 44	1/09	RO-42		
Horaisan M.	May 44	29/02	I-365	Nov 44	29/10
Horaizan M.			I-37	Apr 44	27
Horei M.	Feb 44	23/05	I-371	Feb 45	24/11
Hosei M.	Apr 45	10	I-373	Aug 45	14/04

NAME	MO/YR	DT/HR	NAME	MO/YR	DT/HR
I-4	Dec 42	21/07	Ishikari M.	Mar 42	17
I-41	Feb 45	9/00	Isokaze	Nov 43	4
			Isonami	Apr 43	9/13
I-42	Mar 44	23/23	Issei M.	Jan 45	30/08
I-43	Feb 44	15/22	Isshin M.	Jan 44	2/04
I-44	May 44	26/15	Isuzu	Nov 43	4
I-62 (I-162)	Feb 43	14/11		Nov 44	19/05
I-64	May 42	17/18		Apr 45	7/05
I-164				Apr 45	7/07
I-73	Jan 42	27/09	Isuzu M.	Jul 43	2/04
I-173			Isuzu M. #3	Apr 45	19/09
Iburi M.	Jun 43	25/10	Isuzugawa M #5	Jul 44	1/12
Ichiyo M.	Feb 44	19/23	Isuzugawa M.	Oct 43	10/14
Ichiyu M.	Dec 43	30/22	Itsukushima	Oct 44	--
Ikazuchi	Apr 44	13/19		Oct 44	17
Iki	May 44	24/01	Itsukushima M.	Jun 44	22/05
Ikoma M.	Jan 44	21/22		Oct 44	27/04
Ikomasan M.	Mar 45	16/23	Itsutshima	Oct 44	17 C
Ikuna	Apr 45	10/22	Iwaki M.	Jun 44	1
Ikushima M.	Mar 44	30/05		Sep 44	--
Ikutagawa M.	Oct 44	24/11	Iwanami	Dec 44	4/13
Ilmen	Feb 43	17/07	Iwashiro M.	Jan 43	13/14
Ina M.	Sep 44	1/03	Iyasaka M.	Jan 45	3/21
Inari M.	Jul 45	11/01	Iyasaka M. #6	Dec 44	22
Inari M. #1	Aug 43	20/17	Janbi M.	Jul 44	18/06
Inazuma	May 44	14/03	Jambi M.		
Indus M.	May 43	15/17	Jimbo M. #12	May 43	2/10
Ioshima	Sep 44	19/05	Jinbu M.	Jun 43	11/14
Irako	Jan 44	20/11	Jinei M.	Oct 44	25/04
Iro	Feb 43	28/09	Jingei	Sep 44	19/09
	Jun 43	10/05	Jinmu M.	May 43	9/05
	Mar 44	22/07	Jimmu M.		
Ishigaki	May 44	31	Jintsu M.	Jun 45	10/03

NAME	MO/YR	DT/HR	NAME	MO/YR	DT/HR
Jinyo	Nov 44	17/22	Kaiho M.	Apr 45	19/01
Jinyo M.	Dec 44	6/21		Aug 45	13/15
Jinzan M.	Jul 44	16/24	Kaijo M. #2	Mar 42	4
Jinsan M.			Kaika M.	Jan 44	16/16
Johore M.	Dec 42	11/07	Kaiko M.	Jan 43	--
	Oct 43	24/01		Feb 44	28/16
Jokuja M.	May 44	15/10		Mar 45	9/11
Joshu Go	Oct 44	11/05	Kaimei M.	Sep 42	4
Joshu M.			Kainan M.	Jun 44	12
Jozan M.	Feb 44	17/00		Mar 45	20/00
Jungen Go Shun Yuan	Sep 44	22/04	Kainan M. #7	Jan 45	23/12
Junpo M.	Dec 44	24/23	Kaio M. #2	Jul 44	20/23
Junyo	Nov 43	5/06	Kairyu M.	Apr 45	19/15
	Dec 44	9/01		May 45	25/00
	Dec 44	9/03	Kaisei M.	Jun 45	20/07
Junyo M.	Sep 44	18	Kaishin M. #2	Nov 44	16
Jusan M.	Apr 45	14/04	Kaisho M.	Aug 43	3/23
Juzan M.				Aug 43	22/18
Jusan M. I-Go	Dec 44	16/03	Kaiwa M.	Jun 45	12/08
Jusan M.			Kaiyo M.	Apr 45	19/17
Juzan M. I-Go			Kaiyo M. #2	Oct 44	15
K-XVIII	Jun 45	16	Kaiyo M.		
Kachidoki M.	Sep 44	12/23	Kaiyo M. #5	Sep 44	2 S
Kachisan M.	Sep 43	19/17	Kaiyo M. #6	Oct 44	31/06
Kachiyama M.			Kaiyo #6		
Kagi M.	May 43	26/10	Kako	Aug 42	10
Kagu M.	Nov 44	4/16	Kako Go	Apr 45	14/07
	Nov 44	4/16	Kako M.		
	Nov 44	4/19	Kamakura M.	Apr 43	28/01
Kahoku M.	Jun 43	8/02	Kamikawa M.	May 43	29/01
Kaifuku M.	Nov 43	4/22	Kamitsu M.	Jun 45	26/10
Kaihei M.	Apr 43	15/16	Kamo M.	Jul 44	3/23

NAME	MO/YR	DT/HR	NAME	MO/YR	DT/HR
	Jul 44	17/24	Karatsu	Mar 44	3/18
Kamogawa M.	Mar 42	2	Kari	Feb 44	24
Kamoi	Jan 44	28/24		Jul 45	16/03
	Sep 44	27/05	Karukaya	May 44	10/06
Kamoi M.	Dec 42	10	Kasado	Apr 44	27/03
	Nov 43	26/23		Jun 45	22/01
	Jul 44	1/12	Kasagi M.	Jan 44	27/24
Kamome	Apr 44	27/09	Kasasagi	Sep 43	26/23
Kamome M.	Feb 44	15/11	Kashi M.	Jul 43	--
Hoshi M. #2			Kashii M.	Dec 41	14
Kampung Besar	Apr 44	19	Kashima M.	Jul 42	31 W
Kanan M.	May 42	6		Sep 43	27/06
	Jun 44	21/02	Kashimasan M.	Jun 44	6/11
Kanayama M.	Dec 42	30/03	Kashino	Sep 42	4
Kanayamasan M.	Nov 43	11/07	Kashiwa M.	Dec 43	21/06
Kaneshige M.	Sep 44	11/02		Apr 44	25/12
Kanjo M.	Jan 44	--	Kashu M.	Oct 43	8/03
Kanju M.	Sep 42	3	Kasuga M.	Apr 43	24
	Sep 42	5/02	Kasuga M. #3	Mar 43	13
Kanko M.	Jan 42	10	Kasuga M. #2		
	Oct 43	6 J	Kasumi	Jul 42	5
	Jan 45	5/20	Kasumi M.	May 44	12
	Oct 43	9 J	Katori M.	Dec 41	23
Kanno M. #3	Feb 45	14/06		Jun 44	29/02
	Feb 45	14/07	Katsukawa M.	Jun 44	4/16
	Feb 45	14/07	Katsura M. #2	Sep 43	20/16
Kannon M. I-Go	Jul 44	29/16	Katsuragi M.	Oct 42	1
Kannon M.			Katsurahama M.	Sep 43	22/09
Kansai M.	Sep 43	19/01	Yokahama M.		
Kanseishi M.	Jun 44	15/01	Katsuriki	Sep 44	21/22
Amaiko M.			Kawakaze	Jul 43	12/17
Kanto M.	Sep 42	11	Kawi	Aug 43	19 C
Kara M.	Nov 42	18 C	Kayo M.	Mar 44	4/00

NAME	MO/YR	DT/HR	NAME	MO/YR	DT/HR
Kazagumo	Jun 44	8/02	Kenzan M.	Nov 43	25/12
Kazegumo			Kenzui M.	Dec 44	23/10
Kazekumo			Kibi M.	Feb 44	--
Kazahaya	Jul 43	27/03	Kikaku M. #6	Feb 45	27/09
	Oct 43	6/03	Kiku M.	Mar 45	4
	Oct 43	6/19	Kikusui M.	Oct 44	23/24
Kazan M.	Oct 43	24/19	Kikuzuki M.	Jan 44	27/00
Keihin M.	Mar 45	14/14	Kim Hup Soen	Aug 44	18
Keijin M. #2	Oct 43	18/10	Kimi M.	Jun 45	--
Keijo M.	Jun 42	21	Kimikawa M.	Dec 43	27/12
	Nov 44	8/21		Oct 44	8/01
Keikai M.	Jan 44	27/00		Oct 44	23/17
Keiko M.	Nov 42	8	Kimishima M.	Feb 44	23/12
Keishin M.	May 43	1/09	Kinai M.	May 43	11/06
Keito M.	Jun 45	12/14	Kinei M.	May 45	27/11
Keiyo M.	Feb 43	19	Kinjosan M.	May 42	4
	May 44	10/18	Kinka M.	Dec 41	12
Keizan M.	Oct 42	26/09	Kinkai M.	Oct 42	3
	Mar 45	10		Dec 42	--
Kembu M.	Aug 43	4/19	Kinkasan M.	Oct 43	1/19
Kenan M.	May 44	3/04		Dec 41	12 C
Kenjo M.	Dec 44	6/22	Kinko M.	May 43	5/22
	Dec 44	7/00	Kinposan M.	Jan 43	16/18
	Jun 45	12/09	Kimposan M.		
Kenkoku M.	Oct 43	13/15	Kinrei M.	May 44	4/04
Kenkon M.	Jan 43	21/18		May 45	6/05
Kennichi M.	Jun 44	24/24	Kinryu M.	Aug 44	21/06
Kenryu M.	Nov 43	29/10	Kinryo M.		
Kenun M.	Oct 42	24	Kinsen M.	Jul 43	25/19
Kenwa M.	May 44	23/05	Kinshu M.	Jun 44	17/11
	May 44	23/08		Aug 44	7/18
Kenyo M.	Mar 43	23/04		Apr 45	19/17
	Jan 44	14/19	Kinugasa M.	Oct 44	6/15

NAME	MO/YR	DT/HR	NAME	MO/YR	DT/HR
	Oct 44	7/22	Kobai M.	Jun 45	19/06
	Oct 44	7/22	Kochi M.	May 43	27/02
Kiri M. #2	Jul 45	22/24	Koei M.	Sep 42	21
Kiri M. #8	Nov 44	7/17		Jul 44	31/04
Kiriha M.	Mar 43	6		Oct 44	10
Kirishima M.	Oct 42	25	Koetsu M.	Sep 44	26/03
	Sep 43	25/13	Kofuji M.	Jul 42	24
Kisaragi M.	Nov 44	16/03	Kofuku M.	Jun 42	--
Kisei Go	Jun 45	--		Mar 44	16/16
Kisei M.				Jun 45	11/16
Kisei M.	Jan 45	--	Kogane M.	Oct 43	9/05
Kishinami	Dec 44	4/13	Kogen M.	Oct 44	24/19
Kiso M.	Nov 43	22/09	Kogi M.	Jul 44	5/02
	Jul 44	23	Kogyo M.	Jan 44	11/23
Kisogawa M.	Nov 43	10	Koho M.	May 44	14/14
Kitakami	Jan 44	26		Feb 45	25/21
Kitagami			Kohoku M.	Oct 44	8/04
Kitakata M.	May 42	25/17	Kojo M.	Nov 44	15/20
Kitami M.	Apr 42	16	Kojun M.	Aug 44	13/10
Kiyo M.	Jan 44	5/04	Kokai M.	Jun 45	19/06
Kiyo M. I-Go			Kobai M.		
Kiyokawa M.	Jul 44	26/02	Koki M.	Jul 23	4/04
	Jul 44	26/04		Feb 45	--
	Jul 44	26/05	Kokko M.	Aug 43	31/09
Kiyosumi M.	Jan 44	1/23	Koko M.	Mar 45	--
Kiyozumi M.			Kokuei M.	Feb 44	19/05
Kizan M.	Nov 43	23 N	Kokura M. #1	Jul 44	31/04
Kizugawa M.	Apr 44	8/02	Kokuryu M.	Jul 43	3/10
Koa M.	Apr 43	4/12		Oct 44	24/12
Koan M.	Aug 42	1	Kokusei M.	Oct 44	1/23
	Jun 44	14/09	Kokuyo M.	Mar 44	13/03
	Aug 44	13/02		Jul 44	30/01
	Jun 45	15/06			

NAME	MO/YR	DT/HR	NAME	MO/YR	DT/HR
Kola	Feb 43	17/22	Koshu M.	Aug 44	4/04
Komahashi	Jun 45	24	Kota M.	Nov 44	7/17
Komobashi			Kotai M.		
Komei M.	Oct 44	31/09	Koto M.	May 44	31/18
Konan M.	Jun 43	13/22	Koto M. #2	Jul 44	7/24
	Dec 43	21/03	Koto M.		
Konei M.	Dec 43	1/09	Kotobuki M.	Nov 43	28/23
	Aug 44	2/16	Kotobuki M. #7	May 45	26/12
Kongo	Nov 44	21/03	Kotohirasan M.	Aug 45	5/07
Kongosan M.	May 42	4	Kotoku M.	May 42	24
Konri M.	Jul 45	1/12		May 43	6/16
Konron M.	Oct 43	5		Aug 44	25/09
Konsan M.	Jul 44	3/23	Kotoshiro M. #8	Feb 45	13/06
Konzan M.				Feb 45	13/07
Konzan M.	Jun 45	? J		Feb 45	13/07
Korei M.	Sep 44	10	Koun M.	Jun 45	--
	Oct 44	30/16	Koun M. #2	Jul 45	7/14
Kori Go	Oct 44	23/04	Kowa M.	Mar 43	19/09
Kori M.	Aug 45	5/11		Sep 43	22/06
Koryo M.	Oct 43	28/02	Koyo M.	Jun 43	15/03
	Oct 43	31/22		Sep 43	9/05
Kosei M.	Dec 42	10/00		Feb 44	23/23
	Mar 43	13/22	Koyu M.	Jan 44	20/08
	Apr 43	7/24	Kozan M.	Sep 43	4/00
	Nov 43	11/12	Kozui M.	Oct 43	14/17
	Jan 44	27/00	Kuma	Apr 42	--
	Oct 44	13		Jan 44	11
Koshe M.	Jul 45	4/07	Kumagawa M.	Oct 43	9/11
Koshin M.	May 43	28/15	Kumano	Nov 44	6/08
Koshin M.	Jan 44	22/17		Nov 44	6/09
	May 44	23/19		Nov 44	6/10
Kosho M.	May 44	22		Nov 44	6/10
Kosho M. #2	Apr 45	13/13	Kumano M.	Nov 44	2

NAME	MO/YR	DT/HR	NAME	MO/YR	DT/HR
	Nov 44	--		Dec 44	6/20
Kumanosan M.	Jun 44	24/00		Jul 45	20/05
Kumanoyama M.			Kyokko M.	Nov 43	15/09
Kume	Jan 45	28/02		Jan 45	1
Kuniei M.	Feb 44	17/04	Kyoko M.	Dec 43	27/01
Kunikawa M.	Apr 44	29	Kyokuei M.	Nov 43	8/06
Kunimiya M.	Mar 44	--	Kyokuho M.	Oct 44	1/11
Kunishima M.	Feb 44	23/02	Kyokuto M.	Feb 44	25/01
Kunitama M.	Nov 43	11/23	Kyokuyo M.	Jan 43	11/21
Kurama M.	Feb 42	9		Jul 43	10/22
Kurama			Kyoraku M. #3	Jul 45	20/05
	Jul 44	--	Kyosei M.	Feb 44	--
	Jul 44	18/00	Kyowa M.	Dec 42	18/07
Kuramasan M.	Nov 44	2/11	Kyowa M. #2	Oct 44	16/06
Kurasaki	Nov 44	14/22	Kyuei M.	Dec 43	27/11
Kuretake	Dec 44	30/14	Lee Tung	Apr 45	8/20
Kuretake M.	Feb 45	7/07	Li Liang	May 45	30 C
	May 45	29/22	Lighter #130	Dec 44	29/21
Kurohime M.	Mar 43	30/09	Lighter #136	Oct 44	25
Kusagaki	Aug 44	7/21	Lima M.	Feb 44	8/22
Kusakaki			Lisbon M.	Oct 42	1
Kusunoki M. #2	Jun 45	18/23	Liverpool M.	Jul 43	4/03
	Jun 45	--	M 4242	Jan 43	4/05
Kusuyama M.	Feb 43	8	Ma 1	Mar 45	27
Kuwayama M.	Feb 43	22/07	Ma 4	Nov 44	20
Kyo M. #1	Jan 45	15	Macassar M.	Oct 44	2/22
Kyo M. #2	Aug 44	7/13		Oct 44	7/04
Kyodo M. #28	Jul 44	4/13		Oct 44	7/05
Kyodo M. #36	Jul 44	17/22	Makassar M.	Oct 44	2 C
Kyoei M. #2	Mar 43	29/12	Madras M.	Apr 43	14/05
	Jul 44	27/01		May 44	31/13
Kyoei M. #3	Jun 43	22/01	Maebashi M.	Sep 43	30/07
	Oct 44	27/23	Magane M.	Jan 44	23/03

NAME	MO/YR	DT/HR	NAME	MO/YR	DT/HR
Maki	Dec 44	9/02	Matsukaze	Jun 44	9/04
Mako M.	May 45	15/21	Matsumoto M.	Oct 44	24/19
Malay M.	Jan 45	8	Matsuwa	May 44	24/01
	Jan 45	25/14		Aug 44	22/06
Malta M.	Feb 44	10/03	Maya	Oct 44	23/06
Mamiya	Oct 43	12/12	Maya M.	Jul 44	17/01
	May 44	6/04	Mayachi M.	Aug 44	12/24
	Dec 44	21/01	Mayasan M.	Nov 44	17/18
Manazuru	Sep 44	9/02	Medan M.	Jun 44	27/04
Manei M.	Nov 44	8/04	Meigen M.	Mar 43	22/19
Manila M.	Nov 44	25/05	Meiho M.	Jan 45	8/22
Manju	Jan 45	31/04		Mar 45	--
Manju M.	Feb 42	27	Meiji M. #1	Apr 43	20/12
	Mar 43	21/05	Meikai M.	May 43	15/10
	Nov 43	29/03	Meisei M.	Jun 45	11/02
	Nov 44	25/01	Myojo M.		
	Jan 45	8/22	Meisho M.	May 44	19/11
Manko M.	Jul 44	31/04	Meiten M.	Jun 43	20/05
Manryo M.	Oct 44	12	Meiu M.	Jan 43	20/20
	Mar 45	--	Meiwa M.	Aug 42	1
Manryu M.	Apr 45	16/09	Meiyo M.	Aug 42	7
Manshu M.	Sep 44	9/02	Meizan M.	Aug 43	27
Mantai	Apr 44	1	Mexico M.	Aug 44	29/02
Mantai M.	Jul 44	16/24	Michel	Oct 43	17/02
Manyo M.	Mar 45	5/01	Michael M.		
Man-Yo M.			Michishio	Jan 44	31/02
Marifu M.	Jun 44	13/15	Nasami		
Masaki M. #2	Sep 43	29 J	Mie M.	Jul 43	--
Mashuye M.	Jul 45	4/07	Miho M.	Jul 44	15/22
Matsu M.	Jul 44	8/07		Sep 44	9/12
Matsue M.	Apr 44	17		Nov 44	11/09
	May 43	30/01		Apr 45	30/22
Matsukawa M.	Jun 44	30/04	Miike M.	Apr 44	27/01

NAME	MO/YR	DT/HR	NAME	MO/YR	DT/HR
Mikage M.	Oct 44	24/03	Miyazaki M.	May 44	8/10
Mikage M. #18	May 44	10/06	Mizuho	May 42	2/00
Mikage M. #20	Jul 43	19/02	Mizuho M.	Sep 44	21/09
Mikagesan M.	Oct 44	24/04	Mogamigawa M.	Aug 43	1/00
Mikamisan M.	Jun 45	2/03	Moji M.	Jul 44	8/18
Mikura	Mar 45	28/16	Momi	Sep 44	27/03
Mimasaka M.	Apr 44	9/17	Momo	Dec 44	15/19
Bisaku M.			Momoha M.	Mar 43	15/12
Minami M.	Apr 44	1/08	Toka M.		
Minazuki	Jun 44	6/22	Montevideo M.	Jul 42	1
Minatsuki			Motor Sailboat	Jun 45	24?
Minekaze	Feb 44	10/03	Muko M.	Nov 43	13/00
Minryo M.	Feb 44	--	Munakata M.	Jan 45	7/10
	Feb 44	14/07	Muroto	Oct 44	22/07
Mirii M.	Jun 44	29/15	Musashi	Mar 44	29/18
Misago M.	Aug 44	13/10	Musashi M.	Jun 42	27
Misago M. #1	Apr 45	13/11		Jul 42	--
Misaki M.	Nov 44	14/22	Mutsure	Sep 43	2/15
	Sep 43	29 C	Myoho M.	Jan 43	19/16
Misaku M.	Apr 44	9 C	Myoken M.	Jan 42	24/12
Mitakesan M.	May 44	11/15	Myoko	Dec 44	13/20
Mito M.	Mar 43	6	Myoko M.	Jun 43	17/07
	Apr 44	16/02	Nachi	Sep 43	6/21
Mitsuki M.	Dec 42	20/23	Nachiryu M #12	Nov 44	15/12
Mitsuyama M.	Apr 45	19/17	Hachiryu M #12		
Miyadono M.	Jun 43	19/16	Nachisan M.	Nov 43	13/06
Miyagi M.	Aug 44	4/01	Nachizan M.		
Miyakawa M. #2	Sep 44	25/22	Nadakaze	Jul 45	25 C
Miyako M.	Aug 44	5/13	Naga M.	Jun 45	19/06
Miyama M.	May 44	14/06	Naga M. #11	Jan 45	26/14
Bisan M.	May 44	14/06	Nagara	Jul 43	15
Miyasho M. #1	Jun 43	19/04		Aug 44	7/11
Miyaura M.	May 44	20/17	Nagara M.	Mar 45	5/05

NAME	MO/YR	DT/HR	NAME	MO/YR	DT/HR
	Feb 44	25/03	Nansatsu M. #2	Aug 44	22/02
Nagaragawa M.	Jun 44	22/13	Nansei M.	Aug 44	18/13
Nagashige M #2	Jun 43	6/19	Nanshin M.	Oct 42	20
Nagata M.	Oct 43	28/02		Jun 44	16/09
Nagisan M.	Feb 43	6/15		Aug 44	27/19
Nagoya M.	Jan 44	1/03		Feb 45	11
Naka	Apr 42	1		Jun 45	20
Naku M.	May 43	4/07	Nanshin M. #12	Feb 45	--
Name Unknown	Jul 42	24/16	Nanshin M. #19	Feb 45	2/23
Namikaze	Sep 44	8/21	Nanshin M. #20	Aug 44	--
Naminoue M.	Oct 42	7	Nanshin M. #21	Mar 45	20/15
Namman M.	Oct 43	27/22	Nanshin M. #22	Jun 45	8/03
Nanei M.	Feb 44	19/05	Nanshin M. #25	Aug 44	27/19
Nanho M.	Feb 44	24	Nanshin M. #26	Jan 45	30/08
Nampo M.				Feb 45	17/12
Naniwa M.	Aug 42	3	Nanshin M. #27	Sep 42	4
Nanka M.	Feb 44	1/01		Aug 44	27/19
Nankai	Jul 45	16/05	Nanshin M. #28	Oct 44	3/18
Nankai M.	Dec 42	25/22	Nanshin M. #3	Aug 44	27/19
	Sep 43	1 N	Nanyo M.	Feb 44	20/02
	Sep 44	--	Naruo M.	Dec 43	24/07
	Sep 44	12/05		Nov 44	12/02
Nankei M.	Dec 42	25 C	Naruto M.	Aug 43	8/07
Nanking M.	Sep 43	9 N	Naryu	Feb 45	16/06
	Mar 45	17/02	Nariu		
Nanko M. #8	Aug 44	25/18	Nasami	Jan 44	31/02
Nanman M.	Oct 43	27/22	Nase M.	Mar 45	28/13
Namman M.			Naze M.		
Nanmei M. #5	Jul 45	10/05	Nasusan M.	Jun 44	24/24
Nanmei M. #6	Jun 44	24/00	Natori	Jan 43	9/10
Nanpo M.	Jun 42	15		Aug 44	18/05
Nampo M.			Natsukawa M.	Jul 44	17/02
Nanrei M.	Oct 44	14/08	Natsushio	Feb 42	8

NAME	MO/YR	DT/HR	NAME	MO/YR	DT/HR
Nekka M.	Nov 43	23/05	Nigitsu M.	Jan 44	12/19
Nenohi	Jul 42	4	Niho M.	Jun 44	29/01
Nichian M.	Mar 44	29/05	Nippo M.		
	Sep 44	8/21	Niho M.	Jul 44	16/02
Nichiei M.	Aug 42	17	Nihonkai M.	Jun 44	17/13
	Jan 45	6/20	Nipponkai M.		
	Nov 44	14 C	Niitaka M.	Jul 43	12/04
Nichiei M. #2	Jan 45	--	Nikkai M.	Nov 43	26/19
Nichiho M.	Oct 42	21/14	Nikkaku M.	Jul 44	16/02
	Oct 44	27/04		Jan 45	23
Nichiman M.	Sep 44	8/21	Nikkei M.	Aug 42	8
Nichinan M.	Dec 41	23	Nikki M.	Feb 44	22/22
	Nov 42	16	Nikkin M.	Jun 44	30/01
	Mar 44	27/09	Nikko M.	Nov 43	20/01
	Nov 44	19		Jan 44	16/20
Nichinan M. #2	Nov 44	8/22		Jul 44	1
Nichiran M.	Jul 44	12/05		Apr 45	9/10
	Dec 41	23 C	Nikkoku M.	Dec 41	14/18
Nichiran M. #3	Jul 44	12/03	Nikkyu M.	Jul 43	4/16
Nichirei M.	Mar 44	9/01	Ning Hai	Sep 44	19 C
Nichiren M.	Mar 44	16/21	Nippo M.	Jun 44	29/01
Nichirin M.	Feb 44	19/19	Nippon M.	Jan 44	14/13
Nichiro M.	Aug 42	21		Jul 44	16 C
	Feb 44	17/22	Nipponkai M.	Jun 44	17/13
Nichiryo M.	Dec 43	1/21	Nishiyama M.	Aug 43	22/13
Nichiun M.	Jan 43	29/16	Nissei M.	Nov 42	17
Nichiwa M.	May 44	17/19		Sep 44	25/21
	Oct 44	1/23	Nisshin	Sep 42	28
Nichiyoku M.	May 44	18	Nisshin M.	Apr 42	10
	Feb 45	22/09		Feb 43	7/15
Nichiyu M.	Mar 43	3/24		May 44	6/07
Nichizan M.	Jul 42	12		Apr 45	2/08
Hiyama M.				May 45	13/05

NAME	MO/YR	DT/HR	NAME	MO/YR	DT/HR
Nisshin M. #2	Apr 43	--	Notoro	Jan 43	9/16
Nissho M.	Mar 42	27		Sep 43	20/23
	Dec 42	30/23		Jun 44	29/01
	Jul 42	24	Nozaki	Dec 44	28/12
	Oct 42	24	Numakaze	Dec 43	19/03
	Feb 44	25/03	Odate	Mar 45	27 J
Nissho M. #2	Jun 42	--	Odatsuki M.	Feb 44	15/20
	Mar 45	3/05	Ogi M.	May 44	--
Nisshu M.	Feb 42	2	Ogura M. #2	Sep 44	16/15
	Jul 44	18/07	Ogura M. #3	Feb 44	23/23
Nisshun M.	Apr 43	18/14	Ogurasan M.	Nov 43	26/03
Nittai M.	Mar 44	3/23	Ohio M.	Aug 42	2
Nittatsu M.	Apr 44	30/03		Aug 42	6/00
Nittei M.	May 45	25	Oi	Jul 44	19/13
Nittetsu M.	Oct 44	14/01	Oita M.	Oct 44	11/21
Nitto M.	Jul 44	3/24	Oite	Sep 43	--
Nittoku M.	Feb 44	14/20	Oka	May 45	2/23
Nittsu M.	Mar 43	21/10	Ojika		
Noborikawa M.	Jun 43	1/11	Ojikasan M.	Jun 45	13 C
Noetsutana Sa.	May 43	20 C	Oki	Nov 44	22/00
Nojima M.	Dec 41	27/09	Okikaze	Jan 43	10/13
Nojima			Okinawa M.	May 44	10/06
Nokaze	Feb 45	20/02	Okinoshima	May 42	11
Nomi	Apr 45	14/04	Okinoyama M #3	Mar 44	12/08
Nomura	Apr 45	25	Okinoyama M.		
Nordfels	Jan 43	25/11	Okinoyama M.	Feb 45	7/09
Norfolk M.	Aug 44	21/06	Okitsu M.	Jan 44	26/04
Noshiro M. I-Go	Apr 44	26/10	Okuni M.	Aug 43	18/13
Noshiro M.				Aug 44	31/07
Noshiro M.	Mar 43	13/18	Okuyo M.	Jan 44	1/09
	Aug 44	18/23	Omi M.	Dec 42	28/01
Noshiro M. #2	Apr 44	17/18	Ominesan M.	Mar 44	4/07
Noto M.	Oct 42	31	Taihosan M.		

NAME	MO/YR	DT/HR	NAME	MO/YR	DT/HR
Omurosan M.	Dec 44	22/05		Oct 44	31/09
Ondo	Nov 43	18/23	Palang M.	Nov 44	11
Onoe M.	Nov 43	26/23	Palange	Aug 45	12
Oregon M.	Nov 42	17	Palau M.	Feb 42	--
Osaka M.	Dec 42	31/16		Aug 42	6
	May 44	25/10	Palembang M.	May 43	26
Osakasan M.	Nov 44	18/02		Mar 45	4/02
Ose	Feb 43	21/23	Peking M.	Jul 44	28/15
	Jun 43	24/11	Penang M.	Apr 43	9/08
Oshikasan M.	Jun 45	13 J	Pietro Orseolo	Apr 43	1
Oshikayama M.			Pulo Salanama	Apr 44	29
Oshio	Feb 43	20/08	Rakuyo M.	Sep 44	12/05
Otome M.	Apr 45	29/00	Rashin M.	Aug 45	8/15
Otori M.	May 44	20/18	Reiko M.	Jun 45	18/10
	May 44	22/01	Reisui M.	Dec 44	25
	Oct 44	21		Dec 44	25
Otori M. #2	Feb 43	--	Rekizan M.	May 45	12/08
Otorisan M.	Jul 44	26/02	Renzan M.	Jan 43	1/09
Otoriyama M.			Rikko M.	Aug 44	31/05
Otoshi M.	Oct 44	4/08	Rikko M.	Aug 44	31/05
Otowasan M.	Aug 42	24		Aug 44	31/07
	Dec 44	22/05	Rio de Jan. M.	Jul 42	27
Oyama M.	Apr 43	9/14	Ritsu Go	Apr 45	8/20
Oyo M.	Oct 44	20/04	Lee Tung		
P 1	Jan 43	12/24	Rizan M.	Sep 44	21/24
P 2	Jul 45	25	RO-103	Mar 43	15/17
P 35	Dec 42	22/02	RO-112	Feb 45	11/22
P 37	Jan 42	24	RO-113	Feb 45	13/05
P 38	Nov 44	25/01	RO-115	Feb 45	9 C
	Nov 44	25/05	RO-30	Apr 42	26/10
P 39	Apr 43	23/07	RO-42	Sep 44	16/06
P 46	Nov 44	10/10	RO-45	Apr 44	20/10
Pacific M.	Jan 43	26/21	RO-49	Feb 45	24/11

NAME	MO/YR	DT/HR	NAME	MO/YR	DT/HR
I-371			Ryuto M.	Dec 43	29/03
RO-56	Apr 45	18/05	Ryuyo M.	Jan 44	1/03
Rokan	Apr 44	22 C	Ryuzan M.	Jul 43	30/23
Rokko M.	Sep 44	18/02	Sado	May 44	8/05
	Oct 44	--		Aug 44	22/06
Roko M.	Aug 44	11/17	Sado Go	Apr 42	10
Ronsan M.	Feb 44	12/21	Sado M.		
Roshu M.	Oct 42	--	Sagami M.	Nov 42	3
Rossbach	May 44	7/09		Jun 43	19/17
Ryoei M.	Mar 45	5/19	Sagara M.	Jun 43	23/05
Ryoei M. #66	Mar 45	6/10		Jul 43	4/22
Ryoga M.	May 42	--	Sagawa M.	Jun 45	9/20
Ryokai M.	Aug 43	15/01	Sagi	Aug 43	31
	Aug 43	22/14		Nov 44	8/07
Ryotoku M.	Sep 43	23/09	Sagiri	Dec 41	24
Ryotaku M.			Saigon M.	Sep 44	18/10
Ryoyo M.	May 44	2/13	Saikyo M.	Jun 42	28
Ryua M.	Mar 44	13/14	Sainei M.	Jul 44	17/03
Ryuei M.	Sep 43	4/03	Saipan M.	Jul 43	21/13
	Jan 44	3/01	Saishu M.	Jan 44	3/10
	Jul 44	7/14	Saisho M.		
Ryufuku M.	Dec 42	30/23	Saitsu M.	Jul 45	8/09
Ryuho	Dec 42	12/11	Sakae M.	Nov 44	23/01
	Dec 43	4/06	Sakishima M.	Jul 45	10/04
Ryujin M.	Apr 42	13	Sakito M.	Feb 44	29/20
	Jun 45	4/21	Sakura M.	Dec 41	12
Ryuka M.	Sep 44	8/02		Jul 45	10/05
Ryuko M.	Jan 44	15		Dec 44	22 C
Ryunan M.	Oct 42	20	Samidare	Jul 44	--
Ryuosan M.	Nov 43	4		Aug 44	26/18
Ryusei M.	Feb 44	25/21	Samui	Mar 45	17/03
	Nov 44	8/21	San Clemente M.	May 43	4/17
Ryusho M.	Mar 45	--	San Luis M.	Oct 44	9/17

NAME	MO/YR	DT/HR	NAME	MO/YR	DT/HR
San Pedro M.	Jul 42	5/10	Sea Tan M.	Mar 45	3 C
	Jun 44	25/03	Seattle M.	Jul 44	16/08
San Ramon M.	Nov 43	27/00	Seia M.	Apr 43	30
Sana M.	Oct 43	20/15		Jul 43	22/24
Sanae	Nov 43	18/23		Aug 44	1/13
Sanaye			Seian M.	Oct 44	1/10
Sanjin M.	Jun 45	13/17	Seiho M. #15	Jul 45	11/09
Sanju M.	Aug 44	7/14	Seikai M.	Aug 42	24
Sanka M.	Mar 45	10		Jan 43	19/11
Sanko M.	May 42	22		Sep 43	16
Sanraku M.	Jun 43	15/13	Seiki M.	May 43	28/09
Sansei M.	Sep 43	16/00	Seiko M.	Aug 43	1/06
	Dec 43	8/02		Aug 44	3/02
	Jun 44	28/08	Seikyo M.	Oct 42	23
	Sep 43	29 C	Seinan M.	Mar 43	20/17
Sansho M.	Aug 44	17/03		Jun 43	11 J
Santo M.	Sep 43	29/10		Jan 44	22/17
Sanuki M.	Mar 43	21/11	Seiner No. 20	Jul 43	9 N
	Jan 45	28/02	Seiryu M.	Apr 43	15
Sanyo M.	Dec 41	14		May 44	11/04
	Nov 42	21	Seishin M.	Dec 44	3/06
	May 44	26/15		Mar 45	5/10
	Jan 45	8/20		Mar 45	--
Sapporo M. #11	Jul 45	5/11	Seisho M.	Nov 44	18/03
Sapporo M. #12	Apr 43	12	Seitai M.	Aug 43	20/19
Sarawak M.	Jun 44	29/15	Seito M.	Oct 44	26
	Jan 45	24/06		Oct 44	26
	Jan 45	24/07	Seiun M.	Jul 43	--
Sata	Feb 44	17/22	Seiyo M.	Aug 44	10/09
Satsuki M.	Mar 43	25/06	Seizan M.	Aug 43	20/17
Satsuma M.	Feb 44	11/23		Jun 45	14/07
Sazanami	Jan 44	14/13	Seizan M. #2	Dec 43	24/07
Se Go	Feb 42	8	Seki M. #5	May 45	20/24

NAME	MO/YR	DT/HR	NAME	MO/YR	DT/HR
Sekko M.	Aug 43	9/06	Shinki M.	Oct 44	9/20
Sendai M.	Nov 42	10	Shinko M.	Aug 44	12 C
Senkai M.	Oct 42	7	Shinko M. #1	Nov 44	18/22
Senko M.	May 42	25		Jan 45	9
Senyo M.	Aug 42	25	Shinko M. #10	Jun 44	? N
Sen-Yo			Shinkoku M.	Aug 42	17
Setsuyo M.	Oct 42	4		Oct 42	5
Setsuzan M.	Jul 44	6/05		Feb 43	20/21
Shanghai M.	Apr 43	9/06	Shinkyo M.	Mar 44	2/23
Shibazono M.	Jan 45	3/21		Mar 44	24/23
Shichisei M.	Dec 43	29/04	Shinmei M.	Jul 44	5/15
Shiga M.	May 44	30/09	Shinnan M.	May 45	13/14
Shiganoura M.	Nov 43	29/03	Shinpen M.	May 45	4/13
Shigure	Jan 45	24/05	Shinpo M.	Aug 44	12/07
Shigure M.	Oct 42	10	Shimpo M.	Aug 44	17/19
Shikinami	Sep 44	12/07	Shinroku M.	Jun 44	7/23
Shikisan M.	Oct 44	24/08		Jun 45	9/11
Shimakaze	Jan 43	12 C	Shinryu M.	Jun 43	26 J
Shimotsu M.	Nov 44	8/24		May 44	18/05
Shimotsuki	Nov 44	25/03	Shinsei M.	Mar 43	20/12
Shimpo M.	Aug 44	12/07		Aug 43	28/04
Shimushu	Nov 44	25/19	Shinsei M. #1	Oct 44	24/05
Shinai M.	Jan 43	19/05	Shinsei M. #3	May 43	7/03
Shinano	Nov 44	29/03	Shinsei M. #6	Aug 42	21
Shinano M.	Jan 44	--		Aug 44	11/00
Shinbun M.	Dec 44	6 S	Shinsei M. #83	Jul 42	24/20
Shinei M.	Jun 43	6/23	Shinsen M.	Jun 45	12/08
	Aug 44	10/10		Jun 45	--
Shinei M. #3	Jun 45	19/06	Shinsho M.	Jul 42	9
Shingetsu M.	Sep 44	5/16	Shinshu M.		
Shingo M.	Dec 42	16	Shinshu M.	Oct 44	13/09
Shini M.	Nov 43	26/10		Jan 45	2/07
Shinju M.	Jun 43	15/14	Shinten M.	Aug 44	7/18

NAME	MO/YR	DT/HR	NAME	MO/YR	DT/HR
	Sep 44	8/22		Oct 44	7/03
Shinto M.	Dec 44	6/23	Shiretoko	Oct 44	7/05
Shinto M. #1	Feb 43	3/06	Shiretoko M.	Sep 44	5
	Feb 44	19	Shiriya	Sep 43	21/21
	Mar 45	26/09	Shirogane M.	Sep 42	19
Shinto M. #2	Apr 45	--		Jun 45	21/06
Shinyo	Nov 44	17/22	Shiroganesan M	Aug 44	6/02
Jinyo			Shisen M.	May 44	30/18
Shinyo M.	Jul 42	13	Shoan M.	Jan 43	27/14
	Sep 44	7/17	Shobu M.	Mar 44	8
	Jan 45	8/17	Shoei M.	May 42	12
Shinyo M. #3	Jun 45	11/03		Apr 43	4 N
Shinyo M. #5	Feb 42	17		May 43	26/00
Shinyo M. #8	Oct 44	7/06		Dec 44	8/00
Shinyu M.	Oct 42	25		Dec 44	8/00
	Apr 44	15/23		Dec 44	16
Shinyubari M.	Sep 43	21/20	Shoei M. #6	Jun 45	10/13
	Feb 44	23/09	Shofuku M. #1	Aug 42	7
Shioya	Jan 44	--	Shofuku M.		
	Jun 44	8/17	Shofuku M. #2	Jul 42	27
Shiraha M.	Jan 43	14/12		Mar 44	--
Shirahane M.			Shogen M.	Sep 43	6/06
Shirakami M.	Sep 44	2/17	Shohei M.	May 44	10/06
Shirakumo	Mar 44	16/21		Feb 45	6/12
Shirane M.	May 44	5/10	Shoho M.	Dec 43	31/12
Shiranesan M.	Feb 44	8/22		Feb 44	28/23
	Oct 44	18/22		Nov 44	25/05
Shiranui	Jul 42	5	Shojin M.	Jun 43	20/10
Shirataka	Aug 44	31/07		Mar 44	13/15
Shirataka M.	Mar 44	20/02	Shoju M.	Aug 43	5/03
Shiratori M.	Apr 45	12/00	Shoka M.	May 42	25
Shiretoko	Sep 43	13/07	Shokaku	Jun 44	19/11
	Nov 43	13/08	Shokei M.	Sep 44	8/22

NAME	MO/YR	DT/HR	NAME	MO/YR	DT/HR
Shoken M.	May 44	29/02		Jan 44	29/02
Shoko M.	May 43	30/01	Shun Yuan	Sep 44	22/04
Matsue M.			Shunko M.	Oct 42	14
	Dec 43	1/01	Shunsei M.	Apr 42	1
Shokyu M.	Feb 42	21	Shunsei M. #5	May 42	31/03
Shonan	Feb 45	25/02	Shunsen M.	Jan 45	5/20
Shonan M.	May 42	13/10	Shuntai M.	Jan 44	29/02
	Aug 44	6/04	Shunten M.	Nov 44	17/04
	Sep 44	9/03	Shuri M.	Jan 45	20/24
Shori M.	Mar 45	11/04	Shuttle Bt 833	Jun 45	23/02
Shoryu M.	May 44	4/01	Comm. Ship 833		
	Sep 44	9/16	Shuyo M.	Nov 44	23/09
Shosei M.	May 44	20/16	Siko M.	Mar 45	4/09
Shosei M. #15	May 45	13/04	Soerabaja M.	Jan 43	20/20
	May 45	13	Somedono M.	Jan 43	20/20
Shosei M. #5	Jul 44	10/08	Song Giang Go	Apr 44	29/23
Shoshin M.	Mar 43	7/05	Song Giang M.		
Shoto M.	Aug 43	31/09	Soryu	Jun 42	4
	Jan 45	3/21	Soryu M.	Dec 41	23
Shotoku M.	Jun 43	28/13	Hayataka M.		
Showa M.	Aug 42	25/07	Soya	Jan 43	18/05
	Jul 43	7/02	Soyo M.	Dec 43	7/16
Showa M. #3	Feb 45	13/07	SS 3	Mar 44	28/13
	Feb 45	13/07	Suez M.	Nov 43	29/08
	Feb 45	13/06	Sugi M. #5	Aug 44	22
Shoyo M.	Sep 43	21/21	Sugiyama M.	Jun 44	7/23
	Jan 44	18/03		Nov 44	15/02
	Jun 45	9/21	Suiten M.	Mar 45	3/20
Shoyu M.	Mar 45	5/05	Sumatra M.	Jan 43	--
Shozan M.	Dec 42	31/18		May 43	12/08
	Jun 43	26/06		Oct 44	27
	Jul 44	17/03	Sumida M.	Apr 44	15
Shuko M.	Jan 44	26/22	Sumiwa M.	Dec 44	--

NAME	MO/YR	DT/HR	NAME	MO/YR	DT/HR
Sumiyoshi M.	Oct 42	14	Tahure	Apr 44	30/00
Sunosaki	Aug 44	1/11	Taian M.	Sep 43	28/15
Surabaya M.	Jan 43	20/20		Oct 43	8/01
Soerabaja M.				Jan 44	23/02
Suruga M.	Feb 43	15/21	Taian M. #2	Jul 44	11/01
Suwa M.	Mar 43	28/07	Taibin M.	Oct 44	4/08
	Apr 43	5	Otoshi M.		
	Jul 43	27/11	Taibu M.	May 44	4/03
Suzukaze	Feb 42	4			
	Jan 44	26/00	Taibun M.	Aug 43	30/15
Suzutsuki	Jan 44	16/11	Taichu M.	Oct 43	18/10
	Oct 44	16/22		Apr 44	12/02
Suzuya M.	Jun 43	13/15	Taiei M.	May 42	6
Sydney M.	Nov 43	28/03		Aug 44	21/06
T 104	Dec 44	12/24	Taietsu M.	Jan 45	31/04
T 105	Oct 44	11/09	Taifuku M.	Aug 43	27/03
T 111	Nov 44	4/16		May 43	5/23
T 12	Dec 44	12/24	Taigen M.	May 42	6
T 129	Aug 44	14/02	Taigen M. #2	Jun 45	10/02
T 138	Oct 44	27/01	Taigen M. #3	Feb 44	26/19
T 146	Apr 45	28/07	Taigen M. #6	Feb 44	21
T 15	Jan 45	17/14	Taigen M. #7	Aug 44	14/01
T 151	Nov 44	22/24	Taigyo M.	Feb 45	7/03
T 18	Mar 45	18/03	Taihaku M.	Oct 44	26/04
T 3	Sep 44	15/18	Taihei M.	Jul 44	9/11
Tachibana M.	Apr 42	24	Taiho	Jun 44	19/08
	Sep 44	27/07	Taihosan M.	Mar 43	12/02
	Oct 44	9/02		Mar 44	4/07
Tacoma M.	Feb 44	1/01	Taijin M.	Feb 44	20/05
Tade	Apr 43	23 C		Mar 44	12/09
Taga M.	Nov 43	9/17	Taijo M.	Apr 45	2/08
	Jun 45	10/13	Taiju M.	Apr 44	23/07
Tagonoura M.	Sep 43	3/20	Daiju M.		

NAME	MO/YR	DT/HR	NAME	MO/YR	DT/HR
Taijun M.	May 44	23/05	Taishu M.	Apr 45	29/09
	May 44	23/08		Nov 43	22/03
Taika M.	Sep 42	7	Taishun M.	Aug 45	--
			Daishun M.		
Taikai M.	Oct 44	18/22	Taisoku M.	Feb 44	27/03
Taikai M. #3	Nov 44	16/06	Dairen M.		
Taikei M.	Feb 44	19	Taiten M.	Oct 44	24/11
			Taito M.	Mar 42	5
Taiko M.	Jul 43	11/05		May 44	25/10
	Sep 43	25 J		Aug 44	16/22
	Sep 43	25 N		Jun 45	20/19
	Jul 44	14/12	Taiu M.	Jun 45	4/15
Taikoku M.	May 44	17/00	Taiun M. #1	Jul 45	1/12
Taikyo M.	Jan 45	23/04	Taiun M. #2	Jul 44	1/23
Taiman M. #1	Jan 45	24/20	Daiun M. #2		
Taimei M.	Nov 44	3/01	Taiyo	Sep 42	28
Tainan M.	May 43	26/14		Sep 43	24/08
	Nov 43	26/10		Aug 44	18/22
	Jun 44	24/24	Taiyo M.	May 42	8
Tairai M.	Feb 45	4/16		Oct 44	26/07
Tairiku M.	Feb 45	21/03	Taiyo M. #3	Feb 44	15/07
Tairin M.	Oct 43	18	Taiyoku M.	May 44	4/01
	Jul 44	3/13	Taiyu M.	Nov 43	26/10
Tairyu M.	Jan 42	10	Taizan M.	Dec 41	13
Taisei M.	Sep 43	--	Taizen M.	Oct 44	14/01
	Apr 45	19/02		Feb 45	20/02
Taisei M. #6	Nov 44	29/12			
Taishi M.	Jul 44	13/07	Tajima M.	May 44	4/10
Taishin M.	Feb 44	5/22		May 44	6/13
Taisho M.	Oct 44	26/04	Takachiho M.	Mar 43	19/09
Taisho M. #1	Jul 45	--	Takamisan M.	May 43	30/01
				May 43	30
Taisho M. #5	Dec 44	14/07	Takamiya M.I-Go	Jul 44	6/23

NAME	MO/YR	DT/HR	NAME	MO/YR	DT/HR
Takamiya M.			Takunan M.	Oct 44	1/04
Takane M.	Oct 44	30/16	Takunan		
Korei M.			Takusei M.	Oct 42	14
	Oct 44	30/20	Tama	Oct 44	25/22
	Oct 44	31/01	Tama M.	Jul 44	4/04
Takao	Oct 44	23/06		Apr 45	2/10
	Jul 45	31		Apr 45	7/19
	Jul 45	31	Tama M. #6	Aug 44	8/23
Takao M.	May 43	9/05	Tamagawa M.	Feb 42	2
Takaoka M.	Jun 44	5/17	Tamahime M.	Jun 44	5/17
Takaosan M.	Mar 43	25/05	Tamahoko M.	Jun 44	24/24
Takasago M.	Apr 42	26	Tamanami	Jul 44	7/02
	May 42	8/16	Tamashima M.	Jan 44	30/23
	Apr 45	29	Tamatsu M.	Aug 44	19/04
Takasago M. #3	Oct 44	21	Tamon M.	May 43	--
Takasago M. #7	Oct 44	26/06		May 43	2/02
	Nov 44	--	Tamon M. #1	Jul 42	3
	Nov 44	--	Tamon M. #15	Jan 45	26
Takasago M. #8	Apr 45	--	Tamon M. #5	May 43	7/11
Takasaki	Jun 44	5/10	Tamon M. #6	Sep 42	27
Takashima M.	Jun 44	13/23	Tamon M. #8	Jan 44	4/16
			Tango M.	Nov 43	--
Takatori M. #1	Jul 44	1/15		Nov 43	8/16
Takatori M. #2	Feb 44	--		Feb 44	25/20
Takatori M.			Tanikaze	Jun 44	9/21
Takatori M. #8	Jul 43	11/17	Tarakan M.	Apr 44	2/04
Takekawa M.	Apr 44	29/21		Jan 45	6/01
Takegawa M.			Tarushima M.	Jan 44	16/23
Takekun M.	Sep 44	10		Jan 44	17/07
Bukun M.			Tatekawa M.	May 44	24/14
Taketoyo M.	Aug 44	21/06	Tateyama M.	Feb 43	15/09
Taketsu M.	Aug 44	--		Mar 45	1/20
Taki M.	Mar 42	4	Tateyama M. #2	Apr 43	--

NAME	MO/YR	DT/HR	NAME	MO/YR	DT/HR
Tatsuaki M.	Nov 44	12/06		Aug 44	12/07
Tatsufuku M.	May 42	28/23	Teikyu M.	Sep 42	2
	May 42	29/03	Teiryu M.	Jul 44	19/08
Tatsuharu M.	Mar 45	19/02	Teisen M.	May 44	3/12
Tatsuho M.	Mar 42	30	Teisho M.	Mar 43	--
	Aug 42	22		Mar 43	24/21
Tatsuju M.	Oct 44	23/04	Teishu M.	Apr 45	29/18
Tatsumiya M.	Aug 43	11/05	Teishun M.	Aug 42	26
Tatsumomo M.	Feb 45	24/11	Teison M.	Oct 42	14/15
Tatsuno M.	Jan 44	15/22	Teiyo M.	Aug 44	18/22
Tatsushiro M.	Oct 44	5/15	Tekkai M.	Nov 42	3/02
Tatsusho M.	Nov 44	12 C	Tekka M.		
Tatsuta	Mar 44	13/03	Tempei M.	May 44	22/01
Tatsuta M.	Feb 43	8/22	Tenpei M.		
	Feb 44	--	Temposan M.	Dec 43	29/05
Tatsutake M.	May 43	10/09	Tenposan M.		
Tatsuura M.	Oct 44	26/07	Tenkai M.	Sep 43	5/03
Tatsuwa M.	Feb 43	4/04	Tenkai M. #2	Jun 43	28/11
	Feb 44	10/22	Tennan M.	Oct 43	24/01
Tatsuyo M.	Jan 45	8/17	Tenryo M.	May 45	29/22
Shinyo M.			Tenrei M.		
Tazan M.	May 42	17	Tenryu	Dec 42	18/22
Taizan M.			Tenryu M.	Oct 42	10
Teia M.	Aug 44	18/23		Dec 42	--
Teian M.	Jan 42	9	Tenryugawa M.	Mar 43	17/23
Teibi M.	Oct 43	10/14	Tensan M.	Jul 42	8
Teibo M.	Sep 42	25	Tenzan M.		
Teifuku M.	Dec 42	26	Tenshin M.	Jul 44	31/20
	Dec 42	22/14		Oct 44	24/01
Teihoku M.	Aug 45	11/02	Tenshinzan M.	May 44	7/01
Teikin M.	Jul 43	27	Tensho M.	Oct 44	26/04
Teiko M.	Feb 44	22/17	Tenyu M.	Sep 42	4
Teikon M.	Feb 44	23/04		Jul 45	--

NAME	MO/YR	DT/HR	NAME	MO/YR	DT/HR
Terukawa M.	Aug 43	15/04		Apr 45	16/15
	Dec 43	21/06	Tokushima M.	Sep 44	16/13
Terushima M.	May 43	18/18	Tokuwa M.	Oct 44	9/17
Tetsuyo M.	Apr 44	25/07		Oct 44	9/18
Thames M.	May 42	17/17	Tokyo M.	May 42	25
	Jul 43	25/19		Nov 43	10/15
Toa M.	Nov 43	25/15	Tomitsu M.	Oct 44	22/07
Toan M.	Aug 44	24/04	Tomori	Oct 44	27 C
Toba M.	Apr 42	25	Tonan M.	Nov 43	28/03
Tobi M.	Jun 45	1	Tonan M. #2	Oct 42	10
Toei M.	Jan 43	18/02	Tonan M.		
	Feb 44	1/04		Feb 44	9/12
	Aug 44	13/12		Aug 44	22/19
Toen M.	Mar 43	2/15	Tonan M. #3	Jun 42	25/10
Tofuku M.	Dec 43	24/07		Jul 43	24/12
Togo M.	Apr 45	11/05	Tone M.	Sep 42	20/16
Toho M.	Mar 43	29/04	Tonei M.	Oct 43	1/19
	Jan 44	15/22	Toro M.	Dec 41	12
	Jun 44	1/05	Toryu M.	May 45	2/22
	Feb 45	7/09	Tosan M.	Jul 44	26/02
Tokai M.	Jan 43	26/17		Dec 41	12 C
	May 43	5/08	Tozan M.		
	Aug 43	27/15		Jul 44	27/10
Tokai M. #2	Apr 45	--	Tosei M.	Oct 42	1
Tokai M. #4	Oct 44	27/01		May 43	7/03
Tokiwa M.	Jun 43	19/08		Dec 43	12/08
	Apr 44	26/23		Apr 44	3/15
	Jan 45	20/07		Aug 44	24/07
Tokiwa M. #1	Dec 42	25/15	Tosei M. #2	Sep 44	19/09
Tokiwa M.			Toseki M.	Aug 44	10/12
Tokiwasan M.	Sep 44	9/16	Toshin M.	Feb 44	19
Toko M.	Jan 44	30/02	Toso M. #1	Sep 44	2
	Oct 44	12/14	Totai M.	Dec 43	13/23

NAME	MO/YR	DT/HR	NAME	MO/YR	DT/HR
Toten M.	Jun 44	11/24	Tsukushi M. #2	Jul 44	11/07
Tottori M.	Apr 42	--	Tsukushi M. #3	Mar 45	18 U
	May 42	17/17	Tsuneshima M.	Dec 43	20/17
	May 45	15/00	Tsunushima M.		
Toun M.	Aug 43	22/23	Tsurigisaki	Apr 45	19 C
	Oct 44	23/04	Tsuruga M.	Jan 42	24
Toyama M.	Jun 44	29/07	Tsurumi	Mar 42	1
Toyo M.	Apr 43	3/13		Aug 44	5/12
	Jun 43	26/05	Tsurushima M.	Mar 43	2/10
	Nov 44	15/22		Jun 44	--
Toyo M. #2	Apr 43	2/22		Jun 44	30/02
Toyo M. #3	Aug 44	23/04	Tsushima M.	Aug 44	22/22
Toyo M. #5	Feb 44	2/10	Tsuyama M.	Sep 43	11/02
Toyo M. #8	Feb 44	2/10		Oct 44	2/22
Toyohara M.	May 42	15	Tx1	Feb 42	28/22
Toyohashi M.	Jun 42	4		Mar 42	13
Toyohi M.	May 44	3/23		Mar 42	--
Toyokuni M.	Mar 44	9/01		Oct 42	5
Toyooka M.	Sep 44	9/02		Dec 42	22/09
Toyoura M.	May 44	6/12	Tx2 #1	Mar 42	1/20
Toyu M.	Jul 45	10/11		Jun 43	18/03
Tozan M.	Dec 41	12	Tx2 #2	Mar 42	1/20
Transbalt	Jun 45	13/02		Mar 42	--
Tsubame	Jun 43	19/22	Tyokai M.	May 44	28
Tsugaru	Aug 43	5/10	Chokai M.		
	Jun 44	29/14	U-163	Mar 43	21/01
	Jun 44	21 C	U-168	Oct 44	6
Tsuki M.	May 45	25/21	U-183	Apr 45	23/13
Tsukikawa M.	Mar 44	11/15	U-537	Nov 44	10/08
Tsukiyura M.	Mar 45	9/12	U-859	Sep 44	23
Tsukuba M.	May 44	22/18	Uchide M.	Feb 44	29/24
Tsukushi	Nov 43	4	Udo M.	Nov 43	19/06
Tsukushi M.	Aug 44	23/11	Uga M.	Aug 44	21/07

NAME	MO/YR	DT/HR	NAME	MO/YR	DT/HR
Ugo M.	Oct 44	20/03		Nov 42	10
UIT-23	Feb 44	14		May 42	17/17
Ukishima	Nov 43	16		Jul 42	24/16
Ukishima M.	Jan 43	26/20		Jan 43	26/20
Ume M.	Nov 43	2/04	Unryu	Dec 44	19/16
Ume M. #56	May 45	15/08	Unryu M.	Dec 44	31
Umikaze	Feb 44	1/13		Jan 45	--
Unkai M. #1	Jan 42	7	Unyo	Jan 44	19/12
Unkai M. #10	Jul 44	18/02		Sep 44	16/24
Unkai M. #12	Nov 44	1/08	Unyo M. #1	Jan 42	--
Unkai M. #15	Jul 45	28/04	Unyo M. #3	Jul 42	2
Unkai M. #5	Jun 42	30	Unyo M. #5	May 43	--
	Nov 44	14/22	Uragami M.	Mar 44	21/23
Unkai M. #8	Jun 45	10/03	Urakami M.		
Unknown	Apr 42	3	Urakaze	Nov 44	21/03
	Feb 43	20/08	Ural M.	Sep 44	27/07
Unknown M.	Mar 42	4		Sep 44	27/12
	Mar 42	26	Usa M.	Jan 44	4/05
	Apr 42	17		Sep 44	--
	Apr 42	23		Jan 45	19/01
	May 42	9/14	Ushio M.	Jan 43	26/13
	Jul 42	28	Ussuri M.	May 43	2/02
	Aug 42	12	Tamon M.		
	Oct 42	21/14		Jun 44	27/04
	Oct 42	27/22	Usugumo	Jul 44	7/17
	Oct 42	31/18	Uyo M.	Dec 42	10/00
	Jan 43	17/10		May 43	9/08
	Jan 43	22/06		Jul 43	20/03
	Mar 43	23/05		Dec 43	21/12
	Nov 43	26/23	Uzan M.	May 42	2
	Dec 42	20/23	Uzuki M.	Feb 45	24/14
	Mar 42	27	Usuki M.		
	Dec 42	30/23	VanVollenhoven	Nov 43	27/16

NAME	MO/YR	DT/HR	NAME	MO/YR	DT/HR
Venice M.	Nov 42	11	Wakataka	Oct 44	17
				Mar 45	27
Ville du Havre	Nov 42	8	Wakatake		
Volpi	Oct 44	27 C	Wakatake M.	Oct 44	23/04
VP 408	Feb 43	19/18	Wakatama M.	Jun 45	9/15
W 12	Apr 45	6/16	Wales M.	Apr 44	26/02
W 15	Mar 45	5/16		May 44	23/23
W 17	Mar 45	18/03	Wazan M.	Apr 44	26/08
W 20	May 45	4/00	Wuhu M.	Oct 43	29/02
W 22	Feb 43	27 N	Wufu M.		
	Aug 44	23/14	Yachiyo M.	Jan 43	17/22
W 25	Jul 44	17/03	Yae M.	Apr 42	1
W 27	Jul 45	10/11	Yaei M.	Jan 45	3/21
W 28	Oct 43	2	Iyasaka M.		
	Aug 44	29/04	Yaei M. #6	Dec 44	22
W 3	Apr 45	9/13	Iyasaka M. #6		
W 34	Jan 45	--	Yagi M.	Aug 44	9/04
	May 45	21/02	Yahiko M.	Jan 44	10/23
W 38	Nov 44	20/05	Yaku	Feb 45	23/10
W 39	Jul 45	20/23	Yamabato M.	Mar 43	29/04
W 41	Apr 45	25/01	Yamabiko M.	Jan 44	10/06
W 5	Nov 44	4	Yamafuji M.	Oct 42	20
W 7	Apr 44	15	Yamafuku M.	Nov 43	29/01
Wa 102	Jan 45	27/04	Yamagata M.	Apr 44	16/02
Wa 104	Apr 45	12	Yamagiku M.	Jun 44	28/06
Wa 105	May 45	25	Yamagiri M.	Aug 43	28/01
Wa 3	Apr 45	26	Yamagumo	Oct 44	25/19
	Apr 45	26	Yamaji M.	Apr 45	2/11
Waka M.	Feb 45	--	Yamakaze	Jun 42	25
Wakae M.	Jun 45	18/07	Yamakuni M.	Jan 44	14/01
Wakamiya	Nov 43	23/04		Dec 44	6/21
Wakamiyasan M.	Jun 45	14/14		Mar 45	20/15
Wakanoura M.	Aug 43	10/13	Yamamiya M.	Jun 44	25/02

NAME	MO/YR	DT/HR	NAME	MO/YR	DT/HR
Yamamizu M.	Mar 44	27/20	Yodogawa M.	May 43	11/08
Yamamizu M. #2	Oct 44	6/14	Yoko M.	Sep 43	11/01
Yamaoka M.	Jul 44	4/21	Yomei M.	Oct 42	1
Yamashimo M.	Feb 44	22/15	Yomogi	Nov 44	25 C
	Feb 44	23/01	Yoneyama M.	Jul 43	1/24
Yamashiro M.	Sep 43	23/09	Yosei M.	May 45	13/04
Yamatama M.	Aug 44	7/14	Yoshida M.	Feb 43	20
Sanju M.				Jan 44	18/20
Yamateru M.	Aug 44	17/03	Yoshida M. #1	Apr 44	26/03
Sansho M.			Yoshida M. #3	Aug 44	23/04
Yamato	Dec 43	25/05	Toyo M. #3		
Yamato M.	Sep 43	13/01	Yoshino M.	Jul 44	--
	Nov 43	22/09		Jul 44	31/04
Yamato M. #2	Nov 43	23/00		Jul 44	31/05
Yamazato M.	Apr 43	22		May 45	14/12
Yamazuru M.	Jan 44	14/20	Yoshinogawa M.	Jan 43	9/03
Yamatsuru M.			Yoshitomo M.#21	Nov 43	--
Yanagigawa M.	Sep 44	8/02	Yoshitomo M.#22	Nov 43	--
Yanagawa M.			Yoshu M.	Dec 42	22/14
Yashima M.	Jan 43	22/23	Teifuku M.		
Hasshu M.			Yowa M.	Sep 43	18/00
Yasukuni M.	Jan 44	21/23	Yozan M.	Jun 45	12/09
	Jan 44	31/05	Yubae M.	Jan 43	9/18
	Dec 44	6/23	Yubari	Apr 44	27/11
Yasushima M.	Mar 44	28	Yugure	May 43	16/13
Yasujima M.			Yuho M.	Nov 44	26/15
Yawata M.	Nov 43	2/01	Yuki M.	Jun 44	16/17
	Nov 43	2/03	Yunagi	Aug 44	25/16
	Jul 44	9/13	Yuno M.	Apr 45	30
Yawata M. #3	May 45	27/05	Yura	Oct 42	18
Yawatasan M.	Oct 42	9	Yuri M.	Nov 43	28/12
Yayoi M.	Aug 44	5/06	Yurijima	Jan 45	14/13
	Jan 45	--	Yurishima		

NAME	MO/YR	DT/HR
Yurin M.	Sep 43	4/23
Yulin M.		
Yusen M. #11	Mar 45	--
Yusen M. #3	Jul 44	20/23
Yuzan M.	Apr 43	27/05
Yuzan M.	Jul 45	30/10
Yuzan M. #2	Nov 44	14/23
	Dec 44	--
Zaosan M.	Jun 45	19/02
Zensho M.	Aug 44	4/01
Zenyo M.	Aug 42	2
Zogen Go	Mar 43	19/05
Zogen M.		
Zuiho M.	Sep 44	12/23
Zuiko M.	Jun 45	12/09
Zuisho M.	Aug 44	14/01
Zuiun M.	Jan 45	21/17
Zuiyo M.	Oct 44	1/11
#2115	Jan 45	16

The Naval Institute Press is the book-publishing arm of the U.S. Naval Institute, a private, non-profit professional society for members of the sea services and civilians who share an interest in naval and maritime affairs. Established in 1873 at the U.S. Naval Academy in Annapolis, Maryland, where its offices remain today, the Naval institute has more than 100,000 members worldwide.

Members of the Naval Institute recieve the influential monthly naval magazine Proceedings and substantial discounts on fine nautical prints, ship and aircraft phtos, and subscriptions to the Institute's recently inaugurated quarterly, Naval History. The also have access to the transcripts of the Institute's Oral History Program and may attend any of the Institute-sponsored seminars regularly offered around the country.

The book-publishing program, begun in 1898 with basic guides to naval practices, has broadened its scope in recent years to include books of more general interest. Now the Naval Institute Press publishes more than forty new titles each year, ranging from how-to book on boating and navigation to battle histories, biographies, ship guides, and novels. Institute members receive discounts on the Press's more than 300 books.

For a free catalog describing books currently available and for further information about U.S. Naval Institute membership please write to:

Membership Department
U.S. Naval Institute
Annapolis, Maryland 21402

or call, toll-free, 800-233-USNI.